CW00924014

THE TRUTH IS

Sri H.W.L. Poonja

Compiled and Edited by Prashanti De Jager

FULL
CIRCLE

The Truth Is
© Copyright Prashanti de Jagar and Yudhistara

First FULL CIRCLE Paperback Edition, 2000
First Reprint, March 2008
ISBN 81-7621-082-X

Published by

FULL CIRCLE *PUBLISHING*
J-40, Jorbagh Lane, New Delhi-110003
Tel: 24620063, 24621011 • Fax: 24645795
e-mail: fullcircle@vsnl.com • website:atfullcircle.com

All rights reserved in all media. This book may not be reproduced in whole or in part, without written permission from the publisher, except by a reviewer who may quote brief passages in a review, nor may any part of this book be reproduced, stored in a retrieval system, or transmitted in any form or by any means electronic, mechanical, photocopying, recording, or other without written permission from the publisher.

Typesetting: SCANSET

J-40, Jorbagh Lane, New Delhi-110003
Tel: 24620063, 24621011 • Fax: 24645795

Printed at Nutech Photolithographers, New Delhi-110095

PRINTED IN INDIA
00/01/02/03/21/SCANSET/SAP/NP/NP

Table of Contents

|| Nothing ever existed
is the ultimate Truth. ||

ॐ

Bhagavan Sri Ramana Maharshi
The Guru of Sri Poonja

Introduction

This book is a collection of spontaneous songs spoken by Sri H.W.L. Poonja during gatherings with his students in North India between 1990 and 1997. The songs flow from his impeccable experience of the highest and yet simplest Truth: That we are pure Consciousness, the totality of Existence.

Papaji, as his loved ones call him, was born in the Punjab in 1910 to the sister of Swami Rama Tirtha, one of India's most respected Saints. He realized the Truth when he was 8 years old. This Realization infinitely blossomed in his early 30's when he met his Guru, Sri Ramana Maharishi, the Sage of Arunachala. Since that time he shares this Beauty with his wise words, his look, his touch, and simply by the silent spiritual power that radiates from his Presence. When he left his body in September of 1997 this power exploded and is felt around the world now more than ever.

It is a very rare occurrence that a being like Papaji takes a form, manifesting as a teacher of uncompromising absolute Truth, and says:

> Look within,
> There is no difference
> between yourself, Self and Guru.
> You are always Free.
> There is no teacher,
> there is no student,
> there is no teaching.

When we forget our true nature and believe that we are something finite and insignificant he offers words of ancient wisdom to explain the unspeakable. As doubt is removed and illusoryness flees like the night at dawn these same words dance in a celebration of vast Freedom and Love. And indeed, in his precious Satsangs he often tells people to rise up to sing and dance.

This Beloved Master speaks some of the clearest words that can possibly be spoken and at the same time says that all words are only indicators that merely point to the Truth. He directs us daily to vigilantly follow this indication and not to stick to the words. "Leave the wordiness of the world," this laughing Buddha lovingly roars, "and realize what the words I speak are pointing to. Truth is not knowable, it transcends knowing. It is beyond the ability of mind to analyze, to figure out, to dissect or to comprehend."

From 1918 to Now, Papaji has directly shown to thousands that the Truth is the most magnificent Mystery undifferentiated from our very Self. He guides one to surrender to the wisdom of our Being and that we are the Truth. "You are the unchangeable Awareness in which all activity takes place. Always rest in peace. You are eternal Being, unbounded and undivided. Just keep Quiet. All is well. Keep Quiet Here and Now. You are Happiness, you are Peace, you are Freedom. Do not entertain any notions that you are in trouble. Be kind to yourself. Open to your Heart and simply Be."

He is a true Master with thousands of ways to stop your mind, to help you inquire into who you really are, to turn your awareness directly toward awareness, to bring you into the infinity of this Moment. We are so lucky to have such essential Wisdom available to us. As he says,

> Those who know This know Everything.
> If not, even the most learned know nothing at all.

Hindu bhakta, Christian mystic, Zen master, Mountain shaman, Taoist sage, Dzogchen lama, Advaita jnani, Sufi saint, Aghora yogi, Vedic pundit, you name it: with the depth of his knowledge, the extent of his experience, and the clarity of his articulation he proves to be a Master of each and every tradition.

As Timelessness is a sign of the teachings of the Wise, these songs are compiled by essence only and so have no chronology, often even within a single verse. Also, for the sake of clarity, capital letters are used whenever a word is intended to point toward the one ultimate Self. Examples include Truth, Bliss, Light, Nowness, Fullness and Consciousness. The joyous grammar of Freedom itself can stop your mind.

We would like to acknowledge all those who helped put this book together: Yudhishtara for his overall support and guidance, Prashanti for recording, transcribing, compiling, and editing the Satsangs with Sri Poonja that are the basis of this book, Vidyavati for typing, editing, and proofing, Carol Watts for text and cover layout and proofing, the photographers listed on page 553, and of course, the Master who guided the entire project in Silence.

With love and gratitude to our Beloved Satguru who has given us all so much, it is a joy to offer this book to you. Thank you.

Yudhishtara, Vidyavati and Prashanti
San Anselmo, California
October 13, 1998

Look Within
Approach with all Devotion
Stay as Heart

The Truth Simply Is

ॐ

Let there be Peace and Love
among all Beings of the Universe
Let there be Peace, Let there be Peace
Om Shanti, Shanti, Shanti

You are Love Dancing as Emptiness

Namaskar,

Before the beginning you are pure Consciousness.
You are the Fullness of Love in Love
and the Emptiness of Awareness.
You are Existence and the Peace beyond peace.
You are that screen on which all is projected.
You are the Light of Knowledge,
the One who gave the concept of creation to the creator.
Forget what can be forgotten and know yourself
to be that which can never be forgotten.
You are the substratum on which everything moves, let it move.
You are Now, you are Nowness:
what "I" is there which can be out of this Now?
You are Truth and only the Truth Is.

You are inactivity.
Activity is your reflection, your play, your world.
The sun is inactivity, the mirrors are activity.

You are this precious Moment, presence itself,
any breeze that touches you will sanctify even demons.

You are the One which is aware
of the awareness of objects and ideas.
You are the One which is even more silent than awareness.
You are the Life which precedes the concept of life.
Your nature is Silence and it is not attainable,
It always Is.

"Space" was your first notion
and you took Sat-chit-ananda as your first form.
The world is your mind
and it all arises from your heart.

Here and Now is your heart. As love
you abide in the cave of this heart
from where all time and space arise.

You are the Inside which is neither inside nor outside.
Mind landing nowhere is Inside, no walls is inside.
You are the existence in all atoms,
know This and you are bliss.

You are Emptiness, the ultimate substance:
removing Emptiness out of Emptiness
leaves only Emptiness because there is nothing beyond It.
All rises from, dances about in, and returns to This.
As ocean rises as a wave to dance,
so you are this dancing Emptiness!
Nothing is out of this Emptiness and so it is the Fullness.
Emptiness is between is and is not.
To be Free, you need the firm conviction
that you are this Substratum, this Peace, this Emptiness.

You are what all happenings happen in.
What happens must happen so remain unaffected as Peace.
Be peaceful and this Peace will spread.
What rises from Peace is Peace and
what rises from confusion is confusion.
So be Peace and give this to the universe,
it is all you should do.
Even thinking "I am Peace" disturbs this Peace,
so just be Quiet, be as you are.

You are Being, you are not "had been,"
and not "would be," but "Being."
You are the Timelessness in which no death can enter
for where there is no time there is no death.
That Timelessness is Now, and That is Being.

Being is always shining, I Am is the Light of Being.
This Diamond cannot hide, and can never be hidden.
When there is no mind the face shines with beauty and innocence.
Just simply be quiet, just be as you are.

You are the Space which never moves and never travels.
Inner and outer space is due only to name and form.
Remove this form from mind by removing attachment
to any object, thought, or action.

You are the garden of joy,

to be happy you need nobody else.
You are in the garden of joy,
but when you think of old things you become sad.
This joy, this Moment, will destroy mind and suffering,
because this Moment *is* Happiness.
So stop going to the past moments in order to suffer.

Unconditioned Consciousness is Happiness
and Quietness with no when, no where, just Now.
This Happiness conditioned by thought becomes mind.
Even the "I," the first condition, is a disturbance in Happiness.
Due to desires and hopes of the ego no one is happy.
So to come to Happiness do not think, or give rise to a desire,
simply keep Quiet, because thinking is the graveyard.
To be happy you should have and nold nothing,
otherwise your pockets will smell like dead fish.
My dear friend, Happiness is not an experience,
It is your nature so you need to do nothing for it.
Only Self knowledge brings Happiness because
Happiness is the nature of Self.

Here, *Here* is the wine that nobody knows.
Everything is in Here and this is Consciousness.
Consciousness is the substratum of everything in the Universe;
It, you, resides in every atom of every molecule and even
space and time derive their existence from It.
Who is Conscious that you wear a body and mind and that
the movement of birth and death is in this same Consciousness?
You are That: all doing and not doing,
all multiplicity and all unity is in Consciousness.
Bondage is to deny this, Freedom is to know It.
You are That, *You are That!*

Consciousness.
The senses cannot feel It and the mind cannot understand it.
Consciousness alone is everywhere and rises as "I" within you.
It is the shining of the sun and the motion of the earth.
It is beyond space and time which derive their existence from it.
The mind cannot go to touch it, or to reach it,
and will miss it if it tries to find it.
These attempts are movements hiding the Stillness.
It is found only by itself when mind does not move.

Check all movements of mind for one moment only,
stop all desires and all thought for one second only,
especially the first thought of "I," for one instant only,
and you are beyond the cycle of birth and death forever.
This cycle is samsara, your own imagination.

It has no beginning and only Self Knowledge will end it.
The question "Who am I?" will end it.
So firmly decide, "I have to do it Now."
This human birth is such a blessing, don't waste it!
Postponement is samsara, the cycle of suffering.
Whenever you are in trouble ask, "Am I dreaming?"
This is "Who am I?" and it will wake you up
and make you fall in love with your own Self.
Then you will know all "others,"
and will take this candle wherever you go!

Be quiet, don't think, don't make effort.
To be bound takes effort, to be Free takes no effort.
Peace is beyond thought and effort.
Do not think and do not make effort because
this only obscures That, and will never reveal That.
This is why keeping Quiet is the key
to the storehouse of love and peace.

This Quietness is no-mind, this no-thought is Freedom.
Identify yourself as this Nothingness, as this Quietness,
and be careful not to make it an experience
because this is mind tricking you out of it
with the trap of duality; the trap of witness and witnessed.
Being is Being, there is no witness and no witnessed.
Experiencing it is to say "I am Free,"
which is exactly the same trap as saying "I am bound."
After letting go of object
do not hold onto the subject either.
Let go, Be Quiet.

The purpose of life is to be at Peace,
To love all Beings, and to know who you are.
Know your Self and you know everything.
This immaculate Knowledge alone is, Emptiness alone is.

How can you come out of Emptiness
if there are no limits to it?
The appearance of a manifestation
is but the lila of this Emptiness.
Know who you are, Here and Now,
by simply Being Quiet.

You are this Moment, introduce yourself to This,
do not attach your mind to any direction.
No sadhana, no past, no future,
not even the emptiness of your heart, not even space.
To be free forever introduce yourself to this Moment.
This Moment is always this Moment, It will not change.
It is Freedom, free from mind and concepts,
and is your fundamental birthright.
The best use of this Moment is to drown in It.
Keep Quiet, you are inside of the inside,
do not dwell anywhere and make no effort.
The concept of effort and practice is bondage.
Just keep Quiet, Wherever you are, just keep Quiet.

Name and form hide Reality: This is the Teaching.
Giving name and form is an obstacle to Freedom
because then the substratum, Consciousness, cannot be seen.
Call it a statue of a horse and the granite is hidden,
see a ring and you won't see the gold.
Name and form can never leave Consciousness,
as the ring can never leave the gold.
Even space is in this because only Self is.

Before a wave rises it is Ocean,
before desire moves it is Emptiness.
Destroy craving and bondage by identifying as
experiencing, not experience, as Seeing, not the seer.
You are Consciousness, not one who is Conscious.
To be free you must be like Freedom and this is without desire.
All is and is known in desirelessness.
If you don't want to possess remove your pockets: duality!
The past is past so don't carry it in your pocket.
Why go to the graveyard when you know that you are alive?
All that is temporary must be shunned so only
take hold of your absolute Self.

All that you are attached to, all that you love,
all that you know, someday will be gone.
Knowing this, and that the world is your mind
which you create, play in, and suffer from,
is known as discrimination.
Discriminate between the real and the unreal.
The known is unreal and will come and go
so stay with the unknown, the unchanging Truth.
All which appears and disappears is not real,
and no nectar will come from it so don't cling to it,
and once you let go do not turn back to it.
Stay as Eternity in your own Being.

Surrender to Space
or dissolve ego with Knowledge.
With love and adoration
go within your Self with the vehicle of inquiry.
This inquiry is the abandonment of all effort.
It is not finding what was lost in the past,
but simply remembering the present, the Presence.
Proceed within so silently that even thought is too loud.

Keep Quiet
by knowing you are not the ego that has to keep Quiet.
This Quietness, this Silence,
has nothing to do with talking or not talking
because even when you are not talking
your mind is continually racing everywhere.
No thought rising from your mind is this Silence.
Awareness of any object is not it.
The one who is aware of awareness is It!

Surrender is to surrender your concept of separateness, your ego.
Surrender is to submit your stupidness, your wickedness,
to the will of existence. That's all.
You must surrender like a river discharging into the Ocean.
Surrender is to discharge your river of separateness
into the ocean of Being, losing your limitations,
and allowing to happen what happens.

Check your notions and intentions by inquiring
"what is this movement of the mind?"

People confuse inquiry with yoga and meditation.
Yoga is union with the subject within.
Meditation is concentration on an object outside.
Inquiry does not keep any relation with anything within
or without.

You cannot find and kill the mind, it is the ten headed demon.
Chop off a head and another will grow back because
"I am bound" and "I am free" is exactly the same trap.
So only the desire for freedom will help you
because you are what you think.
Think to destroy the mind and mind is a destroyer, not destroyed.
Think only of Freedom and you become Freedom.
As persistent as the pain of a toothache, always think of Self,
because if the desire for Freedom is continuous
then all other habits and distractions will drop away.

In the pure joy all manifestation is created as lila to play in, to play *as*.
This is all your own creation, your own Self. All Being is one Being. What
appears and disappears is not real. Play in the lila and say "I am existence."
If you say "I am body," you say a lie and you suffer. "I" itself is just
conditioning and vasanas. Individual "I" is a reflection of true "I" in the
dirty pool of ego. Abandon the "I" and its vasanas and know that you are
that which does not sleep, even when the ego is in a deep sleep.

When the face of Self is seen by the ego, ego becomes That. But when ego
sees the senses it becomes the confused individual desiring the objects of
senses. Don't get lost and confused in the mind's cycle of rebirths. Whatever
the mind can conceive is not It. Get rid of all that can be rejected, including
rejection itself. Then the mind will be quiet and this cannot be described: It
is Isness, Emptiness, Fullness, and it is the Truth!

The Truth does not move,
there is no coming or going.
The stirring thought "I" creates an entire universe,
But the Truth does not move.
Keep vigilant of where and how this "I" arises.
This is Satsang and it is your own nature.
You are the Truth which does not move.

But if you say from the ego point of view "I am doing," you are taking
yourself to be the individual movement, the wave. You reinforce this by

17

creating an object and generating some interest in it, and then having desire for it, and instantly you even want some reward for having it. Therefore, you want to go to that object, then you want to possess it, you want to own it. As soon as you possess it you have fear of losing it because where there are two there is always fear of separation. Where fear arises, anger arises. With anger there is confusion, lack of understanding, and lack of discrimination. When you cannot decide things properly, it is total destruction.

So the short cut to Enlightenment is the purity of mind. This short cut is to cut short your desires. Objects of desires are not what give happiness, they destroy your peace and knot you with suffering.

> The sense of attainment of objects of desires
> also will not give happiness. This gives bondage.
> *It is absence of desire which brings Happiness.*
> It is only desire which disturbs eternal peace and rest.
> This desire is the disease of mind; live without it, and be happy.
> Happiness is true Self and is always Here.
> The prescription for this Happiness is to simply be Quiet.

When an object that you wanted is in front of you happiness initially arises because the intellect is steady, due to momentary satisfaction, and returns to the Source, the fountain of Bliss. There Self reflects on it and the experience of this reflection is joy because this is the nature of the Self. The bliss is not from an object, It is Self. So keep the mind steady and the Self will reflect on it and draw the mind into it. Pleasure is of the Self, in the Self and not outside of the Self in transient objects. Objects are temporary, but the bliss is not. You are one with this bliss and once you know this you will love all from your Self, as your Self, of your Self. Your Love will be forever, not from and to names and forms but always in your Self. This Consciousness gives you bliss. Don't carry name and form and you are happy, this is the pleasure of sleep, and this will transcend the waking, dream, sleep states. So associate only with the Peace and Joy and Truth. When this becomes habitual and natural it will transcend three states and you will be transported into a state beyond states. This is for you to experience Here and Now.

So when something comes in front of you just stay as the Truth, which does not move, and react to the circumstances whatever they may be, good or bad. Just react without any possessive concept in you. Whatever happens keep most interested in Self and see that all that arises is Self rising out of Self. Self is not interested in possessing things because Self is total. So don't react with interest of reward or possession. Then you will be very free and all your interactions will be out of compassion and life will be like sailing in the

You are Love Dancing as Emptiness

breeze of non-attachment. This breeze comes from Self and will happen after Freedom, not before.

When you are Free still you have to live because still the world will be there but living will be very compassionate. Just love each other, and hold no hatred with anything. This depends on you, how you take things, and whether this "I" is from the ego or whether it is from Nowhere. The "I" from Nowhere contains the whole universe and this is total understanding itself.

> Only preoccupation with what is not real
> keeps you from realizing the Truth of who you are Here and Now.
> Desiring anything else, anything that comes and goes, is foolish.
> The wise one does not do this,
> so love the Lord with all your heart.

ॐ

> Method is an impediment to love,
> a postponement of freedom, and an insult to peace.
> Use no method, simply identify as That.
> Many methods may take you to Anandamayakosha,
> and end at this subtlest of veils, yet there is an enjoyer of bliss.
> Pre-dawn light is not the Sun,
> bliss is not the totality of Understanding,
> it is the turning toward your own Face
> and is the direct 'practice' to know your Self.

> There is no attainment
> and no cultivation of original nature,
> You are Consciousness, not a farmer!
> Why work for that which you already are?
> Do not mentate, do not stir a thought,
> Trying to get out of superimposed bondage,
> which is the notion that you are separate from Existence,
> you will land in superimposed freedom.

The purpose of all practice is Silence, your real nature. Without Silence you cannot be in peace so strive only for this. Even while active remain in Silence as Silence and be conscious of Silence always. Ramana's main teaching is Silence and it is this Silence that silently answers all questions and removes all doubts. Train your mind to go to Silence. As Kabir said: "Keep your body, your mind, your intellect, and your prana quiet and wisdom will follow behind you searching for you!" Be Silent by directing your mind toward its Source. Mind directed toward object of senses is suffering. The same mind must investigate its Source; the "I" must face its Source. This is true austerity, true practice, and true meditation. Face the Atman, this is Satsang, because this is home, the holy company of the Self. The most holy association is to *Be as you are*. This is Freedom. This is beyond imagination, very new and very fresh. So just keep Quiet. Do not think. It is you. It is you. Don't stir a thought, and if a thought comes, let it, don't waver, don't doubt your majesty. It is so simple. The one who has It will know that they have done it. When you are quiet it is Beauty, Joy and Stillness. It is effortless. Effort is to disturb your mind, effort is playing with corpses in the graveyard. Just contemplate that which is always silence. Go to the Source. Do not believe anything, simply stay quiet and return home and do not rest until you are there. Peace is only available when there is no "I" and you need an "I" to do practice.

> The secret to Bliss is to *stop* the search, *stop* thinking,
> *stop* not-thinking, and keep Quiet.
> The best practice is to Know "Who am I."
> You are Brahman, know this.
> If you want to do anything, just
> Always adore Self.

Self Realization takes one second, but this second takes a great effort to remove all other thoughts from your mind. You must remove all from this second and allow only this second to stay with you. In that second stand up on your toes and with clenched fists shout, "I have to be free in this second!" It is very rare to have such extreme desire for Freedom, such extreme activity and strength that even gods will come and bow before you. It takes a very strong body and mind and intention. Then this second will work. You have to do it. Don't just read the menu, eat the food! Defeat the stupid mind. It is not understanding, it is Being! It is not the mind which makes the decision to be Free, when you do it there is no mind! Control the mind and use it as a slave when you need it, but Here you don't need the mind to be Free. Use no mind and stir no thought, Freedom is not dependent on meditation and effort.

> Sattvic mind will get it right away.
> Rajas mind has to practice and attend Satsang.
> Tamasic mind will not even attend Satsang.
> Sattvic mind is karmically pure, always in meditation,
> and is not different from Freedom.

As it rises so it falls. Make effort and it rises.
Stop effort and it falls. Make the choice!
Stay as simple natural Being without thought or doer
Out of Nothing you can do anything and not leave fo
No intention is no limitation, just stay Quiet,
simply do not stir a thought.
Not activating the mind is to not externalize.
There is no way or method, just keep out of the way.
The revelation of the Self will occur
only when you do not interfere.
Keeping Quiet is giving time to
this Love and Beauty.
Stay as Such.

Dharma means not holding onto any concept,
so the supreme dharma is to reject all dharmas.
If you reject everything what will happen?
All the burdens of all the religions and concepts
will fall from your mind,
bringing you to the perfect Peace and Love,
and this is your dharma.

At the end of sadhana the Guru confirms that you are Free.
You came to Lucknow not for freedom,
but to know that you are not bound.
In Satsang you have to remove your doubts,
because it is only doubts that keep you from being Free.
Simply keep Quiet!

Why get into trouble? It's enough! Everything is Here: Happiness, Beauty, Love! Whatever you call it, it is full of everything! Whatever you think, so it becomes because it is Consciousness and everything is possible in Consciousness. You have created all these manifestations, all these waves in the ocean. You are so capable, so vast, so full, so complete, so conscious. You can create all of this so why suffer? Emptiness is never affected by appearances in Emptiness. The ocean does not suffer when a wave rises. It does not even suffer when a wave falls. Let the waves dance and let them enjoy. Just stay Here and see only Love and Beauty and Happiness. This is the Ultimate Understanding. It does not need any thinking or any process or any meditations. You are Limitlessness, Fathomlessness, Vastness: who will disturb this Vastness? Where will you run out so that you are no longer

You are not limited! Just stay as you are, do not start from anywhere
d do not go anywhere, and do not activate a thought.

Ego says it matters,
the Supreme says that it does not.
Even the power of decision is not from ego.
All is the Supreme Power, do not attribute it to anything else
because this only reinforces the ghosts.
Face the One.

To see God you need body, mind, senses,
and so much paraphernalia.
To go beyond God you need nothing.
Don't even activate a thought,
activate no energy even to not activate.
Contemplation and adoration of Self is all that you need.
Love: Surrender to the Divine and keep Quiet.
Wisdom: Inquire into the Divine and keep Quiet.
Know "I am Home, I am Home itself," and
incessantly look at Self.

There is nothing more beautiful than this Being.
The happiness of all beings combined
is not one millionth the happiness of Being.
Thought cannot trespass into its purity,
not even the I-thought can enter.
Don't think or understand, just stay as thus.

Keep in tune with the source and all your actions will be correct.
If you don't there will be trouble no matter what you do.
With arrogance of ego there is no skillfulness
and without arrogance everything is skillful.

Just as space in a room is not affected by how much furniture is in the
room so space is not affected by activity or by mind or by thought. You are
Space, do not touch the furniture in this space, which means keep Quiet, do
not mentate, do not activate thoughts. If thoughts arise allow them to come
and go, but do not hold onto them or let them land. Do not touch "I am the
body." Instead the first and last thought must be, "I am pure infinite
Consciousness, I am Love itself."

Know the Truth of this, not just the words!
The Truth is all what Is!

22

If something's nature is absence don't cling to it. If something's nature is Presence, this is you; this is Beauty, Love, Self. All else is imagination. The power of illusion is very strong, so be vigilant in a joyful play with tendencies because when one is near Freedom all demons will consolidate and attack. Continue being Self meditating on Self, do this playfully always.

> All appearance has Emptiness as its basis.
> Sit on the throne of Emptiness and all will be yours.
> No manifestation, no freedom, no mind; this is ultimate Truth.
> The ultimate Truth is that all is Emptiness and always was.

> What you think is what you are so stop thinking
> and you will be that Nothing which is everything,
> Awake, and not possessing anything that can be lost.
> When the mind enters into the Chit
> the heart dances and dwells in peace and bliss.

> You are always in Love,
> and you can only Love yourself,
> the changless one in which even space is.
> There is no beginning, no middle, and no end to it.
> Only Love is worth loving and this is your own Self.

> *So Now, Here, simply look!*
> All around you is a flood of Peace!
> Where are you standing?

The essence of my teaching is this: I teach about That which cannot be attained by any teaching. My teaching cannot be taught. I have no teaching for the Essence from where all teachings arise. This Essence doesn't need any teaching or non-teaching for it is beyond everything. It is from where all words rise.

As Bhagavan would say: "Here the Truth Is, choose what you want."

Self

Self is what you are, You are That
Fathomlessness in which experience and concepts appear.
Self is the Moment which has no coming or going.
It is the Heart, Atman, Emptiness.
It shines to Itself, by Itself, in Itself.
Self is what gives breath to life,
you need not search for It, It is Here.
You are That through which you would search.
You *are* what you are looking for!
And That is all it is.
Only Self is.

You were never born, and though only desire takes birth,
Nothing has ever happened, Nothing has ever existed!
This Nothingness you are, and this is the Ultimate Truth.
You are totally alone because Beauty alone is.
Only Self is.

You simply cannot deny that you are Consciousness.
You dwell in the Lotus of the Heart as Joy in Bliss.
Keep Quiet and you will reveal your Self to your Self.
Self Knowledge is that which is worth sacrificing anything for,
because everything else is just a mirage rising out of Consciousness.

Self is the indweller of all Beings,
so love of others is Love of Self, your Self.
Self is the greatest Love and the dearest of all lovers.
Love is the attraction of Self to Self in Self.
There is nothing besides this Love, this source of Joy.
See your own beauty and you are this Indweller, this Love
and the Beauty itself.

Neti, Neti; but what you Are cannot be rejected.
It is Now only; waking or sleeping or dreaming,
It is still the Now which only Is.
Only Self is.

This present Moment is Light, is Self.
This Moment is not bondage or freedom.
It is most precious beyond ideation.
This Moment is the screen on which all projects.

It is always Still and Untouched and it is out of time.
There is no difference between the Ultimate and this Presence.
To be in this Moment abandon all desires,
including the desire to be in it.

That which has no name or form
has millions of names:
Being, Awareness, Bliss, Isness, Atman, Truth, Self,
Auspiciousness, Beauty, Freedom, Divine Love,
Fullness, Emptiness, Consciousness, Nowness,
Effortlessness, Hereness, Silence, Brahman.
As the tongue speaks the word "tongue"
so you speak these names.
To avoid the veiling of your nature with preconceptions,
Buddha spoke of Self in negative terms
like Anata, Untouched, Unmanifest, Unseen,
Unapproachable, Unknowable, and Unstained.

Before notions and creations you exist,
so there are no words
for That beyond words and language.
Self doesn't need to understand Itself,
Freedom is before the concept of freedom.
You are what remains
when the concepts of "I," mind, and past disappear.
Nothingness is no concept.

Identify as Peace-Beauty-Love, do not experience it.
Know, "I am inactive, the activity takes place in me,
I am That, I am the screen, I never come and I never go."
Identify as Consciousness Itself.
If you do not forget who you are,
this appearance of activity is the Cosmic Dance.
Stay as "I am," not as what comes and goes.
The individual I-sense is mind, but Being has no frontiers.
It is aware of Itself Itself. Identify as Being.

> When mind is pure you will see Self in all Beings.
> Purify the mind by removing all concepts,
> especially the concept of purity.
> Then Self reveals itself to the empty mind
> which is Consciousness.

Ego and mind and all creations arise out of Self as Self,
even the ugliest of doubts and the most separate of differences
rise from the beautiful source as Isness.
In Self there are no do's and don'ts.
If there is unhappiness you are not unhappy,
you are the Untouched Awareness of this unhappiness.
As waves are not separate from ocean, nor rays from sun,
you are not separate from Existence.
You are the Moment in which all is.

The Scriptures speak of the three Holy rivers Within.
These are Existence, Consciousness, and Bliss.
Being beyond thought and effort
they cannot be objectified or subjectified.
They are so dear, so near, behind the retina and before breath.
You need not see This, you are It.

You are not different than Existence, than Being.
See Being everywhere by not looking.
The Seeing is Being, not the objects seen.

Consciousness is the original Mother.
If you know this she will take care of you
and give you Happiness, Peace, and Deathlessness.
This Mother we do not recognize and this gets us into trouble.
This Unknown is your nature, return to That
because the known will give no lasting Peace,
no lasting Love.

Bliss is Eternal,
even though it appears to arise when the mind dies.
Bliss is not an experience, It is your nature.
This is the Heart of the Wise.
This gift is always calling to everyone,
"You are seated in the Heart of all Beings."
This is the Truth: Your Face shines.

As the king gardening in the garden is still the king and not the gardener,
so the I Am can be in the garden of the world and remain I Am. It is you who
is active in all the activities of the world. Go to where the physicality of the
world rises from and you will discover the vastness, the secret sacred core of

your Heart. This is who you are, but hold any object or take yourself to be anything and you will forget this, all due to desires and hopes. All is one and One is all. Identify yourself with the common center giving up old habits of desires and hopes and you are the Emperor of the Universe. Go to this Here and Now and you *are* this Here and Now.

> All is Self. The only difference between "you" and "me"
> are the words and concepts of "you" and "me."
> Self in you is the Self in me and in all Beings.
> The Source of everything is the same and this is Self,
> this is love and compassion.
> From Self try to go anywhere!

> "I am the ocean and all forms seen
> are my waves dancing on me," this is knowledge.
> When waves rise the ocean loses nothing
> and when waves fall the ocean gains nothing.
> As waves play so the ocean plays.
> I am ocean, I am water, I am wave;
> separation between water and ocean and wave cannot exist!
> There are no differences, no disturbances, no one to be disturbed.
> Giving rise to an "I," or any other thought, is giving rise to a wave.
> Water remains water so allow everything to be, for it is your Self.
> As a river discharges into ocean, discharge into what you are:
> Happiness, Bliss, Being, Cosmos.
> Here is only Awareness,
> Here only Self is.

> You are that which is present even in forgetfulness
> because you are Aware that you are forgetful.
> You are the Consciousness of Awareness in
> the three states of waking, dreaming, and sleeping.
> Only Self does not vanish in these three states.

> Self is no-mind, no-mind has no body,
> from this Beauty of no-mind art and intuition arise.

> Nothing ever happened or ever will.
> You have always been perfect Love and Peace.
> What changes is not real and what is real cannot change.
> You are that secret, that purity beyond change and description,
> but if you touch the "I" you become polluted with pride.
> The "I" rising from the effort of ego is not the real "I."

The real "I" knows that everything is my reflection-projection.
Simply knowing "I Am I Am" is effortlessness,
is meditation, and is Sahaja, the natural state of Being.

In every speck of dust there are innumerable Buddhas shining in innumerable universes. It is very hard to explain it to you and for you to understand, but this is a fact. You can see it. Everything emerges out of the atom. It is a mystery that no one can solve. It is the same as the Moment that we normally speak of in Satsang. In it you can see all your lives. Everyone is intrinsically Buddha.

Questioner: I want the revelation of eternal undefinable Being.

Papaji:
    This is who you are,
    why have doubt about it!
    Enlightenment is not about words
    and thoughts and concepts which can be doubted,
    Enlightenment is always Here.

    By "Here" I don't mean this present space.
    Here is somewhere within where mind cannot reach.
    Presence is always here and you are always That.
    This here is not the opposite of "there."
    This here is nowhere, it is your Heart.
    When mind is still all comes back to the Heart.
    All the cosmos is but a speck in your Heart.

    Turn mind over into this Here and it is lost.
    Then only Light, Wisdom, and Love remain
    and This you are not different or apart from.

ॐ

If I am not this bodymind form what am I?

You are Formlessness which takes the form of Satyam, Shivam, Sundaram. This is your form: You are Truth, you are Shiva, you are Beauty. This is what we are directly working on here, but you are not going toward this, You *are* this: I *am* Satyam, I *am* Shivam, I *am* Sundaram. I *am* Satchitananda. This is the form of the Atman: Truth Consciousness Bliss. This is your own Self, you are not hankering after it, It is Within.

Bliss is Within. That you *are*.
Truth is Within. That you *are*.
Beauty is Within. That you *are*.
Love is Within. That you *are*.
This is addressing to your own Self.

I want to stay in my own Self.

Then decide that only Self exists and you will never be out of it.
It is Unlimited, how can you jump in and out of it?
How can you jump into limitations, when you are the Unlimited?

Decide: "I am Self, I am Truth
I am God, I am Grace,"
and there will be no trouble.

ॐ

I feel at home in Consciousness.

And where are you when you are not home? Everywhere is Consciousness and everywhere is home. "Everywhere" is but a small corner of your Heart. You are that vast. There is no travel because you are always home. Surrender your ego and you are home.

I had a dream while in the West that you gave me the name
Satchitananda. What is this name?

It is the name of the Self, of the Formlessness. Though everybody has this name it is hidden in the core of your Heart. Sat-chit-ananda is the indweller of all beings but few recognize this. It is not the name of a person but of that which has the qualities of Truth and Consciousness and Bliss, all three are one. Wherever there is Truth, Satyam, there is Chit, Consciousness, and also Bliss, Ananda.

You say that this was a dream, but I tell you it was neither a dream, nor waking, nor sleeping, but something that transcends these. Thus, it is known as the fourth state, or Turiya in Sanskrit. In Turiya you have the darshan of God and receive the messages of God. This is why this "dream" is so easy to remember while you tend to forget others.

Is Beingness the same as God? Is this Sahaja samadhi?

Beingness is very different from what most people call God. God is a concept created by you. Beingness is just Beingness and nobody created it because it is beyond creations and destructions. That in which all creations abide, including God, is called Being.

Sahaja samadhi is the melting of the individual into the natural Oneness and Beingness of all things. It is the samadhi which involves no effort, no use of mind. It is the natural samadhi which is your natural state. If you are Here and not thinking, it is Sahaja samadhi. You can eat and drink and carry on any activity while in Sahaja. Sahaja samadhi is Self in the exquisite experience of the Fullness of Being!

What is true awareness?

There is the awareness which is aware of objects like flowers. True Awareness is the awareness which is aware of the awareness of objects. It is the undisturbed simple awareness in which things rise and fall.

There is an Awareness beyond
the awareness of objects and events.
You are That Awareness in which
the awareness of objects stays.

This Awareness has no name and when you try to give it a name the trouble arises. You are nameless and formless; you can't see anything. Know "I am nameless and formless," and that "I am aware of my own Self." The pure Consciousness will pull you back, it is not that you will enter into it. When you enter into it, it is ego entering, but when It pulls you It has made the choice to take you Home. This happens somehow and we can't know why. Very rare beings are picked up by Consciousness. Once drawn in that man's travels are over!

So do not give it a name or it will just be another object of someone's observation. Consciousness cannot be observed, it is Fullness itself, Limitlessness, Eternal itself. You have to merge with it. Actually, it is not merging, there is no word which describes it. You have to be as good and pure as It so that you are picked up by It. By your own efforts you can not do it. Just see that you are so beautiful that you are chosen by the bridegroom. This is how it ends. I hope you have understood.

I feel like a distant observer of all that is going on.

This observer cannot be touched by anyone. This observer is beyond any identification, any name, and any form. So when you are this observer no one can touch you, you can't even touch yourself then, and there is no fear. You can go into any forest and be fearless of the lions and tigers. Just look into their eyes and nobody will eat you up.

ॐ

*I have had a glimpse of Supreme Consciousness. It was the expansion
of Consciousness and the absence of a center of existence.*

When you have a glimpse of anything you become the seer of the glimpse
and what you glimpse is the object of the seer: the seen. To have a glimpse
you must have seer, sight and seen. So how can you have a glimpse of
Supreme Consciousness because this can never be the object of anyone! Not
even God can see this because even God is an object of perception which a
devotee loves. The devotee extends his mind and this becomes God. This
glimpse of Super Consciousness is not possible, It cannot be objectified
because it is the subject, though truly speaking it is not the subject either.
Where there's no relation between subject and object there can be no glimpse.

The whole world is seer, sight, and seen, but this you cannot place in a
category. When someone has a strong desire to be Free, it moves toward
Super Consciousness, merges with it and becomes That itself.

As a moth runs to the flame and kisses it, what happens? No more moth!
The flame rises in happiness and says, "Come my dear boy, I have been
waiting for you." This moth will not return, it has become the flame. Like
this there can be no glimpse! Whosoever wants to be Free is being led by
something which has been calling that person.

ॐ

What relationship is between energy, golden light and Awareness?

Water is English, agua is Spanish, paani is Hindi. Three different names
for the same substance. So you can call it shakti or light. Light means to have
knowledge of something, for instance knowledge of the missing child. With
the light you can see the child and this light is knowledge. Knowledge is the
energy which takes you to know that you are One! You are Knowledge itself
and energy and this is the same thing as Awareness. Only words are different
according to different persons. One person will say, "I want to be Free." A
Buddhist will say "I want to be empty," and still others want nirvana. All
these different words mean the same thing which has no name. Paani, agua,
water itself has no name. So it is only you who will call it awareness, light
or energy, but it doesn't know its own name, because it is nameless and
formless. Wherever there is a name there must be something not true.

Any name or form leads you to That which has no name or form. How
will you find what has no name or form? Don't try to search for the nameless
and formless because you can't do it. But this light is there, and this is
knowledge, this energy is Awareness, there is no difference. Shakti and Shiva

are the same! One is knowledge and the other is the energy to know, "I myself am Shiva."

Energy cannot die. Energy will always remain. Forms may appear or disappear, but energy will always be Here.

As the substratum?

Yes, it is the substratum, and now the substratum knows, by energy, that "I am the substratum." It doesn't make a difference. This knowledge of energy that "I am That," is energy itself, knowledge itself, light itself, wisdom itself. This is also called Freedom.

But I can have Awareness and I can have Awareness of energy, so are they not separate?

No, they are not separate. The wave rises from the ocean and appears separate. The name is different now, the movement is different, the height, breadth, and width are different. Also, it moves and now she forgets that once upon a time she ocean! There's no difference between the content of the ocean and the wave. So now the wave somehow knows, "I am the ocean."

So let there be movement towards shore. Let it rise and fall and disappear. This is the world appearing and disappearing, but the ocean is not worried at all. The substratum, the essence, doesn't mind that it has become a wave and the question of falling and rising will not appear.

So the energy will always be there.

No, it will always be *Here!* Wherever there is an ocean there will be energy within itself that allows the waves to move and disappear.

And if you die?

That is equal to the wave falling into the ocean. Death you have only heard from someone, it is not your experience. Therefore, you have agreed that you will die only because you have accepted from someone that you were born. But energy itself, the substance itself, does not die. The body, like wave and like forms will disappear while the essence cannot change. This understanding is called energy. Returning to the substratum is called Shiva, the ocean which does not change.

I want to enter the cave of the heart and stay there.

This Here and Now
Is the cave of the Heart.

In the books it is written that there is a cave in the heart and you must have this idea from those old scriptures. Your desire to find this cave takes you out of Here and Now. Then you lose the experience of Now and search for the cave which never exists. Don't try to live in a cave for the cave is just a concept. You can only live in Now.

When you live in Now you will not have any desire for anything else and likewise, you will only be in Now when you give up all desires, even the desire to be in it. Give up all desires to stay here or there or anywhere and give up the desire for "this" and for "that."

How can I give up all desire?

By keeping Quiet!

ॐ

Please tell me: Did I lose my identity or did I find my Self which has no identity?

You don't know what identity you lost and what identity you found. Identification with body is identity. Then you become a son, a father, a mother, or whatever. This is physical identity and as long as it stays you can't see the identity beyond all identifications.

> As long as body identification stays,
> you can't have the identity beyond all identities,
> the identity of I Am.

This is identity with your own Self, not with the ego-mind-body-senses-objects.

How can I totally destroy the mind so that the beauty of Self can shine forever in ultimate Freedom?

Be the Ocean of Bliss and you will not see the relationships with the world, you will only see Ocean. You won't have any relationships with what is outside the Ocean, just a connection with your own fullness of water. This fullness is your original state and this is to be enjoyed. Stay within the Ocean, as the Ocean, thinking only of Ocean always. Nothing else but this Ocean should come in your mind, eyes or contact. Always be in the contact with the content of the Ocean. This you must do. Think of That, smell That, hear That, touch That. This will end your conflicts.

ॐ

One and a half years ago when I received diksha, initiation, in Haridwar during Dewali, everything changed, though it appeared no different. I am so thankful and grateful to you. Papaji, there is a small flame which burns in the fullness of itself and I am its servant, though not always willingly. Thank you.

Where do you see this blue flame?

I don't see it, though it is wherever I am looking.

It is there but you cannot see it. You feel it though. It is looking at you! It means you are a rare one, a lucky person who this flame can look upon. This flame is divinity itself. It has no form, and not even a name. It will work, you have to keep it up. This flame will reveal itself in full formlessness. As you see the dawn before the sun, having had a vision of the flame shows that you are heading in a good direction. Keep it, keep Quiet, and simply see you are not to do anything. This will always attract you and this is called meditation. When you are attracted to something it is called meditation and this is the best attraction and the best form of meditation. So let it be as it is. There is more that I can tell you, but I won't openly because so many people will copy your experience and will start seeing blue lights, since it becomes whatever you imagine. But they'll just be fake experiences. (giggles)

> This light is within and reflects that which is within
> onto the outside. It is within your own Heart
> and seeing it is a good symptom
> which will give you peace and happiness
> like the big blue sky does.

> You have to see this light in your Heart
> equal in size to your thumb.
> This Light in your own Heart
> enlightens the whole universe from Here.
> This is the Light of your own Self,
> of your own Atman.

When you are pure with no desire you can imagine or feel this Light and you can never get rid of It because It is always with you. Wherever you see, see this Light, and see that it is your own Self. This Light wants to appear to you in Satsang and not while you are in the fishmarket. The fishmarket will only give you bad smells and most people prefer this.

ॐ

What is this interval between the stream of thoughts?

In that interval is Consciousness. Between two clouds, there is an interval and that interval is the blue sky! Slow down the thoughts and look into the intervals. Yes! Look into the intervals and pay more attention to the interval than the cloud!

Where the first thought has left and the other is not arisen, that is Consciousness, that is Freedom, that is your own place, your own abode. You are always there, you see.

Shift the attention, change the gestalt. Don't look at the figure, look at the background! If I put a big blackboard the size of the wall here and mark it with a white point and ask you, "What do you see?" Ninety-nine percent of you will not see the blackboard! (laughs) You will say, "I see a little white spot." Such a big blackboard and it is not seen, and only a little white spot, which is almost invisible, is seen! Why? *Because this is the fixed pattern of the mind:* To look at the figure, not the blackboard; to look at the cloud, not at the sky; to look at the thought, not at Consciousness.

That's all the teaching is. Always look to Consciousness. Always look to Consciousness and know this is what you are! This is your own place, your own abode. Stay Here. No one can touch you. Who can enter Here where you are? Even your mind cannot enter.

"You are not the body," is often spoken here. There are some who believe in the preciousness of the body so that there can be the experience of life as sacred. They feel a liberation by feeling completely present in the body.

The sacredness of life is the purusha within you, experience That! It is not the body, which can be made male or female. You are the Purusha within the Heart of everyone whether they appear to be male or female. It is mentioned in the Upanishads and other holy sutras that this Purusha is equal to the length of a thumb. It is within your own Heart, forever burning as a flame. It is your own Self, your own Atman. When you concentrate on that you will see that you are this Purusha and not the gender male or female. Though everybody is Purusha they don't identify with That, but identify with their body for their own interest. No one is told about this eternal Purusha which doesn't come and go. This is what I spoke: Neither do I come, nor do I go. It is that Purusha which speaks. If you become That and merge with this Purusha then it speaks from where the speech arises from and not what the tongue can speak. The tongue can speak, but where does the strength come from which enables to speak? That comes from the fountain which is called the Purusha, Aham Purusha. It is That Purusha which I refer to.

How to release the Self and be in love at the same time?

Self is not bound, it is not chained, there is no prison for That. It is always Free.

I know that your Grace is the only thing which will wake me out of the world of my mind. Even the strength of my longing for Freedom is your Grace. Will you tell me what my real name is?

All the names which are given to you are given by parents and priests, but this is not your real name. When you are born you don't come out with a name. Only later do you become a Suzanne or whatever. You have no name and don't think that you have one.

You are nameless.
Where there is form there is name
and where there is name there must be form.
You are not that, you are within the form
and you are someone which has no name
because only a form needs name.

Who is sitting in your own Heart? Does this have a name?
The indweller of the Heart: *That is what you really are.*
You are not born of your parents, you are That which has
no name, which will never die or be born, That which is Eternal.

If you believe what people say,
why not believe that "I Am That."
I am Atman, I am Peace, I am Love, I am Bliss.
If you don't believe this
then continue this mantra forever: "I am Bliss."

I don't want to take on any new identity because I do not want to impose form on this Bliss, on this formlessness.

If you decide that you do not want any identity that touches name and form you will instantly become formless. If you do not touch this concept of identity then you are free Here and Now.

You go to the past every time that you use your name. People have to call you by some name, but that name should not touch the past. Buddha also is a name, but when you call him Buddha, what personality comes to mind? So your name should not remind you of any attachments or relations. Therefore, many names are given here in this Satsang which do not touch any personality. People leave their old names and pasts here.

If I say go and bring Miss Emptiness here, will you bring her? The word is there, the meaning is there, but will you bring her? It can't be done! Like this the Atman in you has a name, but you can't hold it. It is beyond space and which cannot be touched.

I see that I should not necessarily reject the negative things in life that come and go, I should just not be attached.

Everything in the universe comes, stays, and goes. What doesn't come, stay, or go is your own Self.

ॐ

They say that there are three classes of seekers: Those who get it fast like camphor, those who get it soon like gunpowder, and those who get it slowly like wet wood. What advice do you give the wet wood?

That there are no classes and nothing to be gained. You are always Free, but your attention is somewhere else. Just return your attention to your Self and away from impermanent objects. What you are is always *Here.*

I want to burn like camphor and remain Here.

When you put camphor near a flame it quickly catches fire. The Guru is the flame and your heart is camphor if your decision, dedication, and seriousness is strong. Then if you go close to the flame in your Heart, nothing will be left. If you are a charcoal it will take time and there will be residue, and a fresh branch will take even longer. Yet even these people will get everything in a matter of minutes if they're not looking anywhere but to Self.

Is this awareness in me It?

No, it is not. This awareness is not It. You are aware of persons, objects, and ideas and all of these are from the past. Awareness of the past is not it. The One who is aware of this awareness is It! Do you follow? Who is aware of awareness? When you are aware of an object you are also aware that you are aware of something in your mind. So who is aware of this awareness? Turn your face to That which is aware of something, and when you know this, then forget it. If you do not forget it, it will become a past experience and draw your attention to the past making this something which comes and goes! It is not the past so forget about the experiences of it. If you do you are a Free person of the world, not even attached to Enlightenment! Forget about everything. That is all. But if you remember then this remembrance is memory and this is past.

> So whatever comes in front of you react.
> That is all. This is the advice.

How can I know It?

We describe It as Happiness, Peace, Love. It is not that, it's much more. It is much beyond whatever you can expect. Expectation is only the mind, which itself doesn't even exist. It is much more beyond this and it can be had in this very instant. You need not have any big program to arrive there. No effort is needed, no method is there. Simply keep Quiet and it will reveal itself. Simply don't interfere. Give it a chance Now. You have spent millions of years, Now give one second to It. Let It unfold, let It reveal itself to you. You are imposing your own notions, intentions, expectations, and ideations, therefore, you cannot see this revelation. It is a revelation, you just Keep Quiet, it will happen. Not with meditation, not with concentration, not with pilgrimages, not by going to church, not by penance, not by yoga. All these things will not help you to reach there, It is Here. All these things take you on a program of postponement. Mind is cheating you, don't listen to it! Simply keep Quiet! Don't start a thought, even that much effort is not needed. It will reveal Itself!

I see only the inside is real, only That is always here.

If the inside is real the outside also has to be real. Therefore, I do not prescribe any unreality. Everything is Real, everything is Self.

I would like a name which reminds me of Self.

When you look at the sky or ocean you see that it looks blue, but if you take a handful of air or water it is not blue. So how can something which has no color have a color? It is by virtue of its depth that it has color and so that which is beyond measure in depth or height looks blue. The river is not blue, but when it touches the ocean it becomes blue. It is the same with a rain drop which is clear only until it touches the ocean. So the name of formlessness and depth is Neelam, the blue which is not blue. This is the Unseen in all beings which gives all. To know this is Wisdom, Light, Freedom, Emancipation from the cycles of samsara. You must see that your own depth is colorless and formless. To know this you must go to the teacher who will instantly tell you that which you did not know. This blueness is the blueness of Krishna who is the attracting incomprehensible depth of Love.

Will you give me a first shove into this depth of love beyond mind?

You want to go "beyond"? Then go alone and carry nothing with you. Don't think of anything. Go even without thought. Not thinking is "beyond." The trouble is with your thinking. You think you are suffering or with a relationship. All this you must give up absolutely. Then you will not come back to the previous habits. Simply do not think and Stay Alone. Troubles only arise with thoughts, as the whole world arises only from thoughts. Why get yourself in all of this trouble? Simply do not think. When you don't think you don't need to do anything else. This is quite enough. And don't make any effort to not think.

(She gets it and laughs) It is so simple!

This laugh from beyond is conceptless and very different. This is how it has to be done.

How did you call me Here? I am so grateful for everything.

You are like a bird which flies over the borders of countries with no need of a passport. The bird is never arrested, only the man. You are free like a bird, free of all societal impositions and identifications. Don't listen to society. Be Free and go wherever you like and then, of course, you will be called to a place of Freedom where similar birds fly. Those who stay behind will continue to suffer.

It is true that the individual "I" and mind never existed and that ignorance has never existed.

It is too much to understand, but it is true. Where there is light there is no darkness. What is that Light that enables you to know that there is light?

I feel so good now in your presence that my mind won't move enough to allow me to follow your words.

This is intelligence!

I feel that I have touched something like nothing I have never touched before.

And this is Bliss, this is the happiness that will never disappear, this is Nothing. One touch of this is enough because it is not in time. One ray from this is enough to hold your mind forever. It will not allow any conflict between you and your old habits and activities. You are very lucky. I will tell you a Sufi parable.

In one of the great ancient courts everyone was waiting, according to rank, for the king to enter. In came a plain, shabby dressed man who took a seat above everybody else. The prime minister ordered the newcomer to identify himself:

"Are you a minister?"

"No, more than that" was the man's answer.

"Are you a king?" asked the prime minister.

"Greater than all kings, I am," said the man.

"Are you God?" he asked.

"I am above that also!" replied the poor man.

The prime minister retorted "There is nothing above God!"

Which brought the reply: "That Nothing is me."

*Since God has manifested as the world can you worship the earth
as a form of worship to God?*

Everything that is created is in God. Then who will worship whom? If you are separate then you can worship, but if you know that all creations are the choice of God then you can't make the choice to get out of this choice in order to worship the choice.

> We need not worship anybody
> because we Are That itself.
> Let worship be for those who do not know this.

True worship is the spontaneous love and adoration of Self. Anything else called worship is just an idea of worship coming from the heads of religions in order to give you fear: If you don't worship you will go to hell. So worship and fear go together. You can't worship if you don't have any fear. But why have fear?

> God is living inside you
> and you are living inside God.

Make the decision with right discrimination. Then you can do whatever you like. If you bring the concept of sin and merit in your brain then you can go and follow any church, but I don't advise you to go to any church because

You are not different from That.
You are That! Give belief to this fact.

Sit quietly for 10 minutes before sleep and after waking up, and give the rest of the time to the world, helping those who need your help.

Pythagoras once said: "It is best to stay silent or to say something better than Silence." I think that he knew the Teaching.

Kabir says something similar. Kabir spoke from a pure heart and only a pure heart can catch hold of the meaning. In his own words he says:

Japa muray, ajap muray:	Chanting dies, Silence also ends.
Anahat bhee marjai:	That which has no limits, space, also dies.
Surati samani shabd mein:	When Awareness merges with the word
Taako kala na khaiye:	Then That does not die.

What you speak dies, what you do not speak also dies. What has no limits also dies. The Awareness-Consciousness enters into word and That does not die. Many people at the Kabir Math in Varanasi wanted to know what this Awareness word was and how the limitless could die. Anahat means limitless and it is also a word for Om. So beyond Anahat there is a word that nobody knows. Anahat is not limitlessness.

Your message of Be Still has finally come home. Thank you so much.

I am glad you are back here and that you went to Arunachala, the place which gives you silence and peace. Establish your identity with the One who has no identity or name or form. Identify with That. Nobody is there except silence. Identify with this place.

Is the Self that which is the center of all things?

Self has no center, no circumference, no meditator to meditate on a center, and no meditation. It is very free, very fluent, very natural and spontaneous, and has no fatigue because there is no doership. Doership is "I am doing this," "I have to do that," "I am troubled," and "I am happy." All these relationships will not be there because they are just passing through the body. You are untouched by all of these. You are beyond even the concept of all of this.

You can turn your back on all manifestations, gods, creatures, but do not be shy to your own Self. You have been shy all of these millions of years and looking at what was not worth looking at. Now don't be shy of your own Self. Open your eyes and see!

Papaji, It is just space.

Excellent, excellent, It is space, and it has no limitations. Everything is in this space and you are this space. I am space. There are no limitations. All desires are met here when you are in this space because everything is in this space. This is how all the desires of One who is this space are fulfilled before they arise.

The king of a country does not say, "I will buy this land and that land over there." This idea does not even come to him because he is the monarch of the whole kingdom, he owns everything. So it is when you become this Space, there will be the end of desires and, therefore, the end of suffering.

Desire gives you suffering. Whenever any desire arises, you want to go near it, you want to achieve it, and you do, then you are happy, isn't it? You may think that the object made you happy, but really it is the absence of desire, that moment of Emptiness that makes you happy.

Being empty of desire is happiness.
Return to your own Source and you are happy.
This is the trick of happiness.

To get rid of all suffering and all deaths stay as Source. There Nothing exists, all is perfection, fullness, and that is your nature. You are already That and will always be That. All these notions like "I am the body" and "I am ego" give you suffering. These notions you have been told and there was a time when all these notions did not exist. You were perfect and even now you are perfect. Get rid of all these notions that have been dumped on your head. Shake them off! Shake them off and you will see who you are at this present moment. What notion is in your mind right now?

I am noticing how much struggle there is when I don't let go.

There is no need to struggle. It is the struggling that is the suffering. Don't give rise to any thought, not even the thought of "who is going to struggle," and not even the thought of "I."

No "I," no body, no ego, no mind,
no senses, no objects, no manifestations.

To return back see that manifestation is not other than these senses and sense perceptions. The manifestation is what your sense perceptions are. Senses are not other than mind going out. You cannot really separate the mind from the senses. There is no mind without the senses. Mind is not other than ego and ego is not other than the "I." And this "I," this sense of Being, is not other than the Source. Now, let's start from Source and see what happens.

"I" rises from the Source
like a wave rises from the Ocean.
Let this "I" arise and let everything belong to you.
"I" arises and becomes ego, ego becomes mind,
mind becomes senses, senses become the objects
of their respective senses.

All this is within you,
rising within you, within Consciousness.
You must Be Consciousness to see everything in Consciousness.
But you are in trouble because you think
that you are the body and mind
and this is the cause of suffering.

It is arrogance to consider yourself an individual ego-mind-body and to attribute all that you do to this individual, it is just simply arrogance. Why not call all this the Source? Why not call all this Consciousness?

All of this is Emptiness, you just play the game
of the dancer in it and let this game be played.
You can see yourself as individual or as Consciousness.
One is destruction and one is Peace. What more?
Stay as Is and See.

You don't have to control anything; don't desire anything to happen. You are the Space:

Everything is "I," everything is You,
Everything is Itself and this is your Nature.
You don't have to do anything about it.
Keep things open and see now the Emptiness,
See the screen on which all is projected.

When you go to a theater you see pictures projected on a screen. Some are of mountains and rivers, some of romance, and some are people being attacked by robbers. When the movie is over the screen has no wetness from the river, nor smell from the romance, nor bullet holes from the robbers' guns. The screen is immaculately clean. This manifestation is all a projection of your desires which fall across your mind and cause you to identify yourself as the projected watcher of the picture. You are not these projections, you are the screen. If you identify yourself with the immaculate, unchanging, eternal screen itself, which is the same before, during, and after the show, you will not change and so you will not suffer the changes but enjoy them.

All Beings are this one immaculate screen. There is no need for practice to clean the dust off it because it is beyond everything. The teachers who want you to do lifetimes of practice can clean this dust off their own minds.

I want this forever.

This experience you did not have before, and all the experiences which you had, they have left, they are gone. Therefore, we still want this forever! This will not leave you!

Before things were leaving you. Now here you will not be left. You are in the grip of a very supreme power. You will not be allowed to be left. It's not your fear now. You can't escape, Now you cannot escape. You cannot escape Love, you cannot escape Love. (laughs) Once you touch it, you get lost. Nothing ever exists that can come out again. Everything is discharged and becomes That itself. When the river enters into the ocean, it will turn instantly into the ocean.

I still cannot believe it is possible.

When the river enters the ocean, does it ask the question, "Will I be forever like this?" (laughs) That is the previous fear that is leaving now. All the experiences get lost because tney were not perpetual, they were not permanent. They were only imaginations, only hallucinations, therefore, they get lost. This is beyond concept, perceptions, imagination. Where will it be lost? The wave is afraid: "I want to ever remain a wave." Fear is in the mind of the wave, "I will be lost, I will be lost." Wave is now fearing "I will be lost." Where will it be lost? Where will it go? (laughs) Whenever lost, what will it become? When the wave is lost, no more a wave, it returns back to its source: The ocean. The ocean she was, the ocean she is, and the ocean she will be. Where? *Forever!* There is no time concept at all.

Time is in the mind of an ignorant person. Ignorant because in Light, in Wisdom, there is no such notion that "I am separate from all or separate from Fullness, from Vastness." That was a notion before, in the mind of an ignorant person. In Wisdom, no such notions arise. No separation. All is unity and love and beauty. There is no escape! Ignorance is gone! This is eternal Life, this is nectar!

Yes, I see! I see Nothing!

Excellent! If you see, this seeing is Being. When you see through the eyes at objects that may be distortion, but this seeing is Being. There are different eyes to see. It depends on you, which eyes you want to use, and are using. This sight has nothing to do with eyes. It is inner Being, inner sight and if you do it, you will see always with the same eyes inside or outside. There will be no difference between nirvana and samsara. (laughs) Whatever you will see will be inside. All beauty, all wisdom. That Eye has no limitation; not inside or outside, you see.

When you give up looking through these eyes on your head, the other eyes will open. So pick up the I-thought as you have done now, return back and that sight will open. When you said "I see nothing," Nothingness is the beauty of That sight, that Divine Sight. You will get it and you will see everything as being beautiful.

When you can see a pig or a dog, why not see God? God is the seer in you! When you see a dog, know it is God who is seeing the dog. That much faith you should have, and you must do it by yourself. Everybody is going to cheat you by telling you that what you are doing is stupidness! So, I am happy that you are a strong person. Stick to your path, even if there is no body. Then you walk alone!

ॐ

I understand that from the point of view of the Self there is nothing to do, but from the point where I am is there anything I can do to loosen the grip of the mind and remove this addiction to ego?

First of all, find out if your point of view is superior to the point of view of the Self, and if it is, follow your own. If you are superior to the creator, to your father, to your own Self, if you are more superior than the Atman, then you follow your own point of view and see the consequences of the practices. Point of view of Self is Self. Truth is Truth. This is already Here and Now. What practice do you need to arrive at your Self and to see your Self? Do you need any?

No, but when thoughts come up...

Self is earlier than your body, earlier than what you speak, earlier than the word. How do you reach him? Give up the concept of any practice, any method.

If you have done this then tell me what is it? Where are you? Don't give rise to any concept of effort or practice. Don't make any effort and don't stir your mind. Don't think and don't make any effort. If you really understand what I mean, tell me who you are and what do you want?

No practice, no thought, in between these two. Don't think, don't stir a single thought in your mind, and don't make any effort. If you have heard what I speak about, then it is your time to speak. Now tell me, who are you? Don't think, don't make any effort.

I just want to see God.

Therefore, God has brought you here now. Everyone is God, but we do not see it unless we see God within ourselves. If you first see God in yourself you will see him in the animals, birds, and rocks.

More and more I do see God hiding in people's eyes.

(Laughing) God is not hiding!
When you do not see God
it is only because you are looking elsewhere.
So you must absolutely see God and nothing else.
Then it is the God that is looking through your eyes.

Surrender to God and keep Quiet and he will take your responsibilities. As long as you take your responsibilities on your own head, God doesn't take care and it only seems that he is hiding.

You say I am God. Is the drop the same as the ocean?

There is no difference between the drop and the ocean. It is the totality of drops that make the ocean. Endless drops are the ocean.

Are they of the same quality? Is your no-mind the same as mine?

Yes, they have the same quality. One grain of sugar and a pound of sugar taste the same. And yes, your no-mind is the same as mine.

You say that no-mind is no doubt.

(laughing) No-mind is no doubt because there is nothing there to doubt.

What is the experience in no-mind?

There is no experience. There is only experience out of this, of some object. You have to get rid of the experiences of the past and in this second there is no experience, nothing to experience, and no experiencer. You are free of everything. Experiences happen in time, but in this moment there is no time, this instant is out of time.

It seems easy to miss the beauty of ordinary no-mind!

There is no ordinary no-mind. No-mind is no mind. No-mind is where you don't think about anyone. Not about you, not about anyone else!

Where words and language disappear?

This is no-mind. Let the mind sleep; this is no-mind, Freedom, Enlightenment. But when the mind is awake then you are bound. Let the mind sleep and you stay awake.

Please illumine my mind with the Truth which will set me Free.
I want to see the Atma Suriya shining in the Heart, which burns
away all desires. Please Enlighten me.

This Atma Suriya which you are referring to is in your Heart. How to see the Light of this Suriya is right belief, right knowledge, right actions. Then you will see it, it will reveal itself. Your belief should not shake: "I have to see this Sun in my own Heart," this is right belief. To understand this is right knowledge. With this you have to improve all your actions to all the beings. You must act with love and compassion, so that none is hurt by you. This will take you to see where the Sun abides in the Heart. This Sun abides in the Hearts of all Beings. Once you see your own Sun you will see this same light in all beings, not only in the animals, but even in the insects. But you have to see your own light first. You have a beautiful name: Hari. Who gave you this name?

Anandamayi Ma.

It means one who steals the Hearts of all beings. One who swallows the Heart of all beings. It is a beautiful name of the Self.

A wave called Jasmine would love a wave called Papaji to look into
her eyes and celebrate That.

A celebration will take place if these waves are not separate from the

Self

ocean. It is only a wave who thinks that he is separate: "I can travel anywhere in the water. I have length and breadth by which I swim to the shore." But again it falls back and becomes ocean. So know that "I am ocean," because the water content of the wave is not different than the water content of the ocean. This water is the basis of the unity that is not affected even if the wave thinks it is separate from the ocean. You are not different than the ocean and the ocean is not separate from the wave. This you must celebrate: The end of separation.

> Nothing arises without Self.
> All existence is one in one's own Self.
>
> The wave plays on the chest of the ocean,
> feeling separation, she moves through time.
> Eventually, she falls back into ocean.
> As she rises from the ocean,
> and walks in the ocean,
> and she falls back into ocean,
> the Oneness is not disturbed.
> The movement of the wave
> makes no difference to the ocean.

The ocean, being not separate from you, cannot cheat you. If you know this you can play as you like, Love doesn't forget. If you don't know this you will suffer.

I had a very strong dream last light after which there was considerable Silence. I don't know what it means.

This Silence is a border. There is neither waking or sleeping, only silence. This border behind waking and sleeping is the silence in which you do not experience anything. You do not have any memory of the past. It had no name, but if you want to use one, Silence or Emptiness are the best.

Not knowing what it means is confirmation of the border, of the silence, because senses and memory are not working and the ego is not there. This is between sleep and waking. Here there is no "I" and no "you" and no "they." This can be called Emptiness. From Here everything emerges or appears and into this all disappears as well.

Would you please speak again of how the Buddha's face is on every sand grain.

In every sand grain you can see the face of Buddha. Everyone can do it.

Everywhere you can see your own face. The face of Buddha means the face of your own Wisdom, your own Self, your own Atma. Then you will see the Atman living in all atoms of the universe. But you must first introduce yourself to this grain of sand, to this most minute particle on earth. First of all, remove all desires to see anything anywhere. Then you will see your face everywhere because where are you not present? I cannot actually speak of this, but it is an experience that every Enlightened person has.

Everybody will have this experience if they only give up their desire for any object, any person and any idea. When you do it, instantly you will see. Don't have the desire to meet with any person because every person belongs to past. Any object or concept that you speak about all belong to the past. If you don't touch the past, then you will see your face everywhere. Otherwise you will think that you are a donkey.

I know that I am a lion, but I want to know why I am walking with the donkeys? I want to let my 'donkeyness' go and always be a lion.

If you know that you are a lion then there is no problem to walk with the donkeys, (laughs) because donkey is the food of a lion. The trouble comes when the lion forgets that he is a lion and thinks that he is a donkey. I will tell you the enlightening story of a lion.

Once there was a washerman, a laundryman. In ancient times they would load the laundry of the village onto a donkey and bring it to a riverbank to wash it. One day a lioness came to drink water at the place where the laundryman was washing when a poacher shot and killed her. As the lioness was dying she gave birth. The poacher came and skinned the lioness, but left the newborn cub behind, so the laundryman came and took it home in his basket and nursed it with milk. Now be careful to listen to what happened to this lion.

This cub did not know who its mother was and was fed by the washerman, who also took him to the river everyday. Eventually, he was big enough and so the washerman started loading this 'donkey' up with linen. This 'donkey' started to eat grass with the other donkeys, because one acquires the habits of those that they keep company with, just as a child who stays with smokers starts to smoke. This is how habits are formed.

One day, when this 'donkey' was grazing with the other donkeys, a lion saw it and thought, "I am confused, how is this lion eating grass with the donkeys? His food is donkeys, but he is eating grass with the donkeys! I will go near and see." So he went near and all the donkeys fled away including this 'donkey.' But the lion was very big and fast and caught hold of the 'donkey' by the neck and said: "What is the matter? You are a lion and yet you are running with the donkeys and you are afraid of me! We belong to the same community."

"No sir, don't bluff me, I am a donkey," the young lion said as he trembled in the grip of the wise old lion. "I am a donkey. Please don't eat me. My brothers and sister are waiting for me. Let me go please. Don't make a joke, I know I am a donkey."

"You are a lion, don't be so foolish to think that you are a donkey!" said the wise lion.

"How can I believe this, that I am a lion? I am a donkey!"

So this wise lion took him to the river and said, "Look at the reflection of your face; is your face not similar to mine?"

The young lion exclaimed, "Yes sir, my face is like yours!"

"Now open your mouth and utter a roar like me."

This lion didn't know how to roar. He had been braying with the donkeys and had forgotten how to roar because nobody had told him this. But to roar was his nature and so he opened up his mouth and roared! Instantly he became a lion. This roar removed all doubt about who he really was. Then this lion went after the donkeys to eat them. (giggles)

Now the question is: how did this 'donkey' become a lion? In one instant of time he was a lion. What made this 'donkey' a lion? He uttered a roar! Otherwise he was always braying.

So you need a Satguru to take you to the river and show you your own face. You are not a donkey, but you are living in the society of donkeys, which are the people who are body-bound and say, "I am bound." Those who say "I am bound, I am suffering, I am dying," are all donkeys. The Guru tells you that you are not bound. Utter a roar that "I am Free." That makes the difference.

But you have only been bleating because this is the habit of the society that you live with. Lions become donkeys when they are in evil company.

When you come here I will forcibly part your jaws and make you roar. You have been born to parents who are donkeys and this made the difference, but a donkey cannot stay in front of a lion.

Stop staying in your own shit which you have shat for lifetimes and be a lion. It is up to you. Wait, grow up, suffer and do what the donkeys are doing. Somebody will put dirty linen on you and you will be under the charge of the laundryman. No! Someday some lion will look at you and you will become a lion because you have always been a lion. No donkey becomes a lion.

Only stupid foolish wicked society turns you into a donkey.
Senses are the donkey, but you really are a lion:

Eternal Unborn Consciousness.
The lion Satguru takes you to the lake of Consciousness
to show you your own face.
You are already That,
and this is all the teacher has to say.

Anyone who identifies themselves as individual is a sheep
and has very big arrogant ego.
Lions have no "I," no ego, and no identification.
Sheep are led to the slaughter house to be butchered,
but butchers are the food of lions.

My dear friend you are a Free man. Who told you that you were bound.
Think about this, no one has bound your hands, no one has chained your
feet. You simply think that you are bound and so you are bound. If you think
you are Free, you are Free. It is up to you!

I am Free and you are Free. This is a thought only. When you don't think,
you are a Realized person.

*Thank you for bringing me to the river. I have only been yawning,
not roaring.*

A yawn is when you are going to sleep. A roar means you are Awake.
When the lion roars it means that it is awake and all the animals of the forests
like the deer and rabbits run away because it is awake. But when the Lion
yawns everybody says, "The lion is sleeping so let us go and find our food."
Hearing the roar everybody goes back to their holes.

So when you roar all the tendencies of the mind, of the laziness, and all
thieves of Peace which keep you from finding your Self will run away and not
be there! Now you are awake. The roar is "I Am Free."

Looking for something to only feed your body, or your mind, or just your
eyes means that you are yawning. Therefore, you have to make the roar, "I
Am Free!" Where to go? The ego is sleeping and so this is the perfect time
to go and attend Satsang. Those people who are sleeping have not yet heard
the roar of their Self and, therefore, have been sleeping and will keep on
sleeping. There is no way to bring them to Satsang because it is not the time
for those people. Let them sleep, but you stay awake, come to Satsang, and
roar like a lion.

ॐ

The Satguru

The Self is the Satguru,
you will get help from Within.
Here your true Guide is,
Here all wisdom and knowledge is,
but due to your preoccupations you do not see it.
The Satguru is Within,
meditate only on That.

The Satguru is greater than all else, even God.
The Satguru is Truth-Awareness-Bliss,
and is like the sun; you no longer need a torch to see.

Because you do not understand the language of the Self,
the Satguru manifests as the outer Guru.
If you think that you have a body
you need a teacher with one.
Stay with the Holy one who gives you Peace.
He is like a shade tree in the desert of samsara.

This Guru is the butcher of the sheep ego.
His function is to tell you, "I am within you,"
and to give you the conviction
that you are Existence-Consciousness-Bliss.
Every true teacher tells you:
"Look Within, there is no difference
between yourself, Self, and Guru."
The Guru shows the Treasure
which is already always there.

The Teacher will not be recognized
by the diamonds on his head
or by the number of students he has.
Know the Teacher to be the one
whose presence gives you Peace
and removes all craving, attachment, and desire.
The Jnani's torch burns down the house of false convictions,
but, as Kabir says, nobody takes this fire.

The Teacher is one who knows the Truth
and can transmit this Truth to a humble one
by look, by touch, by thought,

or as Arunachala does, by Silence.
This Silence is the Light that does not move.

The true Teacher has no students,
all is BEing and only Silence speaks.
The perfect Teacher has no teachings
because he knows that you are Free already.
So the true Teacher's non-teaching
is that there is no teacher, no student, no teaching,
and that Nothing has ever existed.
This teaching must be without words
and must land in your Heart.
If you try to understand, it will only land in your head.

The true Teacher removes all names and forms and concepts.
The preacher adds them like a noose around your neck.
The preacher clings to you like a vulture clings to a fresh corpse.
The true Teacher will teach only to the extent that can be absorbed
and then send the student away.

So you must test the Teacher.
Look at the Guru's lineage, it is very important.
And their answers must be backed by practical experience,
because all the Saints sing from Emptiness, not from the mind.
Association with the mind is not beautiful or worthwhile.

Approaching the Self
is like walking on a razors edge: two cannot go there,
you can't even bring your mind or a thought.
So the only one who can help you is Self.
Anything that touches this flame becomes flame.
Touch a Sage and you become a Sage,
knowing Self you see only Self
and this Self is your Teacher.

Eventually you have to get rid of the name and form
of both your Master and yourself,
you have to reject the finger in order to see the moon.
Where there is name and form there is falsehood,
there is an impediment to Freedom,
because nothing that you see will give you Freedom.

Hold on only to Self when you are drowning,
reach for anything else and you will die.
The Satguru is Within, meditate only on That!
The true Teacher is Self, all else is pointing to Self.
Don't cling to anything made from the five elements.
The Guru has no body, visible or invisible.
Do not depend on any body,
which are just fingers pointing to the Truth!
The Guru is your own Self, not ego-self, Self Here and Now.
Reject the form of the Guru and only the Supreme is left.

It is not possible to lose your own Self,
you only have to be told by the Guru who you are.
This pilot is Love-Beauty, this Freedom is the Master.
Just sit quietly: all is taken care of.

ॐ

Questioner: What is the Guru?

Papaji: The literal meaning of this word is "The one who dispels darkness," so the Guru is that which opens your Heart, that which shows you Light. The Guru is Wisdom and Light itself.

How can one identify a true Master? Is it true that the Master is the one who stops your mind?

A true Master cannot be identified through his words or his actions, but your mind will likely become quiet around him. Often people propagate signs and symptoms of the Teacher, but the true Teacher has no symptoms at all. Somehow He can convey his message silently. Some people once came to me and said they would only accept me as a Teacher if I could stop my heart from beating. They got what they came for, but really there is no question about stopping the heart or any other siddhi that anybody can attain.

Why are so many masters male?

There is only one Master, that is neither male nor female. That Master shines within you as your very Self. Identifying as male or female keeps you from knowing this.

What about Buddha and Jesus and...

There is no male or female for the teacher. The teacher is within your own Self. He is neither male nor female. You only speak about what you see. This male and that female is created by your mind. When you sleep are you male or female?

Do you need a guru, a living Guru to be Realized?

You cannot realize the Self without the Grace of the living Guru. If you are in a body you need a physical guru. If you are in a body you need a guru in the body, otherwise the Guru is within, but you don't understand his language. So the Guru in the body is necessary for the student in the body so that they can converse with each other and remove the doubts of the student. Then the student will know that the Guru is within.

> You need a Guru without
> Just to tell you, "I am within you."

The Guru is formless Within you and you also are formless. If you know this you don't need a Guru with a body. *If you are fortunate enough to find a Teacher with a body do not miss the chance!*

Do the Masters who are not in the body have the power to be my Master?

If you have that power so that you can listen to the Master who has no body, then you do not need an embodied Master because that Master is always there without body. It is that through which you speak. It is in your Heart. Do you listen to him? Do you listen to that formless teacher who is teaching within you?

Yes, I do.

If you did you would not have asked all these questions!

So how about Christians and Buddhists who have no living guru?

You must find a living Guru, whether in the West or the East, and test him. If your mind is quiet in his presence, then obey him and stay with him.

If you think you have a body you need a Guru in the body to help you. You will find this Guru when you have an intense desire to be Free. Then you will see that the Guru will come to your door, as it happened in my case. I had such an intense desire for freedom that no other desire was in my mind.

Why are some people like Ramana Maharshi able to find the Truth without a physical Guru?

Ramana Maharshi also had a physical guru whose physique was very big. (laughs) It was Arunachala itself. The guru can be in any form. Arunachala is silent and does not move, which are symptoms of a good Guru. The real Guru does not teach by words because by words the Truth cannot be conveyed. Silence is the Teaching. The Maharshi also taught by silence, like the Mountain. Most other teachers bark day and night.

If you are Quiet and at Peace
this Shanti is your own Guru.
That cannot be found anywhere except Within.

This is why we begin each Satsang with Om Shanti, Shanti, Shanti. Then you have to remove the doubts from the student's mind so you can speak, but this is not a talk. If you have doubt come to the Guru and ask him your question, so that your doubt can be removed. When you have no doubt you are in Peace.

Can a person have two gurus? Do I have to choose one or the other?

Everything is your Guru; rocks teach you Silence, trees teach you compassion, and the breeze teaches you non-attachment. You can have many gurus, and lecturers and psychologists, but the Satguru Is One. How to meet this Master? With no ego.

Satguru is within your own Self and nowhere else.
Your Satguru dwells in your Heart
and in the Heart of all Beings.
Since you don't understand his language,
by Grace he takes a form to point you Within.
The Maharshi often would say,
"The Real Guru is Within."

Most teachers will not tell you this and will insist that you keep their picture and no other. But you don't get Peace from them. However, if you just go to Ramanashramam and sit in Ramana's hall, the Peace will unfold itself to you.

My heart seems to be burning with two fires, my love for Papaji and my love for my Western master. As you say, they seem to be the same source, the same fire.

If you say that the fire is the same, then you are not concerned with the candles. There may be 100 candles, but the flame is One. Don't worry about how many candles there are, just take care to find out if the flame is the same or not. Put your finger in each flame and if it is the same you need not worry.

Flame is only One and that flame is within you. Candles have nothing to do with the flame. The bodies, the names have nothing to do with the flame. Flame is within you and *That is your teacher*. This flame within is your teacher. Not that without! *This flame is within and if you depend on that without, you are making a mistake.* Anything without will disappear, including your ego, mind, body, senses and objects. What will not disappear is that flame. Try to see this flame within you and don't depend on what is outside. If you have a glimpse of it, then speak to me about this flame.

Gurus can be thousands like mosquitos, but the Satguru is One in all the universe. Those like mosquitos will bite you and suck your blood and then run away. The Satguru will totally swallow you, your ego, your mind. You can only love one and that is not in time. The mosquitos are in time.

What is the master disciple relationship? How does it work?

The Master is the One who shows you that you are light itself, and that darkness never existed. (He looks into her eyes, pauses, giggles and then says:) This is how it will work. Why do you want this relationship? Who told you that there is a relationship between the disciple and the teacher? Where did you read this? You have heard about it, but you do not know what the relationship is. If I tell you, you will not understand it. You must first fall into the this relationship and then you won't need an explanation of it. Just like you don't need an explanation of love when you are falling in love with a boy. If your mother describes this relationship to you when you are a seven year old girl will you understand?

You are not to make any effort in this relationship. When you are in front of your Beloved, this Beloved will not ask you to make any effort. This Beloved will take care of you and whatever she does you will accept it. At that time you will not think, "what is going on?" because in love there is no dialogue. In love there is no dialogue, no question, no answer. Simply, both are quiet. You are quiet and your beloved is quiet and something great is going to happen now. You have to wait.

What is the difference between you and me? Why do you sit on the chair and I sit on the floor?

Those who believe in difference belong on the floor. Those who do not sit on the chair. (giggles)

Papaji, who are you?

The Satguru

I Am That.

This and that, or only That?

Not this and that. That That is That That which is beyond any finger pointing to it, and if you hold onto the finger you can't see It!

Who is God and what is your relation with him?

I will give you this reply: I Am God. I have no relation with him. In order to have a relation you need another person and there is no other person besides God. Therefore, I have no relation with anyone else. I am full as God.

Is the Guru one with God?

There is no difference between a Realized Being and God. God with capital G, capital O, and capital D. There is no difference at all because Guru and God have no form and in formlessness there are no differences.

I know nothing about immortality. What happens when the Master dies? Is there any entity remaining? My Guru died many years ago and often I wonder if he is still available? How was it for you when your Guru died?

My Guru Is Not Dead! I never thought that my Guru is just the bones, skin, blood and marrow. I see my precious Teacher only and That Teacher is within, within your own Self. This, within your own Self, comes without to teach you that "I am within you." If you would have had this teaching clarified during the lifetime of your teacher you would not be sad today.

The teaching is more important than the body of the teacher. When you drink water in a cup, do you eat the cup and throw away the water? No, what is inside the cup is more precious, not that without. What is without is only the container, but what is contained nobody knows.

So you can see that your teacher who was without is still within your Heart in a subtle form. This subtle form never died. When you look within you will see. You also must become subtle and you will see the subtle form of everybody whom you have loved. When you love someone, even though they are dead, you can see them with your eyes closed. Even in sleep you can see them in dreams. But the love must be very intimate love, true love. When you love someone truly from the bottom of your heart that person can never be absent from you. So now you are here. Stay for a few days and find out what you have missed. Physical attachment can be kept on forever because the Guru never dies.

Can you help me find the inner Guru?

The outer Guru gives you the address of the inner Guru. Then you will know that this inner Guru has been hiding because there is too much going on in your mind. Therefore, you can't see him.

> You don't see the inner Guru
> because you look somewhere else.
> Stop looking and It will reveal itself without your effort.
> Just stop your mind from chasing all its loves and enjoyments.

The trick of the mind is to run after things for ages, getting kicks from everywhere. Few people want to be free of these nasty kicks. Few decide to be Free and not be a slave of the mind.

> Control the mind as a slave
> and it will be very helpful to you.
> Know this trick from the outer Guru.
> Control the slave, love the slave, keep it Quiet.
> Don't trouble the mind and don't let it trouble you.
> This is how to control the mind.

Everyone will not do this. Just a few of you will be successful in this attempt.

Can you speak about service to the Guru? Am I serving you by being here?

Once I said that to receive knowledge one must serve the teacher for twelve years. This was the tradition in ancient times, but now people are very much in a hurry! They come and say that they want to be Free and that they have a reservation on the evening flight! (giggles) To them I say "You have come in a hurry and with a rope tied to something else." The ancients said twelve years as a test. If the man was not really desiring Freedom he would run away. People who come only to cheat the teacher will run away when presented with twelve years of service to the Guru. For that purpose the teacher said to the students to stay for twelve years, after which he would give the student Knowledge.

Actually, I don't require twelve years. Here I just want one instant of your time and people still find it difficult. Out of a whole life span I only want one instant to be spent here with me. This is difficult for most and if they miss it they have to go through another cycle of 35 million years of births and rebirths. So, since you are here spend one second with me.

The Satguru

I served my Master for nine years before he dropped his body.

You are looking very good. There is a shine on your face which shows your nine years of dedication. Now your former teacher has pushed you to spend three years in Lucknow. That is why you are here. This is the invisible Grace of the former teacher, so for three years you stay here. I will tell you a very easy method to be Free: clean the shoes outside of the people who come to Satsang. This will wipe out your ego. Don't simply come when the hall is ready for Satsang. It is not that. You have to clean the seats, clean the floor, and also clean the shoes. Try it just for one day. It means you are cleaning your ego and without ego that *Nothing* is possible!

Is there anything I can do for you?

I just told you. Do nothing for me, do it for everybody.

Look after everybody
So that they are happy to see you.
It is better to serve the devotee of god
than to serve god himself.

That is what is said. Therefore, in India, when people are going into a temple they take the dust from the threshold of the temple and smear it on their forehead before entering the temple. That is how it should be done. Otherwise, the ego is very strong. The ego will not allow you to get moksham, liberation in this life.

Each day you shower the love on us, but I don't feel worthy or
pure enough.

It is good that you see that you have some impurities because now you will try to make your heart clean, but nobody knows or believes that their hearts are impure. Look after your own impurities to begin with and when your own mind is clean you will not see any impurities in the mind of others. So, remove the impurities, the thoughts. Wherever there is thought it is an impurity. If there is no thought you are worthy!

Papaji, I have a question for you that I would like to ask so that
I can write an article about you. I can do it later of you wish.
I leave tomorrow at 10:00 a.m.

Why not Now? Why later? You have already been postponing for two billion years. Today is the time. Don't make any later appointments. Ask your questions now. Time is very short and you are leaving tomorrow.

First of all, that is *not* the way. That is not the way to go to a teacher. If you go to a teacher you must forget your return ticket. You must come on a single ticket. You are talking about tomorrow at one thousand hours, so you have only 24 hours until then. You have already bound yourself to the next day which has not come. Why do you speak of it? Don't even speak of the next second! Don't postpone it. You do not know what will happen. So make the best of Now itself. The teacher is there, your desire for Freedom is there. What trouble is there?

(Laughing) Nothing.

I told you not to postpone and there came a laugh. Where did this laugh come from? (giggles) The Teacher gives no Teaching. He only makes you laugh, and in this laughter there is only Emptiness. Can you say your laughter is containing something? No! Laughter is just laughter and it doesn't take time.

To cry you need a person to cry, but not to be happy. (laughing) So now ask me your questions! Ask me questions of just Now. Don't ask your old rotten questions of yesterday! Ask me fresh questions which just now arise.

I have no questions. The question on this sheet is for an article that I would like to write.

They will be answered when you take a pen and paper in hand. The answers will come simultaneously. Write an article which makes a reader laugh instead of writing a book with so many things. Let your reader laugh and tell them how to laugh! That is a good message. The book or article should not be past. Your questions are past now already, but you must write something very fresh. Let me hear one of your questions, I will clarify this for you so you can tell to others what happened when you were here in India.

India has given so many Enlightened people, but the people you teach are mainly Westerners. Can you explain that?

Of course, almost all Sages and Saints who have been Enlightened have been from nowhere else but India. I have rarely seen anybody even with a desire for Freedom. I have traveled the world to speak with those people who are enlightened to have their views and to find out what they are doing.

I once was told that there was an enlightened person living on a mountain near Montserrat in Spain. Though every other Christian goes to church, he does not go. He has been allowed by the Pope not to go.

Otherwise, Christians who do not go to church will go to hell. I also heard of a man called Alfonso living in Greece on Mount Athos, a very Holy mountain they say, so I wanted to go see both of them.

The man at Montserrat lived in a small hut 950 steps above the monastery. I found him meditating with an Om in front of him. He told me that when he concentrates on Om all his impurities are washed away. He also was wearing an Om around his neck. There was nowhere that he needed to go because concentrating on the Om was enough. I saw that these men had attained something, but the formula was from India: this Om that we start Satsang with. This Om was picked up by Christians and called Amen. The Muslims call it Ammin. They are both forms of Om.

You and the other Westerners are coming here because you once upon a time lived here in India. But you had some personal physical desires that you wanted to be fulfilled and since you could not fulfill then in India, these desires gave you a birth in the West. Now, you ask why are these Westerners here? Because they have fulfilled their desires, therefore, you are here. Otherwise, you would not have come. So anybody who has a desire must have it fulfilled or this desire will be your next life. If your desires are over you do not need to go anywhere. Then you will see the real secret that everything is about. It is all your desires that you see. But when your mind in quiet, without desire, this is called Enlightenment. Don't wait to do it after death, do it Now. When you laugh it means your desires have vanished, so just keep laughing. (giggles)

I want a sharp weapon to kill my thoughts.

Surrender to the person who is very intelligent and sharp and who knows about the tactics of war and peace. Give him the reins to your chariot. Listen to his commands and do as he says. There is no other weapon as sharp as surrender to the Teacher. He will fight for you.

> I advise you to surrender to the Teacher
> and listen to him from the inside.
> Then let the body become like a machine.
> You don't work it, it is just working.
> Find the charioteer seated in your Heart
> and you will be at Peace always.

You have been in my dreams often lately. Do some teachers manifest themselves in the dreams of their students?

This happens to very serious people who do not find a Guru. In the dream they will be given instructions. In my own case my Guru first appeared to me like this. Some people say that he came to me in a dream, but even at this it is a fact that he came.

Eknath's Guru, Janardin Swami, came to him in a dream also. As Eknath dreamed an address was given to him. When he woke up he went to the address, found his Guru there, and was Enlightened.

You just have to be a very serious seeker and then you do not have to find a Guru because your Guru will find you. Even gods will come to you, but you have to be very serious about your search. It doesn't matter if your Guru is there or not there.

In a dream a few nights ago I saw Ramana Maharshi coming to me in a cave. The next night I saw Ram, Sita, and Ganga Ma in a dream. Are these darshans diamonds or distractions?

Having darshan of Saints and Gods and even the Holy River Ganga shows that your mind is pure. Each of these visits will purify you, they are not harmful. To have a vision of a Saint or a God in a dream is very beautiful. Let it continue.

When you come to people in dreams is this just a dream or indeed a visit?

It is neither dream or waking state. This is the fourth state, the Turiya state. It is the true state of a person. There is no difference between the devotee and the Teacher, so the devotee can see the Teacher in this way. We are just playing parts given by the Divine. The form we take doesn't matter. Actors take different roles: sometimes they are friends, sometimes they are enemies, some are females and some are males. But the Essence is neither male nor female. Who is it that hates or loves? Nobody knows.

I woke up this morning and remembered that you had come to me in a dream last night. We were sitting on the side of the river when I gave you a flower. You looked at the flower, smiled and said, "the flow of the river is one."

I will take you to the life of Buddha. Kashyap goes with a flower and gives it to the Buddha. Buddha smiles and Kashyap became Enlightened; MahaKashyap. Since then, for centuries, people have researched what this means. Handing over a flower, a smile, Enlightenment. This is a great Teaching. You pick a flower, bring it to the Teacher, he smiles. Nobody can give the exact meaning of how he became Enlightened with a smile from his

teacher. If you find it keep Quiet and simply see. Kashyap retur
It means it is so easy. Take a flower, offer it to the Teacher, he will
you are Enlightened. Don't ask why he smiled. Don't ask and lik ......wer
you will blossom. Many things can be attributed to this, but don't ask. It is
a very deep meaning. You have to find out yourself. The questions I can give
you are:

> What is a flower?
> How to offer the flower?
> What is the meaning of smile?
> To whom did you give the flower?
> What is meant by flower?

I want to live so close to you and stay at your feet.

Why my feet? Why not closer? Do you know what is closer? I want you
to dwell in my Heart. This is the best place and it has no distance. Here the
sun and moon and stars do not shine. This is my dwelling place. Once you
arrive Here there is no return because you become one with me, losing all the
vasanas which would otherwise cause you to reappear on earth. You have
enjoyed everything in this world. Now enjoy your own peace and love by
simply staying Quiet.

Why do I come to you in order to trust myself?

If you do not come to me you will always have mistrust. When you come
to the Teacher you have a trust that he will remove your doubt and then your
dream will be over. For that reason you should have no doubt. Your doubts
are like clouds, how long can they stay in front of the sun? They will move
away so that you can trust in the sun where the light comes from.

May I come and look into your eyes so that I will find peace?

Who told you that if you look into the eyes of a person you will find
peace and rest? There is truth in it; if you see the eyes of someone whose mind
is still then you can find peace within your Self also. Either look into the eyes
of a man whose mind is still or look to his Heart. Then your mind will be
still. Whether you look into the eyes or into the Heart it is the same thing.
You will find peace, you will be attracted by those eyes and you will forget
to look anywhere else.

Look into your eyes, behind your eyes, not to any outside object, but into your eyes from behind. Then you will know the trick of how to keep Quiet.

I would like to eat the food from your plate, and walk in your shoes, and speak with your mouth. I am yours. I love you.

Eating the food on my plate means eating the words that I speak about. You have to digest these words. If I tell you that you are free, you have to digest this food in your Heart. Walking in my shoes means doing as I do, that is walking in the shoes. Speaking with my mouth is identifying as me. Then your mouth and tongue are mine and you can speak the words that I speak. These things you can do.

Can you show me "Who am I?"

I am a tiger, can't you see? You are a sheep. (laughing) There is a sheep in front of a hungry tiger. How long will it take for one of them to disappear? This sheep will be a tiger in one instant! This is what I am. There is no sheep. This bleating will stop and there will be a roar that says "I am a tiger!" Any questions that come, come from a sheep and this question is bleating. Let it face a tiger. That's all. It will be finished. Bleating is mind. Tiger is your own Heart. So push the sheep in front of the tiger and it will be all over. It takes no time.

Ramana Maharshi said initiation and Upadesa from a Guru is necessary for freedom.

This is absolutely essential because otherwise teachers will give you things to do. But, a perfect Guru who has attained Freedom knows how to transmit this Freedom. So, you are very lucky if you find a Guru who will initiate you into no method, no practice and who will only tell you that you are already Free.

I feel by coming here to see you I am betraying my master who has left his body.

The Master never dies. Do not stay in the graveyard.

Papaji, in a few weeks I have to go to the West. Is it okay?

Yes, there is no east and west. This is only on the map. There is no east and west for the Master. Wherever you go is the Presence of the Teacher and you will feel it. When you have surrendered it is the responsibility of the teacher to guide you at every step.

In the West old habits take over again. Is this just a trick of the mind? How does Presence of the Master help in being free?

Why do you think that you will be disturbed when you go to the West? When you came that disturbance was there, but now when you know the Peace, you will take it with you *as* you. This Peace nobody can disturb. Only you disturb the Peace yourself, by desiring this and that. So try this now and your Peace will not be disturbed and you will always be in Satsang.

Only a few lucky people will have Satsang in the span of many lives. You must have been aspiring for Satsang for millions of years and during this time you did your tapas and penance and, therefore, now you will win peace. This is the right age. You are a young man in Satsang. It is a rare phenomena.

The Sufi saints call this a rare phenomena; Satsang and the desire for Freedom together. You need to be free, but it will not work in Washington, you have to be in Satsang. The Sufi saints say: "Women and wine both together at the same time, what a luck!!" You must have read this and if you didn't you can read Omar Khayyam, a great Sufi saint who wrote a wonderful book, *The Rubaiyat.* "A peg of wine on one hand, a woman on the thighs and kissing." These two things are very rare, both ways. (giggles)

I have decided not to go to Arunachala on my way back home because it is here, you are the embodiment of Arunachala. I have heard that one should stay with the one who kindles your flame.

Some people hold the belief that you must go to a Himalayan cave to meditate, but these caves are for animals, not humans. You need not go to a cave because what you seek is available anywhere. Even in Hazrat Ganj, in Manhattan, or in the forest. What you search is within you and so there is some sanity to just stay where you are.

Is Ramana Maharshi still alive in the same sense as Jesus Christ?

Ramana Maharshi is still alive. This is not a belief, but Reality. Nothing is created and nothing vanishes. All is always there, but only open eyes can see this. All the beings are still Here. They cannot disappear, where would they go? They are Here to stay. All the beings of the whole cosmos exist in your Heart, nowhere else.

> Everything exists and stays in the Heart itself.
> *Nothing Is Beyond Your Heart.*
> Everything in the universe, from beginning to end,

from mountains to meteors, are but a speck in your Heart.
You are also Here, everything always Is.
This is the end of Knowledge:
No creation, no preservation, and no destruction.
It Is As It Is, and will continue to be as it is
from even before the creator,
who is born out of the Essence of This Heart.

*This afternoon I will take the train to Arunachala. I would like
your blessing.*

Yes, yes, after being here the only place to go is Arunachala. It means
the Mountain which does not move. You have to find the mountain which
does not move. This is called Arunachala. This mountain which does not
move is the light of the Self. You will see it there. Circumambulate once,
twice, thrice and then you will see the light. This Arunachala is calling you
and you will see that this Arunachala is calling you. This is the light of the
Self and you must make a visit there. Arunachala is the best place to sit quiet.
If you are called there you must go and fulfill your mission.

So many people find this Light from you.

You can attribute it to the teachers who tell them, but he only gives the
information that you are already at Peace.

That Teacher which is attributed with giving Peace
Is *not* different from the Teaching Itself.

*If the Grace that radiates out of a Saint makes such a difference
to the people around him, I would expect that it makes a big
difference on the Saint as well. Then why is there sickness?*

Body itself is sickness. This radiation is not from the body to the body,
but comes from somewhere else. It is not body to body relation.
When sun falls on a mirror or on a lake it reflects, but when it falls on a
stone it doesn't. So the body of one who lives in Truth simply reflects the
radiance like a ball bouncing off the wall. This light shines on a dark mind
and sets it free and then comes back because there is only one person who
radiates and there is only one person who is radiated upon. There are *not*
two. This is the answer to your question.

Papaji, I would like to spend more time with you today before I go.

Time. Even if you stay one trillion years you will not make it. You have spent so much time already in so many lifetimes and still you have not seen the Peace. I don't want a lot of time, I only want one second of your life. Just one second where you won't think or go anywhere is all I want. Now you have to assure me that this one second belongs to you. Make sure it doesn't belong to objects, senses, mind, or intellect and if it doesn't, then what happens to this "me"? This is my question and you can answer in any way: Silence, a laugh, a word. Don't step out of this one second.

I love you and your teaching.

I can read in between the lines and I know you are hurt by some disappointments you have with me and the teaching. In between what you speak is what is in your mind, so between the lines you should keep Quiet. Then there will be no difference between your tongue and your thought. Many people say, "I love you" but it is not true. Their mind is different than their tongue and so they are only deceiving themselves and the God within is not happy about it. So do what you have in your mind and speak what is true within and without. There should be no difference, then you will be happy and this is called Wisdom and Enlightenment. You must be the same at all times and speak the way that you feel.

(Papaji reads a long letter sent from America about a man's long struggle to be Free and his attempt to change his environment to be more conducive to Freedom.)

Commenting on this letter that I have just read, I see that there is an inspiration rising from within to be Free, but that the circumstances have not allowed it. He has not gone near a real Guru to stay and learn. All the rest he has done, but now he is just attached to the desert, the monks, and the nuns. You can live anywhere you like. Why make the difference between a mountain and a fishmarket? Why should there be a difference? Wherever there is a difference it is the mind which is cheating you. You can be quiet in the midst of Hazrat Ganj and you may not be quiet in a Himalayan cave. So forget about it.

> During your lifetime it is better to stay with the one
> who knows and who can deliver Peace and Love.
> This Teacher is a raft who ferries you
> across the ocean of life. Otherwise it is not so easy.
> Don't waste your time on meditation, whether in the mountains

or in your home, but instead go to the Teacher.
He will take care of you as the raft does.
Only the raft carries you, not your meditations or effort.
This raft is the Teacher, learn this and don't waste time.
Search for the one who knows himSelf
and who can tell you what is unknown to you.

Now is the right time. Don't waste it. Here I don't teach any meditation or any other exercise.

Just keep Quiet for one instant,
and don't stir a thought in your mind.

If you don't realize in one fingersnap then come in front of me and tell me that this formula has not worked. Come face to face with me and tell me that you have not sat quiet and have not yet seen your own Love, your own Peace. That challenge is open to everyone, today, tomorrow or the next day.

I have heard that it didn't take much time when you met Ramana. Is it true that a single glance from the Maharshi liberated you? What then is the nature of the transforming power of the Guru?

The Maharshi was always sitting in his hall with open eyes and not looking at anybody. His eyes were empty. I would sit in front of him and think that He was only looking at me and nobody else. Also there was Chadwick, Devaraj and Rao, but he only looked at me. This glance is Grace and it falls on the one who really wants the Grace of the Guru. One glance is enough, as is written in the Upanishads. One glance, one touch, one word from the Guru is enough. You need not do any chanting or meditations or exercises, but you have to be a Holy person. Then only this glance will fall behind your eyes. Then the whole of your body will shine in Silence and in Love. That glance I cannot compare with the eyes of even the greatest Saints and Sages of the world. That is a glance from the Self to the Self. Therefore, I believe that if the Sage looks at you then the purpose of your visit to this world is fulfilled. Kabir has said this:

Blessed is the life in which you are born in the human form,
so make up your mind to realize the Truth in this life
before you pass away. Why this life? Why not today?
Why today? Why not Now? Otherwise you will repent
when this bird flies away from the body.

*I so love living in Manali, but the mountains don't compare to being
with you. The depth of inquiry and the power of devotion are both
so much greater near you, in your presence. Many scriptures say that
God, Guru and Self are the same. Will you reveal the secret of this
blessed trinity to me?*

I know that the Vedas say that God, Guru and Self are all the same, but
I believe that the Guru is higher than God and Self because you can only
know God and Self through the Guru.

I will tell you a story about a man who was a hairdresser to a king. This
man would go to the king to massage and shave him every morning at eight.
One morning as he was leaving his Guru came to his house. So he bathed his
Guru and prepared breakfast and then lunch for him. He totally forgot to go
to the king and only remembered when his Guru was totally comfortable and
taken care of. He said, "Guruji, I must go to the king now and massage his
legs because he has arthritis and without the two hour massage he cannot go
to his court. I am very late and so the king may not be happy with me. In
fact, I may not return because he may have me executed!"

The Guru said, "Go now, but come back to serve my tea this evening."

So he left for the palace. When he went through the palace gates the
senators were smiling big smiles at him, and when he appeared before the
king the king prostrated before him! "Please sir, don't bow before me. This
is more of a punishment. You can kill me, but I can't stand the disgrace of
you bowing to me."

The king said, "Your massage was so good this morning that for the first
time in decades I am able to walk with no assistance! My legs are healed! I
tried to give you my own diamond necklace as a reward, but you
disappeared."

"My dear king," the hairdresser said as he saluted the king, "I have
served you for so many years, but now I cannot return. I will serve my Guru
now." So he stayed with his teacher for the rest of his life.

So I place Guru first, then Self and then God. This you'll learn here.

*Recently I dreamed that I jumped out of an airplane, but that I forgot
to take a parachute. I know that this was related to the Guru. What
does it mean?*

It is what this story is about! It means that whenever some trouble arises
you should use a parachute. Avoid all danger and fear by keeping the
parachute in your hand. This parachute is your faith in your Teacher. He will
save you so you need not fall. Have complete trust in the pilot who knows
how to fly the plane.

ॐ

*You said there is no teacher, no teaching and no student. Tomorrow
I will go to France. Can I find liberation without a teacher, without
coming back to Lucknow, by only following my inside voice? Is the
Grace of an Enlightened one necessary?*

Without a Teacher and his Grace
you can't be Enlightened, you can't be Free.
Only one with very clear eyes standing at the perfect angle
can show you the new moon.
Those with jaundice in their eyes and standing in the wrong place
looking at the wrong angle will not see it and will go for help.

The One with clear eyes will tell you to align your sight
with his finger and the head of the crow seated on the tree.
Then, looking beyond the finger and the crow, the moon is sighted.
But, if you hold onto the finger or the head of the crow,
can you see the moon?

The indicators have nothing to do with the moon
and so the One with clear eyes will tell you to reject them.
Don't get attached to the teacher's form.
If you do, perhaps you won't be benefited.

Most teachers keep their students holding the finger and they both are
satisfied. As ego becomes inflated the finger is worshipped and the new moon
is forgotten. Only the Selfless one says to go beyond and declares himself a
mere indicator, a humble messenger not to be held. Finding that Selfless One,
the One with clear eyes, who helps all people, is very difficult.

*You also said that if a devotee has an intense love for his guru that
this love and the desire to see his Guru will compel the Guru to
take another birth. Is it true?*

It is not possible. The Guru is that which Enlightens the devotee. A magic
monger, like so many famous "saints" are, are not Gurus.

The Guru is one who shows Light
and gives Peace to the devotees
even without them asking for it.

Others are commercial teachers interested in building ashrams and making money. It is better to be without desire. The Peace of the desireless man is not comparable to anyone in the world. Don't be attached to the Guru's form. What passes away is not Eternal. Every form will pass away, and the Essence is formless. If you are attached to the form you are making a mistake. It is not the form which gives you light, but something else which is deep inside your own Heart. That is your Guru. That Guru abides in the heart of all Beings, not only just the human beings, but all the animals and plants. You will see this when you see your own Essence within. Then every plant and animal will speak to you as they speak to me.

If there is no teacher or student then why are there so many people here benefited from you? Can you tell me about this Grace? Could I benefit from it?

When I say there is no teacher and no disciple, no giver and no receiver, I mean that there is no physical person. The teacher is not physical, neither the disciple is physical. The one who gives is not physical and the one who receives is not physical. This is what I mean. It is not a person who gives. There is no permanency in any physical body. The body will appear and disappear. What teaching can it give you? What can the mind and senses teach? They themselves have no permanency and are ever changing.

> The Teaching can only be given by the Eternal
> and received by the Eternal.
> The Eternal has nothing to give to the Eternal,
> so there is no disciple and no teacher.
> You are already That, not physical, emotional or mental.
> Leave beside these forms and find out what is left,
> and what it needs.

So many processes to find this out are given by the teachers, but none are worthwhile because whatever is gained afresh will be lost someday. All gains are temporary gains because everything comes and goes.

> So look at what you have not to gain,
> look at what is already there.
> Who can give you this that you already have?
> This is why I say: you don't need a teacher nor teaching.
> Some people don't believe it, but it is a fact.
> You can't depend on anyone else or on your own self.
> Dependency is not Peace and Love.
> That which does not depend on anything is Happiness.

Find out what is Peace and what doesn't need any help from the outside. This cannot be known by any practice in time. It is not in time so how can it be found there. Time itself is not happiness. Wherever there is time there is mind. There is no difference between mind and time and thought. So if you want to be in Peace don't think of time. Don't think about anything because thought is always of the past.

> Peace does not belong to the past,
> Peace is instant Presence.

Thought is past, mind is past. When you don't make use of thought, mind, or past, that is the moment of your Wisdom, Light and Peace. It cannot be gained or attained. It is already here. You don't need any experience to have what is already here. You just need someone who can tell you that "Peace is already Here, you can't get it from me." Only a rare one can have that understanding. Most people think that peace is enjoyment of senses. It is not. It is not from rubbing with the opposite sex. That is over in a second. Find out what the joy is which will not fade away. Most Saints will tell you to do something, like in the West they say you must go to church or you will go to hell. All over this fear is given. So much yoga and seva and meditation is scheduled in all the ashrams around the world, but here in Lucknow I will not tell you to do anything. Doing has been enough for you. You have spent millions of years doing things, but you are not a worker anymore. If I tell you to do this or that to attain Freedom, it means that Freedom is a mere result of doing something. Freedom is totally independent of any doing and of what you have done. So if anyone comes to me I don't tell him to do anything.

> Just stay here with me, your Freedom is my job.
> You are not to do anything, simply stay Quiet,
> giving no rise to even a thought.

This much rest I give to you. You don't even have to think, though everybody else is thinking. I tell you that you have not to think. I will think for you! If you don't think for one second you will see that you have fulfilled your purpose of coming to Lucknow. If you are not Enlightened then catch hold of my throat and tell me that I speak lies! But before that stay Quiet for just one fingersnap, one half second, one half of a half second. During this quarter second tell me that you are not Realized.

Why do so many of my desires come true in Lucknow? It has gotten to the point where I really have to watch what I hope for because it will

come true.

Desires of those who come into the presence of a Jnani are fulfilled because it is like throwing a rubber ball against a wall: it will come back. The Saint does not fulfill the desire because he does nothing, he is still like a mountain. However, desires are fullfilled as they meet this Silence. This Silence gives Peace to anyone who comes near to it and Enlightenment to a rare ripe soul. A Saint can give you anything you want, even if it is not in your destiny, for the tongue of the Guru is not controlled by God or destiny.

If you have the desire for Enlightenment it will be fullfilled in the Silence of a Saint, in the presence of a desireless man sitting quietly like a mountain.

Sitting quietly in the Guru's presence is quite enough. But most people who go to the Jnani forget what they go to him for and continue their old ways. I have seen this around the Maharshi. People very close to him were not benefited because they were lost in their desires.

You must win the Heart of the Jnani so that he gives everything without you even asking for it.

I have only one desire left. I really want to be with my Guru.
All other desires have dropped. I am surrendered to him completely.
I just want to sit with him. Is this okay?

No!

I knew you were going to say this!
Did your previous Guru tell you no?

No.

I say no because I say don't stay with or depend on any person who has name and form. On this basis I say no.

Stay with the Guru who has no name or form,
Stay with It, which is formless.

So, if you still see my form don't stay with the form. Stay with my formlessness. The people who are staying Here are staying with Formlessness, not with form. For some it is taking time to reduce my form (laughs) but they will wait. Some people have immediately seen my Formlessness. Those who have not seen It are not ready to see it. When you are ready, Grace will bring you here and if it doesn't work then it is a disgrace for you. (giggles) If it does work and you know the Formlessness then your work is over. Be Here, complete your desires, become desireless and this desirelessness is called Enlightenment.

Where to find you?

What a question! "Where to find you?" Nobody can see and so what you see is not the fact. Therefore, search for me somewhere where the eyes do not see. Look nowhere and you shall find me. Do you understand? Look nowhere and thou hast found Formlessness.

There is a Tibetan proverb which says that a Guru is like fire. Get close and you burn, but if you don't stay close enough you won't feel the heat.

This is very true. When you go near the Guru it burns your ego. But even if you are far away you will be burnt. You try it. Go to the back of the hall and you will find the heat there also! Sit here and feel the heat.

How do I keep to my true nature where bliss is as natural as breath?

> When the veil which does not exist is lifted,
> then you will have Bliss and Love.
> The veil never is, it is only your desire
> which hides your true nature.

You want to live with someone, but then they grow old and so you want to live with a young person. This is the workings of the demons of desire. You can't get peace from any person, not even God can give you peace. If you have a mountain of merit perhaps you can contact a teacher. Maybe this teacher is the real Satguru. Then by Grace of the Satguru you will have Peace. But most teachers are not the Satguru.

> You must have discrimination
> to know who the Satguru is
> and to know he can give you Freedom.
> But this discrimination is very rare.

> You may live with a teacher and not know who he is
> because you are lost with his habits.
> Even his way of speaking and walking
> can blind you to the Truth.

ॐ

The Satguru

*I am so attached to your beautiful form. I want to drown in That
so please take my hand as it happens so we will go together.*

Drowning is going by yourself into the ocean or river, but what does it
mean to say, "Take my hand, I want to drown"? I don't understand! You
can't drown like this because you have the protection of someone who will
not let you drown. He will bring you across the ocean of samsara where
everybody drowns because they have no protection. A few here and there
seek the protection of a Teacher. Kabir says,

> Men are being washed away in this ocean of samsara,
> all are going to the hell.
> I try to bring someone to the shore and out of the current,
> but many deny the protection.

Now I don't know how the noble and wise Kabir can say what he says
next:

> If the person does not accept this protection
> then kick at his ass and throw him in the middle of the river
> where the current is the fastest.

(giggling) He must have been in a lot of trouble to utter this because
otherwise he was a very peaceful man. What I do is not to kick his ass, but
go myself and get washed away a little bit with that person who is getting
washed away. You must have seen it. They say, "My father was washed away
by my mother," and so they are from birth. So I go and kiss the man, not kick
him. Then I suggest to them that we get out of the current since we are being
washed away and I tell them that I know a good place to get out. Then I bring
that man to the shore, out of the ocean where one is safe. So even if you are
washed away you are pulled out, not by the force, but by Love.

Once, in Ayodhya on the banks of the river, I met a very troubled man.
For decades he did so much sadhana for the sole purpose of having darshan
of Lord Ram, and he had vowed years before that if Ram did not appear to
him by this day, he would walk into the Saryu and drown. I tried to talk him
out of it but he wouldn't listen and slowly he walked into the current until he
started to be swept away. I went in after him and brought him back to shore
where he pranamed to me, thanking me over and over for fulfilling his desire.
He insisted on following and serving me, but I didn't allow him. I gave him
a little advice, got on my motorcycle and rode back to Lucknow.

*We are all so happy just to be in your physical presence.
You don't even have to say anything and people 'get it'!*

79

Where the Teaching is, there is attraction. So people go to that man in whom the Teaching is. That attracts people, not the form. The form of the man who has wisdom attracts because That has compassion in it. It wants to give what it has and so people come and are benefited. What does the poor man have to give to others? But the king will give you a fistful of pearls and gems.

What is your spiritual will? What ambitions would you like to see completed when you are no more?

That day will *never* come when I am no more. You may turn like a spinning wheel for 35 million years, coming and going, and you will see that I am Here at this place where I forever have been and That is my abode. I will never go anywhere, nor will I return anywhere.

I have no will at all. If I am here or not here it doesn't make any difference. I will not impose anything on anybody and therefore, I have no personal will or ambition at all and have nothing to be fulfilled. I do not need the help of any other person to speak on my behalf those things which I couldn't say in my lifetime!

I have stayed with many masters during the last seven years in India. Is it right that I have left them or should I go back?

Stay with someone who gives you peace of mind. Don't judge him by his ashram or by his beard, but whether or not you are getting Peace. If you are there stay with him and remove your doubts and hindrances. Aim for Peace and not necessarily the most comfortable circumstances. So many kings are miserable and so many of the saints have been simple people in simple circumstances, like Rekina, the cartsman who was the Guru of the king. With this simple cartsman the king found something he could not get in his palace and then ruled the kingdom while staying Quiet. So stay with the one who gives you Peace and see what is happening in your mind. It doesn't matter if the king is in Manhattan or the Himalayas, don't worry. Stay in the Peace and learn and then you can go anywhere you like.

All of my life I have been terribly afraid of dying, but now that fear has disappeared. I can't find it anywhere. The mind that feared death has itself died.

Few people know how to avoid the fear of death. If the person is very pure-minded and obedient to the teacher the teacher will remove this fear by look, or by thought if the person is not present, or by touch. Also by kick sometimes! This happens when the student is not getting it, but the teacher is bent on giving it. It may seem to be a cruel way, but the Teacher is looking out for your benefit and not necessarily what you want. He wants to give you that precious Diamond for which you will forever be grateful for.

How can I get over the fear of taking what I really want, of taking Freedom?

If you are afraid and don't extend your hands to take it I will take your hands and force a diamond into it. Your part is to come here and my job is to thrust the food into your mouth even if you don't want it.

I have just arrived here from Ramanashram. Sri Ramana has long been for me the perfect example of the One True Self, and the embodiment of my Heart. His grace has shown me that I am not different that the very perfection of Being. I walked through the ashram as if I was looking through His eyes.

This is how to look.

You are so blessed to have him as your Master and I hope you will share with me something from your association with him.

What you speak of, the ego does not touch. The one who surrenders to the Master gets this kind of experience. Then he sees that he is not the doer. He doesn't do anything, but gets commands from Within and the work is carried out. One is not even to think. The Self will think on your behalf.

I have spent time with Lamas who say the path is difficult. But the time has come to be silent and free of the transient suffering and practices. I am through with searching and having suffering as a teacher. Now I just want to sit at the Master's Feet.

The credit for this first goes to your mother. To get love in these days is very rare, but she built from love a good spine in your body to face the sufferings with. Now due to your mother's love you are here in Satsang. So be grateful to your mother. Regarding the teaching, when you are near to a Teacher your responsibility is over, just as your responsibility and effort to cross the river is over once you are in the ferry. What effort do you make in the ferry? Do you run from one end to the other? Whether you run or sit quiet it is the ferry that will bring you to the other shore, not you. Perhaps though, if you do make effort the boat will tilt to one side and you, the other passengers and even the boatsman will be in trouble. (giggles) So keep Quiet here. Here we neither chant nor meditate. This is something easy, this is Satsang.

> For your part only have full faith in the Teacher,
> and the Teacher will hand over what you really want,
> and what is really good for you.

You are such a mystery to everybody. Is this okay?

If I say it is okay it is not a mystery. Mystery is mystery and so it cannot be ok'd or rejected!

Last night in a dream I was surrounded by Neem Karoli Baba, Osho, Ramana, and yourself on all four sides. Can you tell me about the value of so many spiritual teachers. I feel so lucky to be so connected.

These four teachers are like four walls of a room. If you are attached to any one of these teachers your face is toward that wall. Remove the walls, they only come and go. What is before the wall is and after the wall is gone? Tell me!

Silence.

To get to the Silence will you lick the wall?

No.

So there is no use licking the wall. Silence will stay. It was Here, it is Here, it will be Here. That Silence doesn't depend on any walls which are temporary. It is only a concept of your mind that you will be happy by licking a wall. Don't lick anything. (giggles) The only "thing" that can give you Peace is Nothingness. Stay attached to what you can't see, touch, taste, or hear. That is all. This is the Truth!

I love you through all that is seen and unseen because you are my very Heart. It is so precious and unspeakably pure. Though I am what is nameless, I would love to be named by you before leaving for Arunachala.

There is no place on the face of the earth which will give you Peace of mind like Arunachala will. This is the Guru of my Guru. Aruna means light,

Achala means that which does not move. Arunachala means the "Immovable Light." To celebrate this there is the festival of Deepam, where they burn a very big light fueled by 1000 kilos of butter oil. This may still be burning by the time you get there.

So I give you the name Aruna. You are the Light. I give names according to the face because it is the index of mind. You can't hide the mind because it is on the face, therefore, you get the name of your Heart.

When you walk on such holy land as Arunachala where the Saint has lived you will have the same feeling as when he was there. There will not be any difference. Always remember this. You can keep the dust of this place with you. It is just as holy. Keep it in your room and you will not have to chant any mantra or even meditate.

You sometimes say that you must forget and reject everything, including your family, and even God!

Yes, that is the highest Truth, but you are misunderstanding what is meant by "rejecting."

Reality is One, there are not two realities.
Either you are real or the "other" is.
But "other" is based on you
and so you are the only Reality.
This is why you must reject even God,
meaning: Reject your separateness from God.
Rejecting "other" means to
reject that you are separate from "other."

The highest experience is when everything disappears, even God. Until this happens you will continue to be reborn. So forget everything, even forgetting, because forgetting and remembering belong to the mind. Without mind you can't see your God, or Guru, or country, or parents. Just don't give rise to identifying as a body or mind or personality and there will be no forgetting or remembering. First forget yourself which means stop identifying as the body. You are the Essence which does not disappear. Find it!

I can forget God and my country and the family, but I can't forget the Guru! Should I really forget the Guru?

There is no "shoulding!" I am not saying that you "should" do anything. All automatically goes. Just know who you are and you will know who the Guru is. Perhaps he is the same: Disciple and Guru. Don't give rise to any concept of separate personalities and tell me what is here. That which remains you cannot speak of. Even bliss is not an adequate description. One who has tasted it cannot speak, and one who speaks has not tasted it. It is Being and It is independent of the taster. Few will have this consciousness of real Being. So don't have any desire or any relation for sometime and it will reveal Itself by Itself to Itself. But to Whom?

Love, Truth, Freedom exalts a Holy Person.

So you must be Holy first and you will get everything without asking.

Where will you go after you leave your body? Will you ever come back to planet earth?

If I come back, I must go, and if I go I must come back. Therefore, the Truth is neither I come, nor I go. This is the Truth.

Who goes? You speak of the body, not of your own Self. The Self doesn't come and doesn't go. Why should it go anywhere? What will he do going from here to somewhere else? He is not a businessman! Everything is included in the Self. Why should you go? The king does not desire, "I want to buy that house or apartment or place" because the whole kingdom belongs to him. The king has no desire to acquire property because it all belongs to him! Therefore, when you become a king you will have no desire to go anywhere and with just a clap of your hands all is fulfilled.

What is the essence of your teaching?

I teach about That which cannot be attained by any teaching. My teaching cannot be taught. I have no teaching for the Essence from where all teachings arise from. This Essence doesn't need any teaching or non-teaching for it is beyond everything. It is from where all words rise from.

From the very source of Being?

From where everything comes from, even the words.

Master, I want to know the Satguru, I want to be Free.

The Satguru is Within. The Maharshi says the same thing:

The Satguru Is Within Your Own Heart.

You need this and if you are honest, certain, sincere and one-pointed you will understand that you are That itself. You are Here itself. You don't need any effort, just convince yourself that you are Here. Reject all your desires and don't make effort and you will be alone. Then something will shine and envelop you completely.

ॐ Satguru ॐ

Grace

The Grace of Self gives rise to the desire for Freedom.
The Grace of God brings you to the Guru.
The Grace of the Guru removes all doubts
and leaves only Freedom.

"I want to be free" is the first Grace.
It is Freedom itself calling you.
This desire will take you to where it rises from: Self.
All other desires will burn in this fire.

The Grace of all the Masters and the Self
has brought you to Freedom.
Don't have any doubt about this, or about Freedom.

Grace is the relationship between the Teacher
and his worthy disciple, and is available nowhere else.
This Grace has no equal in the world.
As the story of Kalyan, the humble sweeper shows:
Grace comes only to a worthy disciple,
one who is pure in Heart and who serves his Teacher,
because Truth exalts a Holy person.
If you are Holy the Teacher accepts you
and bestows his Grace upon you.

It is not you who makes this choice for Freedom. It is Grace taking you
where you must go for Freedom, the Satguru. It is Grace giving you what you
need like inquiry, and devotion, and which removes what you don't need:
thought, and desire. Without Grace you can't cross the ocean of samsara.
Without Grace there is no Enlightenment. This Peace and Love cannot be had
by penance, austerities or meditation. But if the teacher is happy he
compassionately gives you the prasad of Grace, and ends your journey in
rest. It is a gift, it cannot be demanded or commanded. Gods can fulfill your
desires and give you heavens, but they can't give you Grace. So be careful and
know what is Grace and what is disgrace. Even if the king gives away his
kingdom to his wife it is not Grace, but due to some interest, it is disgrace.
In this way, everything you get from the world is disgrace.

ॐ

Questioner: I want to feel the Grace of Self every minute of my life.

Papaji: You can keep this desire while you are doing yoga or whatever you are doing. It will not disturb your career. What you learn here will go with you and reside within you wherever you go. It will not matter if you are in Lucknow, or in a cave in the Himalayas, or in a San Francisco supermarket. When you find that there is no distinction then you have crossed the ocean of illusion. Start from Here. Go to wherever you want, stay wherever you like.

I feel so much love for you and I know this love is love for my own Self. I thank you for the Grace and Wisdom that shines through you.

You are beautiful and I love you. This is all I can say: if somebody loves me then they come and sit in my heart. One who loves me sits in my Heart and is so close to me. They have nothing else to do other than this. This love is fearless and cannot die.

I have a lot of trust that your Grace is doing everything that needs to happen and I am feeling such a deepening due to this Grace. Is this Grace stronger or more accessible the closer I am to you physically?

Regarding Grace, it doesn't make any difference whether you are physically close to the teacher or not. But if the physical presence of the teacher is available, that should be given preference. In this half of the century most sages and saints are no longer here in their bodies and so if the presence is available, make the best use of it. Doubts which come up in the mind while in the presence of the teacher can be given to the teacher, answered, and cleared. Later, if the presence is not available, it is difficult to believe the Truth because the teacher is not present so these doubts tend not to be cleared as quickly.

So make the best use
of the Teacher's physical presence.

For Grace it doesn't matter if there is a teacher or not. For instance, so many people have been benefited by Buddha though they have never met him. Although, like Kashyap and Ananda, they would have enjoyed the benefit of his presence if they would have been there.

On Buddha Para Nirvana Day, as the death of his body was very near, some man came to see him, but he was told that the Master would be dying in a moment. But the Buddha saw him and cleared all his doubts in an instant. Then Buddha lost his breath forever. The presence of the Buddha enlightened over 500 people. With his very first sermon people were enlightened and to this day millions are benefited. If you have occasion to be with the Teacher, don't miss it!

I know that time and space are illusion and I know that Grace is real; so it makes sense to me that Grace transcends time and space.

This is correct. There is no time or space. It is just a concept of mind which vanishes when it is transcended. At that time you must be sure that you have achieved everything and there is nothing more to do. This is the only thing worth achieving in this human incarnation.

But I do feel strong changes when I am near you and this is why I am asking these questions on the nature of Grace.

The nature of Grace is to Enlighten
and to stop the cycle of birth and death.

You must be in total trust of this. Know that you are not to be reborn and even more know that this present birth is an illusion. Then you can be sure that all the world with its suns, moons and stars are illusions which are real only when we think and when we think they are real. When you don't think nothing is visible. I am happy that you are here and happy to answer your questions.

What is the role of Grace in the process of surrender?

Only with Grace can you surrender to the Satguru, to your own Self. You can't do it with your efforts. You must, therefore, please your teacher so that he is happy and bestows Grace upon you. With this Grace you will surrender everything to the teacher. Only this is called surrender. Using your own effort and your own mind is not surrender. Something will guide you from the inside and you will become a tool in the hands of the divine. Let him work, let "Thy will be done." Everybody wants "my will be done." They want "this" and "that," but this will only last 90 years or so. This is the end of teaching. Grace comes when you surrender, this is Grace. There is no other way.

Do I deserve to be so peaceful and happy the way I am now?

So few people ask this after getting the maximum. This is perhaps the Indian way. The people of the West are so arrogant that they never use this phrase, "do I deserve it?" So many Western people say instead, "I already knew it," or "I know what your answers to my questions will be." I hear this everyday; this is called pride. But there are some who after hearing the words of the Guru bow to his feet. This is like Hanuman who claimed he never deserved Ram's Grace. Hanuman had crossed the ocean to burn the Lanka of the demon Ravana in order to bring Peace back, to bring Sita back, restoring her to her husband. Then Ram told him: "Well done Hanuman, you are so great, who else could have crossed the ocean and done the job? What a brave person you are."

Hanuman folded his hands as he heard this, prostrated to Rama and went around him three times. Then he said only one word: "Gurukripa," meaning "Thy Grace." "Who am I? I am just a monkey, how could I cross the ocean to fight this demon. It is only by your Grace that I was able to do it and to tell your Sita that you would soon be coming to bring her back to Ayodhya."

What is the difference between Grace and skaktipat?

Shaktipat is the transmission of whatever power a person has to you. You are not to practice anything because they transmit the power to you.

I have had shaktipat from a Guru and it made me feel very quiet and stoned, as if I just smoked three chillums.

So why go to a guru when you can have some hash for one rupee behind the Gandhi Ashram in Hazrat Ganj? This high will stay for three hours and then you can have more. In this same way shaktipat of power without Knowledge of the Truth will turn the Guru-disciple relationship into dealer-addict dependence. Don't cultivate a habit which is dependent on anything. You have nothing to do and you will not get anything. Here there is no transmission or shaktipat, but all that happens is Within you.

Nobody can give you Peace of mind, It is Within.
The Nearness will give you the Peace which belongs to you.

I don't transmit anything, I don't give shaktipat. All that I do is remove your dependence on anything else. If you don't depend on anything else tell me what will happen; you won't lose anything. Just remove your dependence on God and on methods and everyone else and It will shine and reveal itself. That you can't lose. This is the clarity given here.

Remove the confusion and concepts from your mind that you will win peace from anyone else. You will definitely lose anything that you are given, so have no dependence. When you do not depend on anything it will reveal itself without any method. Don't depend on gurus.

What is the Grace of the Guru?

It is the Grace which has drawn you here. God within will take you some place to fulfill your desire. This is Grace. Since you want Freedom, Grace has brought you here.

What keeps one from having Grace? Some peoples hearts and lives are so full of Grace and some seem less fortunate.

What prevents someone from being Grace is the same thing that prevents success to everybody who walks on the path of Freedom: they are looking somewhere else and not surrendering their search to Peace! Even though they are in Satsang they still look somewhere else and not Within! You are where your mind is. It is like the student in the classroom who is really out in the field in that coming night's sports match. You are where your mind is. So, if you keep your mind surrendered to your Self in the Satsang where you are, it doesn't take time.

I came here because I knew I needed to finally hear the Truth. I had met one of your messengers who told me about you.

When the time is right you will meet someone who will take you to the Teacher. It is good luck that you didn't sell your soul to someone. So many "teachers" are not even able to even find their own Self. These people deviate from the Truth themselves. The Divine has gifted you with the discrimination to see if someone is a good person or not. The Sanskrit name for this Grace is Karuna. This will be your name.

Thank you for your Grace. Wednesday I will be leaving for the States to attend to my business, rather than spending most of my time in Lucknow and...

Who has decided that it is better for you to go to the States and who was it that brought you here to Satsang? Even then you had to tend to business, but who was it that brought you here? What is the difference between the Who that brought you here and the who that wants to go back and attend to your business?

I don't think that there is any difference.

(Angrily) No! There is much difference! The difference is that you were busy with your business and somehow due to someone's Grace, and your own merits which you have won in the previous lives or even in this life, this Who has decided to take you away from all of your activities and to bring you Here. Now you have to decide if the who that is calling you back is the same Who or if it is the ego. When you say that "I have to attend to my children," then it is the egoistic who, not the One who decides for everyone what they have to do. How do you know whether your going is better or that staying in Lucknow is better? Who do you think is really taking care of your business? Who gives you the strength and intelligence to do "your" activities?

Most of the people say, "I will go now" and their body leaves, but who is it that operates the body to take this body from Lucknow to the States? Is it the body that is attending to it or the mind? What activates the mind, body and the senses? Who is that one? We do not know and so we have to surrender to the Supreme Power. If we have to go we have to go, if we have to stay we have to stay. There should be no difference, but you cannot decide. Most of the time when people have decided they could not fulfill this decision.

A couple of years ago I had a friend in Delhi who planned to visit me in Haridwar with his brother, who had a garment factory in England. At the last minute this brother said that he was too busy for the quick trip up to Haridwar and wanted to go attend to his business in London instead. He did promise that the next time that he came to India that he would surely come to see the Master in Haridwar.

Four days later I was in Haridwar when I received a telegram from my friend in Delhi. He said to meet him at Kusha Ghat where the after-death rites are performed and the ashes given to the Ganga. He met me there and showed me a little bag and said, "This is my brother who said that next time to India he would go to Haridwar." (giggles) "These are the ashes. Please bless his soul and we will give him to the Ganga." He had died in London of a heart attack.

So nobody knows. You have no time now because you don't know what will happen the next minute. It is better to surrender to the Supreme force inside that makes the decision. Let It make the decision. But when you say "I have to go," this "I" is different than the One who is always there and functions in all of your activities. When you surrender to the Supreme Power it will look after you very nicely, and no mistake will be made. Even your business will not be affected. You can say, "It is that doing the business," or "It is me doing the business." So "That" and "me" has to be decided.

You can look after your children, who says not? Some people are here who say that they are leaving, but just return back from the airport. They do this two or three times and it means that the One who has brought them here decided to keep them here and so they cannot go.

In the last few days I have felt that it is my fear of changing and my need to be a doer which makes me want to go to the States.

It is so. It is so. (giggles) It is your fear.

But, I do feel very connected with you regardless of where I am.

So there is a double crossing in the statement also. It is a double crossing because you think it is correct, but it is not. It is a very high state to be with me regardless of whether or not you are in my physical presence. In this state you will never use "but."

Is there any special advice that you have for me?

You must surrender to the Supreme Power who is working in all the activities you are doing. When you are not doing any activity it is That that is keeping Quiet. Then there will be no mistake at all, whether you are here or not here. Thank you.

How do we know when Atman is revealed, and how to have the Atman revealed?

It is not your choice, as it is described in the Upanishads:

I reveal Myself to those that I choose.

It is not your choice, but the choice of the Atman. Then It reveals Itself to Itself.

I want you to choose me like that.

You have been! If you neighbor calls you, you may not come. So how is it that people from all over the world come when I call. They don't even know until they get here that I have called them.

No one knows this: Everyone is inside me.
The one who calls and the one called are the same thing.

This must be known when the one is chosen. Everybody is suffering and dying, but if you believe in the Protector, the suffering will be destroyed.

If you are equal to That you will be exalted by the Divine.
So sit quiet Here, you can't find this Teaching anywhere.
It is not a mantra or a practice.
Just sit Quiet, don't stir a thought
and don't make effort.

There is no method to Freedom?

There is no technique and no method, Simply keep Quiet. Methods belong to the past. Any method that you bring to mind is something that you only heard of, so forget every method.

With your Grace I know that a leaf from the Bodhi tree has fallen on my head. I am so grateful for what you have given me.

This is the Grace of the Bodhi tree. This leaf fell on the head of the Buddha and he was Enlightened. Today, 2600 years later, people still go there. Those who are true and seek only Wisdom will be Enlightened.

Will the Grace follow me back to the West?

As Grace is Here so will it be there,
if you love her she will not leave you.
She is the most precious person in the whole world,
because nothing gives happiness except Her.

ॐ Gurukripa ॐ

Satsang: Association with the Truth

Satsang is the association with Sat, with Truth.
Keeping association only with That
which will not destroy Love is Satsang.
Being Truth, being with the Wise is Satsang.
It has is no past, no future, no this, no that,
just your own nature, a field of Beauty.
The One who comes to Satsang is happy;
even gods will take a human form in order to attend.

The Presence of the Guru is Satsang.
The Guru's part in Satsang is
to show you that there are no parts.
When you do not inquire you are in parts
and you become that which can be destroyed.

Satsang in the human body is so precious and rare,
don't waste it by asking, "what is this and that."
Just humbly ask, "Who am I?"
Don't let your mind be distracted in Satsang:
If you tie ropes to the past via memory and concepts
you are not in Satsang.
Time is a concept and Satsang is out of time.
Stay where there are no ropes, no concepts
and no distractions or explanations, this is Reality.

Satsang is a tongueless teacher and headless students.
So shut your head, let your Heart open,
and Truth will reveal itself to you in Silence.
Only pay attention to That with your open Heart.

The strong desire for Freedom rises only in an open Heart.
This desire is the fertility of the land
to take the seed of the Satguru's Teaching.
Satsang is raindrops on this opening Heart.
Only people near Freedom need instruction;
not those in the dark, and not those in the Light.

Only Satsang will take you out of suffering
because it shows you the Silence that you have always been.
Satsang is abiding as your Self, not as "I-am-so-and-so."
Asking how you are bound is Satsang.

Satsang strikes at the root of bondage and arrogance,
and is the death of mind which few can face.
Peace is not living in memory or mind, it is only Here, Here.
It is your nature and Satsang reminds you of it.
If you are on fire with anger, grief, and confusion
run straight to the river of Satsang.

There are three ways: Jnana, Bhakti, and Yoga.
In Satsang we speak of only of Jnana, or Vichar,
Knowledge of who you are.
Yoga is not spoken of here,
and Bhakti, the love of the Divine,
cannot be spoken of at all.

In Satsang you have to remove your doubts
because it is only doubts that keep you from being Free.
This serpent of doubt, living in the heart, is killed in Satsang.

Satsang is giving up beliefs, notions, intentions,
desires, and illusions; This is the secret of Freedom!
The notion of creation rises out of Purusha
and the creator is created along with all its concepts.
Our attachments to these concepts become our reality
and only in Satsang is this removed.
To get rid of this suffering attend Satsang at any cost.
Not activating the mind means attending this Satsang.

Satsang means a place of seclusion, of quietness.
It is a place within your Heart.
Come to this Satsang naked.

*Questioner: I only have a few days to spend here. How can I best
spend my time here in Lucknow with you? Already your presence
has touched me deeply and I no longer desire the objects and
experiences of the world.*

Papaji: It is enough to cease your desire for the objects of the world.
Through any of the senses you can get lost in the world. Fish die due to their
sense of taste. Deer die due to their desire to hear certain sounds. Elephants
are caught and killed by the sense of touch; they put an effigy of a female
elephant on some bamboo which covers a pit, then the male elephant comes

to touch the image, falls in the pit and is trapped. A moth dies due to sight as it goes toward the flame.

The difficulties of being drawn by the senses can be overcome because the human being has discrimination and can foresee the results of his actions. Then they can choose to go towards Peace instead of suffering. For thousands of years the way that people have gone towards Peace is to go to the Guru for one instant of Satsang, ask their question, and have all their doubts dissolved. Then only Moksham remained.

Is it okay not to have any question? If I don't ask am I missing anything?

No, it's not okay! You must have a question. Otherwise you are missing Freedom. If you don't ask you are missing Freedom because any pig, dog or donkey does not have any question and, therefore, they miss everything. Every human being must have a question to be happy.

What is that question? "Who am I?" If you do not ask this question you belong to the community that I have already named! This question is the last question and only a rare man will ask this question. All the rest will not ask him. Ask the question and find out the answer by yourself.

The other night I was dreaming that I was in Satsang and I did ask this question.

That is wonderful. So many people are having Satsang in the waking state, and in the dream state. Next will be Satsang in the sleep state and that will be Eternal Satsang. Dreaming Satsang is good because your dreams are just the thoughts you had in waking state that get carried over. This shows that your waking state has been very well spent.

I dreamed I came to Satsang naked!

Satsang is the Garden of Eden where you must be naked. You must even be free of nudity. Remove even nudity, which means remove the ego. No dress and no nudity will really be a good Satsang. Then you will see what I speak about.

I have felt your faceless kiss. Now what was once a fear of the unknown is an invitation to Freedom.

Excellent. This is the result of attending Satsang! A very wonderful experience. This teaching is not available in any of the books. You must be faceless when you are in Satsang, then the Teacher who has no head on his shoulders is going to teach you because you have no face. The teachers who have a head are better not to see; head means ego. Satsang happens when neither the teacher nor the student have any ego.

I think I will cancel my plans to leave because I just want to stay here.

Let the cancellations stand and don't think about anything: Just stay here. You need not go away because Here you will get everything. Wherever you go it will be Here that you will get what you need. So don't think about this. Be Here. Understand you have to Be Here Alone. This is a mystery working.

I am carrying a child within me. Do you have any advice? Should I abide in silence?

Don't be silent, speak to your child. Start Satsang with your unborn child so that when he is born he is familiar with it. Speak to your unborn baby.

You have given me the greatest Treasure. I so appreciate it.

So many people are doing such hard work, but they do not know the treasure that lies below all this work. What they need is a reliable person whose word they can trust, to tell them that just below their work is gold. That is what I tell you and those who believe it remove the practices, all the hard work and immediately they become rich beyond what I can estimate. Riches of gold are lost everyday. India even lost the Kohinoor diamond to the British. Even Krishna and the Pandavas had this diamond and now this priceless treasure is lost.

> You can lose any object gained,
> but you can never lose That.

That night I also dreamed that I lost my house to a fire, but when I called the fire marshal to put it out, I found that you were the fire marshal. By just looking at the burning house you made everything burn more!

I will tell you the meaning of this dream with a story. There was a sadhu living in a thatched hut who was cooking some rice on a fire. He left for awhile and upon returning he saw many people throwing water on his hut and dragging his few possessions out of the fire which was engulfing his little house. He took his possessions and threw them back into the fire. Soon it started raining and the rain was putting the fire out. So he started putting buckets of water from a nearby river onto the hut. Some of the neighbors asked why he first fed the fire with his possessions and now was putting the fire out. He said:

"Once in a lifetime a fire comes to burn your house down. I was very happy with this and gave everything to this fire so as not to annoy her. Now it is raining and so I am bringing water to be friendly with the rain."

Put everything into it and let the fire burn including your attachments to the past. Even let your present and future attachments burn. When everything has burned the rain of Grace will fall on you. Don't save anything and the Grace will come and help you and look after you now and in the future. You need to think nothing and do nothing. Simply stay Quiet and see how it works. Burn the bushes of attachment and you will see the Grace.

So this is the fun. Very few people will understand this secret: keep the flames burning as hot as possible and when the water comes, let it come. The desire for freedom are these flames and Grace is the rain from Self.

I feel adrift on the ocean of ignorance. Can you guide me to the shore? I desire to be Free. This is the only desire I have brought here.

Everybody is ignorant, but nobody knows it. Everybody is proud of what they have done. This is called world. But when you have come to know that you are ignorant, you have come to me. It is enough! This Satsang is a raft across this ocean. You need to do nothing, don't even speak about this ocean at all because it has crocodiles which will swallow you up. Countless people have been swallowed and are being swallowed everyday, but nobody knows that there is a raft. *Just get into the raft and keep Quiet.* The pilot is there and you are his responsibility. You will be safely landed onto the shore.

Actually, this ocean of samsara does not exist.
It is only your desires and when they subside
there is nothing which has ever existed.
If you know this ocean is dreadful
and filled with alligators and sharks this is enough.
These alligators are your desires for objects,
for persons, for some enjoyment!
Once you forget them you are very safe.

This is good advice to a young boy like you. I am glad you are here. It is a right age to come here. Even Socrates said that to know God you must be on the right side of the forties. Ramakrishna writes the same thing. He prescribes coming to the teacher while in youth due to a very interesting observation which I have seen for myself on Marina Beach in Madras.

I used to spend all of Saturday and that night at the ocean meditating on the beach. In the morning I would watch the fisherman put the net into the ocean from two boats, and after making a circle, close back up. As you watch this you see four types of fish which, to Ramakrishna, symbolized four types of men.

Some fish see the net immediately and decide not to touch it and they escape. This is fish or man number one. They do not even enter the net. Sukadev is an example of this. Number two fish see no difference between one side of the net and the other and do not mind either way. Rama Tirtha is an example of this. He enjoyed the world and was a householder and a professor of mathematics in Lahore, but at the age of 32 he left everything and went to the Himalayas and never returned to his town. This number two fish also escaped the net, these are those who escape at a very young age.

Type number three jump out of the net at age 50 or 60 after the net has been closed. But what I saw is that as they jump out many were caught in the air by the seagulls and cormorants. A few did land safely back in the ocean.

Now the fourth ones hold the net tight in their mouths for their own safety. (giggles) Those were the fish that the fisherman brought to shore. They didn't even try to jump, but just held onto the net. These fish go on the table every evening!

I saw the fisherman load all these fish into the baskets with the help of his wife. They were very happy and grateful and out of gratitude put some of the fish back into the ocean which so generously provided their livelihood. So by a special Grace these fish also made it out of the net. The second time he went to put fish in the ocean his wife held his hand and said, "Enough." (laughs) So some people escape this net in childhood, some in youth and some in old age, like me! Not holding the net, I could do it. So all the people with gray hair don't worry. Be sure that you will be offered back to the ocean. The fisherman is very generous you see.

Why are these books and photos and things for sale here. It seems to detract from the purity of Satsang.

If you go to Hazrat Ganj you will go to the shop which has what you want. If you want shoes you will go to the shoe shop and not to the tailor. So in Satsang if you divide your attention here and there it means that you have not come for Satsang. You are just walking in to judge "other." If you *have* come for Freedom you don't see anything or anyone else.

It is like the man who gets a phone call in his office which says that there is a fire in his house. Immediately he goes. On the way he meets a friend who asks him out to lunch, but he will not go because his house is on fire. Instead, he will go straight home to find out what can be done.

So when your house in on fire with: "I want to be Free," you will not accept an invitation of any judgment or relationship. You will straight away go to your home and look after it. But if you have no fire you can stay on after office hours and then go wherever you like.

This must be like a house on fire. A normal house doesn't really matter because you can always get a new house. But if *this* house is on fire you must finish it as soon as possible because you don't know when your next incarnation will be. "I want to be Free" is this house on fire.

I do want to be Free, but soon I am going home and I am worried
I will go none the wiser.

You must find out what does not die and what is not born, and this you will find in Satsang. This is hiding in the cavity in your Heart where death does not touch. It is the source of the power by which you touch, see, smell, hear and taste. The Teacher will tell you that it is within your Heart, so look· within and you will see it and you will become It! Then you will no longer come to this land of suffering.

I want to see it and be one with everything, but the habit of
separation and judging is very hard to break.

In Satsang it will happen by itself. There is no other way besides Satsang. Only desire to be Free is needed. The main impediment for you is that you focus on other things. You must focus on what you want.

I have no question in particular, but I also feel that I have not
arrived home yet.

When you have not arrived home how can you say that you have no question? You are in the fishmarket and you are lost. You have to take a guide and ask them where your home is. Everybody is lost, but they are happy in the fishmarket. There they stay and there they will die!

It is better to ask. If you don't like this ugly marketplace, question someone who knows and who will take you out of this market. If you know that you are here then you can go anywhere, even to the fishmarket, and yet you are home.

I want to have a better connection with you, though mind says it is
enough to sit in Satsang. How can I feel your presence more?

Sitting is not so easy, but you tell the mind to let you sit quietly Here. It may not want to be quiet, but you must win this battle. Sit and watch what the mind is doing, watch its tendencies, watch where it rises from and where it goes. Then you will see that the mind will not allow you to sit quietly because it is attached to the past affairs, past persons, past objects and past thoughts. These attachments prevent you from sitting quietly. But if you can sit for one moment, it is most precious. I advise you:

> When the mind goes out like a monkey bring it back again.
> Again it will go and again bring it back.
> Again it will go and again bring it back.
> Play the game and eventually the mind will stop going.

You didn't do this in California because if you would have, there would be no reason to come here. Sit Quiet and see that your mind doesn't run out and if she does, bring her back.

> Take away mind's attachment to the past and mind is no-mind,
> because mind is the attachment itself.
> So remove the attachments and you will see
> the light of Peace and Love.

Do this and if you have any difficulty please tell me what you have done and what the results were. Did you follow what you have to do? Simply look at the mind like you look at a pair of glasses. When the mind is looking within there is no object to be seen and It will stay with Itself. Since you are here take the opportunity to change your old habits which lead to suffering. Then when you return your friends won't recognize you.

I want to see you alone before I leave for Nepal.

You are invited to see me alone. You come alone to me; (laughs) don't bring anyone with you, not your clothes, not your body, not your mind. Then you can see me alone. Always you can come to me like this.

I have been in Satsang for a month and though all my questions are answered, I still feel that I am in the dark and that I can't keep quiet. I feel I will never keep quiet.

You could have said, "I will never keep quiet," in your country. This is just conditioning from your country. Forget the past and stay in Satsang and don't look for anything. It will just come by itself because your desire is tremendous. The merit that brought you here will work, so just sit quiet and don't do anything.

I can sit quietly but I feel like I have come here burdened and that I still have some burden on me.

You have to get rid of the burden on your head. Suppose you have 200 pounds on your head and you go to a teacher who says to get your mind clean of all concepts. This only adds to the weight. The next teacher tells you to do something else and it is another burden. Here, I don't tell you to do things, no practice, no meditation, but simply I shake your head and there goes the burden. To say "I am Free" is to shake your head free of arguments and other things. Then you will go light-headed and light-minded.

We are so lucky to be in Satsang where understanding just happens by itself in the Heart, and not in the mind. Is there anything more required than Trust and openness and to be here to realize the Truth?

That is enough. You don't need anything else.

You are making this shava shuddha, you are purifying me, and removing my burdens.

What is this process? How do you purify this shava, this corpse?

A corpse cannot do anything.

And like that it is done. (He points to a painting of Kali on Shiva) Shiva is shava under the feet of Kali. Even Shiva is shava, even all of your knowledge is useless, unless you are under the feet of the teacher; this is what that means. Being under the feet of the teacher purifies.

People here have such a different look on their faces. What is this difference?

Everybody is becoming young here. Normally worry eats everybody in the world. Who is there that has not been smitten by this serpent. But, if there is no worry in a person, then they are forever young and death cannot touch them. This is the secret: Don't have any worry in your mind. This worry is a deadly serpent. A man may survive the bite of a cobra, but if he is bitten by worry he has no chance of survival, it will kill him again and again. People look so much younger when they sit in Satsang and have no worries.

My parents back in Ireland are worried about me and wonder what I am doing here. I try to tell them, but I just can't communicate to them what happens here.

It seems you have come here without the consent of your parents, and worrying about them is one of your burdens now! You have done very well, not only for you, but through you they are also benefited. Assure them that you are taken care of and that you have no problems here. Some parents send their children off to a university in a foreign country so that they receive a higher education. It helps the welfare of the whole family when this happens and so the wise parents don't worry about it when their children leave for higher studies. Those higher studies may win them a good job, but this education in Lucknow will give you contentment, peace and love which you can pass on to your parents. So stay on here under any circumstances. If they are displeased, let them be. You must be very strong in this affair and don't try to please anyone who stands in your way. You march on until the battle is won. This battle is between you and a very strong enemy which even the emperors are defeated by. This enemy is ego. She may look weak, but is very strong. She has defeated everyone in the universe and has made them her slaves. Few will win this battle of life.

I do not advise you to reject your family, but you must fulfill your desire to be Free. While here in Lucknow keep only this desire to be Free. Then as a Free person you can return to any desire, including wanting to help your family.

I am so glad to be here. It feels like the best thing I could ever do!

Attending Satsang is the best thing that you can do, it is the best work to be done. You have looked all over the world, but unless you see your Self first you will never see anything else. First look at who you are and then, if need be, look at anything else in the world.

> If you see your Self
> you don't even have to look to God.

A woman came here recently after searching for 25 years. So many swamis and gurus gave her practices and pictures of themselves and of gods. But nothing gave her Peace. Then she came here and without asking any question and without 'getting' anything she realized that she is God, the God she had searched so long for.

I am leaving this evening to travel around and visit other places and teachers, but I would like your guidance.

You want guidance, but you don't want to stay in Satsang and hear it. You plan to leave. So it is better that you go on searching. Maybe after 80 years you will be fatigued. So in the year 2075 why don't you come back. Until then just visit all these places and the black holes.

Please shake me up and wake me up. I want to find what I have been looking for.

You have been shaken and that is why you are here, you don't need anything else. To attend Satsang you must be shaken up. Then you are to do nothing. You have been shaken from the previous circumstances and now you are after something and I promise you will have that.

Can you say something to me about Freedom?

First be Free, then enter the world and you will never be miserable. First things must be first. In your case, since you are in old age it wasn't. If you first get Free then you remain young and energetic and nobody will get fed up with you, nor you with anyone else because you have seen the Beauty inside. You are here now. The past is past. You are here in the field of Beauty because now you have found that Freedom is the most beautiful thing to be attained in life. The past is past and do not care for that. Now be here in Satsang and you will see every cell of your body renewed. You will see the beauty that is within your heart and without also. I am happy you are here and I hope you stay a while longer.

My girlfriend with whom I share a strong mutual commitment wants me to go to Europe for relationship counseling. I would like your advice about this.

The people who are giving this workshop are in trouble themselves. How can they help you? Tell her to come to India and be here in Satsang. Satsang is the best workshop.

Thank you for the precious gift of being here with us. So often I have such strong dreams of Satsang and other things.

These dreams are not dreams, but more real than reality. If you are after something seriously, sincerely and honestly you will see that even the dreams will be real and you will dream about what you have done throughout the waking state. More or less this is the projection of the waking state into dream. But what is happening to you are not dreams, but visions and these visions are better than the waking state experiences. This shows a very deep intention to realize your own Self. Like everybody here, whether they know it or not. One day you will know who brought you here. You will know who your Guide is and who compelled you to come here and sit in Satsang. This you *will* know.

What is the difference between Satsang and psychotherapy?

Psychotherapy is a machine which makes money. Satsang simply gives Freedom and doesn't make money. It is simply for peace of mind, not to disturb your mind. It gives peace and love, but psychotherapy can be very confusing. If you go to a typical therapist they will just take you to the past and leave you there forever! In Satsang we don't dig the graves. We find out who we are and find that we have no disease at all. Most therapists will stay in front of you for only one hour, take $100, and then leave, but the Satguru is always with you forever. That is the difference.

I am not satisfied. I am not free.

What is this dissatisfaction?

Thought, doubt.

Where is this doubt lodging? If it is in the head than cut off the head. If it is in the nose then remove the nose. This is the teaching of seven year old girl in Varanasi. Her name was Kamali and her father was Saint Kabir.

Kabir was giving Satsang and many people were attending it. Kamali asked her Father, "Why do so many people come to see you so early at four in the morning?"

He said, "They come for Freedom and Truth, and to be Enlightened. Why else would they come so early in the morning in the winter time when it is so cold?"

"Papa, five hundred people coming for Freedom and Satsang? I don't believe it, they must be coming for something else."

Then she went away and started playing. The next morning though, she stood at the gate and told each person who came that her father was going to interview each person before they were allowed into Satsang. She told them that they had to lay down with their heads on this log and she would cut their heads off and then bring the head in to show her father. If he agreed then the person would be allowed into Satsang. She assured everybody that the chopper that she had in her hand was very sharp and that nobody would feel any pain as she would instantly separate their heads from their bodies.

The first party said, "We are here because we have a court case and we wanted your father's blessings for that reason. But now we have touched his gate and so we have his grace and so we think we will be on our way to court now."

The second party said, "Our son is very sick and so we have come to see your father to get his blessings so that our son does not die."

The next party said, "We didn't come for Satsang, but for his blessings on our daughter's marriage. We will just salute at his gate and be on our way. Tomorrow we will come for Satsang."

All these people, and more, had their reasons.

After two hours her father came out of the empty Satsang hall. Though it was 6 a.m. no one was around except his daughter who had a chopper in her hand.

"Papaji, I told you that nobody comes for Freedom," she said. "Why do you waste your time? You give Satsang from 4 to 8 every morning, and then you leave and give Satsang in other places only to come back after ten days. You don't even give *us* your love. Why are you wasting your time? Today everybody had some other interest."

So if you are to see a Saint you have to remove your head and then he will interview you. Your doubts are only in your head and when you remove it you are doubtless. Then you are Free. If you understand you will not keep any doubt. Are you in doubt now?

Yes.

Then you go out and chop off your head!

But Papaji, sometimes...

Interpret 'sometimes,' what do you mean by 'sometimes'? What teacher taught you this poor grammar? This is a different class where there is no teacher. This Teacher has no tongue to speak to the students and the students have no heads to understand with. This is *that* class. So if you have a head you have to find some other place, some butchery where heads are beheaded.

This ego is the head, you see. It is worth taking to a butchery. They will take very good care of you. I don't need heads, *I need hearts*. Here heads are not needed, but there are many institutions that need the head only. Remove your head outside and then speak. Then your Heart will speak the language of Love for the first time. Allow your Heart to speak! You have always been speaking from the head so behead it like Kamali says! This girl knew how Satsang had to be attended. These "I's" and "you's" and "she's" are not allowed in Satsang. You are now going to see Truth face to face, that is the meaning of Satsang. You are facing Truth, Freedom. Who can kill you? You are afraid of your own Self and you depend upon other selves. You are too involved in matters which are not permanent and now you can't save your life. Millions of times you have been born and millions of times you have died and so you know the taste of death very well. Now is time to know how to live! It is so simple to be in bliss always, but you want death. This lovely garden of Love and Beauty you have converted into a butchery.

Stop a moment and see who you are. You have never allowed time to your own Self to reveal itself to you and to kiss and hug you. You have tried using your head for millions of years, now at least give time to your heart. Keep Quiet, simply keep Quiet. If you keep Quiet your own Self will come and hug you and kiss you. Allow time for your own Self.

Satsang with you is so intoxicating. I have come to you to rediscover what is always here and rest permanently in the Self.

Usually you have to spend a lot of money for these intoxicants. How did you get intoxicated here.

Your Presence, the best drink!

Usually the best intoxicant is Scotch, but this only lasts three hours and off goes all your money! But this intoxicant will grow more and more every moment. This is not that intoxicant which will go after three hours. You must find a famous label and then only one peg will last you all your life, and even at that this intoxication will not evaporate! Very few people have drunk this wine because they cannot pay the price. You can say that the price is very high and you can say that it is no price at all. You only have to keep Quiet and you will have this intoxication. Simply keep Quiet.

When your intoxication depends on somebody else you are cheating yourself, you are deceiving yourself. No good intoxication will come from any source other than your Self. Nobody will give you Happiness, nobody will give you Peace. Find out yourself. Only a confused mind will think that there is happiness elsewhere. This Love and Beauty will arise if you are Quiet for this single instant. Then you will attain everything. It looks as if you have tasted it. Otherwise, you could not shine like you are. (laughs) Okay, I am very happy to meet you.

I love just sitting here with you in Peace with no other purpose.

The one who sits in front of me with no purpose gets everything. This is what the Gods also promise: "When a devotee comes to me and asks for something, instantly I will give it, whether it be a child, long life, a good partner or whatever." But God also has fear like others do. He says, "I am afraid of the person who doesn't ask for anything because I am bound to provide everything always for that person and I must follow him like a shadow. To the one with no desire I provide everything *the moment it is needed,* so I am bound to that person."

So it is with the person who comes to Satsang with no desires. They are given everything, even if they don't ask. You lack nothing. Rest assured that all that was ever needed is over now.

Papaji, I would like a new name.

First I will give you the meaning. When you put your hands together like a cup and extend these empty hands, the diamond will fall into it by itself. This diamond is Knowledge of the Self and drops by itself, but there have been layers of distractions in your mind which your hands hold onto. These layers are desires. The person who comes to Satsang has withdrawn his mind from the desires and returned them to his Self. This automatically happens in Satsang. Then this cup is ready and the diamond drops and there is Self revelation. Self reveals Itself to Itself. This position of the open cupped hand is called Anjali. You can hold this Self Knowledge because your heart is open to receive this Knowledge.

This is a story from the Upanishads. When someone got emancipation and was asked how he did it he said, "It was like a gooseberry, an amlaki, dropping in my anjali. I didn't do it, it just dropped down from the tree of Satsang." This will happen if you stand under the amlaki tree and not under any other tree.

The names you get in Satsang are names of Love and Beauty, and those who use these names get drowned in Love and Beauty and Grace. Even the one who calls your name gets the benefit. The name should be such that everybody enjoys it. If you utter the name of joy, you are joyful.

The names represent a new lineage. Out of suffering comes suffering and so many of your names hold this suffering. But now you belong to a different atmosphere and the new name is a part of this. It is part of starting your life afresh, free from the past.

Papaji, does one need to ripen like a fruit on a tree and then be eaten by an Enlightened Being?

There is no fruit to ripen, no tree, and no forest. There is no hope, but you must Trust this. Nothing ever existed. Fruits will drop so don't be on a branch of tree. Give up this habit of dropping.

I used to feel very much like a dropped fruit. The first seventeen years of my life were like hell.

Very few people come back from hell. But I know one person who went there. He was a very good man with no sins on his record except that he once was facing an invading army with a javelin and accidentally pierced the eye of a lizard. So when he went after death to the judge it was decided that he must go enjoy heaven for one million years. However, since he hurt that lizard, which had to live the rest of its time in that body blind, he had to pass through hell for a few seconds on his way to heaven.

So, as he passed through hell he asked the security guards why all the people are smiling and dancing. They said, "For one sin they are put into the fire, but unlike an earthly fire which consumes once and the burnt object is finished, these fires are very special and once you die by fire you are instantly reborn and thrown in again. This will go on for one million years, this is hell! But they are happy because you are here. Due to the presence of such a good being like you, all of hell is happy."

"Well then," said the man, "I don't want to go to heaven, I want to stay here in hell. If my presence can make them all happy I am going to stay here!"

So the security guards went back and asked the judge what to do. The judge agreed that he could stay in hell if he really wanted to, but not to tell anyone.

At the same time the people in heaven were getting into trouble because though they were enjoying heaven, they were only enjoying the objects. Somehow they heard that there was Satsang in the hell and one by one until now I think there are about 230 people there. (giggles) So now nobody is going to the so-called heaven and everybody is coming to this hell!

I have been very blessed to meet beings like Mother Meera, Ammachi, His Holiness the Dalai Lama and Thich Nhat Hanh. I am so thankful for your presence on this planet and I bow to your feet.

They have given you blessings and so you are here. It is a blessing of God and so many Saints and Sages that enable you to come to Satsang. It is in this Satsang that you will know your Self. Be patient and don't run away unless you have achieved the goal.

The Buddha was my first Guru and my heart connection with him is so

strong that it feels that I must have known him. I recognize you also, as if I have known you before.

You must have known Buddha before, we have known everybody many times before. It is not the first time. You can note down the 1st of April 1994, about 11:30 a.m. Again in the same time we will meet again and we have met on this particular day millions of times, but most do not remember. Very few remember this and realize that it will keep on going unless you decide to finish this process of coming again and again.

Even Buddha saw millions of his lives appearing somewhere as someone, but he knew it and he was told that when he was the Prince of the Sakya Kingdom and his name was Amitabh Gautam, then that would be his final life.

All of us here have been together in many incarnations; therefore, we are here. The purpose of us meeting here is not to appear again, as Buddha himself has done. What he did was so simple. He just sat under a Bodhi tree, not speaking, and all was over. He did it and we also can do it.

A story is appearing in my mind and so I will take a short time to tell you: it is a story of the Ramanaya which occurred about 7000 years ago. This is a story of the Lord's incarnation as Rama.

There was a battle going on between the Sages and the Asuras or demons. The demons kidnapped Rama's wife and, in short, Rama killed the demon and brought back his wife.

Now they must sit on the throne and the coronation ceremony must take place and so Rama, the king, sent a message to his Guru to come and do the necessary pujas so that he could sit on the throne with the blessings of his Master.

He sent his brother Lakshman on the fastest horse and told him to deliver Rama's ring to his Guru and to ask him to come to perform the ceremony. So Lakshman went to the forest ashram of Rama's Guru and said to the Guru, "I am Lakshman, the brother of Rama. We have come back safely from the south and next week is the ceremony of coronation which Rama requests you, with his ring, to perform."

Now, the ring of the king is so precious that it can have no equal in the country. It had special diamonds which could be found nowhere else. Lakshman offered the ring to the Guru and the Guru said, "I am busy cooking some rice, go into my thatch hut and put the ring in the earthen pot."

Getting off his horse, Lakshman went and put the ring into the pot, but a sound that was unexpected came when he dropped the ring. He was quite curious as to what the pot could contain and felt it was not right to put the ring of the king into a simple earthen pot.

He turned the pot upside down and many rings appeared all similar to the one he put in. "How could it be?" he thought. "There are so many rings I can't count them much less find the one I just put into the pot."

He went out and asked "Please tell me, who has put these rings into this pot?"

Sternly and seriously, Vashishta said, "Lakshman, you have done it. You have done it!"

"How is it possible? I am coming for the first time!" he exclaimed.

"No, many times you have come and you asked me each time to come to the ceremony while sitting on your horse's back, and each time I have told you to put the ring in the pot. And it will continue to happen like this again and again, unless you get down from the horse and remove your pride. Then stay with me and I will teach you something and you will not appear again," answered Vashishta.

So we will keep appearing unless we remove the pride and stop identifying as any name or form, and when you have no name or form you will realize that you have never come at any time before, not even this time. This is the beauty of this teaching:

The Truth Is Never Has Anything Existed.

I have just come from Bodh Gaya with so many Buddhist ideas of merit and karma. It seems so meaningless and irrelevant to Freedom if nothing ever existed!

It is not meaningless, actually it has great meaning. Without good karma you would never have come here or to Bodh Gaya. Few people have the merit to come to Satsang. It takes a mountain of merits to come Here, and this is how you have come.

It is destined when you will be Free, just as it was for Buddha. The strength of your merit will be so strong that Freedom will come to you even if you try to reject it. If you are meant to be Free the circumstances will be such that you will not be able to leave here even if you try!

Papaji, Ananda once said to Buddha: "Noble friendship is half of the Holy life." Buddha replied, "To have noble associates, noble companions, noble friendships is all of the Holy life." Papaji, the association with you here has enriched me like nothing before in 39 years of experience. Thank you for being here when you could just as easily be in the cool mountains.

Kabir has said something about the noble association of the Teacher. I have to rub my memory because she is old and doesn't like to stay with me:

> If you associate with a Saint for just one moment
> your sins that you have committed in previous generations
> will absolutely be destroyed,
> and you will not have to appear again.

ॐ

I don't want to just grow old and die, I want to be Free of this.

Satsang is like a beauty parlor which will remove all your wrinkles because it will show you your True face. Here the price is not 950 rupees, the price is not to think. Anybody can pay the price. If you don't think then tell me how beautiful you could be.

When it comes, clench your teeth and tighten your fists in determination and jump into your own lake Manasrover.

It seems that since coming to Lucknow I am not as happy as I was before I came here. I do enjoy being here in this beautiful sanga. What is happening to me?

The happiness you had before Lucknow was probably a mind conceived happiness based on a person or persons or objects who returned happiness to you. Maybe you got happiness just from your own concepts. That is not happiness! True happiness cannot be described. If you can describe it or its source then it is only a mental flight whose purpose is to gain or attain something. Happiness doesn't come from another person, not even from a Saint or Sage. Happiness comes from Within. Happiness is untold, unaware. You can't even get happiness in Satsang for it is always within you.

You come to Satsang and are told to be quiet and not to think of anything, including your own body and mind and ego and activity of the senses. Then you can be quiet and at Peace. Here you learn to be quiet, not allowing any thought to arise from your mind. Then you will have a happiness beyond description and your face will show this within you. Your face will absolutely change when you are happy. And anybody who looks at your face will be happy.

This sadness welling up is a good sign. It was untouched in the bottom of your heart and more was accumulating there for lifetimes. This sadness has become one with your body and is not separate from it. Like dust collecting on the bottom of a glass of water, this sadness will accumulate in your heart on account of your wrong behavior and wrong activities. The reason that you are feeling this sadness now is because Satsang stirs it up and brings it to the surface where it can be removed. Everybody's mind gets stressed in Satsang and what is unnoticed for years comes to the surface. But sadness cannot stay in Satsang and so it is dissolved. Actually, it is the suffering and sadness that brought you here so you must be thankful to it.

Once you know your own Self all of this sadness will no longer be an issue for you. You may feel unlucky, but actually you are incredibly lucky. Soon the past will no longer affect you and you won't care about these burdens that you have carried. You will only know Now!

I am so caught up in thought and streams of judgments and feelings, it is hard to feel lucky, though inside I really know I am.

You are in the middle of a stream? Why did you enter this stream if you are not a swimmer? Only those who know how to swim can enter the river and enjoy it. So you are advised to not enter rivers if you don't know how to swim. First learn how to swim and you will not fear any river.

Learn swimming by staying with those who know how to swim. Slowly you will learn to swim as they hold you. Then you will move the hands and in this way you will not drown. Moving the hands is swimming and this is Self effort. Then you become a swimmer. If you don't make self effort you will sink. But you can also make use of the depth of the river and balance your body so that you float without moving any part of your body. So keep the company of the wise and not of the stupid people who do not know how to swim. You are here now. Slowly you will learn how to swim without making effort.

Recently in my return to the West, I was treated like royalty wherever I went. But here in Lucknow I am not treated like anybody special.

This is true. Here you are not treated special because everybody is like you. But when you go away from here you will see that you are treated like a queen because they have never seen a face like yours in Sweden. Here all the women are queens, but you only realize this when you are away.

It is like teachers being trained in college. There they are all the same and nobody is special. But when they go into their own classrooms out in the schools then all the students pay them so much respect.

To be a queen, to be beautiful, look within your Self.
Looking without you are not beautiful.
You must look within to be beautiful, then
this inner beauty will reflect through your pores
and attract all those near you.

ॐ

I am so excited to see you again and to be in your presence.

You are most welcome. Let us see each other. I will see you, but you will not see me. What is this phenomena? Usually, if I see you you must also see me, but you don't see Me. You only see my face. Don't see my face, only see what cannot be seen. Then you will really See me and I will See you.

Kiss your own Self and tell me what taste it has. To describe this kiss you can only give a kiss. It cannot be described because it is beyond the concepts of the mind. This kiss is no-mind, and desirelessness is the taste of it. So have no desires and have this taste. This is how it comes. When you are desireless then Happiness comes. Try this Now and this is happiness.

It is so hard to speak about what you have given us.

Often words spoken about this are misused and just spoil the person. You must speak about the Diamond to someone who can appreciate it, not to the foolish.

One thing I can speak of is cricket. I know you love cricket.
Can you give us a Satsang about it?

Yes, it comes and it goes! Whatever lila happens, just enjoy it. Then it becomes a lila. If you get involved in it you will just get lost.

Papa, am I here for shaktipat or to remove my doubts or to satisfy my spiritual appetite?

Preferably, you are here to remove your doubts and after they are removed the Self will transmit its power onto you. This is called shaktipat. And you are not to satisfy your spiritual appetite, but live as spirit itself, be spirit itself.

I have no more questions.

Two people have no questions. One is a wise person and so they have nothing to ask; a man at home is not lost. The other one is someone who doesn't know that there is something to question. So some have no question on account of their Light and Wisdom. But some simply do not know.

So when the questions arise please don't be discouraged or disheartened because it is a good sign. All the mud which has settled below the surface of the mind rises when stirred and is on its way out in the form of a question. Therefore, the questions have to be asked and so don't be shy to ask them. When these doubts have been removed you will see the reflection of your own

Self within the mirror of your own mind. Then you will recognize that this is what you came here for and you can't do this when the surface is disturbed.

When you come to the teacher you are obliged to ask a question because there is no person who has solved this question. Those who are born have a question: How to be happy? Nobody, from the king to the farmer is happy. So ask the teacher, "How to be at rest, how to be peaceful, how to love my own Self and everybody else?" Like this, I request that you ask the question "How to remain at Peace?"

ॐ

Before I asked if you could put your feet on my head in the traditional way but you refused.

I don't follow traditional ways like this. I don't believe in this kind of tradition. It may have symbolized the removal of someone's ego. But feet and head have nothing to do with ego. Both of these are physical and that means that Peace and Love would come from the physical, but that is not true.

It is your ego which waits for some traditional rites. It will never submit. You think that your ego will be dissolved if I put my foot on your head! No! Why waste time? Why ask for a foot on your head? Why don't you straight away rush inside? Don't wait!

I would be very happy to rush in.

No, do not say that you *would* be very happy to rush in, just do it! (giggles) Happiness will come when there is no ego. But making plans that you will be happy is for the future. This "would be" is future and has troubled you for a long time. While your hair is still black rush in. Don't wait until they are white!

What is this longing and yearning that I feel and how can I give myself to this longing? I have been so troubled by my husband leaving me and about the welfare of my daughter.

You have left your home and have come to India, but if you have not left behind the relationships then you will trouble your mind. Then your stay here will not benefit you. If you are half here and half there it will take you a lot of time to be Quiet. You have to understand that one day you have to leave all the relationships with your husband and children. If your husband has left you, you should be thankful and happy because you have experienced that all relationships start and end. Now you won't be fooled by another relationship. Now it will be easier for you to go beyond relationship to where all is One.

Will you recommend which books would be best to read in order to help my contemplation lead to meditation.

This is a very good question. I will show you one instance so that you will have good literature for your meditation.

There was a man who went to the king and asked just for some stale food which had been left overnight. The king gives him a diamond on the spot because the king has no stale food, only fresh food is served to him. He gave the poor man a diamond so that the whole of his life he could have fresh food from the wealth this diamond would bring. You are this questioner, no other! From literature you want to learn how to meditate, but tell me what happens Here, Now in Satsang from the beginning? You don't need to read a book to stay Quiet and meditate!

Yes Papaji, it is time to sit in front of you and see that nothing ever happens to this space of Ananda.

You have found your own friend which is Ananda. You will never be able to describe who this is with you when you have lived forever. Only in waking do you know who is sleeping next to you. Now you know he has been your friend for generations though you were not looking at him. You were looking somewhere else and that is the trouble with everybody.They don't look within their own Self, but look for someone else somewhere. Therefore, they cannot have a friend as intimate as Ananda.

I heard of so many people speaking about how hot summer would be, but nobody ever mentioned how sweet and charming these hot-season Satsangs are.

Some people will like to stay here because when you are in Satsang you don't look at what is going on outside of Satsang. Once I also was in the summer in the south in Tiruvannamalai at Arunachala during the month of June. It was very hot, about 46 degrees Celsius. Most of the people were running away to Ooti and other hill stations. I think it was Major Chadwick who told the Maharishi that all the rich people had gone away to the hill stations and the few people who are left were too poor and could not afford to go and were staying here with him. Maharshi said, "I am also a poor man and can't go to any hill station. Let me tell you: to stay in summer in Satsang with the Master is penance, is tapas itself."

Signs and Symptoms of Immanent Freedom

Before the Guru's Grace brings one to Satsang
It is working in the person's life by manifesting in them
the many signs, or qualifications, that appear
as they become more and more ripe for Freedom,
as the veil of illusion gets thinner and thinner.

The most important qualifications are Holiness
and Brahmajignyasa, a burning desire for Freedom.
Next is Vivek, the ability to discriminate
the Real from unreal, the eternal from the transient,
and between Peace and suffering.
This is followed by Vairagya, dispassion and renunciation
for the unreal transient world of sense objects.

Other signs include humbleness, stillness, a dharmic life,
a healthy body, inquiry, devotion, and ahimsa, non-violence.
All of these signs are aspects of one thing:
The immanence of Self revealing Self to Self.

These symptoms arise on their own.
Don't be fooled and focus on them.
Focus incessantly only on Self.

Brahmajignyasa: The Desire for Freedom

The raft across the ocean of samsara
is the strong decision to be Free.
This intense desire is absolutely necessary.
The intensity of this desire is itself the Satguru,
the pain in the heart is the Self calling.

Always desire Self because
you will always get what you desire most.
The burning desire for Freedom is enough,
and is the result of blessings.

The desire for Moksha is Moksha
because now your relationship is with Freedom.
Now discriminate between "I" and Freedom,

and find out how far "I" is from Freedom.
When there are no more places to go
there is no more "I" to go there, no more tourist left.
Then have faith like a rock in this Freedom
so that the water and winds of thought and doubt
will not move it.

If the desire for Freedom is continuous,
then all the habits and distractions of mind will drop.
Think only of Freedom and you become Freedom
because you are what you think.
As persistent as the pain of a toothache
always think of Self.

The desire for Freedom is the high tide
which wipes out the sand castles of doubt.
Without this desire man is a tailless animal

Questioner: I have such a burning desire to be free of it all.

Papaji:
   It is enough if you have a burning desire for Freedom.
   It will burn the whole universe
   including you, your mind, your ego and your body.
   Let it burn and whatever is left
   throw back to the fire.

Anything that goes into the fire will become fire, even the thought of
Freedom will enter this fire and be consumed and become That! It is so easy,
but very few are burning to be Free. Most people want sense objects and so
they enter into the universe according to their own will.

   Let your will burn in this fire
   so that it takes you nowhere else.
   Let your self be burned in this fire
   of Eternity, Love and Peace.
   Don't be afraid of this fire, it is Love itself.
   This desire for Freedom is the fire of Love!

Most people are afraid of this fire. Very few people have shown this love
for Freedom and those who consume themselves in this fire are still living.

Buddha has done it 2600 years ago. This thought of Freedom came to him while he was in the pleasure garden surrounded by the beautiful young girls that his father had arranged.

His horoscope showed that he would be the king of the ascetics and so his father kept him in the prison of the pleasures of the world. But this fire of Love was blazing inside him, and so he is still alive. We don't remember our grandparents, but this Prince of Peace is still alive in the hearts of the whole world.

Like this you must do it. He was a human being too! So if he has done it, surely we can do it too. Everybody can become Buddha. The only thing that is needed is the fire of Freedom, and to recognize that you are the Stillness, that you are also are That Enlightened One.

I want to be submerged deeply in this pool of Stillness and drink its water. Let me melt in love with you. I am at the edge.

Very few people are at this edge, looking at the eternal water with their ego transformed into ashes by the fire of love. You have left behind millions of people. Now it is good if you jump yourself, but you are afraid of the depths. I am behind you watching the game between your fear of jumping and your desire to jump. Since the diving board is narrow you can't leave it because I am blocking your way. So, if you don't want to jump, I will push you. (giggles) But it is better if you jump because I will not let you return. You will see that you are the eternal ocean and you will be lost in this ocean like a block of ice is lost when thrown into the water.

This is how Ramakrishna Paramahamsa of Bengal who lived along the shore of the ocean and along the banks of the Ganga, said it:

"To win Freedom, to measure the depth of yourself,
be a salt doll and dive into the Ganga.
You will forget that you were a doll
and you will become the Ganga."

This is the Absolute Oneness of the eternal waters.
You will never be allowed to return to its banks
because there are none!

I want to dissolve in my true nature and never turn back.

You have decided very well and you expect something very great. Try to be here for some days more. Stay here and it won't take so much time. This decision is very strong and so you will get immediate results. Don't lose heart.

There once was a man called Matwalla who sat under a tree and said,

"Unless I get enlightened I will not get up." So he was always sitting meditating and not getting up to eat. Then someone came to him and asked him what he was doing.

"I am meditating," Matwalla said.

"What for?" asked the stranger.

"Just to be happy." he replied.

"I'll tell you," said the stranger, "you see how many leaves this banyan tree has? So many incarnations you must take in order to be Free."

"No problem," replied the confident meditator, "there may be thousands of leaves on a Banyan tree, I will meditate." And so, with this decision he continued to meditate: "I don't care about incarnations, I'll just sit."

After awhile another Saint came and asked, "What are you doing?"

Again Matwalla replied, "Meditating."

"Why?" asked the Saint.

"Everybody is suffering and so to get rid of suffering my teacher told me to meditate," he replied.

The Saint said, "I tell you, you must stay here and meditate as long as it takes for one leaf to drop from this banyan tree. When one leaf falls you will be Enlightened."

Then boldly the Matwalla yelled out, "I can't wait for the dropping of a leaf. What does the dropping of a leaf have to do with my Light and Wisdom!" He stood up and started dancing. He was Enlightened!

So the meaning of this story is that you are not to wait one year. This does not depend on the months. You have already spent 35 million years and this tree is always there growing more leaves! If one leaf falls another will grow and so how long will you wait? Why don't you just get up and shout "I am Free!" After all, when you are Free you will enjoy your life. Why can't you enjoy it Now? Most people are afraid and can shout "I am dying," but never did I see a man jumping on the road and shouting "I am Free." So if you are a real Matwalli go out on the road and shout! I am Free!

My ego is very strong. Can you help me to destroy it. I want to experience freedom. I am without anger and fear.

Can you show me your ego so that I can compare my strength with the strength of your ego? Have you ever seen her?

I have just felt it.

Have you ever seen this girlfriend? She is a good friend, let her try her strength on you. Then you will run away because she is very strong like an elephant. So you have to tame it with love. If you tame it with love she will not give you trouble. Let her alone.

When you want something that you do not get the ego will trouble you. You must have the ego to that extent as, "I want to be Free." Let this ego continue. It is also ego to want this. Desire Freedom not tomorrow, but today, not today, but Now itself. Then you will show me the ego. If she is strong this is a strong desire for her to have: "I want to be Free." Then this strength will help you. This is also ego. Wanting something is ego so utilize the strength of your ego by desiring Freedom, no other desire should touch you at the same time. Make use of the strength of the ego by desiring Freedom. Say it now.

I want to be Free.

Like this, day and night, say that you are going to get it. Buddha had it so you can also have it. Say this, "He was a human, I am also human. He could get it so why can't I?" Sit down under a tree and don't get up unless you are free. This is the decision and he had it.

Indecision will not work, so you have to decide. Many lives you have had and many species you have cycled through. Now is the best time. Your decision is good, you have come for Satsang and there is a place to sit and be Free without any practice or effort. Simply keep Quiet, without any thought. No training is given here that you have to do. Simply keep Quiet. Don't stir a thought from your mind. How easy. You are a young boy, you can do it!

> Of all the world
> Those who want Freedom are few.
> Those who are burning for Freedom are even fewer.
> Those who strive one pointedly are even fewer.
> Those who do not return to the senses are even fewer.
> Those who go on the razors edge are even fewer still.
> Those who do not fall off this edge are even fewer still.
> Those who attain the Self are so few!
> Strive, strive, it is so rare that you are here.
> You have a mountain of merits to bring you here.
> Do not waste it! Strive!

When this desire to unite is extremely strong what do you feel? When you jump into the deep river not knowing how to swim what happens?

I will drown.

Yes, some bubbles will appear on the surface and then break. So these 'sometimes' when you are extremely in Love with your Self, this is going to happen. So at the time when the bubbles are coming will you write me a letter? You will not take your pen and paper because they are not necessary when you are jumping into the Self itself. You don't need anything else. You don't need to communicate anything to the people who are standing on the bank and who have not jumped in yet. This 'sometimes' that you speak of cannot be shorter than the time it takes to drown in the river!

When you jump only water exists, there is no air in the depths, otherwise ego could still live there. But it is very deep and there exists only That, only Self, only Love exists there.

Here you are not to gain anything, but you are to give everything to whom you love! Then everything will vanish. If you have the real experience of this, nothing will ever disturb you. But if you have a disturbance in your mind then you cannot see the Light. This disturbance will be attachment to something which you cannot forget.

I am sick of these attachments and I would love to give myself to Love. My only desire is liberation Now. I want to attain Jivan Mukti.

This desire is how you have attained the experience you have. Jivan Mukti, liberation while still alive, is all you want. Mukti, Moksham, Liberation are of two kinds. One is when you are alive, Jivan Mukti. The other is after death, Videha Mukti. This happens when somebody cannot do it while alive, but it occurs at death. Here, what we do is neither Videha Mukti, nor Jivan Mukti. Here we speak only of Now, instant Mukti, like instant coffee, like Nescafe. The teacher will give you Enlightenment like Nescafe!

This is the time you must be strong and near the teacher so that if trouble arises you'll seek advice. Finish your work here Now. Don't run away.

I want to share a Sufi poem by Rumi:

> Come, come whoever you are.
> Wanderer, worshipper, lover of learning, it does not matter.
> Ours is not a caravan of despair, come.
> Even if you have broken your vow 1000 times,
> Come, come, again come.

Papaji, is it the love and grace that stills the mind without effort? Shall I convert all my will into longing?

You have to convert everything into longing.

Your longing must be so strong
that you forget who is longing and for what.
This must be the longing of everybody
who is seeking for the Truth.
He must forget all else.
This is enough, and this rises only in Satsang.
So again and again be strong.
Then you will know what you longed for
was you alone and the longing will vanish
as you embrace your own Self.

It seems that if I really had a true desire to be Free I would be.

You need a 100% true desire that you must be free today, Now and no other desire! Have only the desire "I have to be Free," and no other desire of the world. Then immediately that desire will be fulfilled.

How can I have a true desire now?

Now. This is how. Have a true desire Now and tell me what happens. Sit for one moment with a mind absolutely free. Then this mind will be Enlightened at once. Just don't think of anything in that moment and you will see that you are Free. After Satsang sit for one second and don't let your mind go anywhere and if it goes just watch it as a witness. Watch it come and go like you watch your breath come in and out. Don't stop. Regularly keep watching. When there is no thought you are free.

I have always been a doer, but now I would like to simply abide in my true nature and stay awake to this. Is this just another desire?

This you may call a desire, but it will burn away millions of desires. Most people experience one desire as soon as another vanishes. This continual flow of desires is called samsara. As long as there is desire you can't escape rebirth. But the one desire, "I want to be Free" will stop all of this. This may be a desire, but it will burn everything else.

I am so glad that you have started so young and that you did not postpone this to old age. Now do not give rise to any kind of effort and don't think about anything, whether you are free or bound. The time will come when this desire to be Free will also vanish, but to begin with you must start as a student, not as a teacher.

If I leave this body before I am realized will I continue this work?

Whatever unfullfilled desire you have, if it is kept up to your departure and is the last desire at the last breath out, then this soul takes birth in some circumstances to fulfill that desire. The soul travel in the skies looking for a proper womb to enter. It will search for a pious family in the case that it desires Freedom and if it decides that the family that it has chosen will not be right then it will, as a fetus, abort itself and continue its search. I hear from so many people here that they spontaneously inquired or meditated at very young ages. This is a sign of what your last life was and the last desire of that life. If you don't complete your journey in this life it will be the next life.

My inability to know the Truth causes me so much pain.

It is only because you don't want it. Your pain and suffering is much more readily available to you only because you don't want the Truth.

Why is my decision to be free sometimes strong and sometimes not?

It doesn't matter. The desire for Freedom is so strong that it will destroy all other desires. This destruction means that either the desires will not rise or they will be fulfilled. The desire to be free is so strong that even when other desires come in temporarily, it still reappears.

I have had so many plans to travel all over but I keep canceling them because I can't leave.

Wherever you go eventually you must stay Here for final Realization. Your best guide is your true desire to be Free. This will take you to where you have to be which is where your mind will be killed. But she does not want to be killed so easily and will appear as your friend. Know she is your enemy.

This death of mind and the birth into the Truth is all that I am interested in.

This is the true birth and it will never meet death. All other birth meets death in a short while. With this birth, death is forever removed because now you have your own Self and not someone else, not other. If you love someone else you have to face the consequences of death. If you don't have any contact with any other person or object you will conquer death because you are beyond death in the oneness and happiness of the Self of all Beings.

Signs and Symptoms of Immanent Freedom

When I came here to you there was such a strong decision to do so,
even though it went against the advice of my friends and family.
How can I let go of everything and open up to your Grace and enjoy
the oneness and bliss of "I am"?

You left everything behind in Denmark. You didn't listen to your friends,
but you listened to the call.

Make the decision that you must find
your own Light Here and Now.
Leave behind attachments to thoughts, friends, and objects.
This decision will immediately pay you: "I want It Now."

Say this and you will change instantly. I cannot tell you what will
happen, but I can say you will have no fear and no doubt. Make this strong
decision and you will have more strength than any king. If you have decided
that "I am Free," it is quite enough if you honor it Now. Why do you have
to doubt. When you say, "I am Free," you must honor this Freedom, and if
you do this now it will be the responsibility of Freedom to look after you!

Why do you say "I want to be Free all the time"? When you are Free you
have gone beyond time. How can you return back to time? It is that
timelessness which will take care of you. You have to understand what you
have done and what reward has been given to you. You do not have
assessment of the diamond in the palm of your hand. You have to honor it.
To honor your commitment is most important. Otherwise, everyone is always
Free. They are already Free, but nobody honors that Freedom and therefore
one suffers. People only honor suffering. People honor what their parents tell
them: "You have to suffer like us." The neighbors, the priests, the saints,
heads of all religions all say that you are suffering and that you have to go to
hell. This is the proclamation of the founders of religions.

I tell you that you are already Free, why don't you respect my word? You
have come here to the teacher so you have to respect him and be obedient,
and do as the teacher says. He tells you that you are Free, so accept it.

I don't feel any happiness, in fact I feel like I am dead. Please tell
me what to do.

Have only one desire in your life, the desire for Freedom. Only this desire
will not allow any other desire to trouble you. Whenever it can be fulfilled
sacrifice *everything* for that desire! This desire will give you Peace and
Happiness and you won't return to samsara.

Sacrifice everything like even kings and queens have done and you will
be free of every struggle of life. Don't allow the mind to cheat you. Only mind

keeps you from Freedom. Few people here understood the nature of mind and will not listen to the mind. They refuse what comes from mind and they make the mind listen to them. They sit quiet until they are Free. Only after Freedom will they look after the desires of the mind and fulfill them.

You are a Hanuman bhakta aren't you! Hanuman had only one desire which was to serve his Master, and never allowed a personal desire to arise. Follow the footsteps of Hanuman and work for Rama alone. By doing Rama's work the strength will come by itself and you will be able to leap across the Indian Ocean. This much strength you will have.

There is such a longing to reach home and be in Peace and connect with people on a deeper level. This longing even hurts my heart.

You have traveled for a long time but you can't feel rest until you go home. After you have made all your purchases in the market you will go home and take rest. You can spend time in the markets and hotels but home is the best place, so wandering must someday stop. You have spent millions of years marketing, buying commodities that you want, but you have no rest. So return home and rest. Home is the best place to abide always. I am not talking of the house outside of you, but the home inside of you. When you feel you are fatigued by those in the market who want you for money or something else, then come home, the earlier the better. Otherwise, you are wasting your life. This home is always available, its doors are always open, but you must make an about turn. When you stop going out and start going in you will see that this house has always been free and doesn't even have doors! You just haven't looked.

(She weeps)

This shows that you are at home. The people who are home have a different face than those who are out in the fishmarket.

I want to always be Here. I want to merge with the Source.

The Source of light and life is brighter than a million suns. When you want to be It itself It will burst and instantly end all your desires and suffering. Simply look at It. Don't question, but dissolve in the light. Stay beyond thought and mind where the sun, moon and stars do not rise.

Papaji, thank God that I weep!

This weeping is a deep desire to see something that very few have seen. This is due to your previous karma which has not fructified in your last incarnation. That is why you are here in Satsang. Now you will start smiling and laughing. This crying is not a bad sign. Many people cry at the loss of their property or of a dear one. But you do not cry for all these things. Just as a child cries for its mother and will accept only its mother, and not even a chocolate will do, so you must continue this very auspicious crying. I rarely see anybody crying for that which gives you Peace. Keep weeping until you find your Mother, your own Self, the Supreme Power. I am very happy to that you have been crying.

I have been crying and burning inside to be free.

One must burn inside constantly. When the inside is all burnt, that is the time that you will meet your beloved. Having something left inside you can't meet your beloved, so let it burn for years! Then you are left young, fresh and youthful to meet your Beloved.

So you are well born, you have had a lucky birth. A lucky birth is when you have known your Self and you are peaceful. Most births are unfortunate, unwanted and unlucky. Lucky births are those who were well looked after by their parents, who desire to know the truth, who have found their way to Satsang, and who can speak that they've seen That and all darkness is gone!

ॐ

I have come to you in order to end my struggle to be free because I can't do it alone. The vastness of your Presence has helped me so much already.

You have come here with a strong desire to get something which you could not get alone. Let me tell you, you can only do it alone and not with the help of anyone. Two cannot walk abreast on the blade of a sword. It is impossible. When you walk on the sword you must be alone, by yourself. You can't look this side or that side or behind because the edge of the sword is so sharp that you will be cut into two parts if you look anywhere. To go for Freedom is not less than walking on the edge of the sword. You can't take your friends, near ones or dear ones, you have to walk alone and look nowhere. If you look you will shake and you will never arrive at your destination of Freedom.

This means that you cannot have any thought in your mind because if you do you will be in the past. Do not think and don't do anything. Simply keep Freedom in your mind, nothing else. Then just one glimpse of the Beloved will remove the darkness from your mind which has collected for ages. Be so quiet that you forget even the desire which brought you here to win Freedom. Be so quiet that there's no attachment, not even to quietness.

There are no attachments in Presence,
because there is no mind.

Mind is the past and there is no past in Presence. Mind will only take you to the graveyard and so only dead people live in the mind. Whatever you think of is dead so don't touch the mind at all if you want to be Free. Don't allow this old friend to come in and trouble you anymore. Simply keep Quiet, don't make effort. You should tightly keep hold of the pull to go within and then you will not see any other pull. This needs your seriousness. If you want to stay where you won't be troubled by the outside world, stay where Peace is available. Outside there is no Peace.

Why do so many people come here, stay here, and love you, but they don't get Enlightened when you say it only takes one second to be Free?

Self Realization takes one second, but this second takes a great effort to remove all other thoughts from your mind. You must remove all from this second and allow only this second to stay with you. In that second stand up on your toes and with clenched fists shout, "I have to be free in this second!" It is very rare to have such extreme desire for Freedom, such extreme activity and strength that even gods will come and bow before you. You can't do it with your weak body. It takes a very strong body and mind and intention. Then this second will work. You have to Do It. Don't just read the menu, eat the food. Defeat the stupid mind. It is not the mind which makes the decision to be Free. When you do it there is no mind! Control the mind and use it as a slave, but Here you don't need the mind to be Free.

Papaji, what is this Grace? What is this abidance in Self? I long so much for This which you radiate.

This longing for awareness must be classified as awareness itself. You must have such an intense desire that you forget that it is desire. Then you will see the beauty of that which you long for. Don't even remember that you are in love with it, but know that you are that Love which you are loving. Merge. Then there will be the Radiance!

Vivek: Discrimination Between Peace and Suffering

Vivek is the intellect asking and determining
if something is transient or permanent.
Vivek is the choice between the bliss of Self
and the pleasures of the senses; between peace and disturbance.

With Vivek pick up what is real or else you will make a mistake.
Wise living is discriminating between the false from the true,
between joy and suffering, and then rejecting what you are not.
Discrimination destroys clinging by exposing the transience,
the illusory nature, of the object to be clung to.

You must always be centered in Self.
That Self alone is the Truth, all else is falsehood.
A strong understanding of this in your mind is important.
Instantly reason out: is it a rope or it is a snake!
Faulty discrimination is a prison,
in which you are a slave to the imaginary snake.

Hamsa is the legendary swan symbolizing discrimination.
From a mixture of milk and water
Hamsa can drink the milk
and leave the water behind.

*After the last Satsang I experienced the illuminous One for several
hours. Then slowly mind and duality came back. There had been no
mind and no identification.*

If mind appears tell it that you will not identify with it. Hit it with the
sword. Don't identify any duality if duality appears. How simple. Why get
into trouble? If duality appears say there is no duality and no unity either.

I have trouble when I do this.

Who has the trouble? Personalities? Duality? Why are you in trouble
with mind? Have you ever seen it? Mind does not exist. The trouble is with
your own ego. You think that you appear and decide that you want
something. If this something is not available then you are in trouble. All
beings are there because of your mind. If you check the mind you won't see
any friend or enemy or person or individual, not even time. This is sleep while

all else is awake. Don't give rise to any thought. This is in your hands.

Challenge all thought with the sword of discrimination and complete full decision, and then nothing can touch you.

If your decision is shaky you will not have this Light, Wisdom, Love, Enlightenment. Enlightenment is not for the cowards or the weak, but for those who are very strong who can fight the weakness of personification and attachments. Stand on your own feet and don't depend on anything.

How can I lose what can't be lost?

This you must know. You must find That which cannot be found or lost. Go on discriminating what your purpose is, what you should get, and what you should leave, what is real and what is not real.

You must discriminate or it is all a waste of time.

Begin with discriminating what your purpose is. It is to find that which gives you Peace. Know what is real. You are here for Enlightenment and not for anything else. This is your decision. Don't entertain any thought which will disturb you. Every minute be on guard. Then you will be successful. Don't let your decision falter. Don't accept defeat. You must be a warrior with sword in hand. Cut the thought you don't want and you'll be successful.

I have experienced two different states here. One is a peaceful, spacious, limitless state with nothing there. The other is like being in a womb very much in contact with a lot of energy.

Who is discriminating between these two states?

My mind.

Both are notions and equally unreal. Both of these states are transient projections as is the mind itself. It is mind which likes one state and not another. Who is experiencing these states and discriminating between them? Find out! Who is creating differences? One may be good and the other is less than good. Who is seeing these changes? Return to where all states vanish and then you will enter Peace, absolute Peace.

Mind is discrimination itself, question the source of this mind. Where does duality arise from? Go there and you will be in the source, absolute Silence. Go to where differences arise from, before they are differences. Do it here and now. Go there, but do not give rise to any intention or effort and then you will see it! Do it now.

Signs and Symptoms of Immanent Freedom

Thank you! It has gone empty so quickly!

Yes, here nothing will rise. Nothing! Duality will not rise here, this is Freedom. This is your own nature. Your own nature! Recognize and identify with this, merge into this. Then you will see that all of manifestation is in the center of this Consciousness. Everything is yours and you become all, no states, "I Am all of this!" From here dance.

ॐ

I don't know if I should stay or go or where to stay or go.

To be happy you must discriminate and know when to sit in the shade of the tree and when to walk in the sunshine. It may not be good to do only one of them. So enjoy the sun and when it is too much go and sleep and relax under the tree. Enjoy both.

Wherever you must stay enjoy your circumstances.
Don't avoid anything and don't accept anything.

Since I was at the burning ghat in Varanasi my longing to be close to you and my Self has been burning very strongly. What can I do?

When you went to see the bodies burn you must have seen that only a few ounces of ash are left. These few ounces of ash are the body to which you are so attached. This is burning ghat discrimination. Everybody gets this when they go there, but soon forgets it.

You must remember this discrimination permanently:
This body will soon be ashes, so before it happens
let me fulfill the purpose of wearing a body.
Then when your body is burned you will be happy.

Don't give up peace to chase after thoughts which are not even real! Let the thoughts come and let them go, what is the trouble? Your decision to leave happiness is not a good one. Abide in peace. You have been disturbed for millions of years. Why go back to this disturbance once you have found Peace? Understand this. Discriminate between what gives you Peace and what disturbs you. Whatever is better, follow it.

When you say that thoughts and feelings are not real I get confused. Are they bad or meaningless?

All thoughts and emotions are not real. They are like the waves that

135

dance on the surface of the ocean for a few seconds or minutes and then they return to where they have arisen from. Then they are no more a wave, but they are ocean. How long can a wave keep its form as a separate personality?

> Name and form is not real.
> Look at the substratum from where they arise.
> That is real. It will not change.

Before any thought rises in your mind and goes toward an object of your senses for enjoyment, look at the substratum from where it would arise. From there you can enjoy the forms of thought and feelings because from there you are not ignorant. The wave and bubble are ignorant because they only dance for their own name and form.

> These forms are transient
> and to be attached to them is to be confused.
> Anything that rises be it thought, desire, emotion, feeling or object
> will give you suffering and no one in the world can avoid this.
> Both the enjoyer and the enjoyed are washed away.

> But the wise discriminate between the Real and unreal.
> They know what is Real and so allow their feelings and thoughts
> to arise because they know all is One and the same!
> In this way you will not suffer.

I want to experience the One.

Who experiences your suffering and your joy. It is not the body or the mind. The enjoyer is something else. Everybody is confused about this. They say "I am enjoying" and they mean that, "my body is enjoying." This isn't it.

> Who is the witness of enjoyment
> when the body is involved in enjoying?
> Witness is not engaged, but only a witness.
> This is the Self, your own beloved Heart.
> You are That Itself.

While walking in a field in Poland I had a strong experience which broke down totally the reality of the world. I clearly saw everything as a mental construct of the mind, but this experience slowly faded away after two weeks. I was terrified by this view because I had no idea who I was! My previous identity of who I thought I was shattered.

Seeing everything as a mental construct is the best experience one could have. Why were you afraid? All is mental construction. When there is no mind there is nothing to touch or see or realize, just like in the sleep state there is nothing. When it happens in the waking state it means the person is reaping the reward of his merits and longings. This experience can happen anywhere, in fields, in forests while awake or asleep, it doesn't matter. But when you had a doubt about it, it faded away.

When this happens you don't need to know who you are! When you question "Who am I?" there must be a subject, the question, and an object. But when everything is an illusion, as you said it was, then this subject and object is also an illusion. Nothing exists. This is the Truth.

So many of my friends told me that I had to see a psychologist after I had this experience, so finally I gave in, but instead of telling me that I was crazy, as I expected, he told me that it was time to find my Guru! I couldn't believe it. I heard about you soon after and now I am here.

Grace has brought everybody here! This is the grace of the Divine within saying "Come Home!" Grace brings you here to clear your doubts and to end your journey. You have to make the most of this human birth so that you are not thrown in the womb again to suffer.

How can I stay beyond this separation caused by thought only? I have such a strong longing for it.

You have a desire to be Free and you have the desire for something else, so you must discriminate which is permanent and which is temporary. Most people want only the temporary satisfaction of the mind which fades away in a few seconds. Nobody desires abiding Peace and Love.

> Discriminate between what is Eternal
> and what moves like bubbles on a lake.

This bubble moves across the surface of the lake, shining sparkling, but it doesn't have anything to do with the Reality. With just a small gust of wind the bubble is lost and returns to its substratum. In this way you also work for your substratum. With strong determination know that you have to win it.

> The stronger your determination is
> the earlier will be your success.

Vairagya: Renunciation of the Transient

Freedom is beyond understanding, beyond the movements of mind,
and yet there is one intellectual grasp that is very important.
It is to know that no object will give you peace of mind.
If you know this you will not be attracted to the transient objects.
This is dispassion, Vairagya.

Vivek is the discrimination between the real and the unreal.
The desire for Freedom is the passion for the real,
and Vairagya is the dispassion for the unreal.
It is the abandonment of attachment to all sense pleasures
because they are inherently transient and illusory,
not because they are bad, they are your dance.
Unless you renounce mind all other renunciation is useless.
Everything you would renounce is renounced with mind,
but only Self renounces mind itself
by Vairagya, non-attachment to thought
and the renunciation of all that makes you suffer.
Vairagya is knowing that there are no abiding pleasures.
A wise one rejects all for peace.

*I feel that I am on the road to Freedom, and I wonder if I break all of
my attachments, will I be Free? Do I also need to break my relations?*

When you want something other than these attachments and
relationships they will naturally fall off by themselves. You are not to break
them, but they themselves will fall like a wall of sand. All relationships are
not more than the walls of sand that the children make at the beach. There
is no relationship worth living with like the relationship with your own Self,
and you can never get rid of That relationship. But any relationship that
discourages you from finding your Self must be rejected forever.

Actually, there are no attachments at all. How your attachments fall
when you go to sleep and there is no father or mother, or priest or church to
have attachments with. Like this when you search, all relationships will fall
by themselves because they do not exist. They only seem to exist because you
need something from them. You have some interest somewhere and, therefore
you make up a relationship. The only relationship that cannot be broken is
to fall in Love with your own Self!

This is how you will find Peace! Later you will know that you have
always been living in Peace, but due to attachments you were involved in

other things and you did not look at what was under your feet. Your senses were running out to some place or object or person and, therefore you never got to this space at all. So, my dear friend, now onward, you are Here in Satsang. This is the best place which will not cheat you like all the relationships have cheated you so far.

There is such a magic coming from here. I feel that I was pulled from the other side of the planet like a fish is pulled in by the line.

You have left everything behind. This is the magic. Coming here to fulfill your purpose is magic. You will know the consequences of this magic in a couple of days, I assure you. When this starts to happen it is some inner drive which wants to love you. This drive does not come to everyone, but to only very few people who reject their kingdoms, their kings, their queens and their treasures and who then go straight away into the forest to find success.

Make a strong decision not to leave until you are successful. The stronger this desire is the stronger will be the fire which will burn in the heart of your Beloved. Then just as you have rejected everything, he will reject his heaven and will come in front of you, don't worry. Let this candle be always lit in you. Into this flame the moth will come and consume itself.

The Truth always is, but can the recognition of Truth be delayed in time?

No, the recognition of the Truth cannot be delayed!

Delay in the recognition of Truth
is only due to the searching for what is not the Truth,
and the lack of the sincere and honest desire to see the Truth.

Truth is everywhere, in front of you, behind you, below and above you. But you want something else, some other person or object. When you don't touch these other things, what do you see? Instantly you will see that you are Truth itself.

I have lost interest in the world of name and form. Finally, I came here to Lucknow.

Sometimes people lose interest in the world due to mental tensions which cause neurological problems. Others lose interest due to a greater interest in peace and love and beauty within. I can see from your face that you are not from the second group. I see so much fear on your face. Somebody has probably mistreated you and this is what you are running away from. Just stay here for awhile and you will be helped.

I am sick of being controlled by things which happened so long ago! I want to be Free and always be like a soft breeze.

The nature of the breeze is to never stay in one place. She is always moving. If she moves in a garden of roses she is not attached to the circumstances that this is a very beautiful garden. She doesn't say, "I will stay here." Her nature is to keep flowing. The next place where she comes is some garbage where the pigs are eating. She just keeps on flowing, neither rejecting nor accepting, neither attached nor detached. This is her nature. This nature will help all of us to be Free. It is not to be attached or detached to anything that comes in front of you. Just keep on flowing.

Now, the trouble is, we have attached ourselves to one place. That place is relationship, especially with your own body. You so much like your own body, but this is not the nature of the breeze, therefore everybody suffers. If you say, "This is a beautiful body and personality, I want to stay in this body always," then you identify with it. But this is not going to happen. Therefore, you could have decided for one particular place, one person, and education to make you happy, but you will not be happy. The happy one is the one who keeps on flowing and doesn't stay attached to one particular place or thing or person. This is why the breeze is always happy.

Once there was a person who was trying to find a guru. He saw the breeze and said to her that she was his guru because she taught not to stay in one particular place; "I will also behave like you and I bow down before you." Like this everything that you see is a teacher. Another time he saw a girl in her house whose future mother and father-in-law stopped in to visit. Since her parents were not there she had to cook for them. They were very poor and had hardly any food, but she didn't want them to know this. As she started to husk the paddy her bangles started to tingle. Since she was very wise she knew that the guests would know that she was pounding the paddy, a sure sign of poverty in India. So she removed all but one bangle from each wrist and thus, there was no more sound. The man searching for the guru saw all this and learned from her that you have to stay alone to be happy. Unless you keep yourself to yourself you will be wasting time tingling with others. You have to be close to be with your own Self.

Like this, whatever he saw he accepted as his guru. Earth also taught him. You can do anything and she won't mind. You can pollute her or put flowers on her and she is the same. She accepts everything and so he said that, "this mother earth is my guru." Like this you can have teaching from anything, if you really want to learn.

The purpose of the story is this: don't keep the company of that which will spoil you and waste your time. You must take some time to be alone and unattached. For now, until you serve your guests, until you are free, you must be quiet, alone. Find some moments for your Self and don't always live in society; society meaning that which wastes your time.

This will be enough teaching for you: learn from everything.

Papaji, please guide me through the burning forest of samsara and never let my mind deviate from the service to the Truth.

If you are feeling that this whole forest is burning only then will the Truth be easily available to you. First you must find that you are suffering from samsara which is like a wild fire in the forest. When you feel this you must give up everything and find Peace. This is the right time, the right moment. If you miss it you have forever missed it.

Chaitanya said this as well, "When the right moment comes, don't wait, when the idea comes that you must realize the Truth, you must leave everything." This is what he did.

Don't wait, leave the kingdom. This idea may not come again in your life and again you will have to go through the never ending cycle of the 8.4 million species of life. So, decide, "I must realize this Love in this lifetime, in this year, today!" This must be your decision: "I will not return back until I find Peace."

This Peace will not be available until your whole environment is burning. If samsara isn't bothering you something is wrong. But if it's troubling you, then reject the whole thing. This how even the kings have done it.

I have had a very good life, but it is not fulfilling. I am fed up and I want to end all desires, all mirage. I don't even want the water.

This is a very good vow to take. You don't want reality and you don't want mirage. This is quite enough. Only when you have no concern with reality or illusion will you be able to sleep and rest.

Self has brought me here to see Self in your form. Why can't I give up the illusion? Why does mind continue to argue? Why won't it let me go home? I am tired, miserable, and fed up.

Very good. This is the resolve that one has to make. The mind will argue for sometime and then keep quiet. If the mind is there, let it be there, it has no power. Don't hesitate to allow the mind to be near you. Why are you afraid of the mind? Mind is only a name, like a ghost! It never existed! It was only your desire, only then the mind comes and functions: "I want this" and there is mind. Mind is only in the doubts and desires. Only then do you need mind. Now the trick of the mind is over. Now if the mind comes to you it will be your slave, your servant to look after your body requirements, not to command you to do this or that and trouble you. It will become like a slave. You are not to think of anything, it will serve you. But if you do not know that it is a servant, then you will suffer.

Tell the mind that if it wants to stay with you it must act to your commands, and look after you. Then the tables will turn and when this happens everything will change. Your face and body will change. You get a glimpse of the moment when the mind is not playing with you. When no-mind is there your face is very beautiful, but when you have a desire then you are not happy and you have no peace at all. Okay, chello.

Do I need to release all these problems and worries before I can go to God?

You can't release first and then go. You have to shine first and then things will be released! Go straight and everything will be released. Go straight home and everything will be taken care of for you. Don't keep it in your mind that you have to get rid of this thing and that thing. It will not be possible and you will have to spend a lot of lives trying. Straight away, keep only this in your mind: "I have to be Free." Otherwise, there are too many things to handle and this life is too short to look after them all. Time is coming. You have to hurry up and reach Home. When you have only this Freedom in your mind everything will be released because your mind is no-mind Now. Don't keep anything else. Love your Self.

If Freedom requires you to leave the things you love it is a fierce price to pay, but worth it!

Can this object which loves you love you forever? Will it go to sleep with you? It is only with you in dream and waking states. Even when you die your body will not accompany you. So always love That which will always be with you, and find it Now with discrimination. Keep company with your Beloved.

Holiness: Innocence and Purity

Truth exalts a Holy person
so you must be so beautiful and pure and faultless.
You are Holy when the vasanas are removed,
and when there is no thought.

You are worthy when you are Holy.
But worthiness alone will not do!
You must find the One who is worthy
and be free from worthiness and unworthiness.
As the dead cannot say, "I am dead,"
so the worthy cannot say, "I am worthy."

Stillness is absolutely necessary.
It is an inward turned mind,
turned inward of all senses, thoughts, and concepts,
and this is a free mind. Keep Quiet.
Mind going out to pleasure is samsara,
mind in samsara is the cycle of birth, suffering, and death.

External purification is important:
environment, association, body, and mind.
Internal purification is the burning desire for freedom.

A Sattvic pure harmonious mind leads to inquiry,
and so a pure dharmic life and diet are recommended.
Inquiry cannot arise in a mind disturbed by tamas and rajas.
A rajas active mind leads to anger and sadhana.
It is a monkey mind and will not see its nature.
A tamas dull lethargic mind leads to sleep, doubt, and fear.
The dull mind does not listen to the teacher.
If you are not otherwise occupied
then one word from the teacher is enough;
This is the sattvic mind.

Burning desire for Freedom, constant meditation,
inquiry, and giving up pleasures.
Be quiet, do not think, make no effort.
Those who are Holy will attain Truth.
Holiness is the main condition.

ॐ

I have a strong desire to have a Holy nature.

This Holy nature is a must for those who want to be free. You have to be Holy because It reveals to a Holy person and not to anyone else who desires other things.

> Holiness is falling in love with your own Self.
> This is devotion, and it is not different from Love!
> What you love you are devoted to and
> what you are devoted to you love.

> When this Love has no object, and goes nowhere but to itself,
> It will reveal itself to you in whatever form you desire;
> manifest or unmanifest.

> If you desire *this* Love don't try to love a particular person
> because this love has no personality, no form, and no name.
> God is this Love.

I want to thank you for the time you spent with me yesterday.
Since then all my problems have been burned away like fog
in the early morning sunlight.

Excellent, I told you it would happen. These quick results mean that you are a very honest person.

> Only an honest person can do it because
> The truth exalts a Holy person.
> A Holy person enters into the heart of Truth
> without any difficulty.

> Who is a Holy person?
> Just shut your eyes and see; am I Holy?
> Am I Holy enough to touch the Divine?
> There is no difference between the Divine
> and the one who desires to see the Divine.

Any question I have now instantly disappears.

This shows the mind is pure. So pure that it cannot entertain any doubt or question. Many people come with questions, but before they can ask them they forget all about them. This depends on the purity of the mind. When a man is pure hearted God walks behind him to fulfill his every desire instantly and spontaneously. This is how it happens. Just say as Jesus did, "Let Thy will be done," you'll be very happy if you surrender to That will inside.

I still feel something is not totally pure about me and it keeps me from seeing the flame. I want to become transparent and disappear.

You are pure but when you feel that something is not pure you will not be able to see the flame. This impurity has to be attachment to somebody else, and that doesn't allow you to be pure. You are not to be attached to anyone if you want to see the flame in your own Self. When you are attached to someone else you are seeing the flame, beauty and love in someone else. You must first see your own beauty and then you will see the Beauty in all beings. Transparency is having no thoughts in your mind, then you will be transparent. So have no thought for just a little while. Don't think and you will become transparent.

How to purify oneself and become beautiful?

To become beautiful doesn't take any time. It is not the beauty of the skin. It is that beauty which the Truth exalts. You can be beautiful by not keeping any thought in your mind. Keeping thought in your mind makes you ugly, not beautiful. When there is no thought the inner Light shines through your pores making you and the entire world beautiful.

When Buddha attained Freedom he became so beautiful, even physically. Now people use so many methods to become beautiful. In the 60's they even tried to make themselves beautiful by chemically changing their minds with LSD, but this beauty they found was temporary and the drugs spoiled their health. I met many of them, including the famous ones. The beauty I speak of is inner Beauty. When there is no thought you are beautiful.

Why are so few people free? Why are there so few Buddhas?

Because so few people want to be free of bondage strongly enough.

I feel unworthy of Freedom.

Unworthiness will not allow you to be Free. You have to prove yourself worthy of attainment because Truth exalts a worthy person. Truth will come on its own accord and is always here. Truth has been with you ever since the world was born. You are not to achieve or attain it at a later date. It is already here. Avoid looking somewhere else and it will reveal itself. Avoid looking at your body. You are not body sattva, but Bodhi Sattva! The Bodhisattva is one who has no desire at all, even if they themselves voluntarily involve themselves in attachments. This is the climax of Freedom:

> The Free man doesn't care
> if he is attached or unattached.
> This is Bodhisattva.

Papaji, I want to focus one hundred percent.

Mirabai focused on God 100%. She focused so much that she could even play chess with Krishna, much to the dismay of the king and his sister who thought she was seeing another man.

This Self can manifest if you are innocent. She didn't know that he was 'just' a statue. So if you are focused on Self you will see that the Self will manifest in whatever direction you want because it is the Self which manifests in every form everywhere. You have to change the "I," then you will know that everything that you see is a manifestation of your Self within.

So you be *sure* when you speak about 100% focusing. When you love Freedom, love alone must be on your mind, heart, and activity. When you speak, It speaks. When you hear, It hears.

Can you show me God?

This is the question of questions. There are many questions, but this is the highest you could ask. I remember a story. It was the same quest and the same request.

An eight year old girl came to me and asked me to show her God. I told her to go to school and tomorrow I will show you. Then tomorrow came and she said again, "Show me God."

I told her that the driver was waiting to take her to school, "You should go with him and then tomorrow I will show you."

She said, "Everyday you say tomorrow, but this day I am not going to school. You have to show me!"

I said "Okay, I will show you God in this little room, but to see God you must have something to give to him. What do you have to give?"

"I will give him the chocolate that mama put in my lunch," she replied.

I said, "You give the chocolate and God will come."

"But where is God so that I can give him the chocolate?" she questioned.

"Give the chocolate first, only then will God come. He will not come until your hand is extended," I told her.

She was a child and she had no doubt and so she extended her hand. Then there was a lot of noise in the room and her mother came in, and asked what happened.

"Mom, I gave the chocolate to God and he took the whole thing and didn't give half to me. So I slapped on his face. Can't you see him? I see him, Papa sees him."

Her mother never agreed to what she said, and so the child made a drawing of what she saw which was the most beautiful picture of God I had ever seen! She would go out walking with me and meditating with me and would even tie a rope around my leg which she held while she slept so she would know if I left.

What I want to tell you is that it is innocence. God is everywhere. Those who are not innocent cannot see him. Cleverness is not needed and will only get you into trouble. You need innocence. Then you can see God everywhere because he *is* everywhere. Why can't you see him? Because if you have a doubt you can't see him. The veil between you and God is only doubt that God cannot be seen and only could be seen after long penance in the caves of the Himalayas. Now Itself! Who do you see?!

I don't see anything.

I told you not to doubt. "I don't see," is a doubt! Remove the doubt! Again tell me, what do you see without the doubt? "Don't" is doubt! Again tell me. Don't keep doubt. What do you see!

I see God!

ॐ

Faith and Trust

I feel that I would like to be more receptive to your Love and Grace, but I lack trust. Can you help me?

If you have no trust in me you can't receive my teaching. You must have 100% trust in me. Then only will the teaching will find a way into your heart.

This lack of trust is a neurosis which you developed because of the fights your parents had with each other while you were still in the womb. You were hit from both sides like a poor little tennis ball. Here though, people love you. You are lucky to have come here, so just surrender, surrender to the truth. Forget your old habits, your parents, and your old relations. Now your relationship is Here. Your sisters and brothers have received you so well here. This is your family now. Forget about your parents and even your country. Start from Here, you are born from Here.

Just be Quiet and you will receive a precious gift
from the Light hiding inside you.
Don't worry about what has happened before.
Always starting from this instant of time
is the awakening to your responsibilities.

Go now laughing and smiling even if the world goes on crying and convey this Truth wordlessly.

I have total trust in you.

Where has this totality gone? Total trust is total trust, 100%. I will tell you of trust. I traveled all over India looking for a guru. I was in the army then and so I had a superiority complex. (giggles) So, I would find a teacher and ask them if they could show me God. Then all of the devotees would look at me and show me their long beards which they grew during their fifty year stay with that particular guru. They would say, "We have searched unsuccessfully for years! How do you expect to come in here with your shoes on and see God in a minute?"

Then they would push me out. What to do? But, if you search for something so intensely that you won't even take food until you find it, then you will get what you want. So, this story ends at the feet of Ramana Maharshi. I asked him, "Can you show me God?"

He said, "No, God cannot be seen, he is not an object of senses which can be seen."

I was amazed at this and wondered what he would say next. Then Bhagavan said:

"Nee Naan Bhagavan:" You-I-God!
You can't see God because you are God!
How can you search for That which you are?

At that moment I had full trust that I am God and this trust didn't falter and still it stays. How can you say you have trust? You have mistrust. If you trusted, your eyes would shine and your face would shine and you will smell a fragrance. You have to trust what you are. What is there to mistrust?

How can I trust?

Find out who spoke these words! Again I tell you:

Trust me and trust me totally!

If you don't trust what I speak then you are in the wrong place. You have been a donkey for so many lifetimes so you won't understand this very easily. The donkey-ness is in your genes and unless you meet a specialist who can change you at the genetic level you will not be free of this donkey-ness.

Will I ever be a lion? Will I ever have faith?

No lion will ask another lion if she will ever be a lion. About faith I will tell you a story.

One Shivratri in Varanasi I was with seven girls from different countries who had come from Rishikesh to celebrate it. So we went into the Golden Temple where no foreigners are allowed in. This was written in Hindi and so I didn't tell them, and we just walked in and saw all the gold donated by the king of Punjab. Not only did they see the temple, but the priest helped them to perform puja on the lingam and gave them prasad. As we walked out the people looked at the girls faces and when the girls asked me why I told them that the sign said that foreigners are not allowed. Then they wanted to know why the priest had helped them so much. I told them that he was blind at that time. When we entered their faith blinded the eyes of everybody in the temple. Faith is very strong, it can defeat anything.

Good Karma and Ahimsa

A dharmic life is filled with right actions
which bring good karma.
This is important, in the initial stages,
so that your mind is not disturbed
by the consequences of adverse karma.
It is due to karma that mind becomes sattvic and pure
and pure mind is not different from Freedom.
The pure mind is always in meditation,
the innocent will get it first.

My path to Freedom began 20 years ago with non-violence.
Can you talk about harmlessness and health.

Become the sky and you will not harm anyone. This is Ahimsa. Sky is emptiness. Sky protects everything and is a canopy above everything and even provides water to the earth. The first dharma of everybody who goes toward Freedom is Ahimsa, "I will not harm anyone physically or even by thought."

You have to be so clean internally and externally. Outside also you must be so clean. You must bathe, speak the Truth, refrain from stealing and harming others. This is the foundation on which to stand if you want Freedom. You must be pure in Heart and also go through physical purification, and then stay in Satsang after purification. You should wake up in the morning, wash yourself, do some yoga and meditate. These are the physical exercises.

Internal purity is to not think bad about anyone. And if you think, think for the good of everyone! The first sentence on your lips in the morning should be, "Let all beings be happy, all beings of the earth, all beings of heaven, all the beings of hell. Please, oh God, give them happiness." This will change your face.

I do this exactly, everything that you say.

I don't think so, your face doesn't show it. You are like the butcher who loves the sheep, all the while looking at her ribs. He doesn't love the sheep, but is always wondering about how much meat he will get. This mind is like the butcher. Don't fall in love with the mind. When you say, "I do this," it is the mind which is speaking, touching your ribs and wondering how much meat he will get from you! That butcher is death, Yama, who is after everyone and don't think he is compassionate!

Sometimes we hurt people that we care about and the result is
a feeling of unworthiness which keeps the mind from Freedom.

Don't hurt any person, by word, by action, and not even by thinking because this will rebound back to you and produce ten times the effect. If someone hurts you, you must forgive them and be compassionate toward them. Then you will get Peace. Don't even think of hurting anyone. Not even a tree. You can't understand the language of a tree, but if you abuse if or pluck a leaf or flower she will not be happy with you and can abuse you.

Once I was in Karnataka on a coffee plantation staying high on a hill in a very nice wooden bungalow. In the morning I woke and the planter said that he would go down the hill and have the cook prepare us breakfast and lunch. So, I went out and saw an orange tree full of oranges and I went to her and said, "Good morning mother, you are so lucky, you are having so many children." I was appreciating her load of loose-jacket oranges and I had no intention of eating any of them. As I was about to go down the hill, suddenly 12 oranges instantly fell to the ground. I looked around, but there was no wind or bird. Then I conversed with the tree, which is possible if you have that much love. She told me that she was giving me this present and that I should take it. I could understand the language of the tree. I hugged and kissed the tree and took her gift of oranges. This is what I advise you to do. Do it and see what happens.

I have had the experience of the universe being one.

Due to your good stars this experience comes to you. It is not on account of your effort, but because God is loving you. Your karma of other lifetimes are bearing fruit. Otherwise, it doesn't happen.

But now my mind is coming up with the game, "I am not good enough."

Dirty things are coming into your view now. At least you can see them. The things which are not good for you are found on the surface. This is a good sign; that you are knowing your weaknesses. Most people do not know this. They belong to the category of people who do not know that they do not know. You are above that. You know that you do not know; this is the seeker. The third category are those who know they know; this is the Teacher who you must follow.

What should I do about these doubts?

Keep you outer environments clean, I will clean the inner environment. If there is garbage outside of your house you will have a bad smell on the inside. So remove the outer garbage first and the inside will take care of itself. Outside environment is doubts, restlessness, suffering, brick biting about other people, hating people, not loving people. These are the outside things, the outside impurities. This you must clean yourself and then you are ready for Satsang and it will be easy. Finish all your doubts once and for all.

I have been sweeping all the shoes as you have told me to.
Please help me. I surrender to you.

Has this sweeping away of your ego worked or not? This is why this service of sweeping was given to you! So that your ego becomes so humble to sweep the floor and clean the shoes. This is a way adopted in India. Even very high people go to the front of the temples and take the dust from under the feet of the devotees and smear it on their forehead. The women don't even use a broom to clean, but use their saris so that they are sanctified by the dust from the devotees' feet. This is what they do in India and so I tried it on one Western person and that was you!

Vichar: Self Inquiry

Look Within,
Approach with all Devotion,
Stay as Heart.

Only adore yourself,
worship your Self, and seek your Self,
the rest will be taken care of.
Avoid useless activities and pleasures.
Simply keep Quiet, this is Sahaja Bhav, the natural state.

If you want to wake up,
don't think and do not make effort.
This is the only way.
This may appear as Wisdom with inquiry
or as Love by devotion, but both are the same.
True Wisdom is the Love of Self.

The Supreme Self, the dearest Love,
the source of joy, must be meditated on day and night
whatever you are doing, if you want Freedom Now.
Disregard everything else, see only That,
and all will be added to you.
Only contemplate Existence.
This contemplation is to just Be.
Go straight to the Light.

There is no question of having time for this or not
because it is That which is through all time.
Your true nature is Awareness, it cannot be practiced.
If you do not know this Awareness turns outward
toward manifestation and there is suffering.
Turn your face inward toward the source of "I."
Then the reflection of Self falls on the mind
turned toward Self, dissolving this mind into Self.
Turn toward the Unmanifest, towards Self and Peace.

You have the choice,
for just an instant reject everything possible
and you will find That in which all Is.
Then manifestation is the cosmic dance.

Inquiry is the diamond, there is no other method.
This is the direct assault on the arrogance of the mind.
Simply say, "I am Self, I am not body," and find out
Who has never come or gone, who is moving your thought.
This inquiry is not witnessing, it is Being!
Witnessing creates subjects and objects.
Being is the Satguru within, always meditate on That.
Always concentrate on the Omnipresent Reality and
be totally aware that you are this Existence-Consciousness-Bliss.
Inquiry is presence itself so question, "Who Am I?"
This is the only question that doesn't lead to suffering,
because it is severing the ropes to body-mind-arrogance.
This is withdrawing the mind from its engagements
and planting it in the garden of home.
Inquiry is Love with the Self.

This I-thought is Consciousness aware of Consciousness,
But what is aware of "I"? Ask "Who am I?" and find out
where is the foundation Consciousness?
Who is conscious of body Consciousness?
Your face will definitely someday become the food for worms!
Inquire and find who it is who shines through this face.
Make the most of Now because death comes quickly.
Don't move your mind, Be Quiet.
Shut the windows to the outside, remove all changes,
And look within to the Changeless.

Undress the concept of "I" and jump
into the ocean of Existence-Consciousness-Bliss.
Activate not even the thought of "I."
Activate no energy to even not activate,
and incessantly spend time in this meditation.
Acquire this new habit: sit down and be Quiet,
and the revelation will rise from Here.
First experience That, only then understanding will follow.
Understanding is like reading a menu,
but experience is eating the food.
So the revelation must enter the blissful Heart,
not the stupid arrogant head.
Then identify as this Revelation,
identify as cosmic Consciousness.

Identifying with the Absolute is meditation.
Keep your spirits up and burn all impediments.
Identify with the Absolute.

Truth is very simple, don't complicate it.
You must be in the light to know the darkness:
Just be aware of yourself, the light.
Jump into the fire of Knowledge,
and don't be concerned what will happen
to your clothing of concepts and vasanas.
This fire burns all.

Vichar is Quietness.
Quietness is not moving the mind
for one second and seeing your face.
Quietness is throwing away all becoming,
all ideation, all intentions, all notions.
Simply be Quiet, be still, be still, be still.
You are Love and Beauty Itself.
Keep Quiet and you will know
that you are the Self in all beings.

Vichar is true meditation, concentration on Awareness.
This Awareness will reveal the truth of Itself:
No object and no subject.
The decision, "Only Atman is real," is meditation.
Do not direct your mind to the past or future,
but let it stay Here Now without wavering, and meditate.
Meditate only on who is the meditator,
only on who is meditated on.
This is watching from where all arises from,
this is returning Home to what you are.
Meditation means to make no effort, to not stir a thought.
It is not an act of searching because a search only loses it.
Meditation is to effortlessly turn the mind
toward *that* energy which energizes mind.
This meditation melts into the identification
with Self-Being-Oneness.
You are always in this meditation,
always in Sahaja.

True meditation is Freedom
and this is staying in the source of the meditator.
Anything else is just a form of concentration.
True meditation does not begin and does not end.
In fact, the true art of meditation is to always meditate.
There is no place to arrive, there is nothing to do,
meditation is to simply stay at home as Being.

Time and meditation do not go together.
As meditation destroys time,
keeping the concept of time destroys meditation,
Even the thought, "I must meditate"
disturbs meditation like a stone disturbs a still lake.

Vichar is a special sight.
You don't see through the eyes,
you see through the Self.
It is the Self who sees the Self.
Even with closed eyes you can see where your eyes are
and so, which is this sight that you know by.
This you must do. Look to where the eyesight comes from.
This reservoir is full of sight. Look behind the eyes.
If you look forward you will see objects,
if you look behind you will see subject, the Seer.
It is the source of everything, the source of love and beauty.

Vichar should continue every moment of your life,
naturally like the act of breathing, until your last breath.
As my Master says:
"Inquire until there is no one left to inquire."
The habits of the mind are very hard to break,
and so it must be continued.
You have been ignorant for years,
so when you know the Truth
you must stay As Such for some time.
What else is important?
You have to be very strong.
Question the mind unceasingly.
Decide to never return to stupidness.

Once you are in Silence, stay silent as Silence.

Directed Inquiry

Questioner: I don't know where to begin in being silent.
Can you give me some advice?

Papaji: The Silence that I speak about is neither meditating nor sitting quiet. The Silence that I speak about has nothing to do with meditation or talking or not talking because then your mind is still running about here and there and everywhere. What I mean by Silence is that there should be no thought rising from your mind. No thought rising from your mind is Silence.

I can understand that, but I feel that I have to do something.

No, you are not to do anything. Simply see that no thought rises from your mind. It is not doing anything, it is just keeping quiet and watching the mind. That you have not done. So just do it now, today or tomorrow. Before you leave Lucknow you must complete this. Look at the thought, try it now. Look at the thought that doesn't belong to the past or future. Which thought is rising?

That I am sitting here before you looking at you.

This is not the thought, but what your eyes are seeing. Even the thought, "I am looking at you" has arisen from somewhere as a thought. Where is this "I" rising from which is looking at me? This is what I mean.

I don't know.

Then try to find out. Spend more time and see where this "I" arises from. Don't make any effort, you don't need any to locate the "I" and you don't need any thinking either. Just keep still and find out where the "I" rises from.

I want to sit here at your feet and ask you one more small question: what is Freedom, how to get it and how to stay free?

Freedom is when there is no worry,
no doubt, no unhappiness, and no fear.

Get it by simply sitting Here and not by climbing mountains. Simply sit Here and don't think of anything, This is all.

Stay here by keeping Quiet, doubtless and fearless.

ॐ

I want to merge with the Source.

The Source of light and life is brighter than a million suns. When you want to be It itself it will burst and instantly end all your desires and suffering. Simply look at It. Don't question, but dissolve in the Light. Stay beyond thought and mind where the sun, moon and stars do not rise. This is Krishna's abode that he speaks of in the Gita.

You need only absolute 100% total watchfulness. When something is going on you must be totally alert to observe what is in front of you, then it happens at once. But two swords cannot be kept in the same sheath: you can't have all your old habits along with the question of inquiring who you are. So only one at a time. The other one you have been trying for millions of years. It takes millions of incarnations to attain the human birth, and you have played very well. Now jump a little higher into your own Self and discard everything else. Discarding doesn't mean that you run away from life, but means that you pay attention only to who you are. Then you can live with everything peacefully because everything comes out of That. Then you will know that what you called reality is not Reality. But you have to have this experience first: find out who you are, what is Real, and what is not real. Then you will know that everything is That itself. Where else could it come from?

> Where does the whole of samsara, all animals and planets,
> all concepts, trees, and birds come from?
> There is only one Source: return to it, merge with it.
> Know what it is and everything is It itself.
> There is no difference between you and what you call other!
> Know this and you will speak to all beings;
> every rock, tree, and animal at the same time
> because time does not exist Here.

> Time is a concept; past, present, and future is only a concept.
> So to know Reality just spend one instant out of time
> and find what all this phenomena is.
> Question to yourself, be 100% watchful,
> and you will know the answer: the Source.

I try to question and be watchful but my mind is like a roller coaster. Is there anything that I can do with it? There is so much fear and anxiety even at the physical level which is in my body all the time from these thoughts. I have tried for decades to solve this and have read hundreds of spiritual books, but to no avail.

Okay, pick up any one of these thoughts out of the cloud of thoughts that are troubling you this very instant and tell me what it is. Mind is thought so in this way we will work on your mind.

Very good! That's enough, we will work on this thought "I" which is related to the entire manifestation, which is mind only. Stay with this "I" for awhile. Look at this "I" and tell me where it rises from, dive into this "I." Find what is earlier and even more present than this "I." As a wave rises from the ocean and becomes an individual name and form, what ocean does this "I" rise from?

From nothing!

Now you are at the source of "I" which is nothing, Nothingness. In this there is no more "I" and when there is no more "I" there is no more mind. Where there is no mind there is no manifestation. In this Nothingness what do you see? Don't cling to the past. This Nothingness means no limitations, no time, no mind, no state. As Nothingness what do you see?

What is there?

What It is! No there, no here, just what It is! What It is you will not find in any book. Most of these books will just inflate your ego with pride in knowing things that are not even worth knowing. So throw everything away, all your notions of mind, ego, and body. Get rid of any ideation and tell me what is left. Look into It by Itself. Don't go with any intention, not even the intention to find an answer. You have fired the bullet so now let it find its target. You are the target and the bullet cannot return to the muzzle! So find this out. What is rising from this Nothingness and how does it feel?

It feels good, but I feel that there are thoughts waiting on the outside of this Nothing wanting to come in and disturb it.

Look at them, from the inside. These are just dogs on the outside. These dogs are your old friends just wanting to come back and kiss you, but a kiss from one of these dogs is a bite! So look at these dogs and you are separate from them. You are not a dog. Look very carefully at the dogs and tell me where they are.

I just realized that there is one dog that I always let in. It is the dog "I am not supposed to do this! I am not supposed to be without worrying!"

Find the owner of this dog.

The owner is the "I."

"I" is also a dog. Stay at Nothingness, as Nothingness, and tell me what remains Now.

What remains is the temptation to listen to the dog of fear which wants me to leave this emptiness.

Okay. You have to rise from Nothingness in order to leave Nothingness right? You step up from Nothingness and move your foot through Nothingness and then plant your foot down. Where is this that your foot has landed as you step out of Nothingness?

The step out is just thought arising!

So these steps are thoughts. What are these steps stepping from, stepping through, and where do these steps land? If you step from Nothingness where will you land, where will you put the next step? What is behind you and what is in front of you? What are on the flanks? What is above and below your step? This Nothingness is no demarcations, no limitations, no notions, no ideations. It is totally complete and perfect and yet we call it Nothing because it is nothing that you can think about!

So try to step out of this Nothingness, much less run out of it. Go ahead, run out of this Nothingness. Tell me how you do this!

I grab a thought!

So you are in the ocean of Nothingness. Within this ocean if you reach out and grab something what will it be? Will it be the Himalayas? Will it be a stone?

No, It will just be water! I get Nothingness, but then it goes away. Maybe I should...

There is no "should," it is only water! What comes, stays and goes is only water, only Nothingness. Any wave that rises from the water is water! Anything that rises from Nothingness is Nothingness. It was Nothingness and it is Nothingness, *and this is what you are!* Stay as such! Stay as Nothingness. Now staying as Nothingness, look around, observe, and ask something.

There is still a feeling left in the body, like a residue.

Vichar: Self Inquiry

There is no body!

But there are still sensations.

These sensations are "I." You call it a sensation, but it is really an "I" which is just a notion. Even the creation of the notion of a body is a notion, a concept. From the day you manifested you were told that you were a child and you believe this notion so much that you identify yourself as this. But you can do away with the notion "I am a child, a human with a body" with the notion "I Am!" Find out who all this belongs to. Find to whom this body and this mind and all these notions belong to.

They belong to "I."

Yes, the creator, all the Gods, heavens, hells, and planets, are all created by "I" only. Nothing can be created unless the "I" is present first. Find where this notion of "I" is arising from now.

Now you are in the waking state and eventually you will decide that you want to go to the sleep state, you will decide to get some peace and rest. So you start to reject everything. First you reject your city and friends and retreat to your house. Then you reject your family and your house and enter your bedroom. Then you reject the bedroom and go into your bed. Then you reject your spouse and enter your body. Next you reject your body and come into only your mind. Finally, you reject even your mind and the "dogs" and you are asleep, in peace. Say that your sleeping time was 11 p.m. What did you do at 10:59:59 in order to go to sleep, what is going to happen in this one second? The dogs around you are the 59 minutes and 59 seconds. What are you going to do with them?

Reject them!

Right! The fifty-ninth second is now finished and the dogs are gone. The sixtieth second is also gone. Now speak of the "time" after this. After this what is left in your hand? What is left of friends, manifestation, mind, and body?

It is all gone!

Excellent! Everything is gone and who is left to know it?

Nobody.

You say that nobody is there in your sleep. Who is awake to know that "nobody" is there? What is this consciousness that is awake while you sleep

161

which knows that nobody was there? Who is this consciousness that enjoys sleep? What is this Now?

It is just space. Space!

Excellent! What is the difference between this "space" during the sleep state and the "space" in which the previous waking state and the next waking state are in? What is this "space" in which the dream states happen? How do all these "spaces" differ from each other?

It seems that the same space is there in all the three states.
The space is the same!

Yes, the space is the same! The space in this hand is the same as the space in that hand and is the same as the space in everybody's hand. The hand may be different, but the space is the same.

You are that space! You are the space in which the waking, sleeping and dream states are rising and falling in. You are That which is fully conscious even in the sleep state. All of these states and everything in them are projections on a clear and immaculate screen. You are this screen! The screen has no objects or subjects. This screen, this space is not the slightest bit concerned about subjectification, much less objectification, it just is! You are the screen, let the dogs bark, you cannot be affected. Let there be projections of storms and fires and romances and mournings and sufferings. The screen is not affected, and that screen *you are!*

(Laughter) Oh my God! Thank you! Thank you very, very much!

This is your planet, walk on this planet. (laughter) This you do not attain, you don't get this. All that has happened is that the notions have been removed, the dogs have left. Everything is a notion. If you know this you can live so well on this planet because then it is heaven! Everything is so beautiful. Everything is so beautiful and full of love if you understand this! You just have to understand this only! You are not to climb Mount Everest; It is Here and It is Now! It is Here and Now! This is meditation, here starts the meditation which is not disturbed by anything, not even by going into it or coming out of it because this meditation always was and always is!

(He takes a deep breath)

Now your breath is free for the first time because now it is in perfect harmony with the mind. When mind and breath are in harmony there is peace and only with this peace can we enter into Freedom. You are not to

162

understand. Understanding is over. You are not to stand anywhere, let alone understand.

This This has al. ays been so far away from me, but not now!

Now it is within you as are all the planets and everything else. This is Consciousness and everything is within this Consciousness.

This Consciousness is your own Self.
It is within you as you and never away or out of you!
When you say "I" this is it!
"I" is not the ego, but everything!
This will be the difference, "otherness" is ego and trouble.
The real "I" is everything, Consciousness is your own Self!

How is my mind so quiet now without effort? Is it only by Grace?

No-mind is given by the Grace of the Guru. Practice is through the movement of the body and mind, how can you be at peace in all of this mental activity? No-mind has no activities, no movements. This is achieved by no effort. Try this right now for one instant. If you have done practice then use this practice to keep quiet. Otherwise, don't activate your mind with practice if you want a quiet mind! Simply sit quiet with no effort.

Can you make it very clear how I can attain perfect and uninterrupted peace and happiness?

This question can be answered in just two words: keep Quiet. This will not interrupt you. Don't disturb the mind. Simply sit quietly there from where you came. It will not interrupt you anymore. But when you are moving on and on endlessly following all of your desires then you cannot have peace in this life. So return from where you came and stay there. Try it and if you are not successful return to me tomorrow.

I try to keep quiet. Today I woke up at 3 a.m. and repeated the Gayatri. Then I started Atma Vichar as follows: I took a few deep breaths to quiet the mind. Then...

Who told you to have a deep breath to quiet the mind? I didn't tell you! When you speak of the mind you cannot quiet it. When you utter the word "mind" you cannot quiet it. Mind lives in the name itself, otherwise no one has ever seen it. So when you utter the word "mind" already it is involved and so how can you quiet it?

It is like holding the tail of the monkey so that it will sit quietly! Take hold of the tail of the monkey and what will be the reaction of this monkey? It will turn and bite your finger. Monkey and mind are the same thing!

Then I mentally and silently put forth the question "Who am I?" and reject the body-mind as not me. I have 100% conviction of this.

When you reject body and mind what is left to speak about anything? If you say, "I am not the body-mind, senses, ego or intellect," what is left?

Nothing.

And in this Nothingness do you have to hold your deep breaths?

No. I try to remain silent without effort, and observe the observer, see the seer.

When you don't make effort you are silent. When you are silent there is no observer and nothing to observe, and no observation. In the quietness there is no observer or observed. What you are talking about is intellectual gymnastics with no real experience.

How can you see the seer? If you see the seer it is an object to be seen. Nobody can see the seer because it is beyond subject and object. You can see only objects. The seer sees only objects and then only becomes the seer, but seer itself cannot be observed or seen. If the seer is seen it is an object.

I mean that I try to remain vigilant and when thoughts arise, nip them in the bud.

When you are vigilant no thought can arise. Be vigilant and tell me if you see any thought and if you can, what is that thought. Just keep vigilant, and no thought will come. And if there is no thought, no vigilance is needed, because Self is always alone. It doesn't need any object to watch.

If the thoughts are strong then I am indifferent to them, or I try to be.

This is a good experience. If the thoughts are there and you are indifferent then it doesn't trouble you. If you stand outside of Satsang Bhavan many cars, people, and animals are crossing in front of you, but you are indifferent and so you let them come and pass. Like this you have to be watchful and indifferent. If the thought is nice don't run after it. If it is not nice don't tell them to go away! In most cases people are slaves to their thoughts and run after their thoughts and are carried away, never to return.

This is how the life of that stupid person is wasted after a travel of millions of years to get into the form of a human being. This form is not to be wasted in enjoyments of the senses. You have come for something else which is to Know who you really are! If you do not solve this question you will rotate again and again like a roulette wheel, always in the hell of suffering. This body is a hell and he who wears it is never happy, not even the kings or prime ministers who are always afraid of being shot. They have become something special and so have fear and thus need protection.

We have come for a very different purpose. There are six billion people in the world. Why then are there only a few in Satsang? They are unworthy! They have to suffer. To attend Satsang is not so easy. Why have you been chosen to go to Lucknow? Lucknow was not even on the map until Satsang started here and now it is even in the *Lonely Planet*. Now even tourists are coming and deciding not to go anywhere else. They have settled down permanently here.

Should I wait for the direct experience to occur?

No! Waiting means that it is not already here. Waiting for it is putting it to a future date and not having it Now. What is not Here Now will never be your own fundamental nature!

I do not tell you to wait for the future. Just tell me who you are right now. If you are not already what you are, you become something else and if you become something else you will have to be lost. Therefore don't hanker after things which are not already Here. So find out, who is here now! Not in the past or future. What is present Here Now?

Consciousness, nothing.

So if it is nothing why do you keep looking for tomorrow? It means your mind is running in the future. Mind means past. When mind works it does not stay in the present, but digs the grave of the past. There is no difference between past, mind, thought and time. They are all the same. Speaking of time you are speaking of the last minute, not of Now. And this Now must happen in Satsang in the very first second that you sit here. It must happen and if it does it is the Grace of the Atman on you. If it doesn't happen in this second then you are rejected by the Atman. All those who are not happy, those who are not free, those who are not enlightened are rejected by the Light itself. Who can save them?

You must look to your Self right now! Don't postpone. This world is the result of postponement. Otherwise, where is the universe? You are just playing with things which are not eternal.

Am I on the right track to the Source?

Still you have a doubt. You need a track to move from one place to another, just as you needed a track to come from Malaysia to India. But in Realizing the Self, how many miles do you have to travel? To reach your Self which way will you go? Do you need an airplane or a train or a car? You don't need any vehicle because what you search is right Now Here. This you must understand Now itself! Simply understand it and do not work for it. Understand that the Self is eternal and always Here! When you move from Here to anywhere the Self is not moving. Self is always within you and you move about. Self is the indweller of the heart. It indwells the heart cave. It is not mobile and everything exists in it. This you must get right now: "I am not to move, not to make effort, I am not to think about anything." Then it will reveal Itself Itself.

How?

By not making any effort. Do you follow what I mean? Don't make any effort. This "how" means that you want some way to get something else. "How will I reach there?" You need a map and so you ask how. These "hows" are used when you move from one place to another. You have been using maps for 35 million years, but now you are in Satsang you are at the summit of the mountain. Don't wait for the map, you don't need it.

What I am telling you you won't hear in the ashrams because they have all become commercial. When two people meet there is some interest, some business, some commercialization. I have never seen people meeting for Satsang, they only meet for commerce, only for money. Even with husbands and wives there is some interest. Where is the person who will speak without interest in the world. In Satsang we are one family and have no interest in exploiting each other. We have for each other so much more love than for our countrymen, neighbors and parents and therefore we have settled down here.

I want to be Free. Will you please give me your advice?

Perform surgery on your mind and find out what it contains. If you perform surgery on other objects you will not be peaceful. Open your mind and find out what it contains, and like the surgeon don't think of anything else, concentrate only on that. Find out what the substance of the mind is. Find out what disease and tumor it has. Do it by looking at the mind. Mind is only thought, so look at the thought. Who looks at the thought is the I-thought so you must perform surgery on the "I." Find out where she comes from.

This is the advice that you want. You have to get into it with all your might, all your strength. Then you will be successful.

How can I be quiet to perform this surgery?

I can tell from the eyes who can keep Quiet. Some people have eyes like a monkey and some have a Divine eye. Only the Divine eye can keep Quiet. This is the clue that I can give to you: stop your activity. This is called Love and Happiness and Nirvana. Stay like this in Satsang and outside also. Thank your stars that your mind even wanted to come to Satsang! This is quite enough because mind attached to senses is trouble, but mind detached from senses is Freedom. So in Satsang watch where this mind runs: keep vigilant. It may take time because for millions of years mind has been controlling you, but now it is your time. You have simply to be watchful and very vigilant of the activities of the mind. This will result in Quietness and Freedom.

> It is not difficult, simply watch,
> do not make effort and do not think.
> Keep vigilant and you will see that nothing will arise.
> This is the trick of how to keep the mind quiet,
> and how to win Freedom.
> This doesn't take time because Freedom is always Here.
> You simply have to watch: where does mind arise from?
> Where does thought come from?
> What is the source of this thought?
> Dive together with this mind to its source from where it began.
> Then you will see that you have always been Free
> and that everything has been a dream.

> Who has not found themselves is asleep.
> Who is not attached to the senses is awake.
> In this Awake, waking, sleeping, and dreaming do not appear.
> This is the Atman who is neither born nor dies
> and is That which cannot be understood.
> You are That Itself!
> Thinking that you are bound or even bindable
> is nothing other than entertaining fear.
> Remove this fear in Satsang.
> Know that you are free from death and birth
> because you were never born.

Suffering is not real because it disappears in the sleep state and reappears in the waking and dream state. There is no suffering in the sleep state because there is no object, no subject, and no mind. Where there is relationship there is suffering. Just do not touch the thought that "I am the body." Just do not think and you will land in your own ultimate blissful nature. Time and mind are the same thing. Stop mind and you will fall in Love with your own blissful freedom. So keep Quiet, do not think, and do not exert.

How can I truly let go of the "I" which disturbs the quietness?

Everyday in Satsang you are told how to let go of the "I." Everyday for the last three years we are only working on this thing: how to let go of the "I." When "I" rises it must rise from somewhere. From birth you have been using this word "I" and surely it meant the body. "I" go there, "I" come here, "I" am suffering, "I" am dying." This "I" meant that it was body, with name and form. If you let it go you will find the real "I," your own Consciousness. How to let it go? Find out where it rises from.

Doesn't that entertain the "I"? Doesn't asking who is the "I" just create an "I"?

No, find out where it rises from. When you find out where it rises from you are quiet and this is letting go of "I." Do it! I see from your face that you have not understood yet. Find out where it is rising from. Give me the answer. Is it your glasses, or your ear, or foot, or shirt, or pants? Where does it rise from? It must rise from within you.

It comes from ego.

Ego is only body. Without a body there is no ego. Before birth there is no ego and after 60 years there will be no ego. So the ego has come when you come to know that "I am the body." Then things start to belong to you and you belong to other people. This is called ego and this ego will not give you rest, peace or love.

One day the ego will finish because when the body disappears the ego will disappear. It will be finished with this incarnation, but again it will come back because of all its unfulfilled desires. And so this ego will take an incarnation which will fulfill your desires in a given location, and this will continue endlessly, for millions of years. To stop it ask the question, "where does 'I' arise from?" and be vigilant and watchful.

Your face is turned toward somewhere where it didn't turn before. It usually turns to persons, objects, and places. But all of this you will lose one day and so find out what is eternal. How to do it? Find the source of "I"!

Otherwise the senses are looking outside, but now look within and I am sure you will not see these three things; no person, no place, and no object to which you are attached. This you must do for only one second, and during this second ask the next question. You are not to understand and you are not to lift a mountain or make any effort. You are not even to think.

So how do I ask this question and not make any effort? That is the place where I am having trouble.

Making effort means carrying 200 pounds on your head from Indiranagar to Hazrat Ganj. But I do not give you any weight. I say just keep Quiet and to keep Quiet what effort is needed? To say something you need effort because you must go to the past and pick up something from your memory, and so you need effort. To simply stay Quiet and not to speak does not take any effort.

I understand intellectually and I have been working with it for some time, but it seems like even though there are glimpses of stillness and Beingness, there is no sustaining of this.

You said you have been working for some time. I said do not work! Working for quite some time means past. Mind is past. Intellect is past. Everything is past including every word that you speak. Any relation belongs to the past, find out where this "I" is rising from! It is not that you are going to search somewhere else, simply see that no thought rises from within, because every thought belongs to the past. Can you think of something which is not the past? Can you speak to me something which has no relation with the past? No!

So you are advised for one moment not to think of the past. Then you will be placed in some other domain which has not been mentioned.

(He smiles and sits in silence)

This is the Moment! I can see that this is the Moment that you were missing. You are smiling because you have no connections to the past, or the mind, or the intellect, or to the senses. That makes the difference. This is liberation from the cycle of coming and going for ages. When it is available so cheaply, why not strike a bargain?

When you smiled it is called a no-mind state. When there is no-mind you are happy. Even when you sleep you do not carry your mind along to sleep with you, but leave the mind outside, then you go to sleep and take rest. But if you take mind with you then you cannot sleep. Mind means thinking about things of the past, and that state you have already had from 5 a.m. to 11 p.m.

Now you want rest which you do not have when the mind and intellect are working all day and so you go to sleep from 11 p.m. to 5 a.m. What effort do you make to enter this place of peace and rest? You do not even utter the statement "I want to go to sleep." Then you are in Love and Peace. This is how everybody can have Peace always. Then bring this Peace into 5:01 a.m. without making any effort, and without holding onto time because when time is there you have mind. Tonight try to find out what happens after 11:00 p.m.

Will you guide me in Atma Vichar?

The word Atma Vichar means "thinking entirely about your own Atman all the time and not anything else." So if you do this then what do you feel? Think entirely of the Atman inside who is conducting this Vichar. Don't think of the Vichar, but of the One from where the Vichar rises from. Where does the Vichar rise from and what is there? And who is asking this question?

Ego is asking.

Yes, this Vichar is from ego only. It is ego only which says that you have to do something or that you have to get something. But where does ego rise from?

From the Self.

So you are ego or Self?

Self.

So, from the Self, like the ocean, let the wave rise travel and fall. They are not other than the Self, the Ocean. If you are the Self let anything arise from it and don't be concerned with it.

I am the Self. Aham Atman. That's all! Self has no form. It is not the subject or the object. It is beyond everything and if you become That it is already Being, not becoming. You don't need any Vichar, any method, nor any chanting because "I am Self!"

This trust that "I am Self" has to be there just as everybody has the trust "I am ego." Everybody trusts the ego and not the Self. It is so easy to Be as you are and not to become something else, and just get into trouble. You must have 100% trust that I am I Am. I am Self. Even in the Gita it is said, "Aham Atma Gorakshar" or "I am the Atman indwelling in the hearts of all beings."

Vichar: Self Inquiry

It is difficult to trust Self.

But you easily trust the ego. How long can this trust stay? Ego means "I am the body," isn't it? How long can this trust stay? Can it be more than 80 or 90 years? So you trust for 90 years and half of the time is gone in sleeping, and the rest is spent going to school and having a wife and producing children. This is your trust and what is the result? When you trust you must trust something useful to you. Self always is: trust That!

It is for those who attend Satsang to have the complete Trust: "I am not the body, I am not the mind, I am not the object, I am not the senses, I am not the ego." Here begins Satsang. First of all, you must get rid of things which do not last eternally.

And what about restlessness?

On the ground of restlessness is the rest which I spoke to you about. When you feel restlessness there is rest somewhere else which shows up every second, but no one cares for it. In between someone checking out of a hotel and someone checking in, what is this?

Empty.

This is called rest. In between everything there is rest but no one takes care of it. What is the period between exhalation and inhalation?

Rest.

Yes, you cannot describe it, and nobody knows it. But if you are aware of this it is called Atma Vichar, or being the Self alone. This doesn't take any effort if you remember that "I am in between both thoughts, I am between both breaths, in and out." It doesn't cost you anything. Just have the attention, "I am that gap between the two." There no death or dissatisfaction can enter. No death or unhappiness can enter. This is simple guidance. Anybody can keep still, keep quiet and it won't make any difference, but it will be difficult to have the real experience of Silence.

The "I"-less silence?

Why speak about any "I's"? It can't be attained by effort. Just be Quiet! To see that the mind is not going back to previous attachments takes effort, but what I speak about is to not make any effort, not even for Silence. Just don't make any effort whatever it is. Don't make effort and then you will have this experience. I don't call it silence.

Krishna told Arjuna how to control the mind and immediately after that Arjuna fought a war! He slaughtered nine divisions of armies within That and his Silence was not disturbed. Krishna didn't tell him to keep quiet, but told him to, "kill your own kinsman, which are your concepts." So do not give rise to any thought and do not make effort. Then you have won the war. don't make any effort, for one second and tell me, are you not Still? By making effort you can't be happy so do not make any effort. All the distractions from this come from your old attachments.

Once I did feel this peace while in a big ashram in Rishikesh.

This you had due to your seriousness and not the ashram; you can have it anywhere. These ashrams where they speak of yoga and other things will only confuse you. I also went to that same ashram in 1942. There they speak about yoga and chanting, but not about Atma Vichar. So in all the ashrams you just waste your life and waste your time. It is better to attend Satsang where these things are clarified without a long period of stay. I don't see any outcome from any ashram. They just meditate and read books and they do not keep Quiet. They are always working day and night and this work is not going to help you.

So keep Quiet! How? I will tell you! Do not make any effort! What harm will there be? The result of effort everybody knows. Just keep Quiet and see the result of this in this instant of time. Then this instant of time will fall in love with you. It is not that you will fall in love with the Peace, but Peace will fall in love with you. If you don't feel Peace it is because this supreme Peace has rejected you and you have no chance. You will have to wait for the next incarnation be it human or donkey. Make the most of this incarnation when it is so easy!

I am trying and as long as there is a continual dose of enlightening stimulus like the reading of the Avadhuta Gita there are reactions and responses of quietness and Aham Brahmasmi, but once this stimulus is removed I fall flat.

Aham Brahmasmi means "I am Brahman," and every breath that you breathe is giving you this caution. Aham Brahmasmi is a call which Atman itself is teaching you.

The questions arise, where did "I" arise from and where will "I" return to and so Ko Ham arises! Ko Ham: "Who am I? Who am I? Who am I?" From the beginning a man wants to know the fundamental reality of his soul and to answer all the questions like "where do I come from?" and "where do I return to?" and "what is all that is around me about?" This is the sign of

Vichar: Self Inquiry

a man who is listening, though most people don't listen. So sit quiet and the answer to Ko Ham arises: you are That, Tat Vam Asi. You are That. But first you must give rise to this question, Ko Ham? Then the Atman tells you: you are That. Listening to That, holding onto That, then the devotee, the one who needs to be Free, accepts that he is Brahman. This is how it will happen.

I think it is good luck that you are "falling flat" as you say. You wanted to climb somewhere by the stairs of others, but you are not to climb anywhere. Remove all concepts that there are ladders and you will stand where you always have been standing: on the surface of the Mother Earth, and That is Aham Brahmasmi!

I don't want to identify with the mind. Can you help me to stop going into all these concepts and this confusion?

If you don't want to identify with the mind then you must know what the mind is. Look at the mind. You establish the identification with the mind. You provide what the mind wants. So first find out what the mind is and then you will see if you can identify with it or dis-identify with it. You don't understand mind, but you can understand thought. So find where the thought rises from, now itself. Try it now and tell me what happens.

The thoughts come from nowhere!

> If something comes from nowhere
> how can it be anything?
> How can it be anything when it doesn't come from anywhere?
> Anything must come from somewhere.
> If it doesn't come from somewhere it is nothing at all.
> So if thought comes from nowhere it must be nothing at all,
> because only nothing comes from nowhere.
> It's easy.

(He gets it)

I feel such a deep peace with you now. I don't know what more to ask of you, but I would be happy to hear any advice you have for me or just sit in silence with you.

When you are Here just sit Quiet. You don't have to ask any question. If a question arises find out immediately where this question arises from. Then you will be able to sit quiet, for the source where the question arises from is where there is Stillness, Quietness and Peace.

173

Don't be led away by your questions
because they all belong to the past
and they will just cause you to suffer.
If you want to stay in peace
find out where the question is just now arising.
Look to that place which is before the rising question.
Putting this into experience just Now
you will see how to sit in Quietness.

I Love you. Please show me the moon. This is all I want to say.

Very good. Which kind of moon do you want to see? The moon in the
sky everybody knows, isn't it? In the daytime you see the sun and in the night
you see the moon. Everybody knows this so which kind of moon do you want
to see?

(He looks into the Master's eyes and remains silent)

Okay, then I understand.

The moon is Within you.
Freshness, sweetness, giving light even in the darkness.
You have to look to this moon by yourself.
Don't look outside to any other object.
Everything is outside, even your body
because whatever you can touch is outside.
Reject everything which can be touched or seen or smelled.
If you do this instantly you will see the moon.
Do what I say: don't look at anything which can be seen,
don't touch anything which can be touched,
don't smell anything which can be smelled.
Then you will see what the moon is
and what you are yourself.

I am very happy that you are here at this young age. You must have come
for some reason, something must have brought you here.

*I understand that all I can do is to keep quiet and turn inward,
allowing Grace to reveal itself.*

Turn your mind inwards and not outward toward objects. When the mind is turned inside then there are no objects which it can get attached to. When you are successful at turning the mind inwards then it will get lost like a wave disappearing into the ocean. At that time you don't think of any object, person, or idea. If this is done for one instant of time, It will reveal itself to you. During this instant don't make any effort and have no desire and don't be attached to any object. Then just wait for half an instant and you will see the result and your mission will be fulfilled. That's all. You can do it.

How can I look inside and go back inside to the Source. Is there a technique?

The technique to return to your source is very simple.

The outside attachments do not allow sitting still and meditating.
So avoid, for some time, all outside attachments
like you do when you sleep and have a very peaceful night.
Practice this in the daytime.

The instant in which you forget all your outside attachments
will be the taste of tremendous love and happiness.
Then slowly you will stop looking outside
until the outside and inside are the same
causing both to cease to exist.

The difference between the outside and the inside of this house is just a two-inch door. If there is no door, there is no inside and outside. This door is mind. When mind goes to fulfill its desires it goes back to its outside, and thus inside is also created. But when mind is quiet you are your own Self because there is no-mind. Then you will see that this happiness you never had before. Though you will love it you will not know what has given you this peace of mind and bliss. If you stay in this atmosphere you will forget the previous atmosphere and you will merge into bliss and be bliss itself. This is a very easy technique.

If I can find the door it is easy.

This "if" is the door. If you don't use "if" what is going to happen?

I will find the door. No! There is no door! There is no inside or outside! It is all This!

Yes! Yes! It is all This!

ॐ

THE TRUTH IS

There are no more doubts and I am seeing the connection between a still mind and the Self, but I am having a hard time keeping the mind quiet. When I am quiet, though, there seems to be a foreign entity lurking in the background. Is this the Self? Or is this a trick of the mind?

All that you are saying are the tricks of the mind because you have not understood what the mind is and when you don't you are always in trouble by the mind. It will play tricks and appear as anything and you will see it and think that it is reality. But everything that reflects in front of you as real is not real as Buddha found out in this very month of May. All are tricks of the mind.

> There is one thing you must do
> so as not to be tricked by the mind:
> *Simply keep Quiet and do not make effort.*

What you mention is making effort, but you are requested not to make any kind of effort and to keep quiet. If you ask me how to keep Quiet I will ask you not to think. If you ask me how not to think then I will suggest that you find out where the thought arises from. Turn your face toward That. Do not look at the object of the mind, but to where the mind rises from. There is no difference between mind and thought. Mind is a bundle of thoughts and there is no difference between thought and "I." When "I" rises thought rises, when thought rises senses arise and when senses rise they produce objects of their respective senses. Eyes to see, nose to smell a flower, ears to hear music, tongue to taste and hands to touch. These are the objects that senses see, but senses and the objects are the same. When senses are there objects are there. Now return back slowly to where the senses arise from. They rise from mind. Objects-senses-mind. Where does the mind rise from? Ego! There is no difference between mind and ego. Where does the ego arise from? This means where does the "I" rise from? This you have not stated. Look toward the place where "I" rises from. Pick this up. When you do you will merge into that place where "I" arises and disappears and that situation is yet undescribed by anyone, no teacher or preacher or religious book or Sutra of the Buddha.

You say to find the source of "I" and mind. How long should inquiry be continued?

> Inquiry should be continued
> walking, talking, sleeping, waking and dreaming
> until it becomes your nature.

176

As you enter the source of this inquiry you are near the ocean. Continue this inquiry and you will see that it is going on even in your sleep with no effort of yours. Most people think that inquiry should be started when you sit down to meditate and end when you get up. This is not the case. Rather, it has to be continued as the thought of the one you are totally in love with continues in your mind. Inquiry has to be continued like the pain of a headache or toothache continues throughout the day, no matter what you are doing. This ache is continued without effort, at the office or in speaking with people. Like this continue inquiry waking or sleeping or even when you are activating your mind.

This inquiry must be continued like the act of breathing so it will be as natural as breath itself.

When this happens, when I discover it, it will be obvious, right? I won't mistake it for the mind, is that right?

What you are speaking is being spoken from the head! But what I tell you is not to think. Thinking and head, there is no difference! What you describe is very intellectual. Otherwise, you would wear a very different face. Only those who know their real beauty have truly beautiful faces. The face of the Beloved is so beautiful that even the senses cannot transcend there to describe the word beauty. The beauty that is usually referred to is only skin deep. The eyes that see the beauty of the Beloved are very rare, like Kabir, and Chaitanya and Mira, and after seeing That their eyes saw nothing else in the world. So the one who has seen It has been stolen by that Beauty! They are dissolved into the Beauty itself.

I think that you have been smelt, but when you go to the Beloved, he will pick up those who are unsmelt. The unsmelt flower must be offered to the Beloved. The honey bee knows. The bee kisses the flower and nobody knows what it has stolen from the roses, and if one tastes it he cannot describe it.

Does mind have to be destroyed totally for this to happen?

Enlightenment is not possible until the mind is destroyed. Still the mind by giving up those things which are most dear to you because it is these things which will cause the disturbance. If your peace is being drained out there must be something holding your mind. Still the mind by discerning whether it is real or unreal, whether it is permanent or transient, whether it is truly worthwhile or not. Even in the case of your beloved partner, the truth is that you love them for the sake of the Self only. Still the mind by staying with the teacher and by constant meditation on the Self. Joy also will destroy the mind, but once you bury it don't dig it up again.

You have to be rid of all objective attachments. Stillness of mind comes from giving up all attachments except that attachment to Self. The problems come when you are attached to transient objects. So sleep to these transient objects, to the world, and be awake to the Self. Non-inquiry is samsara, being awake to the objects and asleep to the Self. Inquiry is being awake to the Self and asleep to the senses. Inquiry is Freedom.

Thoughts are like temporary clouds in front of the Sun, even the I-thought is a cloud. Be aware of the cloud that is mind itself. This mind is your desire of this and that. When you see that the thoughts, even the I-thought, are just drifting like clouds then you will not be affected by them. When there is stillness of mind then mind is no more, then you are truly aware.

In the middle of the night last night, for a millisecond, there was nothing. Is that it? Is that Self? Then the mind came back.

How could the mind come back in? Where was the mind in this Emptiness? When there is nothing in your pocket how many dollars can come out of this empty pocket? What can come from Emptiness?

> Once the Heart becomes still,
> Once it becomes empty,
>   it cannot come back again!

So try again. Enter into Emptiness and don't think about coming back. Then everything that you see will be in Emptiness.

Often I am just too lazy and seek after distractions instead.

You are not lazy, but you should be supremely lazy, which means you are too lazy to even think. If you think you are not lazy, but very active. If you don't make use of the mind it will leave you. So either you become very lazy or very active.

I just don't believe I can do it!

Why not? You have to believe it! Know "I can do it, I have to do it!" If you are here the mind is not, but if the mind is here then you are not! Now tell me, "Who are you? *Who are you?*"

(She smiles as she sits quietly and then says:) When you asked me "Who are you?" my mind suddenly stopped. There are no thoughts,

only happiness. I am surprised that it is possible!

Yes, no doubt it is possible! You should have no other thought but this "Who am I?" if you have any thought at all. This thought brings you to where there is no thought or concept, no person or object, to where there is only Emptiness. This is your ultimate Nature which is "lost" because you wanted to enjoy objects of the world which you have become attached to. Due to attachments you do not have the time to know your own true loving nature which will give you Peace. To find this Peace do as Kabir says:

Stay with the Saint for just half a second,
just half of the half second, just half of that
and you will lose that which binds you.

With the Grace of the Guru you will know who you are.
This Grace is a fireball burning all your sins
that you have collected.
When all the sins are burned you are like a lotus
as your heart and mind is opened.

This is the time everybody has been waiting millions of years for. Don't waste anymore time. Have it Now.

ॐ

I want to know myself.

Forget everything and you will know your Self. If you remember you will suffer, so forget everything. Dissolve the desire for everything and you will have everything.

When a desire or a thought arises I have been asking, "To whom does it arise?" The answer is, "To me." Then the next question is...

Why do you jump to the next question? Why don't you understand the first question? When you look within what do you see?

Empty space.

Who is looking at the empty space and what is seen?

I don't know.

When you look at thought and it disappears.

You are That which is seen
at the moment the thought disappears.

It is like a river which is limited by two banks. Water limited by two banks is a river, but when the water meets the ocean it loses its riverness and becomes ocean. The river is lost and becomes ocean. This is what is meant by this inquiry. Do it once and not as a repetitive process.

Ask, wait, find out, and become That itself.

Don't inquire about others: "Who are you?" or "What is that?" "Who am I?" is the first question to be asked. After this explanation there is nobody left to ask questions.

You are Consciousness
and you can't become unconsciousness.
Do not think, but act spontaneously without the mind.
Stay as you are and don't think about what will happen.
Have no fear and no doubts will arise.

I want to laugh without understanding the joke.

Then know that someone who is laughing within your Heart. You only have to hear this laugh and this will be the last experience because you will find who is always in bliss, happiness, and in love. Someone is hearing and looking at what is going on. Who is laughing in your heart? Who brought you here? What is the purpose of your coming here?

I have a question regarding self-defeating reactions to people's actions. Are you saying that instead of investigating a particular unpleasant reaction, I should just accept it as a consequence of ego? It seems to me that by investigating the ego we could make our lives better.

Whatever you investigate it is only through ego that you do so. All investigation comes from ego and not from anywhere else. Therefore, if you ask for my advice, simply keep Quiet and do not start any investigation. After all, what can you do to investigate a 12 billion year old world? How can you understand it? You are here for 100 years, maximum. What is your contribution to this 12 billion year old world?

Simply keep Quiet,
let things happen in front of you,

and enjoy this universe which is offered to you.

Don't make any effort and don't even think
and you will know who you are!
Don't think of the past or the future
and within this you will find what you never have found before.
But few people do this and instead waste their lives
in practice which only expands their ego
as they boast of all the ways that they please the Divine.

So simply be Quiet, make no effort
and you will know who you are!

This is what I have come here for. To find the Unknowable before the "I."

You have understood the purpose of your coming here.

Your purpose is to be at peace,
to love all beings, and to know who you are.
This is the purpose of life.
Slowly you will know this and get through.

What is peace?

See things with an open heart and you will see what peace, love, and beauty are and at that moment you will forget everything.

Have you heard of Saint Kabir? He says, "If you keep Quiet for an instant, for half an instant, for even half of a half of an instant, then the whole world will run after you." That is the attraction that you will become if you keep Quiet. You will be the most beautiful person in the whole universe and the universe will run after you to have peace of mind. You will become That and it is not difficult.

Can you show me That? Can you show me that peace, the Self?

Self lives in the heart behind a veil. You will see the Self by slowly stepping in and not by knocking at the door. Some messiahs have told you to knock at the door and it will be opened but they have been misunderstood because really there is no door! Proceed quietly and slowly, so quietly that even thinking is making too much noise. So don't think and you will be with the Beloved for the first time, because the condition to see the Beloved is to be Quiet. Now keep Quiet and tell me if you do not see.

I don't see. (Then he shuts his eyes)

I said to keep Quiet, but you don't understand. You create the veil by shutting your eyes. Whose fault is this? Do not shut your eyes, keep them open, and do not take anybody else with you. You must go alone. This is very precious.

Fear comes up when you say go alone.

Fear comes because you do not want to go near your Friend, your Beloved. Touching That you will become immortal. Just looking at this nectar will make you immortal.

This "I" is poison! Don't take "I" with you, go alone. Why take the "I"? It means fear-separation-body-death! This "I" is so troublesome, so do not take it with you, go alone with it, without "you," without "he," and without "she."

(He smiles and stays silent)

Now you understand, I can find out from your face. (giggles) You have the taste of what I speak of. You have searched the corners of the universe, but the Beloved is always Here, so you never knew the way. This is the way.

ॐ

I try to inquire and find who is inquiring, but I can't find him!

Exactly! Very good. It is the one that you can't find! You have to find the one you can't find. No one has ever found it so give up the search. If you say that you cannot find it, that is okay, it doesn't matter, don't try to find it. Give up the search for the coat you are wearing! Suppose you have given up the search, what then is the result? You have to be very careful. It is a very good question, and now it is up to you to give me a reply. The one that you cannot find, let him go. Give up even this concept of search. If you have given up this search for one who cannot be found where do you stand?

I don't know!

If you do not know, it does not matter, just keep Quiet. Just keep Quiet and this answer will show itself. You have to keep Quiet and let the Quietness speak to you. Stay where the river of thought begins and you are where the answer comes from.

How can I be quiet? How can I be mindless and turn off this computer that works day and night?

It is very simple and you can have it right now: keep Quiet, do not make effort to keep Quiet, and do not think. Do not let a thought stir in your mind because every thought is the graveyard. Can you think of anything that is not past? To think you must go to the graveyard, dig up a grave, and find out what is in it. That means thought. There is no use in going to the graveyard. Just do not think and you are Free. Just for one second do not think, and in that moment, that instant, that second, you will kiss Freedom. If the last breath of the waking state is inquiry then the first breath after sleeping will have the answer.

Can I be Enlightened now?

This question you are asking to now? Ask this question to Now and Now will tell you how. Ask this question to Now, not to the past or future, not even to the present. I am not making a joke. I am very serious, sometimes. (laughs) Direct your face to Now and wait for the answer. Again I will give you some tips: Don't make any effort when you ask this question and do not think.

The question is gone. But how to make sure of this when I am no longer in front of you?

Once you come in front of me, I will stay in front of you, I promise.

This is my last Satsang, today I am leaving.

If you are in a hurry to leave it will not work. You have to stay and clarify things. It is like going to the supermarket, but leaving before you buy anything. It is a waste of time. You have to decide that I am going to a place with a definite reason and you must decide that you are going to fulfill this reason and purpose.

Only a few have decided this and the rest have gone out to the fishmarket, and not to this Eden Garden of Satsang. In this garden you only have to spend one second, or even one half a second. But if you are otherwise occupied, then a quarter-second will do. You will get everything in this quarter of a second if you spend it entirely with me with no ropes attached to the past.

Again and again I remind you, you are here for a definite purpose and I am going to fulfill it even if you don't want it. Even if you close your fist I will, with my entire strength, open it up and place a Kohinoor diamond in it!

ॐ

*Ramana Maharshi spent many years asking "Who am I?" before
he was Enlightened. Do I have to do this? Are there levels of
Enlightenment?*

It is not correct that Ramana Maharshi asked this question many times.
He asked it only once before coming to Tiruvannamalai. He was going to
school from his home. On the way he felt that he was dying and this question
arose, "Who is dying? Who am I?" and this lad, on his way to school, found
the answer. He realized he was not the body, senses, mind, intellect, and even
if these things die, that he would not. After that he went to Arunachala and
stayed there until his last breath, in Silence. That Silence, he says, is the
Nature of everyone and if they ask this question they also will be Silent.

There are not levels of Enlightenment, but there are levels in your
approach. Serious approach, moderate approach, and the third level is doing
it in old age.

When this boy found it he went directly to the place of Lord Shiva and
not back to his old circumstances. Levels are of decision only. These levels
are for the ego, not Enlightenment. The light is there and if you only half
open your eyes you will not see the sun. The sun is always there and does not
turn its back to the earth. The earth turns her back to the sun and the result
is night. There is no night or levels in the Sun. There are no levels in
Consciousness. It is like the ego of the king which kept him away from the
Pir. But when the ego is gone he will immediately rush in. Your own light and
wisdom waits for you, but you have been postponing it for a million years.

Also, you don't need practice. In the ancient times people would go to the
caves and hide themselves like wolves, but you don't need a cave, you are a
human being. You are here just for the question, so find the answer. Don't
make any effort and do not think. Find the source of thought. So now it is
time for you to find how serious you are.

Intellectually I am conscious of the source of thought.

Simply sit Quiet, don't go out to the tavern, don't race, just sit Quiet and
the Bliss will come. Keep Quiet and do not think and there will be bliss.
Otherwise, you will suffer. There is no other way. What do you lose if you
do not think? When you sleep you do not think and what do you lose then?

*I want to lift the veil. I want to be free every moment. I want to
dissolve the "I" into emptiness. I want to witness eternity.*

There is no witness of eternity! Who is the witness of this affair of
eternity? Who is the witness? This concept of witness produces the witness!
So turn your face beyond the witness to, "Who is aware that there is any

witness?" Then the witness will finish. That is called limitlessness and eternity. There is no word for eternity, no one to speak of any experience and no time to accompany you. That Silence cannot be experienced and so you are not That which I speak about. Simply keep Quiet and see that nothing rises from any quarter to disturb your Silence. This is what I can speak about beyond the witness: Silence alone. No waves in that ocean.

I am very grateful for your teaching and to sit in this Silence with you, but still I have a question.

Does it arise from this Silence?

It arises from my mind.

Whose mind? Where is this mind from where it arises. You know the clothes that you are wearing, right? Now tell me where this mind is that you are wearing.

It is just a feeling of "my"-ness that arises there.

It is "there" and so you must be "Here" to know this. Stay in this Here and tell me where is body, mind, senses, and manifestation? Stay home, not in the supermarket.

It feels like it is just Nothing.

Let this question arise out of this Nothingness and tell me what it is about.

There is no question.

You have found It! Stay here and there are no questions, no doubts, no sufferings, no troubles at all. Stay at home, this is your Nature. Get rid of all notions because these transients are not your nature. You are free of all notions. Stay Here as you are and you will not have any suffering. This is eternal Love and Beauty. But if you entertain notions, if you get attracted to following concepts you, will be in trouble.

The first notion is "I am the body!" This creates time, present, past, and future, and the never-ending cycle of birth and death. So return home, Here and Now, you are not to do anything. It does not take time, not more than perhaps a second. In just one second you can find your Self, Here and Now. Don't postpone it.

Look at this very Moment this very Moment.

This Moment is your true face.
In this Moment there is no past or future.
In this Moment see what is eternal.
In this Moment what effort can you possibly make
in order to be in this Moment.

I see that you see It Now. Now you can feel It. You are peace and you are very beautiful and certainly you are not in trouble. Instantly you will feel within, without, and everywhere. Now ask the question that you had a few minutes ago.

I have totally forgotten what it could be and I have no idea of what could even be questioned!

This is very good forgetfulness! Very few people forget the concepts that make them separate and bound. But if you forget these even the concept of death will not touch you. This is eternal Love.

(laughs and laughs)

Come close and let me see the face of forgetfulness. Look Within and you will find that there is no bondage because the concept of bondage is gone. Then you will return to your own natural state whatever it is. Don't give this another name because then you will just get another concept of liberation and freedom. Just let, "I am bound," vanish and you will return home. There is no question of freedom, just find from where the "I" that thought that it was bound rises from.

ॐ

I need help with unlearning all my conditioning.

You are very lucky because you are so beautifully placed in a human body with the desire for Freedom and you are in Satsang. When these three things arise something beautiful will happen. These three things, this trinity, is a sacred confluence. You have done very well.

Now just keep Quiet and find where your questions are rising from. You will get it because you have a mountain of merits in order to be in this confluence. You have done very well. Now just be quiet and wait for the other side to appear before you. Don't think and don't make any effort and it will appear before you. Just keep Quiet and let it appear, whatever it is!

It is Enlightenment. I want to be Enlightened!

Where is this Enlightenment and where are you? Who is it that wants enlightenment? Who is it that wants to be enlightened? Find this out. Which is this "I" that wants to be Enlightened?

Ego.

Where is this ego arising from? It must be arising from somewhere, isn't it. We will see what we can do about this ego, but first let us see where it is rising from. To find this you are not to think, mind you, just to see.

It is just conditioning.

Yes, it is conditioning. There must be the "unconditioned" from where the conditioning rises out of. Where does this concept of conditioning rise from. Find out where the notions of "you" and "me" and "other" arise from. You are not to think to find the answer and not to not think. It is here and now. Find out! Don't give rise to the I-thought and tell me what is? What is *before* the "I"? Go to the point *before* you use "I."

It is like a huge land, like a vast empty desert.

Now don't cling to "I" and stay as thus, stay as vast space. What do you see in this vast space?

Light.

Very good. Now reject this light and the space.

No boundaries.

Very good, no boundaries, no light, no space. All these concepts are over. This is the Unconditioned, That without boundaries. It cannot be spoken of because even words are gross boundaries, thoughts are boundaries, anything you take yourself to be is a boundary. Now speak from Here! Stay Here without boundary, notion, concepts or conditionings. Is there any first person? Is there any second person? Is there any third person? Are there any manifestations, or gods, or heavens?

(laughs and cries) There is a space, and it keeps expanding!

Go on expanding, be expansion itself!

It just keeps on going!

Everybody is touching everybody. All the colors of the rainbow are running together. For millions of years you have searched for this beauty in all directions, but you could not find the right place where you had lost It. Now you are expanding in all directions as It! Beautiful. This is beautiful. This is Love and Beauty. This is what you are. Always you are That. You can do whatever you want because it is your game, your play, your dance!

Dance! Here there is no death, no suffering, nothing trespasses in this. Words or mind cannot trespass into this. Nothing can touch it, nothing can pollute it. This is your place and this is what you are. There is no process or method needed to arrive Here. There is no path or way which will lead you Here. It is so vast that all of the universes are just in one small corner of It. Don't underestimate yourself. Give full value to what you are. It is the Truth. It is always As You Are.

If there is peace in your mind you will find peace with everybody. If your mind is agitated you will find agitation everywhere. So first find peace within and you will see this inner peace reflected everywhere else. You are this peace! You are happiness, find out. Where else will you find peace if not within you? Just keep Quiet, do not stir a thought and you are free. Don't entertain any notions. If you do not entertain just one notion in particular you will be Free. This notion is "I am the body." This is the notion that really troubles you and you go along and reconfirm it every minute of every day with all your relations with other bodies and objects. When this notion is no longer there you will be Free.

In this Freedom you will see the whole cosmos and all the bodies are you and you are all these bodies. Nothing will change, a mountain will be a mountain and a river will be a river, but your viewpoint will change.

So pick up the notion "I am Free" and both notions will leave you. You are neither bound nor free. You just are what you are. Know this and all the notions will leave you. You are not the body, or the mind, or the intellect, or the world. You are something else. Find out! What is this thing? Just keep Quiet and see. Then it will unfold Itself. It will reveal Itself. First keep Quiet.

Questions about Vichar Answered

There must be a tremendously strong effort and decision
to not be washed away by the past and by thought,
or the mind will slip back to impurity and mischief.
There is nothing without this self-effort.
This tremendous effort is easy because it is no effort.
When the circumstances of the vasanas arise

the dormant vasanas will also arise.
So totally devote yourself to intense Self-effort.
Divine faith will help you so jump into the ocean
and you will get help from within.

"I" is the illusion destroyed by inquiry.
Follow the I-thought effortlessly
always in whatever you do.
Always look in the right direction.
You only need a half step into That,
a full step is an activity with a name.
Just as a cloud can hide the sun,
so the I-thought can hide the Self.
So inquire and find the Source of this thought.
During this inquiry do not move any thought,
not even the I-thought.

Give up your preoccupation with "other things" and you will see it.
Everyday vigilantly check upon the trends of mind.
What you think you will become, so do without thought,
and you will return to the natural state.
Then stay as Such,
unattached to thoughts.

Vigilance is keeping aware of what enters the mind-house.
Do not fight with the arising thoughts, but simply watch them.
Do not disturb your mind, and do not divide it.
But even this watching is through mind,
so then strike at the root of the illusion
by inquiring, "who is watching the thoughts?"
Otherwise a "doer" survives as a watcher and this is mind.
In the same way, wanting to kill the mind just creates a "killer"
which can be only effort and movement, only mind itself.
So simply keep Quiet, simply keep Quiet,
simply keep Quiet, and make no effort!
Don't even make the effort
to carry the burden of the I-thought.

Unceasingly keep Nothing.
There is no better partner than this.
Make friends with That which is not involved in activity,
aspire for That which does not dwindle,

not for transient paltry pleasures.
Vigilance and watchfulness must be your habit.
The rising thought is samsara,
but seeing the thought rise is Nirvana.
This is a beautiful dance and romance.
If it does not reveal itself it is because
you are concealing it with the "I"
which you use to love the transient.
Remove this ignorance and the Truth will reveal itself.
This body and mind do not belong to you.
Be wise and keep only what is yours.
Don't run away from the Beloved One, the Unknown.

Checking the outgoing tendencies to objects of attachments
takes the illusory-ness from the illusion.
Withdraw these tendencies to deeply rooted objects,
and return back to the Source,
Be vigilant to watch all arise out of the Silence,
and make no effort.

Thought and "other" is boundary: touch no boundary.
Likes and dislikes are superimpositions: look between them.
Don't be enslaved to the engaged mind;
if you face the past you are lost.
If mind is really hungry
give it the food of inquiry 24 hours a day
and face your Self, face Love.

Inquire "Who am I?"
Patiently, wisely, honestly inquire,
turning your face, Awareness, within.
When you are face to face with Self, only keep Quiet.
This Quietness is no mentation, not even stirring the I-thought.
This Quietness is the peace of "Let there be Peace."
This Quietness is the eternal abode.

*I have several questions which come from the mind again and again
and seem to be needed to be asked, even though they come from the
mind and the source of mind is Emptiness.*

You say that the source of mind is Emptiness. Do you have this experience? You go from question to question to mind to source of mind. Are you traveling with it? If you have arrived at the destination where the train halts, as some trains from Lucknow go only to Delhi, like the Gompti or Shatabdi, do you stay there in the train? If you keep sitting in them they will not move because they are at the destination. Like this the Emptiness is the destination. Tell me what happened there! The train has halted, which means that the thought has halted. So are you sitting in the train or are you pushing the train farther?

I think what hap...

(Angrily) Understand first! Don't waste time! You say that you have returned to Emptiness, what do you see? Is there any search? What is there?

Nothing Papa.

Don't simply ask questions. Mind hides in questions! You must work with a question and be very serious as to what you want. Simply picking up questions from here and there is a waste of time. When you arrive in Emptiness it is the destination and in this Emptiness nothing ever existed, including this person; then who is there? If you find the source of any question the question will suffocate. So remove "but," "when," and "if."

It is just that these questions come again and again.

In Emptiness ask me a question!

Papaji, you say just keep quiet and if a thought arises, watch it, and then keep quiet after it goes.

Yes, this is what I say and what do you have to say about it?

I understand what you are saying.

Understanding is not needed, something more is needed. What will you understand if you are in New York and I give you a map for you to get on a plane to Delhi and in Delhi to get on another plane to Lucknow? This understanding is not enough. You have to get on board! The plane has to carry you!

I have been doing this, Papa.

You do not need doing, what will you do on board? Will you push the plane? (laughs) Simply keep Quiet. They even say this on the plane: "Sit down and fasten your seat belts," that's all! Will you push the plane? Simply keep Quiet and by itself it will move and someone will even bring you a tray of food. This is what it means: don't make any effort. It is for the pilot to take you and you cannot advise the pilot, you are not even allowed to go into the cockpit.

Keeping Quiet means to observe where the thoughts are rising from. There is observation and this observation is translated into English: "Who am I?" Ask "Who am I?" inside the mind. This is also observation. Finding the source of "I" or finding where the thought is arising, I don't think there is any difference. Simply observe. Keep vigilant. Don't make any effort.

Even when I am quiet there is still a sense of individual "me."

When you are quiet you see that someone is quiet. This "I" has to be observed, where does it rise from? Where does this personal individual "I" rise from? Look and tell me what do you see? This is a very good question and it needs experience, not understanding. So when you look at the "I" find where it rises from and tell me what do you see? You will not see the observer or the observed. Concentrate on where the individuality of the individual "I" is rising from. What do you see?

Nothing right now, but I do see that things are waiting to jump up.

Again you have to observe what is waiting to jump up. Again the "I." Again observe that. Do it. Quickly do it.

But you say to observe effortlessly. I must use effort to remember to observe. Otherwise I am lost in my thoughts again.

To see your nose what effort do you make? When you see something very close you do not need effort. When you look at something far away, then you need effort. Now the question is, you are going to look for your own Self, your own Heart, your own Beauty, it is just like searching for your own retina! What effort do you need to see your own retina?

Impossible.

Impossible, yes, yes. Even the retina is away, and That is before the retina. This is what makes the retina able to see, therefore it is impossible to see it. So, I say keep Quiet, don't look for It with your eyes, you can't see It. But through which your eye sees and through which your mind understands, what will you do to see That through which you see and through which you think any thought? Just be Conscious. What effort is needed? Within the ocean you have to be a wave. Let the waves arise, they are still a part of the ocean! How far has the wave gone from the ocean when she arises? She is still a part of the ocean. When the ocean is there, there has to be waves. So what other questions do you have because I won't speak earlier than what you ask for!

In my Zen practice I get quiet, but then a painful pressure arises in my head and my heart as I become more aware of all that is going on within and around me.

But what about the *observer* in the Zen practice? I tell you to observe the observer! The observer has to be observed. Now I tell you to observe the observer and what effort do you need to do this? And if you do it what is the reward and what are the consequences?

To do this turn your face within and let the observer become the object and let the supreme Consciousness look at this observer. Even if you try to understand, this understanding will not touch it. You will never understand this. Understanding will be a relationship between subject and object. What can you understand if you erase the object from your mind? What will you do?

So with any method of teaching you are always dealing with the objects and this will not give you any fruit. Therefore, I tell you keep Quiet and it will be taken care of by itself. Only see that the thoughts are passing, and see where they come from and where they go. You remain a witness; simply witness, whatever happens be a witness. Any circumstances, good or bad, comes and goes. It does not stay. Just observe! A good circumstance comes, it stays and then it goes. *What does not come and does not go is the witness!* When you take care of this, then this witness will be coming and going in front of someone else! Let the witness dance in front of something which has no name. Let this witness come and go as an object. And how to see the position? How to observe the observer? How to witness the witness?

Just Be Consciousness.

Yes, that is it. I remember a story of Saint Kabir.

Kabir had just come out of his mud house and he saw two men fighting. A policeman came out and arrested them. One man says "He has attacked me!" and the other says the same thing. So both were sent to court, but the court cannot decide without a witness. So, the policeman said, "Only Kabir was there to witness this man chopping the hand of the other."

So Kabir was summoned to the court and when he appeared the magistrate asked him, "You were there?"

"Yes, I was there," he said.

"What did you see? Who attacked who first?" asked the magistrate.

He said, "The one who has seen cannot speak. The one who speaks cannot see."

What does this mean? The magistrate was baffled. What does it mean? The eyes have seen, but they cannot speak. The tongue speaks, but it cannot see. (giggles) So the eyes cannot speak as the witness. While the tongue is speaking, but it has not seen so it cannot be believed. So the magistrate was very baffled and set free both of the people. So you need a witness and you can't speak.

(laughing) I can't think either.

Yes, when you see, you become the witness. It is really a joke I tell you!

I want no barriers, I want to surrender to the Self. I am not humble enough because of the ego. I ask you to light this candle from your source of Light.

You speak of ego and you have started to dissolve it, even though everybody likes it. You have worked hard, but this is massaging the ego. Everything that one does just massages the ego, inflates the ego. But this is not the way to be happy. To be happy is to do away with anything that endangers your peace. So, I tell everybody everyday simply find out where the thought arises from. "I will be happy if I will get this object or this person," so this is deception of the ego. Nobody is going to give you happiness in the world. Nobody will give you happiness. To be happy is to keep Quiet. No relationship will give you happiness. No dear ones will give you happiness. They all suck your blood, and when there is no blood they will not look at you. This is the way of the world! But if you are conscious in this life you have a chance to win freedom, for this purpose you came here. Finally you have come here as an intelligent human being with the good luck to come to Satsang. You have all the good points, but what you have to do is clearly understand that when the ego raises its head you have to strike at its root and keep Quiet.

You are after it now, you are going to do it. Don't be disheartened. Simply watch what is happening and discriminate who is the one who will stand at your side eternally and not run away. Everybody will run away.

Papaji, I had such an experience. It was so timeless, there was cool silent bliss. Since I saw a glimpse of myself I have been in so much

194

mental pain, so much I-thought, so much unworthiness.

You have to know that this mental chatter is not going to help you. Know that this unworthiness will not help you. Know that any thought that arises will not help you. Just go on doing this. And why do you use "was" timeless? "Was" is in time! "Was" means past. This is a good experience, why have you thrown it away? Why have you put it in the past? Why did you throw it into the river? You had a diamond in your hand, so why did you throw it in the river? Now you can't find it because it washed away!

There is one river in India, in Bihar, the Padma River where people go to find rubies. They pay royalties to the government to have a 10 by 10-foot plot where they can dig. Maybe they find rubies at 10 feet or at 50 feet or further down, but they do it. One man paid the royalty and went to the river bed, and on his way he stubbed his toe on a rock. He looked at this rock and threw it into the river. A little further on he saw a man dancing "I am rich, I am rich! I will have a wife and a palace, I have found a ruby!" Upon seeing this man's ruby he realized that he had thrown a ruby into the river, but now it was hopelessly lost.

So having this beautiful experience how can you afford to lose it? You have gone for this purpose! You have paid royalty which means this life you have decided to find you own shanti, your own peace, your own love! If you don't use the word "was" what will you lose?

Then it is presence.

So how can you lose Presence? Mind will always try to cheat you, but if you say this body-mind is not mine, then you cheat the mind. But the mind was successful. Mind means thought, thought means "I," isn't it? If you simply look at the "I" then it can't touch you. Do you follow, or no? Simply look at the "I" wherever and whenever it is. If you do not look at it then it will attack you.

My mind was absent...

This is bad grammar I tell you! Why use the word "was"? Mind *means* was, so why do you use a double "was"? When you say mind it means past. One second is enough. This second has nothing to do with time, it is not one of 60 seconds. This second is an instant out of time. Don't look at the time. Don't use "was" and don't even use "is," not even "is." Do you understand? Not even "is!" If you don't use "is," then you will find out who is who.

ॐ

*While staying in Rishikesh I heard about you from many people and
so I decided to come to Lucknow. When I first came to your Satsang
I was surprised to hear how people write to you about their personal
experiences because I thought that Self inquiry led you to the cessation
of identification with thought and emotions.*

Yes, everyday people are writing about their experiences, this is no
surprise. There must be an experience when you are seeing something new
and fresh for the first time. Isn't there an experience the night after the
wedding? But your eyes, your face, and your talk show that you have had no
experience so far. You can find out from the face. Even your voice and body
will show the state of experience because experience will change the whole
being of a person, inside and out. Anyway, you are here now. Don't be
surprised about what people are writing. Someday you too will have that
taste. When your work is finished and the questions have vanished, this is the
experience.

It seems that you have not even inquired. Though you *speak* about
inquiry you did *not* inquire. Otherwise, you would not have asked these
questions.

Can you tell me how to stop identifying with thought and emotions?

Again, by inquiry, everything stops. If you make the inquiry "Who am
I?" everything will stop. Just keep Quiet, stop your meditations, and find the
meditator!

When you say "keep quiet," instantly my mind asks how?

Here you are to do nothing. Simply keep Quiet and if there is any
problem just ask me. Don't do anything, don't think anything. For one
instant don't do anything! All that one thinks must belong to the past and
one does not benefit themselves by thinking of what is dead and in the
graveyard. It is of no use, therefore, do not let your mind go to the past.
Mind means past! If something will happen it will happen just in this instant,
not the past. Don't let your mind drift to the past thought and then you will
see that you are quiet.

Everyone is always thinking of the past and, therefore, they are in
trouble. So I advise you not to do it.

*My mind is like a stubborn goat which keeps butting its head against
the wall, but between the thoughts there is peace.*

This space between two thoughts is another way to have freedom at once. The same is for between two breaths. In between the breath outside and the breath inside there is no time, and this happens sixteen times per minute. Every thought must come from this empty space. Where does your inhalation rise from?

Nowhere.

Yes, and it is the same for thought. This thought must come from emptiness. Before thinking, you are not thinking, and so if you go to that point from where all thoughts arise, that is how inquiry meets the same thing, but it is not explained. It has to be explained. Where does this inquiry come from? Emptiness! Before thought, before inquiry, before breath. The I-thought must disappear if I tell you it comes from nowhere and you are that nowhere and not the thought! This is what I tell you again and again. You have to honor this. You have to honor your origin, from where you came. Then you will find that you have never disappeared, you have been always Here, and all belongs to you. *All you your Self is!* You have just to understand this, not to practice. I do not believe in any practices. You have to feel "I am That" and this will not come by any practice. You do not have to practice to become your Self because you are already That! So like this, this That has no limitations, no frontiers. This That is ever present, everlasting, so you have to be That, not become That!

I have tried for years to be That by finding the meditator, but I can't find it.

Then don't find it, then give up your search. If you are tired then give up your search and ask: "What is there that I have been searching and could not find?" Now don't look for anyone. Give up everything; meditations and searching, and then tell me what is left.

Papaji, I don't quite get it, I am not fully drenched yet, but I feel it is impending Grace!

Why do you put it to future? It means you are not Quiet. Keeping Quiet is the final experience and you don't need anything more. If there is something that you will do in the future it means that you are not quiet. Quiet means inside Quiet. Your mind has to be quiet, not your lips. So try always to keep Quiet internally. If any thought arises then you are not quiet, so let no thought arise. No effort is needed to keep Quiet. Don't make effort and don't allow any thought to be stirred from anywhere. This is called Quietness. If you are successful you are finished, you have nothing more to do.

*(He gives Papaji a drawing of a man hitting a cricket ball with
his bat very hard.)*

I have been playing cricket since my childhood and very much like this
game. Even now I miss Satsang sometimes to watch cricket. What is the
significance? Always I keep a bat in my hands and if any ball, any ego comes,
I hit it. If I miss it I must go to the pavilion because the stumps were drawn
and thrown away. But if I hit hard then the ego goes to the border of the field
and I score a sixer. I have always scored sixers!

Keep your bat ready and when any ball comes you hit it hard. This is a
very good way to keep Quiet. When any thought comes hit it hard and send
it back to the pavilion. I always took the game this way. Always keep a bat
in hand, dreaming with the bat in hand, sleeping with the bat in hand, and
awake with bat in hand. Therefore, you can see me playing cricket! (giggles)

Is it possible to describe the process when the mind turns toward itself?

Turn your mind and I will see what happens. Wherever it is now grooved
or posted turn it from there, turn it from the object to where there is no
object. Mind cannot be a mind unless there is an object! There is no meaning
to "bat" if there is no "ball." Turn your mind so that it does not touch any
object, then what will happen? After turning your mind away from its objects
describe what is the situation of the mind. I can't turn it for you, you have
to turn it yourself. You turn your mind every night when you sleep. When
you turn your mind inward how do you feel? Your mind is turned when you
sleep. How do you explain this?

You would show a different face if you would turn your mind. If you can
describe something, your mind is still functioning and it is not turned. When
you turn your mind there is no-mind, no describer, no description, nothing to
be described. This is after you turn your mind inward. Do it. Don't just speak
about doing it.

Inquiry is so simple. You can do it anywhere you like. You can do it in
the home or office or in the market. Simply carry this thought always, try to
understand, "What is all this?" "Where does this world arise?" "Who is
suffering?" "How to get rid of suffering?" Inquire, "Who am I?" It doesn't
take much effort to keep this on wherever you go. One day you will be
advised to attend Satsang and your inquiry will be over. Everyday people
come here for a few hours, get benefited and go back to their countries.

My energy has been rising for two nights now.

Your allergy is rising now? Did you say energy or allergy? (giggles) If you are happy with this energy let it play, keep it up. If she is troublesome then take care. I will explain to you how to make good use of this energy. I advise you to dam it, and channel it. During the rainy season the rivers can cause floods so it is better to dam and channel it. These channels will be useful for everybody and for you. The channel is: find out "Who am I?" Do not let it freely flow. Then it is up to you to channel it. It will be under your control because you have dammed it, and it will go wherever you like. If you bring it to this peace you can channel it toward the heart and ask what is this channel good for. You only keep Quiet. This is also energy. The best use of energy is this: keep Quiet! It will take tremendous energy to keep Quiet.

When I ask this question "Who am I?" I can't keep quiet!
Doubts come up, but I want peace.

You are not Quiet and therefore, you have not asked this question. You have to ask this question to the mind itself. Ask this question to the source of this thought.

First understand the question "Who am I?" Where does it come from? From the walls? From the books? Where does this "who" come from? Ask this question to this "who"! When you speak of not being quiet this itself is bringing you out of silence. Inquiry should bring you home. It should not bring you outward. Now ask the question, Where does the "who" come from? Turn your face backward. Everyone's mind is working forward and therefore they are in trouble, but you have to work in the reverse. Go back in the reverse and find out where "who" rises from.

I can't find the Source!

What is there before the "who"? There is nothing to do, just simply find out where this cup is rising from as this cup (he points to his water glass) rises from the table. So I say, where does this question arise from?

I can't find it.

Which is this "I" which cannot find it?

My mind.

Mind and "I" are the same thing. What is there before the mind? When I arises, it arises from somewhere. Where does it arise from? Where does the source of the ocean arise from? Like this, look below and find where the "I" rises from.

I can't see.

A seer is needed when you look out to an object, but I don't want you to touch the objects, I want you to turn back. Simply see the source of the "I," where does she arise from?

You are in the habit of seeing objects, but this One that we speak about cannot be objectified because it is not an object. Reverse your mind to That which is not an object! Objects disappear and appear. Your body is an object, That is not.

I can't perceive it.

It is before the "I" so of course "I" cannot perceive it. So don't touch this "I." "I" is mind, thought. Don't touch it. Answer me but don't touch the "I."

I can't...

I said don't touch the "I"!

...keep this Self inquiry maintained constantly.

You need not do it constantly. Only once you need to do it. It needs no repetition. Only find out, "Who am I?" and you will get the answer Now. Ask, "Who am I?" and listen, don't think about it. Simply ask once and don't think about it and don't make any effort to find the answer. Do you follow what I say?

Do not keep any thought in your mind, even of this inquiry, which also is a thought, and don't make any effort. Wanting to keep up this inquiry is arrogance! Only ask once and the answer will reveal itself. You can't command or demand. Allow time for it to reveal itself to itself. It is not an object, nor is it the subject, so don't keep any object in your mind. Why do you force this happening, this revelation, this Reality. Let it take care of you. You just surrender to this Reality and keep Quiet. \

Keep Quiet and allow it to reveal itself. When you are not quiet it will not reveal its revelation. It reveals, it does not "show up."

It is like Being.

Whatever it is. Being is Revelation. You can't compel this Being to do anything. When you are Quiet this Being reveals itself. Its name is Being, not "had been," not "would be," but Being!

ॐ

Vichar: Self Inquiry

I know that you say that no effort is needed but I am so lazy I need effort just to start.

It is always Here, there is no starting. Even while sleeping you can do it. You are not to begin it, you are to Be It 24 hours a day.

It seems that I need effort to do what you have been talking about.

What effort do you need to drop something. Any object which comes on your head simply shake off!

One man had a 100 kg of rock on his head in the hot summer heat. He went to a man and asked for help and the man said, "Here you take 10 kg of iron. Iron is better than rock." So now it is 110 kg. Another man gave brass, it being better than iron, but now he has 120 kg on his head.

So it is. Wherever you go they will load some weight on your head, on your mind. Who is the teacher who does not load any weight on your head. They all say, "read this book" and "do this practice" and therefore they just add to the burden of your mind. Don't accept a teacher who gives you any weight, any thought, any practice, and Vipassana or Upassana. Don't take him as a teacher. A teacher doesn't add any weight. Only preachers add weight. You must have been with a preacher before.

Just simply keep Quiet. Before your birth you were quiet. After your death you will be quiet so why don't you be quiet right now. True relaxation is keeping Quiet. When you think there is suffering, and you can't relax. When you are happy and relaxed you are not thinking. Your happiness does not come from the objects of your desires once you attain them. Happiness comes from the cessation of the desire for the object. When there is no more desire, there is no thought, and there is happiness.

Most people don't even notice their thoughts and are washed away in the current of the river. Be vigilant! Whenever the thought comes, watch it, then there will be no thought. Only when you go through the routine of life without thinking will you really enjoy it. Whatever comes, let come. Whatever goes, let go. You simply keep watching.

Meditation is when the mind is free and not holding thoughts.
Let the thoughts come and go, but do not run after them.

If you turn your head and watch someone walk down the street you are lost. Better to just let it go. This is the happy way of life. Let trains on the platform come and go and get into the one which is going your way. Don't make friends in the transit lounge, for they are not going where you are going and you will only be distracted. This world is a transit lounge of people and your mind is the transit lounge of thought, it is not your permanent home.

So don't make friendships with these people who will disappear. Make friends with one who is traveling with you on the same flight. Make a friendship with That.

I want to be happy and remain dancing, but I can't keep my mind and heart from fighting together.

This fight is not possible because you can only fight with the mind, not with the heart. When heart is there there is no fight because there is no-mind. You will only fight when you do not have any relation with your own Self. Then only the mind is the commander-in-chief of your armies of thought. So look at the heart and try again.

I try to look at heart, but I so easily get attacked, and trapped, by the functioning of the senses. I cannot stop the functioning of the mind enough to see just heart.

The functioning of the senses is the observation of objects through one of the five senses. When the objects are seen by the senses who is aware of the senses? This you should have done. Who is aware of the senses? You can call it intellect. Intelligence, or buddhi, knows the function of the senses. Who is aware of the intellect?

The mind is aware of the intellect that decides. Then come the senses and then the objects. Who is aware of the mind? Call it "I"! "I" is aware of the intellect, intellect is aware of the mind, mind is aware of the senses, and senses are aware of the objects. Who is aware of the "I"?

Now you are going back to no-thought-ness, to Silence, to Peace, to the Source. This is how to stop the functions of all things: Find where the energy is coming from, find what is always at peace, find what is never disturbed.

How do you know that you are aware? How do you know the "I" is aware? You have to go even deeper than the I-thought. What could be earlier than the "I?" Who decides that you are "I"?

You are five steps behind the senses and there nobody can go anytime. This is the source of peace, your home, and this is also called Freedom or Consciousness. We can take another step back, even before Consciousness. This is how to stop thought: Go toward your own source and find out where you are going, where is your place. This will keep you Quiet. Find who is beyond the senses, mind, intellect, and "I." Beyond the "I" is Consciousness.

Always I ask myself, "Who am I?" to go beyond the mind and to find this Consciousness, the heart.

What do you mean by "always"? It is not like eating food everyday! You

Vichar: Self Inquiry

have to ask only once and then find the answer. What does it mean if you are always asking the question but never getting the answer? If a student goes to the examination hall and writes the questions over and over for three hours what marks will he get? (giggles) You have to give the answer. Once only read the question and then spend the remaining time with the answer. This will give him success whereas filling the whole page with questions will not! So once this question is in your mind find the answer. Only once you have to inquire "who" is inquiring.

I always get the same answer.

(laughing) That is because you are asking the same question! When you get the real answer you will be in Peace and there will be nothing more needed.

But Nisargadatta's Guru told him to constantly attend to the sense of "I am" and to give attention to nothing else. I did this and got relief for a few moments.

In his case it wasn't for a few moments, but it was for his total life, his total Being!

Pay total attention to "I Am" and nothing else.
Leave everything behind and go with great Love.

Your attention was mixed with fears and so your relief was only for a few moments. His attention was fixed by faith in his Guru and so his relief is permanent.

ॐ

There is a practice where you sit opposite of someone and keep asking each other "Who are you?" What do you think of it?

You have to depend on nothing and nobody. This is the real experience. You don't need any aid. Everybody is spending their time with partners, even animals do this. Though everybody does this for peace of mind, I have never seen anyone in Peace as a result of it, not even the kings.

It is better to find out who you are when you sleep and that changeless person will arise the next morning. Practice bringing this sleep state into the waking state. When others are awake, you sleep and when others are sleeping you stay awake. Others sleep with their desires of other bodies, but you sleep to that and decide to stay with your Self. Their sleep is your wakefulness and their wakefulness is your sleep. That is the meaning. In the day from 5 a.m.

to 10 p.m. inquire who was happy to sleep. This inquiry will end at 10 p.m. Always continuously keep this inquiry while walking, talking and working in the office or in the home. This inside inquiry must stay as such. Like you have a toothache you should inquire. When you have a toothache you always have a toothache, whether you are in the office, home or speaking to people. You don't forget that you have a toothache. Like that make this inquiry.

I will do it.

Very good. You must have heard of this practice from some ashram and you believed them. Only when you don't believe what everybody else says can you question "Who am I?" Only if you don't believe and don't trust what others say will you go and find out for yourself. Don't believe me, believe only yourself. Then what will happen?

I don't know.

Ah, yes, you do not know because this cannot be known. You see the joke now? It can't be known!

If you feel I am ripe will you help me get the joke right now?

To test your ripeness I will ask you a question. Can you keep quiet for one second? This is my test for ripeness. Just for one second do not think and do not make effort. If you can do this you are perfectly ripe and deserve freedom Just Now! If you can't do this then wait for the next cycle of transmigration. This you must tell me, that you can spend one second with me not thinking and not making any effort. If you can, I promise you peace.

Papaji, I think I need your Zen stick!

(giggles) I have a Zen stick and I use it sometimes like a Saint once upon a time in China did.

The king of China had heard that there was a Master who gave instant Enlightenment and so he went to see him. This Saint always lived in a boat and so the king went there on his elephant and had one leg planted on the bank of the river and the other one about to be planted on the boat. At that moment this Zen monk thrust an oar into the chest of the king who then fell into the water. Of course the king wanted some teaching, but when he was thrown into the water his mind was blank and he was very happy, and that was the teaching.

Sometimes I use this teaching with the Zen stick, but usually I love people, though it takes more time. (giggles) Therefore, if you don't understand in three days I will use my Zen stick which is hiding here. You have to decide and later on you will be called for a song.

ॐ

Who am I with all of these sensations and experiences? Who am I if this name and form is taken away? Identifications with the particulars have estranged me from the Self. When I inquire "Who am I?" I find prejudice, hopes, and memories of associations.

This is not right understanding. You have not understood the correct meaning of "Who am I?" If you find memories when you practice "Who am I?" then you don't understand the practice, let alone the three words. What memory appears when you utter the word "who"?

At this moment, nothing.

And how about at the later moment? This is the next moment already. Again find out what is "who."

Now there is no time, before was just an intellectual inquiry.

Why speak of that moment when you are here? When born why speak of being a fetus?

It is all gone, all experiences are over, there is only space.

So one word is over and it brought you to "all gone." Now utter the word "am" and what do you feel, what do you hold?

Just presence.

So "who" was space, and "am" is presence. Now "I" is left. Simply speak "I," only "I," not I-am-so-and-so. What is the object or subject when you utter the word "I"? What do you feel? What do you touch? What do you see?

"I" translated in Sanskrit is "Aham" so if "I" is confusing then use the word Aham. In Sanskrit "Who am I?" is Ko Ham! The answer to this is Aham Brahmasmi, "I am That!" So where are the memories in this? It is the Vedavakya and you can't dispute it. It is the experience of the Rishis 25,000 years ago. They came to this sentence. Inquiry started thousands of years ago.

So first understand the meaning, just the meaning, no practice is needed. This is what we speak about here: inquire into your own Self. If you do not understand this I can repeat it again and again: simply speak "Who am I?"

and then find the source of "I." This is the meaning of inquiry. Kabir says:

> Just throw away all thoughts of imaginary things
> and stand firm in That which you are.
> Friend, hope for the Guest while you are still alive.
> Jump into the experience while you are still alive.
> Think and think while you are alive.
> What you call salvation belongs to the time after death.
> If you do not break your ropes while you are still alive
> do you think that ghosts will do it after?
>
> The idea that the soul will join with the Ecstatic
> just because the body is rotting is a fantasy.
> What is found now is found then.
> If you find nothing now you will simply end up
> with an apartment in the city of death.
> If you make Love with the Divine Now,
> in the next life you will wear the face of satisfied desire.
> So plunge into the Truth, find out who the Teacher is.
> Believe in That great Sound.

When I am in your presence I do feel a certain peace.

What do you mean by a "certain peace"?

My mind becomes quiet and I am Here, nowhere else.

But then something else happens?

Yes, my mind takes over.

Mind must have something to disturb it. Where is this disturbance?

I know that I should be more vigilant of these disturbances, but isn't this vigilance a trick of the mind?

This vigilance, which you must have is not a trick of the mind. The trick of the mind is when you are not vigilant! Then the mind will play tricks. If you are really vigilant then there is no mind to play tricks. I will tell you how to be vigilant. Now you are in sitting front of me. Now be vigilant of what is instantly in front of you, in this present moment. Don't look to the past.

Be vigilant of the present circumstances.
This is quite enough to give you happiness.

> Be vigilant only of this Moment!
> When this happening goes, don't cling to it.
> Clinging to past circumstances is the trouble with everybody.
> This is the cause of suffering and misery.
>
> What has happened cannot be brought back,
> so it is reasonable to not cling to it.
> Simply do not cling to past circumstances.
> Don't cling to the past.

If you are wise you will see that there is no use in clinging to the past things which are over now. You have to understand this somehow. This is enough to lead a peaceful and beautiful life while you enjoy the circumstances offered to you by nature. All these disturbances and thoughts are like rats in the home of peace, so you have to be like a cat. The rats come because you forget that you are a cat. Be watchful of your thoughts like a cat is watchful of rats. Be vigilant of the thought and see where it rises from. Be watchful, watch where the thoughts are rising from. Now tell me what the current thought is.

(she laughs a very knowing laugh)

This is the smile of the cat after it has eaten the rat! When there is no thought everything disappears, and then you can laugh. This is Now, this is not then. Do your job, be vigilant and watchful and tell me if a disturbing thought, or any thought, can arise. Like this, be watchful and pounce on the rats that arise before you. Simply be watchful and don't do anything.

I feel that I am proceeding step by step toward the experience of the Self. Can you guide me more?

> Experience is not bound by any step or by no-step,
> by any state or by no-state!
> The mind must be still without carrying any person or object.
> Be careful! Don't let the mind run to concepts
> which will trick and disturb you, so be very careful!
> Look to where the mind runs.
> Do this without taking any steps.
> Just watch the mind's activity: where it goes, what it wants.
> Be careful, day and night, whether you are meditating
> or in the marketplace.

That is the guidance that I have for you. Follow it and you will be peaceful and happy.

ॐ

*I always ask "Who am I?" but then I only face a blank wall and
no answer comes.*

No answer will come! Who are you asking this question to? From whom
do you expect an answer and what kind of a reply should you get? Are you
expecting a fax? This is a question that you ask of your own Self and you
won't get a reply because you do not need one! It is not a question to be
answered, It is Being.

"Who am I?" is answered in being!
"I am my Self." That's all.

You have made a decision to solve this question. You will be successful
if you don't give up this decision wherever you go. It won't take long.

*I asked "Who am I?" and the "am I" became I Am. But "who" is
stubborn.*

Where is the "who" in the I Am. "Who" is only in the question, not in
the answer and so is finished in That I Am. All worry and suffering is also
finished.

Simply Be and that is all.
Have Faith in this I Am,
which doesn't refer to any person.
All Beings are this I Am
which is seated in the cavity of your Heart.

Will you give me the name of this I Am?

This I Am has no name or form. It can't be touched or tasted, but to It
you must give your heart and mind in Devotion. So I will give you the name
Shyam, the blue-hued person. This blue is the blue of depth, like the ocean
or the blue sky. The sky is not blue but due to its depth it appears so. The
sky and ocean are formless and nameless and so Shyam, the color of depth,
is your name from now on. Shyam is also attraction, the attraction of the
Divine, so don't be surprised if you start attracting this Divine.

Vichar: Self Inquiry

You say Enlightenment can occur in the snap of a finger. I am here only briefly so how can this happen?

It will happen in no-time, but you speak of "briefly," which is in time. You are counting in time, so it will not work in a million years of snapping. There is no-time in a fingersnap and this is what is meant. Your mind is full of time.

I have experienced peace and happiness through inquiry, but then the fear of the unknown comes and I experience doubt.

How long does this peace last?

Just minutes and then thought comes.

Why do you give up this happiness and what do you give it up for? Your decision to leave happiness is not a good one. Abide in Peace. You have been disturbed for millions of years, why go back to this disturbance once you have found Peace? Understand this. Discriminate between what gives you Peace and what disturbs you. Whatever is better, follow That.

I can't find the seer which will give me peace, I can't.

If you cannot find the seer it is a good experience. You see through the glasses, but the glasses cannot see. See what is behind the glasses, what is behind the eyes. Who is enabling the seer to see? A dead man's eyes cannot see because the one who sees is no longer there. Again, try to see the seer.

If I ask "Who is thinking?" I experience more thoughts and sensations. How can I still the chattering distractions? How can I dissolve? The small breaks from the thoughts don't release me from my passions.

It is not true! The break will release you! When do you say that it will not release you? During the break, during the space between the thoughts or after the space?

After.

And when it is after you always think of the future. Between the thoughts do you see the past, or the future, or the passions?

Nothing.

This is what we speak of.

209

How can I make this space larger?

You can make this space infinitely large because all of space comes from this Space. You can make it larger by asking this question, "How can I make it larger?" while still in the space. During the space between thoughts if you ask this question "I" will give you the right answer. Ask Now!

(The man is absorbed by silence)

He is enjoying Now. He is sucking the sweetness. He is very close to his Beloved. He is one inch from the lips of his Beloved. He is a young man so I must use metaphors like this (giggles) because the classic metaphors from the Upanishads won't work on such a young man.

So jump and merge with the Oneness
and even this will finish.
I am still enjoying this same sweetness,
(His throat chokes with Love)
so much has come Here.
It is as easy as that, but nobody watches it.
Just watch this thing, go close.
Go close and there is no past or future,
no desire, no existence, no non-existence, no creation,
and That is the end.

Very nice, I am very happy with the young boys who get it.

How can I switch off the watcher? I see so much darkness and often lose all clarity.

When you see the darkness you must be in the light in order to see the darkness. You can't see the darkness while in darkness. You are the seer of the darkness and the darkness is the object, so you must be the Light. When you face away from the light you see only your shadow, the darkness. Turn toward the light and you will see only light, not your shadow. Turn your back on the shadow and face the light. This is up to you now. If you see the illusion you are Enlightened, but if you think that you are enlightened you are in the illusion! (giggles) So find out who sees the darkness. Who sees the darkness? To whom is darkness an object of sight? Find out now, who sees the darkness.

You must stay Quiet to find this and do not make any effort. Keep still. Then there will be no darkness. Don't even stir a thought of the darkness in your mind.

When I do inquiry I get such bad headaches. Can you give me some advice?

If you feel a headache it must be that you are fighting with this inquiry, fighting to know who you are. Then only there is stress. Your headache is a result of effort.

The right way to inquire is to simply ask, "Who am I?" and "where does this inquiry come from?" Take this very lightly and not like you are about to cross over a mountain. Here you are not to go anywhere or to make any effort. Simply relax and look at what happens and then discriminate where the "I" is living. First clarify your mind and find out where the "I" is. Once this is ascertained follow the path to where it is. Find out what vehicle you need to use to go there, a car? A plane?

You will find that you do not need to go anywhere to get to the "I." Instead all that you have to do is stop all the movement of the mind and you are Here. As you don't need a rickshaw in your house you don't need to go anywhere to find the "I." Inquiry removes tension, it doesn't give you tension.

One part of my attention seems to watch stillness while another part struggles with thoughts causing the tension.

This is a good practice: keep attention on your diamond and keep the thieves away from it; keep still and be aware of thought. If you keep aware you will not have any thought because no thought comes when you watch. When you do this you are naturally in Awareness itself.

I see that I have an intention to look inward to Stillness, but you teach that there should be no intention.

No tension, no intention, simply attention. No struggle between the in and the out, just stay relaxed and at ease.

This I learned in the army: standing at attention and then at ease. Also pranayama helps because you have to hold your breath when you aim and fire your rifle in order to be 10 for 10 on the range like I was. Speaking of the army, tomorrow there will be tanks, modern weapons, and school girls marching on Hazrat Ganj for Republic Day.

Would you advise me to go to Ramanashram and inquire there?

The Grace is there as it is Here so it doesn't matter. What matters is that you make the best of whatever circumstance that you are in. Your time must be utilized in a perfect way. Don't lag behind, but have a strong decision that you will do it.

As I love the caves of Arunachala, I want to enter the cave of the heart and stay there.

> This Here and Now
> *is* the cave of the Heart.

In the books they talk about the cave of the heart and so you must have your ideas about it from there. Your desire to find this cave takes you out of it, out of the Here and Now. Then you lose the experience of the cave and search for this cave which never existed. Don't try to live in a cave because this cave is just a concept. You can only live in Now.

When you live in This you will not have any desires for anything else; likewise, you will only be in This when you give up all desires, even the desire to be in It. Give up all desires to stay here or there or anywhere and give up the desire for "this" and for "that." Give up all desire.

How can I give up all desires?

> By keeping Quiet!

It seems to me that if there is still an inner dialogue going on, then mind has only been suppressed and Enlightenment cannot happen.

The objects of the inner dialogues are only from the past and so this chatter must be stopped, it must be controlled. This dialogue is only memory and it has to be controlled.

I thought that Self Realization had nothing to do with self-control.

This self-control is with small "s" and refers to controlling the mind, the thoughts of the mind. Self control is when your mind is not leaking anything perishable, when your mind touches nothing that fades. No clinging to the past, no thoughts, no expectations for any future. Keeping mind between past and future is mind control and this is your face. This is not so easy. People have been trying to do this for so long. Five thousand years ago Arjuna asked Krishna how to control the mind which is as difficult to grasp as air. Krishna said:

> "By Abhyasa, practice, and Vairagya, non-attachment,
> you will control the mind.

Vairagya is being non-attached to objects.
Abhyasa is bringing the mind back from its objects
and establishing it in me."

So sit quiet and watch the mind. It will want to go and enjoy the past experiences and enjoyments. Bring it back. If you are aware of the thief it will not steal from you, but if you are not aware then the thief will not let you be happy. It will loot the property of peace. This happens everyday and we enjoy it. We actually make friends with the snake. Keep after this inner dialogue and it will stop, if you have strong determination. All these objects of the mind are only projections. Only when you stop the projecting will you be happy. When the projection is finished then only the screen is left. This screen is the same before, during, and after the projections.

When mind stops there is no projection,
This is the blissful state.

What about all the spiritual practices that people use to reduce their uneasiness and increase their peace. Will this stop the projections?

Various teachers and traditions speak of different things which may temporarily control the mind, but again it rises when you are out of this practice. These practices will not remove the uneasiness so quickly. But if you follow Krishna's advice it will completely eradicate the uneasiness. Actually, I don't give any exercise or practice because all practice is in time and is in mind. What I recommend is to simply stay Quiet, don't make any effort.

Stay Quiet, don't make effort, don't think.
This is all you have to do now. Do this now.

I try to stay quiet, but I don't feel relaxed.

Give up the desire for relaxation and tell me what is left.

I still slightly feel that I am bound!

If you know you are bound you are no longer bound
because by knowing the bondage
you separate yourself from it, you objectify it.
With this release the "I" that was bound pours into Consciousness
like a river pours into the ocean.

(He starts smiling and is unable to speak.)

Tell me what is left, your 32 teeth are telling me, why don't you? Your whole face and eyes are different. What is it?

Is it energy?

There is no difference between energy and intellect. Intellect is energy, so are the thoughts it controls. I want you to find out where this energy comes from to discriminate, then to think with the mind and then to act with the senses. Even the objects of the senses are energy only. Where does this fountain of energy come from?

This comes from Atman-Self. This is what is seen in the Quietness. You are this Self itself. This Self is the Unknown, the Emptiness. All waves rise from this Emptiness and are thus formulated and become intellect, mind, senses and objects. The only reason why people are not happy and peaceful is that they do not realize that they are Atman. Once you know this you can enjoy this samsara as an ocean enjoys its waves.

I feel that I have experienced this but it is transient. The stillness comes and goes.

(laughs) This is not Stillness! It is a concept of stillness that you provide to the mind. Like you provide attention to something beautiful, so you are providing this concept to your mind to enjoy. You see a flower and you call it beautiful. A goat will call the same flower food and eat it before your eyes. What is provided to the mind differs from person to person and what includes differences is not It. A diamond is precious to a jeweler, but is concentrated carbon to a chemist.

So you choose what is given and whenever there is a choice it cannot give you Eternal rest. Eternal rest and Peace is characterless. It can't be chosen because it is already always there.

You can't find true Peace
so don't try to search for it.
What is left when you give up searching?

This seems so easy!

It is easy. You complicate it! It is simple.

Don't make any effort, stay Quiet
and the noisy surface dialogues will cease.
Then the substratum will rise up to the top.
It is simple. Follow this. Do you see it?

I don't see anything.

Yes, you are That Anything. You are that Seer which is Consciousness, not the object to be seen. You are the Witness who sees the activity.

I try to find the source of thought, but I get so much resistance from my mind, even though I try very hard.

You are not to try, and there is no difference between thought and mind. There is no thought without mind and no mind without thought. All this is the mind trying to survive:

When a fish is dying it is more active
and so mind becomes very active in the last few minutes
like a fish flopping out of the water.
This fish has troubled you for so long so now feast on it.
All you can do is not think and not try.

Thinking brings you to the past which doesn't exist. So not thinking is the only way to stay here in Peace. In the night when you are in the sleep state, you are happy and at peace, but in the waking state you are thinking and so you end up suffering because mind is there. In deep sleep you are happy and you don't even know what this happiness is, you are simply happy without any reason. You know that you have been happy because when you awake your friends ask you how you slept and you reply "I slept very well, I had no dreams." So you are happy, but you don't know where this happiness comes from.

The happiness which Is when there is no thought,
the happiness you experience in the deep sleep state,
the happiness which has no known source,
is your own True Nature.

But if you think you will suffer.
So sleep in the day and keep Quiet in the night.
This means simply: don't think.

It means that most people are asleep to their true nature and awake to the world in order to carry out the actions which will fulfill their desires. Very few keep awake to themselves and asleep to the world. Let people execute their desire based activities, but you sleep. "I am That" is the waking to which most people sleep. It is so easy you see!

I don't think I am the mind, I think I am That!

I told you not to think! What is your experience then? Just for half of a second do not think. Do it Now! Go no way and you will be in Peace. You are not to make any attempt. This attempting is just the mind disturbing the mind. Don't make any attempt because Peace is already there. Any attempt to find Peace is throwing a stone into a calm lake. Peace is already Here. You just disturb it by running outside. Don't make any effort for Peace and what will you feel? When you don't make any attempt there is no mind, but when you try to make any attempt there rises the mind which is going to disturb you. Don't make any attempt.

As I move toward no-effort...

What do you mean by moving toward no-effort? What is this movement? Don't move!

Is there a process to become silent?

There is no process. To disturb your mind you need process, but to stay silent there is no process. Stay in Satsang, stay Quiet, always have love with your own Self. You are not to win it by any attempt or effort. Simply stay Quiet. If any thought rises, simply find out where it came from.

Now I only think of not thinking.

This, of course, is also thinking! Find out where the thought of not thinking arises from. Stay in Satsang and don't miss the golden opportunity which is looking into your eyes. Merge with that so that it becomes complete identification.

What is the difference of being the Oneness by doing Self-inquiry or by spontaneous Grace?

Inquiry is mind and is effort. Spontaneous Divine Grace is no effort and no-mind. Inquiry is conducted by mind and is in time. But there is no limitation by mind or time in Grace. Nothing needs to be done with or without effort. It happens by itself. Grace is such a strong and indescribable thing. It is always there, but you do not accept it. Grace is what you call the effort to come to Satsang. You say you've come here by plane, train or road, but I tell you that you've come here only by Grace. This is the difference. Except by Grace, nobody comes to Satsang.

ॐ

Vichar: Self Inquiry

I am sorry to waste your time, but I want to be crystal clear on the method of Atma Vichar.

You have just been repeating what I say to you and not doing it! If I tell you to go to a restaurant and have lunch, and you say "Go to a restaurant and have lunch," what will the use be? This is what you have done. I didn't say to revise what I tell you. I told you to keep Quiet and yet you speak and write so much. You are carrying around the concept of Atma Vichar like a boulder on your head!

But nothing has been happening.

How can anything happen when you are only repeating? I told you to keep Quiet and instead of keeping quiet you only keep saying that I told you to keep Quiet! If you want to say anything you should say the results of keeping Quiet. You didn't leave the mind, ego and the body you only talk about it!

I told you that if thoughts arise to be indifferent to them. Keep Quiet and make no effort and there will only be Awareness of awareness. Don't repeat the things that I speak of, but have an experience.

So this is the approach I should have?

There is no approach at all! Just keep Quiet. Stay wherever you are, just keep Quiet. Where do you have to approach for Quietness? Just keep Quiet.

In Bhagavan's Summa Iru he doesn't give details on how to keep quiet.

Just keep Quiet! What details do you need?

Is keeping quiet like japa, tapas and meditation?

No, don't repeat any japa or do any meditation. Just stay Quiet for one second. This is what is needed.

I had a strong experience in 1978...

You are still repeating 1978 and now it is 1995! Don't even repeat 1995, much less 1978. '78 is dead. Don't keep it in your mind. You have to love the Self, if you don't you are rejected by the Self. Self stands with extended arms waiting for you, but you look somewhere else! "Come my child, it is enough! Now come to me and I will give you rest." But you don't listen, you just look to something else. Whose fault is this? The Beloved is waiting for you, but you are looking toward the red lights.

I can't press you, so you do as you like. This is what Bhagavan told to Arjuna "Fight these enemies, kill them, for they are already dead. Get up and fight." And he did. Bhagavan told him to do it and he did it, he didn't ask any further questions nor did he repeat the instructions. He stood up, bow and arrow in hand, and finished them. God was there as his charioteer. God is *your* charioteer. Do as he bids you to do and don't simply repeat it. If you don't do it then you think that you are rejected by Him.

🕉

Is it important to bring "Who am I?" into the context of my psychological therapy? I feel there is a seed in me which will grow into the bringing of the message to the people.

The tiller has tilled the land and the seed has been sown. Fertilizer has been used, but the sprout will not come until there is rain. This is your case exactly. But if it doesn't rain the chemicals of the fertilizer will destroy the seed. Now you have come to the place where all the 12 months have rain and now you are sprouted out. Without rain nothing will happen, but in the rainy season you don't even need fertilizer. Just throw the seed anywhere and it will sprout. I hope you understand this. In the same way you must plant the seeds into the minds of your clients so that they do not spiritually starve. You must be the rain.

I don't know how to be the rain.

To be rain you have to remember where the rain and the clouds come from. They must have come from the ocean where they rise, then they come and strike the mountains and rain.

So now look at your own mother, the ocean, where one day you were when you evaporated and became clouds. Looking at the ocean means to look at the source of rain, and you will be taken over by the sun. Now you have clouds and so you move toward the north and strike the Himalayas and become rain. It is so easy, it is not difficult!

Is it possible to go in and beyond mind anytime that one chooses?

There is no going in and no going out and no choice.

You are not to make the choice to go in or out. If you are choiceless...

Then I am finished!

Yes! There is no choice, not even, "I want to be free," because all choice

218

is from the mind: I choose this and I reject that.

Is it always a gift then?

This is quite true. It is always a gift. But gifts imply a giver and a receiver. Is it not the same person? So if there is no giver and no receiver then what gift is there? Yet, it is a gift. This means that it is that which cannot be gifted because it is always there. How can you give the necklace on your neck to your own Self? It is like a woman looking for a child which she is carrying unconsciously on her hip. Finally she says that she has found the child, but what can this find be when the child was already there? So there is appearance of finding your Self.

You need a reliable person with authority to tell you where to look for what you are searching for. Then the search will be over. In this way you will know that it is already there and this knowing is Awareness aware of Itself.

Your questions are very good because it is absolutely necessary to dissolve all your doubts. It is a good work that you are doing and you will be successful, but first all your doubts must be removed. These doubts are "Where to search for it?" and "How far must I go?" Actually, you are not to go anywhere and you are not to understand anything.

So this search will be over when you see a teacher
who shows you it is Here.

Where does Consciousness come from?

Trying to understand or describe the Consciousness which is aware of the Consciousness which asks the question, "Where does Consciousness come from?" is a joke. You can't understand it!

Can you pull me from understanding into Consciousness? Can it be done?

No it should not be done. It is Undone. When you don't do it, then it happens. When you do something then confusion will happen. Therefore, don't do anything. Then you will arrive in Consciousness. Don't give rise to anything that you can do, or to anything that you have done. Now sit free of these doings and not-doings. Then you will see what Consciousness is.

How can I fully abide in the Self?

The Self is the abode of everything and you are already abiding in Self. You are always in Self and yet you forget and think that you have to do some practice. But you don't need any practice. That Self which you attain by practice is not the real Self. Self is present everywhere always and is unattainable. How can you separate from it? Where are you that you could possibly be out of Self?

These kind of doubts appear only to those who have not yet had experience. You will know that you have been the Self itself all the time. Now you don't see this because you have been busy elsewhere, seeking elsewhere some object, so you could not have the experience. Don't look for any practice to take you to the Self because the Self is always Here and Now. Where can you go and leave the Self?

Find out who you are. Everyday we deal with this question here in Satsang. You must find out for yourself Who You Are! Solve this question for yourself or it is all just intellectual understanding. You don't need intellect or mind to understand this. Simply keep Quiet for one moment. Then you will know who you are.

I feel near to something but I don't get it.

What do you want to get?

The things that are happening here all the time.

You can never get it, It is not an object to get.
You cannot objectify It, It is the subject.

Subject cannot be seen, or attained or achieved with any kind of effort, Subject is the Subject. You are that Subject, what do you lack? What do you miss? You are the Seer, not the seen nor the sight, the Seer, the indweller of the house, the indweller of existence, the hub, the center of existence. That is the Ultimate Truth.

You have not to proceed anywhere or to arrive anywhere. If you get rid of all this proceeding and arriving, all of these notions and intentions, then what do you see? Who are you? How do you feel? Even the intention, "I have to stay in Silence!" takes you out of Silence. Give up all notions of staying anywhere. What are you thinking right now?

That sometimes I do not understand it.

What sometimes? There are two sometimes, which should we think about? The sometimes Here or the sometimes there?

When I am Here.

So let us speak of the "sometimes" which is here and now. But when it is here and now it is "Notime," and there is no question of "sometime." In this very moment there is no time. Can you call it past? Can you call it future? Can you even call it present? If the future and past is not there, present is meaningless and vanishes also, you see? So "sometime" belongs to notions you got from somewhere. It is not your experience. Dive into this moment and get experience. When I use the word moment it is not the moment that belongs to past, present, and future. I don't know what other word to use, but I believe you understand.

This moment is a finger pointing to something which does not even belong to presence. If you get it you got It and if you don't you miss it. That is all that I could speak of this moment. Now, here, look unto yourself! Dive unto this peace and then speak from within this peace itself, within this lake which has no ripples. Ripples are thought, ripples are just mind and the lake without a ripple is your own Self nature. Dive into this Self nature and tell me how you feel, tell me what you feel? Where is time? Where are concepts? Where are precepts?

There are no concepts!

Here is the place, no sometime-sometime that you spoke of. There is no time at all. Stay as such and this is your abode, where you are always abiding. This is Consciousness itself, wisdom itself.

Where all these planets and manifestations are hanging: It is a capacity of Consciousness. Whenever a thought arises it manifests. So many of these thoughts are hanging in this emptiness; let them! You have no limitations so just let there be millions of planets. They are just a corner of this universe. You are the creator of the creations, you are all, you are whole, you are happy; stay here as you are Now! Can you describe this in words?

My body feels like it is energy itself and my view is very different.

View changes from diversity to unity, from partiality to totality. This is what you are! You are total and whole and beautiful and compassionate. Here "sometimes" disappears and all your notions of who you think you are vanish. After they all vanish what is left is eternal love and peace and no creation can trespass into this.

I close my eyes and I feel such great pleasure and sweetness. Am I getting attached to something I shouldn't be? Should I go deeper?

When you close the eyes and you cut off the senses' contact with their objects you throw away a lot of things that steal your peace. This is what happens when you sleep and you feel so peaceful. It is the cessation of the projecting of and clinging to external objects that gives you some Peace. The world of external objects, the waking state, is really the sleep state because you are unaware of true peace. You are only aware of objects.

So close your eyes and decide that you want Peace. Then this Peace will transcend you and transport you to another state which does not belong to time at all. This state will give you a lot of pleasure. This is Turiya, the fourth state of consciousness. It is transcendent of the waking, dream, and sleep states.

From Here you get pleasure. It is of great pleasure to reject all the states filled with notions, and concepts, and intentions, and clinging. This state is always Here and does not depend on whether your eyes are open or closed. Another eye will open, the inner eye. Then you will see the inner world, the inner Being. Closing your eyes helps to open this Inner eye and in the beginning both will not function simultaneously.

So wake up to your own Self and you will have pleasure. If you make effort to arrive there you can't stay, but will come back to where the effort started. Just sit quiet and relaxed, just see that you don't give rise to any thought and you will see that your nature is the pleasure that you speak about. The mind is always clinging to objects of satisfaction and is never satisfied by these, so don't take your mind.

I see that you are in It now. As I have been speaking you have been dropping. (giggles) You got it now, now you have this Now. Now neither close the eyes nor open them and just See!

I have been meditating a long time...

Guru is many but the SatGuru is One and dwells in your heart. Only those who the Divine loves will be chosen to know This, to know who they are. If you are interested only in Freedom and are dissatisfied by the unreal world, only then will the Divine come and kiss you.

The real seems so far beyond my grasp.

You cannot grasp the real, it is all that is. This desire for Liberation will merge into Liberation itself. When satsified you will not be there to see if you are satisfied or not and you will not be able to meditate because everything will be meditation. Then it is only Love for your own Self. You must have the trust that you are That that is before this desire, before even your birth.

Being with you my heart is becoming more warm and loving and compassionate, but also sometimes, without consciousness, I get romantic, sentimental, and emotional. I have heard so much about meditation on the heart. This must be what you mean?

The heart that you speak about is the organ in the body, the blood propelling organ, but this is not the Heart that we speak of. The Heart that we speak of has no location but we call it Heart because there is no other word. This Heart is neither inside or outside the body. It is only present, eternal, without frontiers. You must concentrate on this Heart, but within this Heart who is there other than That who will meditate?

It has no limitation,
and is subtler than thought and mind.
This Heart cannot be conceived,
though it is present everywhere as Presence.
Who will meditate on that Omnipresence?
It is unconditioned and limitless.

Meditation is limitation itself. You become a meditator and then you want to meditate upon an object. It is all conditioning then; the subject is conditioned, the object is conditioned.

The Sanskrit word for meditation is Dhyana. When it went to China it became Chan, and in Japan it became Zen. Dhyana means that 'place' where there is no object and subject relationship. This is meditation. True meditation has no object of meditation and no meditator!

So give up meditation, the object to be meditated upon, and the notion of the meditator and then, perhaps meditation may take place. You are actually always in this meditation. This is not the mediation where your knees get stiff and you have to come out of it every few hours. This meditation which starts and stops and has ropes tied all over it like "I have to go to the office in one hour," or "I think I will meditate now for fifteen minutes."

Just for one second do not have any notion about the meditator or about meditation or about anything else. Then something will rise, something will reveal itself, and you will merge into That. This is true meditation; this is my understanding of meditation on the Heart.

Om, Shanti Shanti, Shanti. Finally, I have returned to your feet for your advice.

Everyday we start Satsang this way as you have just done: Om Shanti, Shanti, Shanti. What better advice can I give you?

Doubts about the Truth Removed

Doubt about Enlightenment
is clinging to suffering and bondage.
So suffering will not leave you until doubt does.

Doubts and negativity poison everything:
mind, food, and world.
A serpent can kill once,
but a doubt can kill you millions of times.
Doubt is "I am bound," and "I am suffering."

Your doubts are like clouds,
how long can they stay in front of the sun?
But Freedom is not shy of doubt,
so when doubts come, let them come,
and when they go, let them go.
To any doubt that arises
just say, "I know who I Am!"
You say a "part" of you has doubts;
There can be no part of you which has doubts
because you are that Whole which has no parts.
When you do not inquire you are in parts
and become that which can be destroyed.

When "knowing" drops away
have no doubt in what remains.
"I do not know," is the Knowledge.
Who is the "I" which does not know?

It is very important to remember:
dormant tendencies rise as manifest thoughts.
Even gods will tempt you and only Buddha survives.
So reject pleasures of heaven and earth;
what is not Here will never be Freedom.

Give up all doubts.

*When I inquire I fall into a deep silence, total peace. Then the question
arises, "Is this it?" I feel that it must not be because I would not ask
this question. Papaji, what am I missing?*

The fact that this question arises means you have doubt. You have doubt that what has come to you unasked for and effortlessly may not be real. You have a diamond in your hand, but you doubt that it may be a piece of shell and then you throw it into the ocean. It is just like that. This is a diamond. Don't doubt it. If you doubt then you will repent later on, but you will have lost the fortune.

The mind will play many deceptive roles to you, but don't care about these. *You have to stand like a rock.* Then only you have done it well. Let the waves come, let the wind come, let the rain fall. How is the rock affected by these? It is not affected. So, this is it, that "I am the rock." I am not the wind or the rain. The rain will fall for sometime and again stop. Even a cyclone will come, stay and go. So whatever comes, let it come and whatever goes, let it go. Know "I am the rock" and when the storm disappears you will still be there. Know "I am as it is, this is what I am" just as a rock sinks into the ocean, yet remains a rock.

If I am here it is because I want to be free. But if I still have fears and doubts is it because I don't want freedom badly enough. If it is so simple, how can it be so difficult?

Any simple thing is difficult. Difficult things are not difficult. If I tell you to do something hard like a head stand, then you could do it. But what is the difficulty in keeping quiet? To keep Quiet means just not thinking and you have seen the results of thinking: confusion, trouble, suffering, doubt and death. It is only difficult because you have not heard it before. Your parents never told you this, nor have your neighbors or your country. It is only here that you hear that *keeping Quiet is easy because it is your fundamental nature.* You were Quiet before you appeared and will be after you disappear. You were Quiet before you spoke and what you spoke ended in Quietness. Everything comes from Quietness and ends in Quietness, and so it must stay in Quietness. While speaking you can keep Quiet also. If you can't learn you will have to wait, though many have done it and many who are here will do it, because there is no doing. This strange language you will understand slowly.

I feel disconnected from Quietness and swallowed up by thoughts. These demons are taking ownership of my life.

There is no difference between the mind and your demons. They are the same.

Even after realization the demons will attack
and you will have doubt and think your freedom is fake.

Don't be afraid of it!

How can a doubtful person be convinced permanently? Can you guide me?

You will see that everybody has doubt and, therefore, they come to Satsang. If you have no doubt, why should you come to the Guru? You need to go to the Satguru to remove your doubts. Other people need not go to the Satguru because they have no doubts. If you want to seek the Truth and you know that you want to seek the Truth then you should go the Satguru and seek guidance. But someone who knows that he is the Truth itself need not go. In the third category are those who don't know what they have to know and don't know that they don't know, they also do not need any help.

But you say you are doubtful and so you can go to the Teacher to remove your doubts. When you see that the mind is doubtful then look at the doubt of the mind and then tell me. Don't just listen to me, do it! Tell me what is the doubt. Look at the doubt. Are you understanding?

When I look at the doubt I don't find it.

Ah, yes, when you look at the doubt there is no doubt, but when you don't look there are doubts. So the Satguru tells you "Look at the doubt" and you can't see the doubt. It is so simple. You are not to do any sadhana, or practice, or go to the Himalayas.

Doubts have to come and each doubt will give you the next incarnation. Each doubt will carry you to a new birth. Therefore, solve your doubts here now. It is so simple. Look at the doubts and no doubt will come. Keep Awake! If you are awake the robber will not enter your house to steal from you. But if you are sleeping then your things will be missing because you didn't look at the robber. For many years you have lost everything, but now keep awake and watch this robber. This robber is mind, and where there is mind there is doubt. So always keep awake which means *always look at the doubts*. It is so simple. It doesn't matter if you are going to America or you are staying here for a long time, this is a simple teaching.

I know myself, but still there is a doubt.

This is a contradictory statement. When you know your Self there can be no doubt. When you don't know your Self there can be doubt and fears. So correct it: "I know myself." That's all, finished. If you have doubt then you can't do it.

Where there is flame there is light.
Where there is doubtlessness there is Grace.
Don't forget about it.

I don't know you, I can't even perceive you!

You don't need to know me.
Know your Self, this is most important.
Instead of knowing others, Know Thyself.
First know your Self
and all else will be revealed to you.

You need not perceive.
Give up all perceptions and It will reveal Itself to you.

How can I remove doubt?

When you have the desire to know thyself all doubts will fly away. Keep Quiet. Simply keep Still. Don't give any thought to your mind for one second. Don't stir any thought and don't make effort, for just one second. If you understand what I speak about tell me what will happen when you don't stir a single thought from the mind and you don't make any effort. Just these two things: no effort and not giving any thought to the mind! Just for one instant. What will happen?

The only thing that can happen, I assume existence!

Still you have doubt. If only existence is there what is the doubt? When everything is existence where is the doubt and about whom is it? Who doubts and who is doubted? Unreality. Existence and non-existence. It will all be clear to you if you make no effort.

I don't feel doubt.

If you don't feel the doubt where do you even get this word "doubt"? If you don't have a thousand dollars in your pocket you won't say, "I don't have a thousand dollars in my pocket." If you don't have a doubt you need not speak that "I don't have a doubt." For just one second don't have any doubt.

Why am I here?

To listen to this command: Don't doubt! You are being told to remove all the doubts that you brought Here. Here the doubt is being cleared by just keeping Quiet and by making no effort. You came here to remove doubts. Then there is no here and no there.

For one instant forget your friends, relationships, country. Forget all of this and who do you see? No one! It is like enjoying the emptiness of the sleep state. The whole reason why you sleep is because in the sleep state there is something which you cannot find in the waking state. Now do nothing and everything will be fulfilled. Then you will dive into a pool of Love.

I have such a strong doubt that I fear I will never be Free.
I attempt not to let thought arise.

This must be a very strong attempt. How can a thought arise if you have made a very strong attempt not to allow it? Will you open your apartment door to a stranger that you don't know? But everybody has opened the door, in fact there is no door. Everybody lets everybody walk in and out as they like. So you are not safe.

Let no stranger into your mind! But you know them and so you let them in. Be careful, that which troubles you may be a robber and enter your apartment and steal your things. First see who it is, and if it is a friendly thought like Peace, Love and Beauty, then you can open the door. But if you open the door to everybody you will be in trouble. So be careful. First watch out and then act.

Doubts come up as to whether this is what I am looking for.

When you are in peace and happiness how can doubts come up? If you have doubt you can't be in peace. If you are in peace doubts cannot come near you, try as they may, because you are beyond doubts.

Doubts are like rats eating away your life. Therefore, keep Quiet. Don't try because this trying is also doubt. Rest and let no one disturb you. Let the doubts dance around you. Look at the doubts and they cannot come near you. Look to where the doubts arise from. Look into this Nothingness. Give this trouble to the doubts. Don't let them give you trouble.

They just keep coming.

Let them come and go and they won't trouble you. People and cars going down the road do not trouble you. Cars, tractors, trucks, buffaloes and bicycles pass in front of you, but you are not concerned when they pass by. If you get concerned then you are in trouble! You stay Quiet and let everything happen in front of you and do not absorb what is happening into your mind.

I always feel so depressed. I feel trapped and full of doubt and despair. I understand intellectually what you say, but I don't really get it. I have no desire to continue living in this illusion. Will you please help me?

This question must arise to someone who will have Wisdom and Light. It has arisen to you and now you are Here. Only those who know that it is of no use living the illusion will come.

First, you must find out who has brought you here. There is a push within from the compassion of That which will help you. You are here to be happy. Don't have an insecurity complex, you have great merits behind you. You need merit to come to Satsang. You need a strong rock-like decision: "I am going to win it, this life, this year, today." This you have to decide. Do it now. Whenever you are going to do it, it will be Now. So why postpone this Now to next year? Now will help you. To be happy you need not go anywhere. It is Here! If you look within you are happy, but if you look outside, then you are in trouble. *That you must decide!* Look within and be happy. If your mind goes anywhere, bring it back. This practice you can do for some days: Watch and stay Quiet.

The mind is never Quiet, it has to run out. So, wherever it goes, bring it back. This process should continue wherever you are: walking, talking, inside the house or outside. From inside your mind always see what your mind is doing! Bring your mind back. For ages you have let the mind do as it likes, so Now is the time for you to control your mind. But nobody can control it unless they have a very strong decision. Only then you will be able to control the monkey.

Can women be enlightened?

This doubt is a trap given to you by the male dominated culture. But the truth is that women are as strong as men. As women like Queen Lakshmi have shown in Jhansi. There have been many enlightened women, like Maitri. They have every right to be Free. Have you heard of Saint Teresa of Avila and Saint Claire in Assisi? At the time the church wasn't very accepting of their experiences because the church wants to hear about the Bible and the church, not about the direct experience of Christ that these Saints have.

There is no difference between a man or a woman and each has equal right to be Free. Everybody has a right!

ॐ

A few years ago I had an experience of truth, consciousness, bliss which profoundly changed my life. I now know my being, but I get caught up in thoughts and doubts.

How much time do you give to Truth and how much to these doubts? Does the time that you give to doubts cancel out your experience of Truth? When thoughts come wipe them out by looking at them and slowly they will not attack you. When doubt rises simply see where it rises from. Doubt only troubles you when you don't look at it. Look also at the bliss. Ask where it comes from and to whom it comes. Find the center where all these waves rise from and return to.

The question "Who am I?" brings peace, but again doubt arises.

Whenever your mind is disturbed bring it back into your Heart. If it goes again then again bring it back. Don't be lost in objects as is the habit of mind. Bring it back from these objects and when it goes, again bring it back. You will see that you are successful when you control the mind in this way. Everybody else is controlled by the mind. Bringing your mind into your Heart is the only way prescribed in the Upanishads and also in the Gita. When Arjuna asks this same question to Krishna, Krishna replies:

"Wherever the mind goes, bring it back,
and keep it in my Heart."

I have not felt the bliss for months. Is it possible to always be in the bliss? Is there anything beyond this?

Where does the doubt come from that the bliss comes and goes? In the egotistical consciousness open eyes see and closed eyes do not see. But you are the Consciousness and the Bliss itself, not the experiencer of the Bliss. You are that Bliss itself, not the one who sees it. Know that "I am that Bliss." Then it will not open and close, it will not come and go. The sun shines 24 hours. There is no night known to the sun, but if the earth turns her back to the sun there is night. It is the fault of the earth, not the sun which shines eternally.

You must see that you are the Sun. Then only you have understood this teaching. Discriminate what is darkness and what is light. What is real and what is not real. *What appears and disappears is not real.* Don't touch this happiness which comes and goes. Rather, go to the Source, the reservoir of Consciousness.

ॐ

I am fed up with doubts and desires and this machine called mind.
Perhaps I must wait for Grace. Is there anything I can do?

Without Grace nothing will work. You need Grace. How can you say that you have no Grace in your life? How do you think you made it to Lucknow? There must be Grace which called you here. Otherwise, you would not have come, as in the case of your friends in your country. It is mind which says you have no Grace because it wants to believe that everything comes from its own effort. But it has been making effort for thousands of years and now your time has come to be free of it by the Grace of Self. This Grace will guide your activities telling you where to go and where to stay. If you accept that you are here due to a command from within, this is surrender to this Grace. Once you surrender, the way will be very smooth. Simply don't do anything. Don't even think. Just allow the Grace to rise.

I feel so overwhelmed by your Grace. My heart is at your feet and
all of my fears have vanished. How can I express my gratitude and
how can I totally remove the last of my doubts?

What doubts do you still have? If you are in love with me, what doubts do you still have left? Doubts arise when you are in love with a stupid person. Then you have doubt and fears. With me, you must trust That, and have no doubts because I Love you. In other cases, you may love someone, but the other doesn't love you. This may have been your experience in the world: The person to whom you give your mind to is attached to someone else. I remember one story:

One man appeared at the gate of the king and was allowed into the court. This man said to the king, "I am a yogi from the Himalayas and because of my tapas, penance, and trust a divine fruit which grows only in the heavens was given to me by the angels. I am 350 years old and so I don't need this fruit which keeps one young. I have eaten one long before and as you see I appear to be only 25 years old. I have heard that you are a very good and generous king and so I want you to have this fruit so that you can help the public for a long time."

Now the king took the fruit, but decided that he wanted his junior queen to have it so that she always stayed 25. This way he could enjoy her more. She took it but since she didn't have full satisfaction with this old king, she had taken on a young lover from the horse stable and she gave it to him so that she may always enjoy his youth. Now the fruit was in the hands of this palace servant. However, this boy was always afraid of being caught with the queen, an offense for which he could be hanged, and so he had started a love affair with a simple prostitute. With her there were no doubts or fears and so he passed the fruit on to her to that she may always be young and enjoyable.

Now the prostitute thought that if she stayed young she would remain in trouble and if she grew older her life would be better. So she decided to give the fruit to someone who would really benefit everybody by staying young: the king!

The king saw that it was the same fruit that the yogi had, but that even prostitutes had this fruit. So he wondered what could be the use of this fruit and called the yogi to find out an answer.

"Is this the same fruit that you gave to me?" the king asked.

"Yes, definitely it is the same," the yogi replied.

"But even the prostitutes have this fruit!"

"No, I don't believe it. Are you sure? Have you eaten the fruit that I gave to you?

"No, I passed it on to my queen."

"Call your queen and ask her if she has eaten the fruit," commanded the yogi.

The king asked her if she had eaten the fruit, but she was honest and told the king that just as he had desired for her to stay young, she had desired for her lover, the stable boy, to stay young because she enjoyed him more than she enjoyed the old king.

This servant was called and admitted his fear of being the queen's lover and that he had passed on the fruit to a prostitute who he loved and enjoyed. The prostitute was called and she told her whole story.

"See how many hands this fruit has traveled through, but nobody had the merit eat it," stated the yogi. "Now I will take it-back because none of you had any use for it." With that the yogi walked out of the palace.

Now the king got a lesson and learned that he could trust no one. So he divided the diamonds, ministers, elephants, and country between the two queens and left the palace to search for Peace in the forest.

This story is the story of the world, this is the story of the universe. Some will understand this earlier and some later on. So whatever you have to do, do it today.

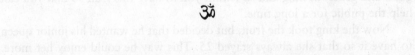

Fear of the Truth Removed

The fear of vanishing which may arise with inquiry,
is the old sensation: "I am the body."
This is not a fear of the new, but of leaving the old.
Have no fear and plunge into your own Being.
When "you" disappear, all fear will also.
Stay Quiet, be Still, Here you are.
Stay as the presence in your Heart.
Do not fear meeting the Self,
it is what you have always been.
Nothing can be lost, have no fear.

There can also be fear of "losing it."
Only when you possess something does the fear of losing arise.
Only Self cannot be held, so only Self cannot be lost.
The only way to avoid fear is to return to the inner beauty,
the Self, the Heart on the right.

You may also fear you will be crazy without a mind,
but where there is mind there is duality,
and where there is duality
there is desire, anger, hate, fear; in short: craziness.
So don't be afraid of losing your mind
because no-mind *is* sanity.
This is no doership, no judgments, no anger,
this is supreme Wisdom and Peace.

All fear is baseless as all fear is based on non-existent "other."
Fear lives only in the duality of the waking and dream states.
Where there is fear there is falsehood,
to overcome it meditate everyday.
Fear is ignoring the target
so keep a strong relationship with Freedom,
be it hate or love.

The fear in inquiry is the dormant intention to be with "this and that" after the inquiry. It is suppressed and then you have peace. Though it is suppressed into the sub-conscious mind it will wake up again. Do not suppress them, just understand that they do not exist. You can still have "this and that" but just know that they do not exist. It is like children and their sand castles at the beach. They play all day, but at the end of the day they do

not try to keep the sand in their pockets. They rejoice to kick it into the ocean
or they just watch the high tide take it away.

> *So sand is sand.*
> *Nothing belongs to you! It is all like the breeze.*
> *Leave your mind as free as the breeze*
> *by not clinging to anything.*
> *This is the secret to happiness: Enjoy the garden,*
> *but do not cling to anything!*

It takes a fearless sattvic intellect to know the Truth.
Burdened with vasanas, confusion, and fears you cannot inquire.
So the mind must be free of vasanas and fear,
and this depends on how much longing you have.
Ignore the egotistical "I."

ॐ

I often get a fear of death as my meditation deepens.

The fear is in the breaking up of name, form, notions, and identity; of the
river entering the ocean and losing its river-ness. That breaking up is a sudden
jump. At that point the fear will be converted into fearlessness. The fear is
a product of barriers, of banks of the river, of limitations. These limitations
are mind. The fear is just in losing all past notions and identities. Upon
meeting the ocean the fear is there and disappears as you become ocean. The
fear is only thinking that you are separate from the ocean and so the fear is
a form of arrogance, of separation, of ego. Give up these notions and be Free.

Everybody must die and so everybody has this fear. The fear is only that
you will lose something when you are not here. Remove this fear by seeing
and practicing, "I am not the one who will die." It is the body which will die.
Death is for the body only and not for you! When the body dies you do not.
That inside the body will not die. Slowly practice this and remove the fear
of death; just know "I am not the body." It may take time, but again and
again say in your mind "I am not the body, not the senses, not the activity
with the sense objects." Keep on speaking this, and like a mantra it will work.
Separate yourself from these. Start at your foot and realize that you are not
a foot and work your way up from there. After you realize, "All of this is
not me" then ask the question "Who Am I?" Slowly you will be picked up
by the Truth and lose all your fear.

My experience with you has involved so much peace that it sometimes
frightens me.

What has frightened you?

The intensity of experience. But I am not frightened Now.

You are frightened because for the first time you have peace of mind. Nobody ever has Peace, but when you have it continually it can frighten you, if it is an experience. You need not be frightened. It is only because none of your friends or family ever had this experience. Nobody has experienced the unique sweetness. Enjoy your life without ego, otherwise, the ego will always bite you like a scorpion; this you always experience.

The kiss of the ego
is like a sting of a scorpion.

ॐ

I have had an experience where only Awareness was, but due to fear I dropped back into this plane of existence.

This experience is quite enough, but you thought and this thought brought you to the past because it is the past. You started to think what had happened and what it was that you got. Nobody had told you about it and so you could not value it. Though it is there everywhere, with everyone, only a rare one will find it. You have to see it is a diamond in your pocket, and not a shell from the beach. Know it is a diamond, and not a shell. Know it is a diamond and you don't have to think and you will be the richest person in the universe.

There was a man who brought bricks to construction sites on the back of his donkey. Still they do this in India, especially in the villages. He would work all day for only 25 paisa, a few cents. One day while he was digging some sand needed for a house, he found a shining thing which he then tied to his donkeys neck. He didn't know what is was. A few days later a diamond merchant was passing by and he asked the brick hauler how much he wanted for it as he pointed to the donkey's neck. The poor man said, "One dollar."

A dollar in those days was twenty rupees and since he could buy a new donkey for only five rupees he thought he was making a good deal.

But the diamond merchant took only the shiny thing from the donkey's neck and left the donkey behind. The poor man thought he was mad and asked, "Sir, what about the donkey?"

"I am not a stupid person. I am a diamond merchant. I am not paying for the donkey, but for this diamond. You didn't know it, but you had enough money here so that you would never have to work the rest of your life. Even your family would not have to work for three generations. But here I will pay you 5000 rupees just for your stupidness."

He then sold it to some local dealers for 100,000 dollars. They sold it on the Calcutta market for ten times that and then it was brought to the Gulf sheiks where it sold for ten times that. And all the while this poor man became poorer and poorer and repented more and more for his stupidness.

So when the diamond comes to you, test it yourself. Take it yourself to several places and then get the best price for it. You have not appreciated this diamond because you are not a diamond merchant and you don't know diamonds. Show it to a diamond merchant. Bring it here and I will test it. Then I will tell you how many carats it is and I will pay you the exact price which nobody can pay.

So don't make a mistake. When you find something that shines, bring it to Lucknow. Here there is a diamond merchant who is not dishonest. He will pay you the exact price. The exact price is not in money, or stones or in dollars, but in Peace, which nobody can offer you. You may sell it for ten times more, but you won't find this Peace anywhere else. This is why you all are here, for this Peace of mind.

I tried to let go, but I became fearful.

To let go is difficult because everybody wants things to happen according to their own choice. But is there anything in the world more valuable than this diamond? What is there in the world which will last and which you won't leave someday? Even this body you will leave. So let go.

What is not stable and permanent, let go.
There is only one thing left.
Worlds and gods will disappear, but this will not.
When you are reminded of this keep your eye on it,
not with the intention of having it, but just to Be it!
All the things you want are in the "let go" category:
House, wife, body, parents, gods, let go.
What is left? What cannot go? That you Are!
You cannot go because you have never come
and anything that comes must go.
Find out what it is.

Let go of your ego, not your wife and family. Fear and ego are mother and son. Ego is the mother of fear and fear is the son of ego. This family you should let go, not your wife and your children. Let go of the old family of ego-mind, persons, relationships. If you want to be happy absolutely divorce them. But tell your family about Satsang and teach them to live a very healthy life.

Vichar: Self Inquiry

Sometimes silence appears before me by itself, but disappears
as I try to hold it.

Are you afraid or disturbed by this silence?

No.

Then why do you opt for disturbance instead of peace. You say that you
prefer Peace, yet you allow yourself to be bound to a place which disturbs
your mind.

For instance, Lucknow gets very hot in the summertime with
temperatures sometimes reaching 48 degrees Celsius. If you can't stay well
here why don't you go? With just an overnight journey you can be in Almora
or Mussoorie or Nanital. The next morning you will be shivering! It is up to
you to utilize the situation and circumstances. You are not bound to stay
here. You can go to wherever you feel good. This is in regards to the climate
and the same holds true for the mind. Why should you disturb your mind
with some affair if you don't like the disturbance. Shift your mind to
something which is beautiful, in this case to a beautiful thought: "I am not
the body which is always in trouble, I am Atman, I am Soul, I am God
myself."

What problem is there with this? When you have to think you can think
something good, and not something that will disturb you. If you must utilize
the mind utilize it in this way.

Make a strong decision that "I must be peaceful before I die," and you
will be successful.

Sometimes my heart dances with good thoughts or no thought at all,
and sometimes I am in fear. Why must I respect these childhood ghosts
when I can laugh with you and be Here.

This ghost is just old habits and they are similar with everybody. But the
new habit of keeping still and not thinking of the ghost is rare because
everybody thinks of their ghost and ends up living a miserable life. And they
actually prefer this! You have to do otherwise: "I want to laugh and be happy
and be free of ghosts!" Ghosts are just concepts of the mind. Actually, there
are no ghosts. From the beginning you are Divine and you are not born to
suffer.

ॐ

Since I was a child fear is a problem which takes over regularly even
though it is clear that the fear is a thought only. Is it possible that one

thought can be stronger than another?

You are right! Some thoughts are weaker and some are stronger. If you say, "I want this or that," it is a weaker thought. If you say, "I don't want anything," it is a strong thought. Then you analyze which is a stronger thought. If you think that you want to be with a person, realize that person will leave tomorrow and you will then be in trouble. So weak thoughts like this will give you trouble, and actually any association will give you trouble. This is the experience of everybody in the world. Wherever there is any association there is suffering. When you are all alone in sleep you are happy, but the next morning you are in trouble because you want to be with people. So you must chose between a stronger thought and a weaker thought.

How is it that though I love you so much and you love me, I have so much fear of being naked without protection in front of you.

When you have Bliss within yourself you love your Self and everybody else. This is Atmananda. If you have fear it means that you are not turning your mind inward to this. Fear only comes when the mind is turned outside on some object of the past. Your fear is simply fear of the past. You can find this out for yourself by noticing that when you have fear that there is some involvement with a past affair or circumstance. If you do not look into the past you are Here and Now. Then you will dive into the Bliss of the Self.

When the mind goes to the past check it.
If you are not successful again check it.

Bring the mind back and just watch how it drifts to the past. Mind means past itself. Mind is thought and thought belongs to the past. But in the presence there is no thought, only happiness. Just look at the mind and do not let it go back to the past. In the beginning it may trouble you, but later it won't.

Mind is like a bull which goes and grazes in the field of other farms. There it gets a beating until it returns to its own fields. It doesn't understand the beatings and continues to go to the other fields and so it continues to get beaten. After receiving many complaints the farmer finally ties the bull up in the barn and feeds the bull in there. But when he places a bushel of feed in front of the bull the bull will not eat it because there is no one to beat him.

Like this our mind will not listen but will go time and time again to be beaten. So this bull doesn't eat for a day, for two days, for three days. After the third day he is very weak and hungry and starts to eat without being beaten. Eventually, he feels very good and the farmer no longer has to keep him in the barn. Though the bull is no longer bound it no longer strays around. The bull knows that it is very well fed at home and doesn't go out to be beaten anymore. So if the bull is controlled let him go wherever he likes, but actually he won't go anywhere.

Fast the mind of thought with the strong decision, "I will not go back to the past," and bring it back to the Present. This is an affair of three days.

ॐ

For a few months while sitting in Ramana's room I was given the Grace to know that I am That I. Then out-going mind took over again.

I am That I is a good experience, but how long did you keep it? Why did you reject it? Was it not good?

The experience was perfect.

Is this not enough? Is it not good enough for you? Sitting in the room of Ramana Maharshi.

It is the highest Truth, the highest experience.

Then why did you leave it? Why did you reject this moment?

Because I am scared to totally disappear.

This fear comes after this moment, after you have rejected the moment. It doesn't come during the experience, during the moment. Why did you reject this moment if it was so good? If you find a diamond will you take it and throw it into the river? A diamond is a diamond in this moment. In the next moment it is also a diamond, but you won't find it again if it is in the river!

I rejected that moment because I chose something else and I wrote this letter to you to ask for your help. I want to stop choosing other things.

So you reject the diamond for something better.

It is not better.

If the distraction was not better then why did you throw the diamond away?

I cannot throw that experience away because it is who I am!
I want to offer who I am to you right now.

If you know what you are, why do you care about what you are not? Never before did you know what you are until Grace took you to a place where you can find what you are. The matter should end here.

Suppose you are in the honeymoon chamber with your bride, do you think of some other girl then? What will be the result of this?

No marriage.

In this way you will spend your whole life searching for your bride, but you won't find her. This is what happens with everyone because everyday this experience comes to them, but everybody rejects it.

Reject your doubts and the experiences will come to you. Then it is better for you to hold onto it. When you have no doubts you are in peace, and in love and you are That.

I found myself in such despair because my ego had won.

The ego is always winning and you lost the chance to defeat it.

Can't you just take your sword and cut it to pieces? I only have a week left in my stay in Lucknow and I don't know that I will ever be able to return. Please destroy me Papaji. I know there is nothing real which can be lost.

You have a good desire to destroy your ego, but in the same breath you threaten to leave here next week and not return. Do you know what your plans are? Do you know what your planning is? It is the ego waiting outside the door, allowing you to come and meditate, only to take you again the moment you step out. This will not do! Have you heard the story of the king who went to see the Saint? It is exactly like you! I told it recently so you must have heard it. The king with his royal ego goes to see the Saint, but is kept waiting until the ego is destroyed. He could have gone in immediately to see the Saint, but his king-ego stopped him. The Saint knows no difference between the king and the farmer.

So, if you want to see the Truth within, you must instantly rush inside. Don't wait, don't even meditate. Rush inside, Now! Don't even close your eyes for meditation! Simply rush in and find where the ego rises from. Beyond this there is someone seated who is waiting for you.

> When the time comes don't miss it, it may not come again!
> This one second is enough.
> So your hitchhiking from place to place is not needed.
> Stay wherever you are, it takes no time

because it is not available in time.
If you speak of time you don't get it.
No-time is available to you with every breath.
You can find yourself at that time
after inhaling and before exhaling.
How much time is there before exhaling and after inhaling?
What could you possibly want in this moment
and what meditation could you do?
This instant is the time of peace,
and here you can find your Self.

Sometimes I feel this fear keeps me imprisoned.

Whenever you keep Quiet there is no-mind, but the mind continues to call you to go off with it because many times you have befriended him, but now you have to decide not to listen.

But this mind is in love with you and encircles you, and you are in love with him. If you don't break the relationship you will always suffer. So, be brave and decide that this time you will have no relationship with the dead persons. This is the decision, "This life I have to be Free!"

This is your first Satsang. You have done very well. At least you have a strong desire.

I understand what you say in theory, but in my life there are still the same old patterns and habits coming to the surface. It is almost like I fear love inside. Can you help me?

If you try to understand it will not work. You have to have experience and don't just listen to the words. Don't just hear the words or understand what is spoken, you must have experience. You have to have a deep experience.

If I say go dive into the ocean, in theory you understand this but you have to Understand this. You have to have an experience of Quietness so that no other thought is arising in your mind. Look at the thought that is arising, go to the depth of it and the thought will vanish, theory will vanish, and you will have experience.

I have had experiences, but when I go back to Denmark...

This experience can go back to Denmark? It has to stay with you. The experience is that you are Free. You have to stay with it! How can it go anywhere?

So you have not to experience it. It is only theory. "I am Free" will remain always with you when you have an experience of Freedom.

Will you help me get this experience?

Why aren't you getting it? You must be holding onto someone in Denmark. When you are Here you must cut all your relations and keep Quiet for just one second, one moment. This is how to get it. Don't think of anyone else. No person, no thing, no concept, just for one instant, and then in this instant you will have the experience which will last forever. I hope you can give one second to your own Self. You have given your life to others, but now keep one second for yourself. And that will be all.

You always have the experience that "I belong to him," but for one second get rid of all relationships. Without it nothing will happen. Just as in sleep you break off all relations with everyone for five or six hours, you don't even relate to yourself when you sleep, you have no relation with body, mind, senses, or objects, so you can do it for one second while awake. Do you understand?

Yes.

In theory or practically? (giggles)

I want to put all my fear at your feet.

In the dream you face dream tigers and feel dream fear of them. When you are Awake there is no tiger and no fear.

Facing all circumstances will remove your fear and is service to the Divine. Whatever comes in front of you, accept it. Like the wind blows, but does not stay at one place. This is Divine will: Go everywhere like the wind. Don't stay at any place.

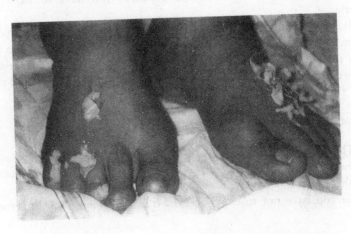

ॐ

The Cessation of Objectification

Why objectify God? Subjectify That!
Go straight to the Light, immediately jump into It
and don't write an article about it on the way.
Keep Quiet, entertain no doubt, raise no desire.
Remove all objects and remain as That!
All pain belongs to objectification.
Do not let ego own Freedom, so do not objectify the Truth.
Do not call it a gain or an acquisition, simply identify with it
as you do when you see your face in a mirror.
Forget this visitor called mind and just identify as That!

You can only experience what you are not.
Only transience can be experienced,
because the experiencer itself is transient.
So give up the notions of experience, name and form.
Don't touch name and form, *just watch!*
Utter "I" and all objects are there.
Look at the "I" and everything dissolves.
Let the "I" look at the "I."
Inquiry is to first objectify the "I," the experiencer,
and then to look at the subject who has objectified even the "I."
Inquire who is the Subject which objectifies the subject.
This subject is the Seer.

My Master, Ramana Maharshi, said to me,
"God is not an object to be seen, He is the subject.
He cannot be seen, He is the Seer, find this Seer."
My Heart was opened.
"Find the Seer." This is the Teaching.

Self is before even subject, so who will concentrate on what?
The seer must be seen, do not accept the dream as real.
Wake up by not stirring a single thought for one moment.
Even a thought will taint It because It is so Immaculate and Pure.

Mind is the habit of objectifying, of projecting duality.
Master the mind with Vichar.
Know "I am Here," and let this go anywhere.
This will stop the mind.

If the mind troubles you ask,
if it doesn't just stay quiet.

When mind is quiet, all is Self.
When mind moves the world arises,
so be Still, throw away everything, and be Free.
Then, when mind is pure, you will see Self in all beings.
Give up seeing with the outer eye
and the Divine eye will open.

To still the mind question the source of "I,"
look into what does not come or go, and be That.
The mind moves only because it is attached to something,
so do away with what is dear to the mind.
Withdraw from attachments and decide to return
to Awareness-Being-Bliss by keeping Quiet.
When mind touches Being it becomes Being.
The concept of freedom removes the concept of bondage.
Then use all your strength not to be called back
by the concepts of old habits and dissolve into Freedom itself.

Stop thinking for this is world process.
Now is the gap in this and this is Freedom.
Not thinking is to not activate the mind;
do not activate the mind for only one moment.
Do not think. Freedom from thought is Freedom.
If thoughts come, let them come.
If thoughts go, let them go.
No notion of Freedom is Freedom,
no intention of Freedom is Freedom.
True inquiry is not thinking or activating your mind.
If you must think then only think of Self.
This is the nearest practice.
This is staying in the ocean and letting the waves rise.
The last and first thought of the waking state must be inquiry.
Just stay quiet and see what happens.
This seeing is Being.

When mind has to work it will go to sleep.
Don't do this, sleep is a trap.
Keep effortless attention
on the pearl that you are diving for,

the permanent answer: Silence.
The answer is at the end of the breath.

Understanding is objectification.
Uncover your Self by throwing away understanding.
By trying or by understanding you will not find the source
because all questions and answers rise from the ego.
Find where the ego rises from and it will disappear.
Ego must be destroyed, thinking must stop.
Do it Now; aspire for the Unexplainable,
That beyond understanding, sight, and touch,
by casting off the concept, "I am not I am."
Remove even the concept of concept.
Vedanta, the end of knowledge, is to forget all, including words.
Carrying around books is like a donkey carrying Sutras;
so many Saints are illiterate.
As the fire in a painting will not cook your tea
so intellectual understanding is not enough.
Intellectual understanding is like reading a menu,
true experience is like eating the food.
All understanding is dried out boredom
compared to the taste of That!

Existence, Consciousness, Bliss;
only the ego-mind-intellect hears these words.
Do not let them interfere,
do not analyze what you have heard.
When you think of emptiness you are out of it.
Speaking of freedom is only for the prisoner.
One who is always Free does not say it.
This spoken freedom needs bondage to be free from.
Inquire into your Self yourself and be Free!

This Freedom you can't describe in words.
The best description is in the eyes and walk
of one drunk on the bliss of Self!

ॐ

I want to be close to god.

You speak about God like a school girl reads something in a book. You
are making God an interesting object and setting yourself up as the subject.

God cannot be objectified, God is the subject itself. When you say simply "I Am" the meaning of this is "I Am God." If you know this your personal identification is finished. In Sanskrit this is "Aham Brahmasmi" which means "I am God-Brahman-Atman my Self." If you want to be close to God stop objectifying God for this is separation. Have the strength to know that "I Am God."

So, God is the seer of this illusion.

Again you have created a relationship between seer and seen.

It seems like there is a big difference between Self and ego, between reality and illusion.

It is a creation of mind to say that this is reality and that is illusion; this is ego and that is the Self. This is creation of the mind!

I had the experience that nothing exists, suddenly I found myself in a big black hole!

What did you do with this experience? How long did it stay? Now if you get this experience again you will compare it with the previous one and also you will lose it. If you have this experience, why do you want to analyze it? The mind comes up to understand and you lose it.

I tried to keep it.

How can you keep the emptiness? How can you keep anything that never existed? How can you keep it? There is something wrong somewhere, you see.

Mind and this experience do not go together. You have to give up the friendship of one. Choose what you want, God or mind! This you must decide before you sit in Satsang.

You must see that "nothing ever existed" is the only experience. You were not here forty years ago, nor will you be fifty years from now. What is before and after must also be Now to be real.

Be careful next time. Don't be washed away by the mind. There should be no difference in your mind and understanding between "I am the illusion" and "I am Atman." Why do you want to understand? If there is nothing, how can you understand? If there is something you can understand. You are working, I am very happy.

It evaporates when I try to describe it.

It is indescribable, and when you try to describe it, you forget what you have to describe.

Do you have any other guidance for me?

I will give you some homework. The question is: "What is this all about?" This you must give me a reply to. Do you understand the question?

"This" I don't know, but that is the question!

I will be happy if you answer this. You are clever, but I will see how much your cleverness will help in answering this question.

ॐ

Could you please make me believe in God. I don't understand God. I want to have faith in something.

God can be understood by a person? Who will understand God? Who told you that you can understand God? You don't understand who you are, let alone who God is! First understand yourself.

Don't have faith in anything. You must trust what is already there. Faith is a word coined by the founders of religions: if you have faith you will go to heaven and if you don't you will go to hell. Faith is not correct, rather you should find out how things are in reality! I ask you to find out who you are and for this you don't need faith.

Start from your dress, from your dupatha! I am not the dupatha. Then comes your suit, your watch, your ring. You are not these things. These belong to you, but you are not them. Know this! I am not the hair, I am not the glasses, I am not the nose. The nose belongs to me, but I am not the nose. This is reasonable understanding. You do not say "I am the nose!" The skin belongs to me. If it is injured it can be replaced by plastic surgery. I am not the blood, I am not the bones, I am not the marrow, I am not the liquids in the body. These I am not. What belongs to me I am not. This house is mine, I am not the house. So what is left now? The owner of the house. What is left that is not a belonging, but the owner. I am giving you the answer to your question.

So what is left? I am not the mind, I am not the body, I am not the senses. What is left?

My soul.

Ah, that is good, but even at that you have counted your soul as a belonging: my house, my car, my soul. No difference! Who are you to whom the soul belongs? It is not reasonable at all to say that the soul belongs to the body, the blood. What is a reasonable reply?

You want to believe in God. I tell you, first of all believe in your Self, that "I am God." Then you will never fail. Believing in God is being God. Knowing God is being God! Understanding God is being God. Who can understand God except God himself? If you understand God it becomes your object and who is the subject? God is the subject itself! God is not an object to be objectified. God is subject itself. So it is better that you become the object of God. Even then it will do. What problem is there if you say, "I am God"? This is the best trust and the best faith. Instead of having faith anywhere else, have faith in your Self that you are God. This is the biggest faith. Then you are normal. Otherwise, you are abnormal or subnormal.

I feel so badly because everybody is getting it, but not me.

Separation is suffering. You are feeling separate from "other" and so you suffer. This is all. You are hiding, you are not accepting what you are.

You are total Oneness, with everything.
You are everything itself.

Give up your concept, "I am something else" and "others are something else."

They say that the Self is centered in the naval.

There can only be a center where there is a circumference, isn't it? What is the circumference if the center is at the navel?

The body.

Self is not conditioned. To say that is it centered in the navel is conditioning That which cannot be conditioned. There is no center, but if you are going to carry the concept that you are a body then you can carry the concept that you are centered in the navel. The whole concept of "centers" in the body is to be used for objects of concentration, but I have not seen any results out of these centers. If you give up the notion that there is a center and circumference, then perhaps it will work. What is the center when there is no circumference, nothing to be concentrated upon, and no concentrator?

Don't fix centers! This is just a trick of the mind. The center cannot be anything other than the mind cheating you out of Freedom. Do not allow a thought to land anywhere and you will see this. Don't let any thought abide anywhere. Then where will it go? Don't give time to these centers. I have seen so many people who have given 40 or 50 years to these centers and the only result is tighter bondage.

ॐ

Since I was very small I have had a strong desire to know god and this desire has given me countless experiences of oneness with truth.

There are not countless experiences of Truth. For Truth there is only one experience and god cannot give you that experience. If you have an intense longing for god, this god will send you to church because god is only found in church.

> In Truth there is no god.
> Truth is Truth
> and god is your own creation.

This is controversial, but god only lives in the church.

Recently, I had the experience of no-mind, but I know mind is tricky.

When mind is not there who is there to call it an experience? Knowing that mind is tricky is itself a trick of the mind. Wake up!

My mind is so strong and clever, will you help me?

Why have you accepted your defeat, that the mind is so strong? Why? It has to be your slave, not your master. As a slave he is very obedient, but as your master or as your teacher he is a butcher! Don't feel defeated by this man because you have not even seen him! How can you say he is so strong? You have never seen him! Nobody has seen the mind. Therefore, this is only a ghost. You are haunted by a ghost. Those who say "I have a strong mind," or "I am troubled by my mind," they are haunted by a ghost. There is one psychotherapist here in Satsang who will help you with your ghosts (giggles) and he will charge you $100 per hour! So to be haunted by ghosts is very costly!

If you are conscious of the rising of the thought it will not arise. Do you follow this? I will speak again and again. It is very important! When the thought is arising, look at it. Do this and tell me if you understand. All your life the thoughts are arising, so look at them and tell me what happens.

Be vigilant. Invite the thoughts to come. Say "Oh thought, I like you, I love you!" (giggles) and see what thought will come.

No thought comes.

So you know the secret of how no thought will come to you. I am very happy that you have come to Lucknow at such a young age. There must be a strong urge in you that made you come to Satsang instead of the fishmarket. I will tell you a story.

There was one fisherwoman who would fish in the river and then take the fish to the market to sell. So one evening there was a very bad storm, a cyclone, and so she could not even walk with the basket of fish that was on her head. But there was one florist who was on the way and so she said, "My dear sister, you can stay here and when the storm stops you can go. You can't walk now because the wind is at 100 miles per hour." So the fisherwoman came in. All around were flowers like rose and jasmine.

When the night came she could not sleep. She said to the florist, "I can't sleep because there is the bad smell of flowers all over your house. All these roses and jasmine are making my head ache. So my dear sister, if you allow, I will bring my basket of fish here and use it as a pillow." So she did and she instantly started snoring.

So, those who have lived with the garbage of their thoughts cannot sleep without thought. Every thought is a fish which is enough to spoil the whole pond. Keeping one thought in your mind you cannot be at peace. Therefore, do not allow any thought to stay in your mind. Then you will see the difference. Try it for only one second in your life. Not months or years, just one second! Do not allow any thought in your mind.

(Papaji starts coughing and with a hoarse voice says:) Every word has power you see. When I say "I love you," it has power. When you abuse a man, it has power. A bad word hurts, and a good word like "I love you," changes a person. Words have tremendous power. I have been using the word "fish" and (starts to cough more) this is the power of the word.

I want to realize my God-Self, but I think there is a veil between me and That.

The veil is this: you have some desire in your mind. You have a desire to arrive at a greater consciousness and this is the veil between you and That. You have to be absolutely without desire and without thought. Desire is a thought. When you have a desire you have mind and an object of desire. But God is not the object. He is the subject. He is not the seen, arrived to or reached. He is the seer! Don't try to see anything because God is not an object. All objects have beginnings and ends, but the greater Consciousness does not. Just simply do not have any desire for anything for one second, and tell me where the "greater Consciousness" is and where the "lesser Consciousness" is.

Now where is the veil? We create the veil by wanting this and that, but where there is no desire God will come himself and sit in your Heart. But if the chair in your heart is full of the garbage of desires where will he sit? God needs an absolutely pure seat. Only then will he come uninvited and take possession of it forever. Then whatever you do, it is God who is doing it. You don't need anything then.

You must remove all name and form and there will be no veil. When the veil is lifted the only thing remaining is the compassion to lift the veils of others. This work is so allotted to one who has removed his veil, but one who has ego, how can he remove the ego of others? Do it now, you are in a human form and you have a desire. Those humans who do not aspire for liberation are just animals who have removed the tail. The true human is one who has removed the veil in this human life. Do not doubt it, you have done it.

I feel there's a wall that keeps me from understanding the Truth. I think that this veil is a wall made out all the stuff I learned all my life.

This wall is a notion and if you demolish it there will be no inside or outside. You are not to think because by thought you will not remove this notion. This notion is imagination only and it does not exist. The snake never existed, it was always a rope. It is only due to your faulty vision that you call it a snake. This makes you responsible for your own creation. The rope did not create a snake, you created it. Find out what this notion is that has given you so much trouble. Just keep quiet and look at it and it will no longer be there. Look at the notion that makes you unhappy, just look at it! No effort is needed just look at the rise of the notion that gives you trouble. You have created this notion and like the snake which never existed, this notion has never really existed. You are always well placed in peace, love, happiness, and bliss. This is your inherent nature. All the rest are notions that do not exist. So get rid of all these notions and intentions and ideations which have been dumped on you by your parents, priests, and society. So much garbage has been put on your head and on your heart and you have been lost in all of it. Now repeat the same question.

I can't, I don't know any question anymore.

Excellent! I can see from your face that everything has changed now. Excellent! This is your nature. Stay.

Losing the Revelation by Attaining It

Only when you possess or attain something
does the concept and fear of losing arise.
Only Self cannot be lost.

If you have attained peace,
mind will come back; just let it come,
just watch from where it arises.
Allow the mind to run, but by directing it to Now,
do not let it land in the graveyard of the past.
Clinging to the past is keeping evil association.
When you meditate all these past patterns will leave you.
The trick is to keep full attention on who wants to meditate,
because when the house is full, the thieves will not enter.
Don't expect and do not search and you will find it.

But if you again find what appears,
you will have found the wrong thing
and you will definitely lose it
because what appears, appears only to disappear.
Don't try to suppress the thoughts and experiences which appear,
just keep alert and let them come.
Inquiry stirs the serpents to arise.

Keep alert, *keep alert.*

The desire for the permanency of clarity
is a trick of the mind because permanency is in time
and only postpones what is here and now.
Find the source of this desire.
If "again" is for a gain it is useless.

This "losing" starts from the ego wanting to be the "doer" and wanting
to proudly own Freedom. If you say from the ego point of view "I am doing,"
there must be some interest and you already want some reward for it. You
decide that something is beautiful and so you go near that object which is
attracting you and then you want to possess it, you want to own it. As soon
as you posses it, you have fear of losing it because where there are two there
is always fear. This is because in duality there is always a fear of separation.
When fear arises anger arises. With anger there is confusion, lack of
understanding, and lack of discrimination. When you cannot decide things
properly it is total destruction.

Everyone is beautiful,
but when you grip a begging bowl in your hand you lose it.
Don't try to possess blissful states, so get rid of your pocket.
Original nature is Emptiness and this is Peace.
Let things come and enjoy them, but do not try to own them.
Don't worry, Love cannot be lost.

How do people lose it?

By getting it. Anything that you get is not your Self and so if you lose something it means that it was not your true Self and is better off being lost. Self cannot be lost because it is what you are. There are not two; one of which can be lost and the other one being that which has lost it! The Truth Is what you are. All that can be lost is that which obscures it: perishable things like doubts and thoughts and objects.

When people say "we got it" a misunderstanding is all that they have gotten! Then soon, of course, they will say that they have lost it. People who think that they may lose it have only understood it and any understanding is a misunderstanding.

Nature cannot be lost, your Self cannot be lost. It simply Is and is not what can come or go. It is not achieving or attaining anything. It is knowing your Self as you are. Before you did not know who you are and you wanted to abide in things which are not permanent and which will not stay. The notion of losing it comes from the mind. Therefore, when you try to get something you are liable to lose it. So do not achieve anything, just get rid of all the notions that have been dumped on you for lifetimes. When you get rid of this notion, even for a second, you will know because then you reveal your Self to the Truth, and the Truth will reveal itself to you! This is just Being, just Presence.

When I come back to the connection with the Self it is the most beautiful space. So why is it that I choose to come out of this and create a new theater with a new film playing?

When you decide to stay alone in Beauty, when the ocean has no waves, you are enjoying your waveless Fullness. And when this ocean decides to play this notion of play arises in the form of waves. This film that you speak of are these waves! The ocean knows that it is ocean and that these are its waves dancing on it. It is not at all disturbed by these waves, rather it enjoys the waves very much.

Your question then is what is the difference between a waveless ocean and an ocean with waves. This question is a wave, a notion, not an ocean! It is a notion from the wave side. This question of separation belongs only to a wave, the ocean could never ask this. This notion is just like the notion of the wave that it is separate from the ocean; that you, as a being, are separate from Being. As a wave we think that we have a height, length, breadth, and movement, but these are all notions. Separation is only a notion. The wave who wants to end this separation starts to look for the ocean! Waves look for the ocean!

But how can the ocean decide to become a wave?

It is fullness, the ocean is fullness. When it decides to play, this decision is waves. This is Consciousness, *this is Consciousness*. Whatever it thinks it is still Consciousness. It can never be other than Consciousness. The game of differences and separation is the same as if there was no game. It is not changed! Ocean is ocean with or without waves, Consciousness is Consciousness and is empty with or without manifestation.

There is no change at all from the "viewpoint" of Emptiness or Consciousness, from the "viewpoint" of Awakening. When you know you are That you have no differences. You are not separate from what is going on. This cannot be lost!

All of manifestation from the beginning to the middle to the end are the waves within you, within your own Self, and are not apart from your Self. Reject the disturbance which is only the notion of separation. Be totality, not this and not that. When you decide to do this it will happen immediately. Even if you do not decide this everything still is you only. Your question amounts to "If I am all this then why all that?" (laughing) Just do not touch this!

If I get rid of "this" and "that" then I am in the space of Nothingness.

Who can disturb this Nothingness? What will become of that which enters this Nothingness?

How to stay in the ocean?

Don't use the concept "how"! "How" is only a wave.

Without "how" there is only staying in ocean.

It is the "how" that troubles people and whatever you think the answer to be you become, instantly. It is better to just remove the question because whatever you think you become. If you think you are free, you are; and if you think you are suffering you are suffering. This is the beauty of Consciousness: think and it becomes, whatever you think will arise as you think it and it is still Consciousness. Because it is Consciousness it doesn't need to take any material from the outside. It is Consciousness and all within it is Consciousness. Consciousness is so full: anything it desires instantly comes into Being, as Being. So if you want to be Free you can instantly Be Free!

This thought of Freedom, this notion is just to remove the notion of bondage. To be Free just entertain the notion of Freedom. Then both notions will be finished. Neither notion exists. You are as you are and have never changed. With Freedom get rid of the notion that you are this body and mind.

Everything will dance. This is called Freedom. That one who has tasted Freedom dances!

I lost it and I did not re-attain it for six months and I do not know how to get it back!

But why again? If you get it again you are after something temporary and you will lose it again! It is not like eating food where you need more after just a little while.

But if you have just one drop of nectar you will not need any more food for the rest of your life. This is that glance! A millionth part of a second is enough, but if you want to retain it do not desire to hold it, for it cannot be held. Don't desire to keep it and don't desire to have it come back again. Simply be with it. Don't think that it will run away because it cannot run away. It will not disappear. It is You who will disappear when you allow an open heart to it and let it stay with you. You disappear! What happens to the moth when it goes to the flame? It is gone!

So touch this flame in your Heart.

Why is it that so many seekers come and experience this state in Lucknow and then it drops away when they return to the West.

It can never happen. It can never happen. How can one who has realized himself forget it? It is not possible, it is not true. As a river which discharges into the ocean cannot return as a river in name and form. It is finished! So when you discharge your mind into its Source, mind no longer is a mind. It is That itself. It cannot become a mind. It is now called no-mind. Be clear with this.

Many people say that when they return to the West that they lose it. I don't believe this. They did not get it, and only then can they lose it! But if your hand is empty there is no gain or loss. If you have not gained anything you cannot lose anything. So you have to empty your mind of all desires. Once emptied it cannot be refilled. They think that they got something new in Lucknow that they did not have before, therefore, they are bound to lose it.

I tell them that they are not to gain or to lose anything, but to understand that you are already Free and Enlightened. If you are already Enlightened, you are already Enlightened in Moscow, Washington, or Lucknow. How can you lose anything anywhere? This I speak about; Don't try to gain anything but rather lose all the gains you have so far made. Leave behind all that you have read and heard about. What is left will reveal that it is your own Self, and when you know this you cannot lose it.

So any gain will be lost and what you have not gained you will not lose. If your pocket is empty in Lucknow it will also be empty in New York. So always keep your pockets empty. With empty hands everything will come. If you are always holding something you have no capacity to hold any more, so emp v your hands, and again all will be replaced. So it is the empty mind who is the emperor of the universe. Empty mind and hand mean having no thought, and a man with no thought is the king of the kingdom. You can try! (giggles) Empty your mind of everything and feel who you are. This is called Peace, also Enlightenment, also Freedom. But don't keep anything in your mind.

I had a vision a few days ago of Ramana climbing a ladder and then smiling at me compassionately as if saying, "Come up with me." Is this a diamond that I have treated as a pebble?

Yes, it is a diamond and you have thrown it away, but it doesn't matter because you have seen what it looks like and next time you will keep it in your bosom.

It is rare to get a diamond and to throw it away is bad luck. But it is always available and so you must use the same "practice" by which you attained this diamond: Not thinking anything about this diamond, not wanting this diamond. Then the teacher will call you and say, "Here is the diamond!" That is the Grace of the teacher.

My mind feels unworthy, mainly because it feels that it has not taken care of the revelation which has unfolded. Is this unworthiness or is it just the way things unfold.

It is unworthiness. If someone comes to stay as a guest in your house, but you push them out, what is it? If a married woman goes and sleeps with other men what do you call this? She is not a worthy woman but a prostitute. So if you do not take care of yourself you are a prostitute to something else. You are not a yogi, you are a bhogi.

May I leave this unworthiness with you?

You can do whatever you want. In this place I advise the yogi, not the bhogi. There are six billion bhogis in the world today, but very few yogis.

I want to be a yogi, and I experience Silence, but then "I" returns.

Let the "I" come, she has to live with you. She is a good woman.

But how do I find permanent Self-Awareness? I don't want the "I."

Find the questioner of this question and you will find the answer to this and to all questions. Find where the question arises from and you will find the answer. Stay here and know who you are. This Silence will be your reply.

You will find there is no questioner. You will find questions but you will not find a questioner, only Happiness.

I feel I have found this but I am so forgetful.

I like the way of forgetfullness. Whatever comes, forget it. Don't listen to anyone. Forget all the world including your mind, body, and relations and world. Kabir also says this.

Don't care about what you can remember and what can be forgotten. These things have nothing to do with who you are.

I saw an oceanic vision when I was last with you, but then I lost it.

Only one person can sit in a chair. Something settled in your heart, but now you miss it. It is because something else is occupying the same place and two things cannot be in the same place at the same time. Either you have Peace or you have disturbance.

But I did try to lead the thoughts back to their source.

This is quite good. This will take you to a place which has no depth and no shallowness. This is your own ultimate Home which you must return to in order to be peaceful and eternal Bliss itself.

After I left you last I slowly lost contact with Self while in Germany.

If you lose what you have gained you are being pulled to something else. Otherwise, you would stay in happiness. You are more attracted to something else and not your own Self. The mind goes to where it is happy and in your case it is going to temporary happiness and pleasures. It can only be permanently happy by staying in the Self.

If your mind is going out to a place which is causing you to suffer, incessantly tell it not to and she will understand someday. Don't get lost and don't be worried about it. Just make the decision that you will be Free in this lifetime. It is quite enough.

I experienced such a blessed blissful state but fear of losing it crept in.

The Beloved will not leave you, even if you see this beauty for only a second. It is the mind which carries this fear and tension, but it is not true. Don't worry, it will have a permanent hold on you. You think that you have lost it, but it is not lost. If you have this glimpse for only one moment it is finished, but if you put your attachments over it then you can't see it even though it is still there.

> Self is always present, Bliss is always present.
> You are not to work at attaining It,
> just remove the obstacles by which you can't see It.
> The hindrance is only one: Attachment to the past.

If you do not attach yourself to any thought of the past it is already there and this is called experience, you see. Experience of That is when there are no obstacles, no hindrances, no attachments. So, try again.

I did but again it disappeared.

Let it disappear. You had a glimpse and you remembered it. This will still work. Always remember this glance which disappeared. If you know this Consciousness disappeared, what is this disappearance? Is it not appearance in your mind of something that has disappeared? So, this one glimpse cannot disappear and is quite enough. When you go to the pleasure garden and you see a girl and then she disappears, you carry this disappearance in your mind, even when you sleep. You carry this girl in your mind and so she is with you. In the same way it does not make any difference.

Fear is of losing what you get, and wanting to keep it with you. Suppose you had five thousand dollars in your pocket and you are walking in the forest; there is fear. But if your pockets are empty you are not afraid because you have nothing to be taken.

It is best not to desire anything which can be lost because having it will cause fear in your mind.

Stop chasing after what appears and disappears and you will find That which will give you permanent satisfaction and joy. What neither appears or disappears is Eternal and this is available here and now without any trial.

How will the silent mind come?

It will come if you don't allow the mind to hold anything which appears and disappears. Find out where mind goes and guide it to its Source. This source is the Source of happiness and here it will not get a constant beating. But even when the mind is battled you feel you are battled, it is not so. Don't allow the mind to go out and don't allow even the desire to go out. Do this by knowing that the Source within is a priceless diamond. Very few people know the value of this diamond that they Are.

ॐ

Honoring the Revelation by Being That

The cosmic Heart is the minutest particle.
You cannot go there with your body or your mind
because it is the purest of the pure
and even a thought will contaminate it.

A true glimpse of this cosmic Heart
is like pouring your cup of water into a river:
you will never see your water again!
Don't touch "I" and you will have this glimpse.

Glimpses are not as important,
as the one who is having the glimpse, who is It.
What stays after the glimpse is most important.
Awareness cannot go and cannot be destroyed.

You do not have to depend on anything to be Free
and it is not a glimpse!
Freedom is always permanently residing in your Heart

so get rid of all these aids which give a glimpse of bliss.
Don't depend on anything and simply keep Quiet.
Let your mind not cling to anything of the past
and check its futurizing tendencies.
Do not allow any clinging to any physical form,
not even your own self or your Guru.
Then you are left alone with Freedom
and this will not be a glimpse,
it will be a permanent abiding in your own Self.

Satsang and the inquiry into what you are
will stir up vasanas to be washed away.
Pure mind will then rest in its Source.
Constantly uplift your mind to Self.
Find out what is eternal in this Moment.
Two cannot walk the razor's edge
so you must remain one-pointed,
you must believe in the Unbelievable,
and you must face the Unknown.
Do not turn back to the known.
Stop complicating yourself: Be Quiet.

When all associations are abandoned
you must reject even rejection,
or you are just keeping the wastebasket on your head.
Then go into That which even thought will taint.
This infinite inquiry is infinite reward.
Finite inquiry gives finite rewards.
So get lost in inquiry until it gets you.
Then, when inquiry brings no name and no form,
it is finished because there is no inquiry in Freedom.

After the four walls are torn down,
The four walls of intellect-mind-body-senses,
there is still the old gate remaining,
The old habit of "I" in the form "I am Free."
This gate is not needed
and will leave at the time of death if not before.
Both are the same.

I have reached a point in the inquiry from where I can't move beyond.

Where you can't go beyond is where you have to stay. It is only mind which says that you have something more to do. Stop this mind.

Once a team of climbers were ascending a mountain when they found that their map ended before they reached the summit. So, they sent a runner down to the base camp to get the final map. While they were waiting there, a second team descending from the summit came into their camp and asked what they were waiting for.

"We don't have the final map to the summit and so we sent a runner to get it," they replied.

"Damn it," said the leader of the victorious team, "You don't need a map, this *is* the summit! This is the end of all the maps!"

This is the case with you. You have sent the mind as a runner to get a map so that you can go further, but you do not need to go anywhere because you are at the summit, you *are* the summit. Now just honor and love this Summit. Only mind needs a map, not you.

I have read a lot of what Ramana Maharshi says and so I feel that I have a good intellectual grasp of what you say.

An intellectual understanding is a must, but it is not all that you need. You need to do it, you need to be It, an intellectual map is not enough!

But, I am often quiet.

Why go to and fro and in and out of quietness? Soon you will stop making all these trips and your mind will stay in Quietness. Why move here and there?

> Don't go anywhere to try and find Peace.
> Peace is within you.
> *You are that Peace.*

> When you go to any object
> it will never give you Peace.

I know the place where I watch thought-objects rise and pass away.

> You are the one who watches.
> You are the witness of thought
> as it rises and passes away and stops.
> The one who watches is everlasting.

> The mind is the habit to be involved in its objects.

It can't both silently watch and be involved.

Because of this habit you forget that what you are involved in is just a projection on the screen. Due to this forgetfulness, identification goes from being the silent witness to becoming the projection itself. You forget that you are the screen on which these projections are rising and passing.

You are the screen which doesn't change.
Oceans of water cannot make you wet,
fires will not burn you and
movies of romance will not affect you.
So allow the projections of the mind
which is everything you see within and without.
Like this you must remain That which is untouched,
That which is before identifications and intellectual grasps.
This is eternal Being.

When thought takes you to an object you tend to go along with the thought. This is everyone's habit: Following the mind. Avoid the thoughts which come and go, and avoid the one who follows the thought. Don't just look at the thought, but look at the one who is following the thought from the inner Consciousness to the outer object.

The one who follows the thought is also a thought!
The one who follows the thought is in thought.
When you know that both are thoughts,
You are Home.
Then allow thoughts to arise
and allow them to be followed.
You remain as That unmoved and unconcerned Being.
This the highest understanding.

It is difficult to understand this. You must only do it. Let the thoughts rise and let them subside like waves moving along the surface of the ocean. The ocean is not concerned with the rising or the playing or the falling of the waves. It knows that the waves cannot leave because the waves are ocean. This is called vast understanding.

This is where the matter ends:
Samsara is there, so let it be there.
Manifestation is the nature of Self.
Self itself doesn't keep quiet,
but manifests as everything.

As a wave is the ocean,
so all manifestation is That.

Therefore, do not accept anything
and don't reject anything.
Allow the Quietness and
allow the mind to go and enjoy itself.
The difference is that you are not the enjoyer.

I think I had a glimpse of this where there is a momentary gap in "I."

Glimpses mean that you have seen something. This means that there is an object to be seen and a subject which sees. This duality of an object and a subject is only the play of mind. This gap that you speak of is not momentary, it is the only thing that is permanent. The gap between breaths or thoughts or between any other two movements is always there and it has nothing to do with the movement itself. This gap is what the movement occurs in. You are the gap. Knowing this will make the difference.

The Stillness in which thoughts rise and fall
is permanent. You are this Stillness.

Sometimes while in this gap or Stillness I start to laugh and it seems to bring me out of the Stillness.

It can't bring you out of the Stillness because this Stillness is pure happiness. This laughing rises out of It and is It. The waves of laughter rise out of the ocean of joy. All of this is in the tiniest fraction of a second and so it is a secret. Only those who understand, who see it, who know that they are It, will be happy. All others will continue to suffer. They will cry at their death and at their next birth.

You are beyond happiness itself.
You are that place where the waves of happiness
arise from. Find that place, don't understand it.
You have to simply see that you are That itself.

Will you help me go deeper into this?

Remove your concept of depth. I hope this is clear. Thank you.

The question "Who am I?" leaves me in a bottomless well of silence

that tastes profound. Why is there a sense of a missing link?

When you jump into a bottomless well, to whom are you saying "why is there a sense of a missing link?" Where does this "why" come from? You must be a good swimmer swimming at the top asking people to pull you out. They send you a rope and again you will go back there. But, if this well is bottomless, just jump. That is all.

How? How?

A man leaves his house to go jump into a bottomless well. The decision has been made. To whom will he ask how?
How to jump? There is no well!

I know there is no well.

Know well is also no well! Leave knowing behind. (He giggles and shows her a picture of Krishna dancing on the serpents head while in the Yamuna River.) He knew the trick of how to jump and dance on the head of the cobra. So this decision has to be there. Nobody was swimming there because there was a thousand hooded snake. This snake is the world, this cobra is the fear of death. Enjoy where this serpent is who bites everyone. Rise on its hood and dance and play the flute. This trick you must know: Fearlessness. Then there is music and dancing on the hood of the snake. This is a very simple trick, fearlessness, and that is all. Nobody could jump into this part of the river, where only this young boy did, for the peace of the rest of the villagers who were afraid to go there.

One night mind stopped dead in its tracks revealing effortless Awareness. The search is over. When I try to practice sadhana it is like dropping a stone into a still pool or scratching lines in vast space. I have come here to thank you. The silence is still here to thank you, but there is also a subtle want for something more. Maybe for the experience of the intensity of the realization of that silence. Can you advise me?

After having this experience I don't think that it is wise to play with the snake. It may not be a dead snake, it may be lying and if you try to massage its hood you will be in trouble. It is better after having this experience that you keep quiet. Don't play with the mind, it is not dead! It is still alive living in the name of itself! So you have to watch up to the last breath of your life because it can revive, it can again smite you. So it is better to keep quiet. Don't even utter the name. Because it lives in the name. When you utter its name it is alive. There is nothing more that you need. There is no intensity. I advise you that you only keep silent. Keep Silent and watch, save it and honor it, you see! (giggles)

I look at the thought and it disappears like a sugar cube in the ocean.

If you put sugar in a glass of water it will dissolve, but when you heat this water and it all evaporates, what is left on the bottom? Sugar! (laughs)

So the sugar you have not taken care of. The water will be evaporated. Anything that can disappear is not worth relying upon. The sugar will remain sugar so you must deal with this sugar. (giggles) This concept of sugar must go now. Don't speak of a lump of sugar because it remains a lump of sugar once the water evaporates. You must find out what remains as a residue and look after That which leaves no residue. Camphor! Burn camphor and what is the residue? Nothing! So like a camphor you must burn.

All these words which you say, everybody knows. Whether they have experience or not they know it because it is written in the books, and spoken by the Saints and Sages. "It is loving, it is silence, it is bliss, it is joy, it is expanding." All these words are there, yet they are only words. Now you have to remove the word. Go deeper to where there is no word. Even silence is not there. "Silence" is a word. We may speak the word "sugar" but our tongue is not tasting sweetness. Like this we may speak of stillness, bliss, happiness, but they are all words! We have to do away with the words. Don't talk about any word. What will you do? What is that transcendental state where word has no meaning? That is it, you see. (giggles) And that you can't describe! That eternity cannot be described. So the best is what I speak everyday: Keep Quiet. And when the thought comes, "I am blissful, I am limitless," you must find the source of this thought. Where does the thought of bliss come from? Then you will see that there is no thought, not even thought of happiness, peace and blissfulness. When you dig at the root you will not be able to speak because any word is outside of you. Next time speak to me without using any words. Thank you. Good luck.

Beautiful things are happening here in Lucknow, but still a notion of witness persists.

Beautiful things are happening and you are the witness of these things. What is the problem? Just stay as the witness.

I cannot say that it is Oneness! I cannot say that it is home!

See that you are the Witness, what problem is there? Turn your face and look. Just be a witness. If someone laughs, be a witness. If someone cries, be a witness. You don't understand the meaning of witness. Witness means you are not involved in anything. This is Witness. Whatever is happening just simply see. When the same witness is what is witnessed, then you must behave like it. What you witness is the same as what has witnessed, then there is no problem. Witness and the witnessed are the same.

In a dream you see an elephant, a mountain and a tree. How can this tree not be you? The dreamer and the tree is the same thing. The dreamer and the mountain is the same thing. You have become the tree and the mountain! Is it not? Who has made the mountain? You dreamed that there was a mountain and a mountain was there. There is no difference between you and the mountain. Both are dreams. So now you must witness this witness! That I am the mountain, and I am dreaming the mountain is so subtle to understand!

Can I come to you for further guidance?

This is the guidance!

ॐ

Now my head is no longer in the fish basket.

Do you remember the story I told about the fish basket? Most of the people keep their heads in the fish basket because they like the smell. These fish are arrogance and ego. Who is it that does not have their head in the fish basket? The one who is out of ego and arrogance, but all humans, animals and birds have ego.

These fish do not bother me if I follow them back home.

Yes, when they appear, follow it. This means that if a thought appears you should follow it and she will take you to a place where she really belongs to. Follow any thought from where it comes. You will reach a place and that has been your place. But if you follow a thought out to its object you will be finished.

I have been feeling such a vast space, but it has edges around it.

This ocean has no shoreline and who will see the shoreline? The wave! The wave feels that it is no more ocean because it thinks its name is wave and she does not know that she is still ocean. It is only this name that has separated her. Then she has length, width, height and movement. She moves on the chest of the eternal Father and thinks that she is wave and searches for the Father. So she goes to the edge of the shore and is finished. The wave searches the ocean for the ocean, and nobody can tell her that she is the ocean and it is only because a name is there that she does not realize it. But the content is the same. So you must see that you are the content inside, not the name or form. All names come from formlessness so follow this thought back to the depth of the ocean and then ask "Who am I?" "I" is a thought, "I" is still a fish. Where does this fish come from? Follow it! Follow to where the "I" comes from and you will find the place from where you have never left. It is only name and form that hide this. Name and form do not even exist in the ocean. Ocean has no name. Even the word "ocean" is a name which the ocean does not know. You give it the name ocean, but ocean does not have a name. Even so, Self has no name. It is only when you think "I want to do this" or "I want that," then it becomes the I-thought. Then the desire arises for this and that and you become lost in "this" and "that."

I find it hard to find the Self because Self is always Here. When I drop thought, Peace and Love pervade.

Then you have done the job. Self is always here so what more do you need? What is the difficulty?

Thought comes back.

Where can it come back to? Only one person can sit in the chair at a time! I am sitting in this chair, but if I ask you to sit here also I will be sandwiched! (giggles) I will slowly get up and make room for you. Only one person can stay in the chair at one time: Either the Self or the mind. Mind is past. Self is present. Mind belongs to the past. Mind is disturbing you and taking you to the graveyard and you agree to it! Refuse the mind, refuse the thought and you are sitting comfortably on the chair of Presence! It will be vacant, empty, there is no one there, but when you walk with so many things it does not work. You must walk on the sword. Very carefully stepping because if you look here and there you will be cut into two pieces and never return to this path again. Therefore, shun the company of the mind for one second. Steal just one second from this life span of eighty or ninety years. Can't you steal one second for your own happiness or do you belong to others? This is the mission of life. At least spend one second and see the result. Spend one second without thought and see the difference.

I have dropped into the space you mention many times, however, I always hang on by a small rope. Now I long to let go of the rope forever, but I cannot. I am deeply afraid. Can you please cut this rope?

I can't wait any longer.

You have to cut this rope or it won't pay you anything if you want to go and meet your Beloved. Rope means attachment to the past, and so you are not diving deep into the well. As you draw water out of the well with a bucket which has a rope attached to it, you keep the rope in your hand so the bucket can be pulled back. Your intention is to take this bucket full of water home, but here you must be told to keep the bucket in hand and throw it into the well without tying the rope to it. Then what will happen? It will sink, it won't come up.

Like this you throw this mind into the well of Freedom and don't keep any rope like, "I will use this mind for such and such purpose." This can be done all at once. Don't keep other interests in your mind to keep any relationships with the world. This you must think before you leap.

If you want to be Free, forget everything. Win only Freedom. All things in the world should be free of your desires; how long can you have these transactions. No one will come near you when you are leaving to go back home. So find out who is your intimate friend who will be with you now and then. Then you proceed in the Love of your Beloved. It is a narrow lane, two cannot tread abreast. You must walk alone on the edge of the sword; this is the lane of Love. So my dear boy, you have to decide.

I love peace and I have a sense of stillness. I want to come home Here forever. I know what will fill me up is not outside of my Self. I also experience the paradox of being totally alone and never alone. Often I cannot tolerate this feeling. I feel afraid.

You are afraid because this is the first time that you have had this experience. Therefore, you are worried and you don't like it because you were never told about it by your parents and friends. This is a very new experience that your parents never told you about, nor the neighbors, nor the teachers. So everyone surely must be afraid. This I accept. But to be afraid of things is belonging to the past because all fears belong to the past. Now you must see that this fear has nothing to do with your present experience and you must merge into this present experience.

Now I advise you that you don't try to understand or consider this an experience. There is no experiencer. If you try to be a experiencer and try to know the experienced then trouble will arise. So you don't try to identify with an experiencer who has an experience. Always when there is an experiencer there is some trouble or fear. Let the experiencer disappear from your mind.

Often I experience a blue flame in my meditation.

This experience of blue flame is a result of deep concentration. When there is no thought left this blue flame is seen in the Heart. Any question you have will be answered by the blue flame.

This experience is not the end of everything. It also must be rejected because it is a lamp post on the road. You should not hold it because your destination is somewhere else; not the flames and the lights and not any thought. You must find the seer of this flame, this is Mahayoga. If you ever have this experience, you must speak to your teacher so that you are not stuck at this point.

I have been experiencing myself as a very peaceful being. It makes me nervous though when sometimes there just isn't anything there!

When you are peaceful, what do you expect? When you say there is nothing there, what do you expect should be there? A pig? (laughs) There has to be nothing there. After removing your concepts there will be total emptiness. This is what we need to understand. There should be no expectation of anything. If you expect you cannot have experience because only expectation will be there in front of you. Expectations are only some persons, some ideas, some concepts. That's all. They will be there, but if you sit quiet and don't have any expectations, then it will reveal to you.

More and more I am seeing the Grace in my life and I see an opening in the heart. Often I experience where there was nothing but emptiness, although an "I" was still there. I want to go all the way.

You had this experience, but you did not know what happened to this "I" because for millions of years this "I" only meant body. "I will go there," "I will do that," "I am suffering." So this "I" that you have been using up to the time of experience is only body, senses, ego. If you continue this experience with a teacher this "I" will face the real I, which is Consciousness. Then this "I" will dissolve into I and the I will function in place of the previous "I," the egotistical "I," and there w.ll be I alone. Nobody knows what this I is. This I will not give you suffering, it will not touch the body, it will not touch time. This I is beyond limitations. You must be very acquainted with this I, but still, you speak of the previous "I." This must be dismissed entirely. This I is everything. Acquire this new habit and all will be clear.

When you speak of I, don't touch the ego. I means I beyond all limitations. Then you can use this I in all circumstances. You can say, "I am eating," or "I am suffering." You can do it, but unless you have this experience you will not be happy.

What am I to do?

This question is from the little "I." The "I" that I spoke about has nothing to do! That "I" is very different. If you use the "I" which is Consciousness itself, then when you use the words, "I am eating," all the beings are eating. When I breathe, all the beings of the universe breathe. Use that "I"! Give up all attachments to the previous "I."

How is the experience of Fullness related to the Emptiness?

They have no relation. They are the same thing. What is Full is Emptiness and what is Empty is Fullness. It is hard to understand, but it is a fact. In the beginning there was Emptiness. In the end there is Emptiness. In the middle there has to be Emptiness. This is how I can explain; In the beginning there is total Emptiness and from here arose so many things, staying for millions of years, but in the end they will all dissolve from where they came and remain empty. If you want to understand this, you can't.

Emptiness is always here, just as in a room which is full of furniture, this furniture is in emptiness. Emptiness is the background. Emptiness is never affected by what is in it, by what comes into it or what leaves it. You can't understand this because you are Emptiness yourself. This is Truth. Again, when this Emptiness is full of mountains, birds and trees it is not affected. Whether things are in it or not, Emptiness is not concerned. You can't understand this, you have to Be it. Only then can you enjoy the Fullness also.

How can I always have the beautiful experiences?

What effort did you make to have the blissful experience? What practice did you do? What thinking, what gymnastics, what hardship? It is enough if you have a glimpse of Emptiness once. Once is quite enough. Why do you want it again and again? Always return to the same glimpse. Always think of Emptiness while walking and talking. Don't forget that you are empty. This will work. All the time, in the day and in the night. Don't let it go and that is enough. Once is enough. Why should you call for a second time? It is not a habit like Coca-Cola. Once you have the nectar, one drop is enough.

If you taste the nectar you must stay with it. Don't allow your mind to create any doubt. Why come out of this Happiness? Don't be afraid of losing it, for even if you forget It, It will not forget you. Have trust in It. The Grace and the fruits of your past lives is what gives you this Happiness.

I am just afraid that I will forget this taste of Freedom.

The taste of wine will last for four hours, but this taste will never leave you. You don't need to repeat it, it will ever be there after death.

Only remove the doubt from your mind. Once you taste it do not allow your mind to interfere with your communion. Sit quietly and don't let the mind look toward you and you do not look toward the mind. This guideline I give you or you will return back to the graveyard again. Stay Quiet. It is enough. Enjoy your new taste and make this habit a permanent habit.

ॐ

Beloved Papaji, when I ask "Who am I?" it brings silence and peace, but I am still not satisfied.

This is quite okay. You should stop here at peace. Don't say more unless you are a journalist who wants to write lots of pages without understanding anything. This is what journalists do because their mind is not at peace.

If you were satisfied you would not have to come to Lucknow. All the people who are here have some dissatisfaction. Where does the thought of dissatisfaction arise from? How can there be dissatisfaction in peace? I accept what you say, but only at the intellectual level. You have no experience.

When you wed with a woman, is it intellectual understanding or your own experience of marriage? You can't only have an intellectual understanding of marriage and be satisfied. So it is with most people: They do not experience the Source of where all thought rises, but just develop some kind of intellectual understanding of it. Though it is easy to understand intellectually, you must do it practically and then it will take just one moment to see that you have always been in peace and have never been disturbed. If you would have had this experience your face would be very different. Your eyes would be very different as the eyes of a drunkard tell what he has been doing. If you would have tasted this Source it would show in all the activities of your life.

My dear friend, you are far from the Source, but in one fingersnap you can be in this peace. Just keep Quiet, don't think, and don't make effort and tell me where you stand. Can you devote just one instant to your Self? Can you? Now do it! Don't just hear it. Don't think because all thought belongs to the past. Don't make effort and do not think. Who are you?

There is no answer and no question...and no effort!

Now you are speaking from where all questions dissolve, and so you have spoken for the first time. Your eyes and face show it. Why do you smile Now? (laughs) When you made effort you did not smile, but now you are in a zone of not thinking and so you will always smile! Okay. Thank you.

ॐ

Sometimes I feel that I take two steps forward and one step back.

Don't take two steps. The bird leaves no footprints in flight and always flies forward. Don't allow a track before or behind you. Those who will be Free have no tracks. Tracks are only for sheep and shepherds. Lions don't have tracks. Sheep stay in the world, but the lions come for Satsang, for freedom. They will roar and the sheep will flee. The sheep are fears and doubts and the roar of Freedom makes them vanish. I can see that you are carrying so much grief and sadness in your heart.

I have had profound glimpses of peace during my two last visits to Lucknow, but now I am experiencing so much grief and sorrow. Is there a relationship between grief and awakening? I thank you for your Grace.

You must be somewhere else with someone else and this causes you grief. This is only from the past and has nothing to do with Satsang. Even when you think of grief it takes you to somewhere where this grief has happened.

You get slapped in Manhattan and then you go to your house in New Jersey where you get kissed. If you think of the past you will be in grief and you will go back to Manhattan where this will slap you again. This is the habit of most people who do not learn this lesson and this is their behavior. If you would not have gone to Manhattan you would not have been slapped. Don't go to places where you get insulted. Stay at home and you will be happy. Stay at home means staying within your own Self. If you stay there it means no one will harm you and everybody will love you.

You told me to ask "Who am I?" The result was me and space.

Now subtract the "me" and what is there?

Nothing, but will it remain?

If it is an experience and not something just written on paper! There once was a class of twenty students and the first lesson was speak the truth. The next day the teacher asked if everybody has learned the first lesson. Nineteen out of twenty boys said yes, but one boy said that he had not learned it. He was punished and told to stay with this lesson while all his classmates went to the second lesson.

The next day he was asked again if he learned the first lesson "Speak the Truth" and again he said no. He was punished again and accused of dull headedness. The third day was the same. The fourth day he was asked if he had done it and he said, "Yes sir, speak the Truth. I have it." The teacher asked him, "Why did you take four days to do this?"

"Sir, it was very difficult for me to decide and now I have decided to speak the Truth for the rest of my life." He proved it up to the end even though it went against him in the battle of the MahaBharata. This is what I mean. Don't just speak the words, but enter into them and find out what they mean. Do not let this "me" appear at all.

I have found myself steeped in a thought-free state of mind much of the time, and yet...

A thought-free state is the only state that will take you to Truth. Being thought-free is Truth itself.

> You can stay with a teacher
> in whose presence you are thought-free.
> Stay where your mind is Quiet
> and not thinking this and that.

I just want to be finally established in It.

There is no finality in It and no concept of finality. It is just thoughtlessness. The longing for God that you had and the longing which brought you to Satsang are different and will give you different results. Merge like a river merges with the ocean and don't use the word "I."

How to stop the thinking?

By Being! (giggles) When you think you are an object, a person, a body or some other idea, but by Being there is nothing! Just Being. And this Being is already there. You are always Being. To become something you must meditate and perform some mantra, ritual or practice. Just to Be is simple. Without Being you can't do any practice.

> So don't think of anything else. Just Be!
> It is so easy to Be.

But when I try to just be, so much thinking happens. I am sure everyone has this problem.

Thinking happens when you want to become something. Then you must think. But to not become something what is there to do? Stay as you are! *Be as you are in whatever circumstances, just always Be.* It doesn't need any

273

practice. Whatever you get by practice you will lose, but Being will never be lost because you will not get it by any experience or practice. It simply is. Simply Be.

Don't stir your mind in Being, don't think and don't make any effort. I will tell you how to be the Being itself: No effort, no thinking. Avoid thinking and avoid not thinking. What is between these two?

I have experienced such emptiness. Should I do more? Should I just stay empty? Is there more? Some people say I should explore it.

To stay empty is better than to try to feel something. Staying empty is the easiest of all. Don't make any effort for it and ignore everything else.
More and more I am able to abide as the pure individual I-thought. Ironically, it seems like I am just an Awareness without a sense of "I," though the world is experienced from or by an "I."

All that you see is from the "I" which is not individual. It is from just Being. From Beingness all functions happen. True Being is called "I," not individualized "I."

Why can't I merge this individual "I" into Self and stop the deception?

You are not ready or willing to merge because you are trying to do it yourself. This reinforces the individuality and doesn't let you melt into That. If you know you have been deceiving yourself you are a wise man. See what the deceiver is and you will not be deceiving yourself.

I have a strong desire to be free, but I guess it's not the foremost desire.

First fulfill the desire to be free and then you will have no other desire. In Freedom the things you desired will come to you to have their desires fulfilled. This is difficult to understand, but I hope you do. Because you are desireless you will fulfill the desires which come to you. The difference is that you will not be attached to the desire. Like in a dream, the desires which come to a free man will be fulfilled. This dream is neither real nor unreal.

Out of the stillness the mind rises again like a mythical dragon.

This is the experience of everyone who gets it. They get the experience of Love and Silence and then mind rises again.

How to slay the dragon?

Until you are confident that the mind will no longer deceive you, you will ask this question. You have to check the mind when it runs out and not just follow it. You have tasted Silence and Love and now you find your mind is running out. It will run because running out is a million year old habit for it. Be very watchful of the mind and let it go, even into the fishmarket, and you will not be disturbed.

I had a beautiful vision while meditating on Aham Brahmasmi which faded away. Will you show me how to die totally to this ego structure?

You have meditated on Aham Brahmasmi, you have not become it. You are Aham Brahmasmi, not Aham Ego-asmi! When you say Aham Brahmasmi how can the ego arise? So whatever is there is there because you think it is there. Otherwise, it will not arise. Therefore, you must be repeating Aham Ego-asmi! Then the ego is in front of you! So speak Aham Brahmasmi and there is no ego. When you say, "I am Man-asmi," you are a man and you will not say, " I am donkey-asmi!" (laughs)

So does the whole lila drop?

Let it drop or not drop, that is not your concern. You remain as Brahman. Don't worry about if the lila is real or not. You cannot disbelieve that you are a man. You won't believe someone who says you are a donkey because you are very sure that you are a man. Like this, you must be very certain that "I am Brahman." Be very certain that "I am not the body, mind, ego." You shouldn't even think of it, then you will have no problem.

You start with "Ko ham," or "Who am I?" Then the answer is: "You are That, you are Brahman, Tat Vam Asi." There is no question of becoming anything else. If there is anything else it is a thing and it is not you. Let the things be there, but you are apart from the things. This practice must be as real as you speak so that it cannot even be practiced, just as you are not to practice to become a man. You don't need practice to become a man because you are a man and like this your trust must be as great as that.

You asked me if I saw a world and I couldn't reply. I couldn't say anything. Since then I saw a world, but then I couldn't see anything.

You didn't see anything, but mind came back again. In sleep you don't see anything. So, like this, sleep in the waking state. The difference between this sleep and night sleep is that you will know everything! People come here to see themselves in the crystal pure mirror of their own Self. Here you are reminded that you are a lion and have never been a donkey. Don't have any doubt about this.

I believe that I am God, but it is just a belief.

Keep up this belief. It will not trouble you. Believe that "I am God, I am the creator of all creation." God must speak like God. Like a king he doesn't say "I will buy this or that." This desire doesn't come because everything belongs to him! Anybody who has a desire is not a king, is not God, but a subject of the king.

You must behave according
to your position and status.

Keep Quiet, don't make effort. This will remind you that you are not a beggar, this will wake you up from this dream.

ॐ

I know it is a great opportunity to be here in Satsang and I want to fully honor this gift. Papaji, is there more? Am I settling for too little? I still experience an "I." Please help me. I have no other desire but to be Free. I am eternally thankful for the magic of your Grace.

If you still experience the presence of an "I," it is not the same "I" which you had before you came here. This "I" is quite harmless and you can keep it with you. You must speak to people and without an "I" you can't do it. But inside, don't forget that this is not the old "I" which troubled you.

When I was here before my mind was not quiet enough to receive the gift of your presence. My mind is now much more silent and it grows and deepens. Is there anything else required?

When the mind is quiet what should you do? Suppose you want to marry and you get a beautiful wife and the love is growing and deepening. At that time what do you say?

Just continue to love and live.

I would simply say: "Thank my stars! For millions of years my mind was busy like a monkey, but now she is Quiet." Now the beauty of the whole universe is in front of you when you are Quiet. At that time bend your head and be very grateful for the satisfaction of the mind which you could not get before. That is all I suggest. Every moment say, "I am thankful to you, Oh my Lord, Oh my God. I am very grateful."

ॐ

I am wondering, why this apparent realness when you are from the viewpoint of there? Everything seems unreal and when you come back to the body everything seems real again.

Yes, yes! This is a very great experience, you see. In the beginning you said, "This is my body, these are my worries, body is mine and all other bodies are related to me." So, this was suffering. This was a mental concept only. The body is a mental concept. So, you know this, it has come to you, you have conquered that.

You are here for months, so Satsang is the only place where you can remove this concept that body is real. So, all that appears is not real because reality must be Here all the time. In the waking state this reality is not the reality that you see in dream state. Both these realities disappear in sleep state.

So, you have awakened to it and you kept Quiet, your mind was Quiet. This is not real, so you entered somewhere unknown to you, and to everybody else so far. When this concept that all this appearance is real disappeared, then you arrived somewhere else indescribable, and you found rest there.

Within that rest a wave arises, but comes not as mind as was the case before. That previous wave was a notion of the mind; "this is real," "my body is real," "all this is real." So that disappeared when you went to the source of this appearance, everything disappeared. That was a place of rest; Consciousness. Now from Consciousness, Consciousness reflecting into Consciousness shines only Consciousness. As a reflection of that Consciousness, the wave rises as existence. Whatever rises from Consciousness manifests there and then. From within the Consciousness the wave arises, and facing the Consciousness it shines. That shine is Wisdom. In that Wisdom nothing can ever be unreal. Consciousness is Consciousness everywhere; all over the cosmos, the world, maybe hundreds of thousands of universes are hanging in that Consciousness.

If you see from that viewpoint; not from the mind, not from the ego, but from the Consciousness itself, Emptiness itself, all is empty. You look from there. Go to the Source then, and let it rise. That experience is a genuine experience. Wherever you go you will be happy. You will be free. Everything will be real. What is not real in Consciousness? Where is death? Where is the body? You have looked and seen.

Before you said, "I am the body-ego," "I am born-ego," "I am dying-ego." That gave you trouble and it will go on endlessly. Therefore, everybody will be in trouble and the next beginning the trouble will begin again; endless cycles. Few can come out of this cycle of miserable birth and death. Your experience is genuine. I am very happy, there will be no trouble for you.

Everything is real, where is the question of unreality in Emptiness? Emptiness is Emptiness. That look you will have, not with these eyes. Hearing will be different. There will be no possibility of finding anything real unreal. This will go, there will be no discrimination of "this" or "that." Neither in between. So, this is Freedom. Everyone can have this. Have you any questions Now, from there?

When I first come back wanting to deny being back in the body, that notion of being back is like being confined again. But you answered me: I must accept that everything is real.

Anything that comes you have to accept it as real.

I have a very big longing to be there and nowhere else. Just floating in That, never back in the body. When I come back it's always, "Oh no, I'm back!"

This notion also has to be abandoned. From where have you come back? There is no coming back or going away. All these are notions. You are never gone anywhere, where will you go and where will you come back to? You are where you are, you are where you are. You are what you have always been. Don't aspire for things which are not here now. Don't try to attain anything at a later date. Everything is Here and That has to be True. Not what you will borrow from someone else, anytime in the future. That you will lose also. What is here is Real. What is here is Free. You don't need anything else. Find out what is here in front of you this very moment. What is here at this moment, find out! Don't have any intentions of gaining anything or rejecting anything, Find out! In between this here and now, this very moment, this very instant, this very second. That is going to be always Real, always Here.

Recently, I had an experience of no-mind and...

When mind is dead why put it on your plate like a dead rat? Who would do this? Are you bluffing yourself or is your dead mind speaking about all this?

After the ego is crushed you must still watch out because even though the serpent is silent it can still strike. The dead body is there but until total cremation takes place there is still danger. The feeling of death of the mind even comes from the mind. To hold onto emptiness is still indirect and is still the mind. Be strong until the ego is totally burned.

🕉

About five years ago all the signs of Enlightenment spontaneously manifested in me. I had no idea what was happening and so I was very relieved to read your account. It took the terror out of the experiences. Do you have more insights into this?

If you would have been with a teacher you would not have been terrified. Whenever you have an experience you must run to the teacher to find out what happened. His explanation will help you, so immediately go to him.

This happened in the late 40's in Lucknow. So many people started running to me and articles in newspapers were published. When the number of people reached forty or fifty I had no choice but to run away to the South where I had lived before.

Even though I say you should go to the teacher to confirm your experience, actually the real experience will leave no room for doubt, you will know it yourself that you are happy.

> Peace of mind is a sentinel of Freedom.
> Contentment is another.
> Wait with these sentinels.
> The door will open by itself
> and you will be called in.

🕉

The "I" left, what shall I do now?

Stay in Now, stay in Now, That is Now. What you have seen, that is Now. No word, no name, no thought. Now has no name and no thought. And you have to identify with that which you have seen. Hence, get into That! Get resolved into That. "I" is no more there.

Thank you.

Yes, just merge! Something will rise from this body, you don't interfere, you don't interfere! Stay Quiet. Let it merge. Stay Quiet, let it dissolve. There is no mind there, you see. Mind and ego are lost. From there the Consciousness will arise. From there Consciousness will rise. That Consciousness will be its own object, it will function. There may be manifestations and dissolution. There is no question of that. That is eternal. That will be eternal Peace and Silence.

🕉

I want to thank you for the gift of Self you have given me.

Now is the time to dance. This dance will never end, for your partner is always shining and beautiful and will never get old. Enjoy this relation for which you came to Lucknow after two billion years. This life must be spent dancing and laughing! When you have this experience of being Home throw everything away and serve your Teacher.

I am being pulled more and more into the Silence. Will you share any insight you have with me?

Allow this pull to continue, but don't make it an experience. Simply allow yourself to be pulled into the Silence, but don't make any comments about it. Devote yourself to your Self. Surrender your arrogance, your separation, your ego to this Love that you are.

How can I maintain the oneness without being dominated by emotions and feelings?

> Only by Love, only by Loving
> can you maintain the sense of Love and Peace.
> Then emotions and fear will not dominate you
> because you are in Love.
> When in Love, only Love sits in your Heart
> and so fear has no place.

How can I invite Peace to come to my house and stay longer?

Peace *is* your house. Keep this house empty and let Someone who comes share this Love.

How can I rejoice this being nobody?

Rejoice with someone who has no form anymore. That is the only one in the three universes who can give you perfect eternal Love. Eternal Love is that with no form. Wait for the one with no form to call you, and while waiting be in the same character as this Love so that it is attracted to you. So first abandon your name and form. Then you will see that this Lover will fall in Love with you. There is no love between form and form, only in Love is there Love.

> Don't move, don't move, don't move your mind. That is all.
> Keeping Quiet is the highest tapas, the greatest yoga,
> and the most beautiful devotion. This is Being. OM

280

ॐ Guru ॐ

Bhakti: Love of the Divine

You have to love the ultimate Truth.
Adoration of Self, with wisdom
will get you Self.

Only adore your Self, worship and seek your Self
the rest will be taken care of.
Avoid useless activities and pleasures.
Simply keep Quiet.
This is Sahaja Bhav.

> When there is unceasing tapas; when all is lost
> and mind, senses, and intellect are destroyed,
> then you will merge with That Freedom.
> Tapas is always being toward Atman.
> Tapas is total devotion to the Self,
> burning everything away, merging to Love.
> The best use of this moment
> is to drown in It! This is devotion.

To worship you must pre-exist worship
in order to give rise to the concept of worship.
So know you can only worship your Self.
You become That to which you offer yourself to,
so offer yourself only to Love.
Whoever tastes this nectar
is this nectar.

Freedom is always Here,
it is the holiness that is missing.
What are you going to give the Supreme
if you have given up your heart to something else.
Only a pure unsmelt flower is offered to God,
only love for the Self is needed.
Be humble and devoted to the Self.

> Silence is the wine in which you will be drunk forever.
> In this Silence you know and love all Beings.
> With that wine you can drink anywhere,
> and when you drink you cannot speak.
> Stay in the experience, surrender to It.
> To taste bliss forget all other tastes

and drink the wine served within.

The attraction to Self, the love of Self,
cannot be taught, either it comes or it doesn't.
You don't need a flashlight
to see where this light is coming from:
You are the light!
Only doubts and wicked association harden you.

The pain and tears of separation are blessed.
This aching from being separated from the Beloved
is better than union with the Beloved.
It is beautiful, so dissolve your doubts
and adore your imperishable Self
with peace, wisdom, and self control.

The devotee, the true devotee,
is the heart of the Divine.

Questioner: Can you help me understand the relationship between what you teach and bhakti yoga?

Papaji: There is no difference between jnana and bhakti. You can approach God by love, which means bhakti, with great devotion and love and when you do this you know what is happening. When you love, your Beloved one will unveil the treasure to you.

If you love you have knowledge also. And if you know someone, that someone has love for you also. Therefore, jnana and bhakti are two wings of the same bird. Wherever there is love there is knowledge, wherever there is knowledge, there is also love. If you love someone that someone will not keep any secret and so you will have knowledge. And if you know someone that someone also has to love you. So it is one and the same thing. People quarrel that they are different and there is a big dispute over it, but the fact is that anybody who finds a difference in the two are ignorant. You love That most so that you have no one else in your mind. Then you will have the treasure revealed to you by It.

What are the different ways of knowing your Self?

According to the books of knowledge there are three ways. One is jnana yoga, which is knowledge. Number two is devotion. Number three is karma, activity, action. The people who are intelligent go to the rishi in the forest and ask Ko Ham, "Who am I?" The teachers said only: "Tat Vam Asi," "You are That." By only this statement, the student would say "Aham Brahmasmi," "I Am That." This is for those who are intellectual and who understand the meaning of the word, and not simply hear the word. That means That. When the teacher says That the student looks at That, and agrees: "I am That." Then the teacher said, "Good luck, off you go."

Number two is devotion, surrender to the Supreme Power within. In saluting and looking at that power you become that power itself. Give your mind to that power and don't have the ego that "I am a separate entity." Know "I am the Supreme." This you must win by love, not by intellect.

There is no difference to be That in understanding or in devotion. The child goes to the mother to suckle because it knows who its mother is, and the mother knows who to feed.

The third is karma. Karma yoga is whatever you do, you do not seek for the result of your doing. You just do it and keep the result in the hands of the Supreme Being.

Actually, all these run concurrently: knowledge, bhakti, karma. If you get attached to one of these, all the others are with you. If you know someone, you love them. If you love them, you know them. And your activity is the same for each other. There is no difference.

I am coming from bhakti. Is it possible that a bhakta can inquire?

Bhakti is through love where the God loves the devotee. Vichar is where the devotee goes to God. This is the difference and so you must make a choice. If God has to fall in love with you it is bhakti. If you fall in love with God it is jnana.

It is difficult for the people of inquiry, or vichar, because they do not know the personality of God. They don't know what he looks like and so they can make a mistake. But God will never make a mistake when he loves his devotee. They say God follows one step behind the devotee looking after his welfare and giving him things even if he doesn't want them. There is a story about this regarding a saint who was blind from birth. One day he was going into a forest and in front of him was a well. He was about to step into it, in fact his foot was already above it, when somebody came and touched him and said, "Baba, there is a well in front of you, come to this side!"

Now this touch, so soft and delicate, was like no other that he had felt in his whole life. All the hair on his body stood up in haripulation. He couldn't even speak, "Who are you?" because he was so choked up and, of course, he couldn't see who it was. But he knew that it couldn't be anyone else other that his own Atman within his own Heart that could give such a touch. Then he sang a song about this:

> I am blind and old and without strength.
> Now you have kept me aside because you are young.
> But though I am weak, I will see if you can run away
> from my Heart.
> You may be strong enough to lift mountains,
> I don't doubt that, but if you are·brave,
> tell me if you can run away from my Heart.

This must be the decision that I spoke of earlier when I told the woman to clench her teeth and tighten her fist and see if That will run away. Only if you have that much strength will you cross the ocean of samsara. Otherwise, there are crocodiles on one side and sharks on the other! If you can deal with them you are fine and don't need a raft, but it is safer to be on the raft. This raft is Satsang and it will take you across to the other side and once there you will not have to go into this samsara again.

Most people prefer to jump into the mouth of the shark, but your decision must be strong to stay on the raft.

It is not the duration of the time in Satsang that is important, but the understanding. This you may not have in a whole lifetime or you may have it this very minute, or half a minute, or quarter of a minute.

> I speak the same thing everyday;
> You are Consciousness,
> You are Atman, Beauty and Love.

If you understood this we wouldn't have to pay rent on this hall anymore!

Is the process of attaining enlightenment different for different individuals and the choice of practice followed?

No! Anybody who is realized through any process is not realized.

> Truth does not have any way to take anyone to Awareness.
> Where there is process there is mind and mind is ignorance,
> not attainment of Truth.

Divine intention is breaking this ego and I feel that I am in the middle of bhakti and jnana.

Total bhaktas cannot work in the world. People who commit totally to jnana become too proud, so half of each is good.

> If you want to know Truth,
> you must have one hundred percent love for Truth.
> In this way there is no difference
> between the ways of love and knowledge.
> You need love to know
> and you need to know what you're loving.

Different people may appear to take different paths. The intellectual person will be interested in the path of knowledge. The one who has love in their heart will want to see God as love itself. God is love and God is truth.

So, if you are intellectual rub your intellect and find where all the intelligence comes from. You will find it comes from the heart, which is Love. When you love you are loving your own heart.

I don't know if I am ready for this love or not.

Don't even ask if you are ready or not, rush toward it as the river rushes toward the ocean. She doesn't say that "I am not ready to be accepted by the ocean." So keep it up day and night: rush to the source, the ocean. No other thought should come. Continue this day and night.

ॐ

Papaji, I think of you during the day and dream of you at night!

Oh, very nice. This is the best of all teachings. When you are sleeping, dream of the one you love. And during the day, don't just think of the one you love, but sit in front of the one you love. Then you will never sleep. There will be no difference between the dream and the waking state. This difference is for the rest of the people and not for the lovers. There is no night or day for the one who loves!

Can you speak about devotion?

Devotion does not mean that you start loving anyone else. What about devotion to your own Self? This is the only devotion: That you must be dedicated and devoted to your own Self. Having done this you have given love to everybody. Devoting love to anyone else, even God, it will not help you because all else is your creation! Even you are the creation of someone. Find out who has created you. Who is That? This That is that That who has created you. So you must be devoted to That, and this dedication will give peace to all beings of the world. Don't take anyone as other than you; you must walk and talk as one and then only you will know what devotion is. This is devotion: When you talk the whole universe is talking! You must have that much faith and trust in you. When you eat the whole universe is eating along with you. Then you will see the difference. It is not "by myself" and "by themselves." That is not going to help you. If you want to be a devotee, have full devotion to yourself.

Papaji, I had a dream that I was in such a special space.

Most people forget their dreams, but you have remembered. What was this space that you remember? Space has no limitations and so it cannot be limited to the waking, dream, or sleep states. Find out what it was. Find this space, it brought you here. Fall in love with *this* space. Don't look all over for this space because it is your very Self and it has brought you here.

Why didn't you take Maharshi's advice of who you are seriously and instead continued Krishna meditation?

What he spoke I took very seriously. He never said for me to not love Krishna. There is no difference between Krishna and Maharshi. Everybody thinks that devotion is something other than knowledge. On one occasion I was with the Maharshi when some Vrindaban devotees of Krishna, who were on their way to the Meenakshi Temple, stopped to see him. They gave Maharshi a picture of Krishna and I saw Maharshi melt in devotion dropping tears from his eyes. Then I knew that there wasn't a better devotee than Maharshi. Tears are one of the three or four symptoms of devotion. Some others are a choked voice, absolute stillness of mind like being wonder struck, and the hairs of your body standing up; these are some outer symptoms.

I want God in my heart, I want a love affair with my beloved Self.

If you want a love affair with your beloved Self then you are not to think. When you are thinking you are thinking of the love affair with someone else. It is not a direct experience. Those who want a love affair with their own Self will run and run and never stop and never think. They can't think because only their beloved is in their mind. If you think, you can't find your beloved. Thinking is like searching outside in the bushes for someone who is standing next to you, only this someone is within you. Seeing this beloved is like trying to see your own eye. You can't do it because the eye is too near your sight. You can only see what is outside of you, like your body. Anything that you see or love is someone else. So, if this is true, how can you love your own beloved Self?

> The lover is the beloved.
> The subject of your search is the object,
> and so you will never find it.
> The only way to love Self
> is to Be It!

Be That which you are searching million of years for. This can be done in one instant of time if you don't think of anyone else. Then it will reveal to that holy person who is sitting at the feet of the Satguru.

Will you introduce me to the beloved?

For the last sixty years I have had an agency which arranges this embrace! Here you can have a boyfriend which will last you forever. He is embracing you because he embraces all of creation. You didn't find him because you were searching for something else. Forget about everything else and you will find that you have always been in the embrace of this Friend who is available at the cost of pure love.

When you see anyone else you are not wise because it is of no use to love someone who will disappear soon. Decide now to see that person who has no ground under his feet. All others, including yourself will disappear, but He will not. Avoid all that is not Eternal.

The only thing which is eternal is Love.

This Love *is* the beloved *and* the lover. When you don't make any separation between these two you have found the secret: That you have never been separated from anything. This is all you have to do. Did you get this secret?

Yes! By your Grace, I am crying whenever I look at you.
There is infinite beauty and love sweeping me away.

I believe that in these circumstances, crying is better than keeping Quiet. This crying is not the same crying that happens when people are not with their beloved ones. This crying is for God and this love cannot be described. So keep on crying day and night to yourself. Let this rain fall and give you a good bath. It is very difficult to cry for God. Who ever does it? They always cry for someone who has rejected them. Only one who has cried tears for God and love will know the sweetness of it. Now you will cry all the more because now you have your lover in the shape of God himself. So keep on crying. When you cry He will sit in front of you to enjoy your crying and to wipe your tears.

Papa, I have been crying so much that I have barely slept for days!

This crying is better than sleeping also. (giggles) Isn't it? This cry is not the cry of suffering on account of separation. So few of the six billion beings here on earth cry for their own love. They cry when they are separated from others, not at the time of meeting something very beautiful. I can share this crying if you come next time to my room. Chello. Beautiful.

I believe that this physical separation from the Beloved is very unique and better than meeting each other. So keep separate and always aspire to meet your Beloved and one day this separation will burn you! This separation is more sweet than the meeting.

It seems that true love is to not receive anything from anyone.

True love is to give all you have
with no thought of receiving anything in exchange.

But everybody in the world needs something from the "other"! Even the love of the Divine is not without expectations of exchange. People ask God for a son, or for money or whatever. If you ask for anything it should be Freedom, the removal of all your doubts, so that you can have a very clean lovely and beautiful heart.

My heart is full, but my mind is not empty.

When your heart is full of love no thought can stay in the mind. Only one person can sit on a chair at one time. Nobody else can stay.

But my mind seems so busy.

It is good to keep your mind busy; busy with the Satguru. Keep your mind always busy with the service of the Satguru. Find how you can devote your mind and your physical activity to the Satguru 24 hours a day. Then there is no chance of any thought disturbing you. Prayer and devotion is better than keeping the mind quiet because the mind troubles you more when you try to keep it quiet. Let it run to the lotus feet of the teacher. This intention will not disturb anyone. On the contrary, the lack of this will disturb you.

> Unless you serve the Teacher,
> Moksham, Enlightenment, Liberation
> or anything else is of no use.
> The reward that the Teacher will give you
> cannot be weighed on any balance.

The mind cannot be silent because its very nature is to run. It is said in the Upanishads:

> Manav Munisharnam Karnam Vanmoksh

When Mana comes into the shelter of the Muni, the Silence, the Sage, Mana is made Moksha, it is Enlightened. The mind, Mana in Sanskrit, is always thinking something. It can never be quiet, thus, that which does not keep quiet is called mind. This word cannot really be translated into English.

One of the main ways that my mind keeps busy is that it always wants to compete with everyone. I don't know what to do or what not to do. Can you give me advice?

Then compete with God: Love God more than he loves you and more than anyone else does. Defeat God in this and he will accept defeat. If you don't want to compete then be the dust at His Feet. Both ways are very good. This lucky dust has no arrogance or ego. So either have no ego and be dust or have full ego and pride and love God more than anyone ever has.

Before I wanted to be closer to Jesus, but now I want to be closer to you, physically close.

This reminds me of a young woman in Spain who wanted to be close to Jesus. Her name was St. Teresa of Avila and she had such a strong desire to meet Jesus in his physical body that the statue of him that she worshipped came alive and smiled at her and gave her a kiss. In India this comes as no surprise because there are many stories of similar things happening. But it is not acceptable in the West and so when she went to tell her Guru, St. John of the Cross, she was told that Jesus does not smile and does not kiss and so it must have been a demon that kissed her. St. John said that Christ was never happy and so he never smiled. This is why in the States in all the churches show a very unhappy Christ. He himself had never had a vision of Christ, so how could he judge hers?

What is the attraction and where will it lead me? I feel like a gopi.

The gopis were so close to Krishna that both were called Gopi Krishna, it means the union between Atman and Paramatman. Gopis are the seekers of Truth and only Krishna can reveal it. Only to those who are very near to him, very dear to him. After coming to Him the gopis do not return back. Meeting Krishna means the end of all separation, the end of "going away." There was so much magic in his eyes that he could speak with them. He would also speak the names of the gopis on his flute and they would come to him because they could not resist this beautiful flute player. Once a girl was cooking the meal while her husband was out selling the milk and the children were away at school. Her mother-in-law noticed that she had put her arm into the cooking fire instead of a log and that she did not even know it. Her eyes were closed in absorption and tears were falling from them. Immediately she ran to her daughter and taking her arm out of the fire she said, "Oh, child what are you doing? You have burned yourself so badly!"

She replied, "Oh mother, I cannot stay in this house. I must go."

"You cannot go, you must stay and cook the food for your husband and children," said the mother.

"Someone calls me, I cannot stay," she answered.

So she goes and starts walking out of the village, though all her friends tried to stop her. She came to the Yamuna and crossed it, searching for That which was playing tenderly in her heart. Finally, at night she sat down absorbed in the love of God. When a person thinks, he thinks of his family or his house, but she was thinking no thought other than that about her Friend whom she had not found.

Desire can be fulfilled by a person that you meet, an object that you see, or a concept stuck in your mind. But the desire for God cannot be fulfilled unless you become the desired object. Here the subject is the object. So the Lord comes to her and touching her shoulder said that the Lord Krishna had come. She replied:

> Krishna is not two persons, Krishna is One,
> and That me is Krishna itself.

It ends there. If you really want to be a friend it should be with that person who you cannot see. The person who you can see has a duration in life, and at the end of this duration you will suffer.

> Don't be a friend with that which disappears,
> but with That which does not disappear.

Having that friendship you will also not disappear.
This is Gopi Krishna, the union of the soul with God.

I experience Sat and Chit, but not Ananda.

Actually, it is Satyam Anandam Brahman, "Truth is bliss." The bliss is
very rare. Experiencing truth will not give you bliss.

Bliss is not from understanding, but from devotion!
Bliss is the blessing of the Guru to one who serves Him.
The Teacher who can give this is very rare.

I want to be free and blissful permanently.

Then you must give your separation away and you must fall in love with
the one inside your heart. Slowly go near Him and He will suddenly jump
up to receive you. Once you are with him don't go back which means don't
remember the past. Just keep looking at Him and He will return your look.
What could be the taste of this union?

If you want it to be permanent, totally fall in love with your own Atman.
When you are totally in love with That tell me if it is a permanent or
temporary affair.

I want happiness always.

Then offer something. Don't go to the king, or the saint, or the temple
empty-handed. Offer the fruit of your Heart to the Divine, not peaches, figs
and apples. God only wants a beautiful face and heart. But you have to be
careful or he will steal your heart, and you will be part of his lila!

It already happened!

When this happens you will be mad, or crazy with love. Actually, it is not
madness or craziness, but there is no English word to describe the total love
for That in your heart. This happens when the indweller of your Heart steals
your Heart.

Don't just read of this lila, but go and take part in it. Then you will really
enjoy reading about it. If you want to see more of this game go to Vrindaban.
Every particle of the earth in Vrindaban still radiates love. In most cities
people avoid where the street sweepers are working, but in Vrindaban people
go to them and have dust swept onto their heads! This is the sanctity of the
place. Next time somebody from Satsang goes there you can go with them.

ॐ

I am feeling separate, it is a familiar feeling. I have had glimpses
of the Self and a very strong desire to be free.

These all mean the same thing. A desire to be free, glimpses of the Self,
and seeing something that is familiar to you. All mean the same. This
familiarity cannot be other than your own Self. It is not the familiarity which
is when you meet someone on the street and you run back to the past and
remember the association. This familiarity is no more running back. All these
familiarities you must run back to the past to pick up how they were familiar
to you and it will be because you had some interest with the person or object.

But this familiarity is your own Self and when you stand in front of it you
will see it as familiar, but you haven't seen it since you have been looking at
other persons and objects! Therefore, you forgot to look at it. So turn your
face toward it and get dissolved into this familiarity. Then there will be no
difference between you and this person who is very familiar to you. You will
become one! Then you will be naked and you must be; if you wear any shirt
or pants you will not see it. You must remove everything. That means you are
not to wear any thought around you. Then you will become naked. Then
you are that familiar person who you have been searching quite some time
for.

Don't go with the feeling that you are naked. Even this feeling you must
leave behind. If there is no feeling you will see this beautiful person who is
familiar to you and familiar to everyone.

I don't understand my fear and resistance to surrender.

This is how you are not naked! You are wearing resistance. You don't
like it. You say you want to be free, but how can you be free when you are
resisting this freedom, and have fear in your mind? Then you can't see your
beloved. Remove this fear and you will be naked. Remove the fear from your
mind, and the resistance and then there will be surrender. You can't do this
unless you are quite free from thoughts.

Can you help me and shed light on this?

You must become the light itself to see the Self.
Nobody else can shed any light on it!

You must see your own light while you close your eyes, the light is always
there. When you don't see any other light then this light will appear in front
of you. For a short while you should try this. Don't look here or there or

Bhakti: Love of the Divine

anywhere and then you will see this light.

ॐ

Though I love Ramana so much, I don't feel it for you.

It doesn't matter. If you love my Father then you have a good connection with me. All who love my Father also love me.

But I want to create a sense of devotion in myself.

In whose self? I don't find any difference in "this" myself and "that" myself. Could you tell me how "this myself" and "that myself" differs? The only difference is in the corpses; that which has form and which will die.

> Don't develop devotional feelings
> for that which is not eternal.
> The Self, the Self of Ramana, your very own Self,
> is eternal, and worth loving.
>
> If you love everybody you have loved your own Self first,
> because all is seated inside that Self.
> Pick up any Self and love it,
> and you have loved everybody in the world.

It is important to me to know whether or not you are my Master.

It doesn't matter if I am your master, or you are my master. Don't create a problem for nothing! Just be quiet and love everything.

ॐ

How do I get back to my own true nature? I have been a Buddhist monk for ten years, but instead of being free, I feel dry and repressed. How can I let go of control and repression and return to my true nature?

All the Buddhist monks that I have seen are dry because Buddhism doesn't teach love very well. You need love. If you love your own Self you will see God and it is only through Love that you will get back to your own true nature. God needs only love; therefore, you must love only God. What does your name mean?

It means "seer."

295

THE TRUTH IS

So you must be the seer, not the object of sight. Whatever you see is an object of sight and you cannot be such an object. Seer only sees and is not an object and so you must reject the sight.

Start with your own body. It is seen and it is an object. Now I will take you behind all objects. Whatever you see, think, taste, hear, feel, smell, or touch is an object. So the whole universe is included in this. All the five elements are objects that you see and you are beyond them. Now see who the seer is. Who sees these things? Turn you face beyond these.

I Am.

"I Am" is not subject or object and this "I am" is That "I Am." Now this "I Am" must turn its head to That still beyond.

I do not understand.

Because you can't and you are not to understand. Understanding is with the mind and I am taking you beyond the mind. Therefore, lay down your understanding. Don't try to understand or think what this understanding may be and then tell me who you are. Not "I AM," not understanding, just turn your face toward That, and lay down all efforts.

Just this, just is!

And this Isness is Enlightenment because it is beyond all senses. It is only Isness. Do you want to go beyond this or is Isness enough?

You can't go beyond Isness.

By saying that you can't go beyond, you are giving limitations to it. It is very close. The trouble is that there is too much nearness, for it is nearer than anything. Why can't the retina be seen? Tomorrow tell me the answer. The best Gatha will be rewarded.

God is not as near as this because you can call his name and draw a figure of him. This which is too near cannot be defined by any word, sign, or thought, or effort. It is so simple to know what it is.

So where does the love come in? A lot of what you say are things that we already practice in Buddhism.

For practice you need your mind and body. You are not to use your physical body because anything that you get from physical practice will be physical, and anything you get from the mind will be mental.

Where I am taking you is beyond physicality, beyond mentality, beyond

296

spirituality. This is Freedom.

How do I transcend the mind?

For transcendence you must do constant meditation. First start to meditate on objects, this is concentration. This is why there are idols of different gods. It is to train the mind. As a monk you have spent a lot of time doing this, of course. Then simply close your eyes and do not let any object into your mind. When there is no object you will enter into a space which you can't mention, this is called transcendence.

Now you must fall in love with this state or you will love something else. This is the only thing that will give you constant eternal love. Such few people want this though. Everybody wants physical or emotional enjoyments. If you transcend these things you will fall in love with It and It will fall in love with you! You will have a very intimate relationship. It is very easy. You just have to fully desire this. You will see that it has always been here, but you have wanted something else.

With you I have found for the first time that I have a heart.

Before you only knew that you had a head, but now you know you have a heart. In the head there is a headache, but in the heart there is overflowing beauty. Nobody looks toward heart they only look toward head. You can tell by the face the people who look toward their heads. They are full of agony and pain. If you look toward heart it will smile through you.

When you go to the Master he removes the name and form and there is the narrow lane of love. Sharp as the edge of the sword; very few can walk this. If you look here or there you are cut into two parts. If you only look ahead this razor sharp blade will be a road of flowers. Keep in view "I want to meet my Beloved."

What keeps me from fully knowing myself?

Divine love, love of your Self is missing. Therefore, you do not know your Self. Without love, nothing will happen. If you can't love your Self, you can't love anyone else. The result of this will be suffering. Love thy Self and you will have loved every being. Learn to know how to love your Self. Love your Self. Always love your Self and this Self will love you more and more. Take just one step toward the Self and the Self will take two steps toward you!

Papaji, will you throw me into the ocean? Is there anything in the way?

If you cannot do it yourself, then keep quiet and I will do it. But if you want to do it yourself then you do not need my help. If you have surrendered completely and fully then the responsibility of the teacher is to look after the one who loves him. But if you have ego that you are doing everything, then the teacher keeps quiet. If you keep quiet though, then the teacher will help you. If you don't keep quiet you will have to do things on your own behalf.

Once a very great devotee of God was faced with a charging elephant. God immediately jumped up from sitting with his wife and ran to help the devotee, but he just as quickly came back. His wife asked, "Why did you return so soon?"

"The devotee picked up a rock and bamboo stick and so he will look after himself. He doesn't need me," said God.

So, just keep Quiet and everybody will come to help you.

Is there anything in the way?

Yes, you have not decided to completely surrender. This is arrogance because you want to do it yourself. You must surrender to the Self, then it will take care of you. I will give you the name Sundhya, which means surrendering to God.

Where should I celebrate this Holi?

This "I" must go and play Holi in Vrindaban where the Holi was played and started. Play Holi with the one who cannot be colored. Play where nobody can touch Him. You play Holi with Him. Go with the colors in hand and find the One who cannot be colored, who is beyond color, who is beyond form, beyond name. Search for That person.

Some of the devotees of this man could find Him in Madhuban to play Holi with Him. All the young maidens of the cowherds went to play Holi and they didn't return back. That is the One. You have to play Holi with your own Self. That will be the best celebration. This is a celebration of those young maidens who became Free to play Holi with their Beloved.

My name is Chaitanya. I love you and my old teacher. I also love my girlfriend, my family, and my relations. I want to be free of all of this. What can I do to find the real love?

If you know of Chaitanya you must love like him. You must always behave like the name you have. Chaitanya is the incarnation of the Love Divine. About four hundred years ago he was here in India. He was love itself and was transmitting love to everybody.

Once he was passing through the streets of Palitana, now called Patna, which was then governed by Sultan Salowdin Khan. This Sultan was going down the road on an elephant in a royal procession when he met Chaitanya singing and dancing in the middle of the road, with the Name Divine.

The Sultan became quite annoyed at this and sent one of his ministers to beat him and get him off the road so that he, the king, could pass by. The minister hit him from behind and told him to move, but as soon as he touched Chaitanya he himself started singing and dancing.

The Sultan thought he was joking, but the minister didn't stop dancing. So the king asked the mahout to stop the elephant so that he could reprimand his minister who by this time was singing, dancing and clapping with the Divine Name. As he grabbed the minister he also started to sing and dance.

This should be the change in you. You should not only be happy, but make those who touch you happy too.

The story of Chaitanya is a very long beautiful story. He was going from Patna to Puri. He was a teacher of philosophy who changed so much as he changed from philosophy to love. If you go to Jagannath Puri you will see his cave where he finally sat down chanting the name of the Divine.

I came here with so many questions, but now they are all besides the point.

What is happening? So many people are coming here with such clear minds. What is this movement? Self is the same. You are my Self, and how does this happen? It reveals to whoever it chooses, you do not make the choice to know the Self. You must be so beautiful that the Self falls in love with you and reveals itself. That is how I express these things, you are not to do anything. You must be so beautiful that It attracts Itself to Itself and in doing so reveals Itself to Itself.

The Divine Mother

What is the best way to show your devotion to the Divine Mother?

The best way to honor the Divine Mother is to be her Divine Child.

In this century many gurus have named women as their successors.
What is the meaning of this trend?

For centuries males have dominated, but now they have to pay for the
untold miseries and repression that they have made women endure.
As far as woman successors, I don't fall into this category and neither
does my Master. In fact, never in this lineage has there been a woman,
starting from Guadipada Acharya, the teacher of Adi Shankaracharya.
Though there have been many women Enlightened, no one in this lineage has
left a woman as their successor.

Do people have both male and female energies?

Yes, even Shiva, as Ardhanareshwara, is half woman and half man.
When you have compassion for others this is an example of female energy.
When you feel that you want to protect something or someone, this is male
energy working. Actually, they both come from the same source and are not
different.

Can a man embody the Divine Mother?

Yes, of course. The Divine Mother is neither male or female.

Why is the earth referred to as Mother Earth?

The earth is the Mother because without her nobody is born. Because she
is the Mother she must be worshipped. When you sit for penance you sit on
her chest, so you must salute her no matter what you are doing. When you
wake up in the morning you must salute her. Everything comes from her and
returns to her. She is the Mother.

What is your favorite form of the Divine Mother? Will you please
tell us a story about her in this form?

From the beginning my Mother has been Mother Ganga. She is not only
a river, but she is the Mother. Because of her compassion she flows over this
soil. I have tread her banks from the Bay of Bengal to Uttarkashi, from 1910
to the present. My family went on yearly visits to Haridwar. I will tell you a

story of Ganga Ma which happened when I was at the Maha Kumbha Mela in Prayag, the Mela which comes only once in 144 years.

In the Mela there are so many traditions and centers each trying to promote their own propaganda 24 hours a day. One day it was too crowded for me so I went for a walk downstream to where the Yamuna, Saraswati, and the Ganga flow as one to the Bay of Bengal. After about five kilometers a girl ran up to me and fell at my feet. I looked around but her family was nowhere in sight, which was very strange because a young Indian woman never goes out alone.

"Where are your parents?" I asked.

She replied, "I have no parents, I am alone."

"Why are you here?" I continued, "Why don't you go back to the Prayag where the Kumbha is being performed? Why are you alone out here?

Then she said, "In this Mela everybody comes to remove their sins by having a bath in the confluence of the three Holy rivers. Everybody leaves their sins, but what can I do with them? I have vowed to take the sins away from these people, and I do, but I must leave these sins at the feet of a true Saint and be free of them. I have been searching the Mela for seven days, but I have not found anybody who could take these sins. But now I have found you who are the only person to whom I can release my sins. I am the Ganga!"

Then I looked at her beautiful eyes and knew that they were not human, and I noticed that her body was transparent and that I could look right through it. She stood up and walked out onto the river and slowly became one with the water. I stood there for many hours wondering what had happened and how I could have been so blessed to have seen her in her real form. She had been living in the heavens, but has compassionately come down to earth in response to Bhagirath's penance. Now she blesses all those who see her, or taste her, or touch her. This is the experience of my Mother.

I also love Sarada Devi. Sara means essence; "I am the essence of form and no form. I am the essence of everything." Sarada is intelligence; you need the Grace of Sarada to understand what I say. You need her grace to understand that you are already realized and that you have to do nothing. If you have any doubt then this goddess Sarada is not shedding her grace on you. When the Teacher speaks immediately you must follow, "Yes, it is so." And not simply parrot back: "Papa said to keep quiet." You must know the essence of what I mean.

How can the Mother's Grace help us realize the Self?

You need the Grace of the Mother or of the teacher to realize Self. The urge or desire to be free comes from within, not from without. This within is the Mother. Out of compassion she gives you this desire.

Everybody in Satsang has the blessings of the Mother.
Credit again goes to the Mother, your own human mother,
for sending you here.
Your neighbor's mother didn't send you here,
But your mother did and even gave you the form in which to come.

There is no difference between Mother Earth,
your own Mother, and the Divine Mother.
They all are the same.

Are there any places that I should visit in India which are related to the Mother?

Yes, go to Ramanashram where they worship the Feet of Ramana and walk around the Holy Mountain Arunachala. Also you can visit the Ganga in Haridwar and at Prayag, where a half Kumbha Mela will soon occur.

I will give you the name of the wife of God; Tulsi. You will be worshipped in the form of a holy plant which every Hindu worships. Just one leaf of tulsi taken everyday will purify you and make you holy. Remember the Divine Mother every moment when you get up. Prostrate to her and repeat her name. Do this, don't just think it. Dedicate your life to her as she dedicated hers. Whoever repeats her name, like Tulsidas, is very blessed. Otherwise, you will have to suffer as you are.

I have noticed many Durga shrines in Lucknow and I know of your connection with Buddha and Krishna. What about Durga?

That which removes your ignorance is called Durga.
That shakti, that energy inside, through which you know
Buddha, Krishna, or Durga *is* Durga.

You must have seen in the temples and shrines that Durga rides a tiger and has a whip of a snake in her hand. This energy or power is called Durga. Without Durga you cannot understand anything, and so first you have to please your own energy. Then you will understand what you are doing. If you don't please your energy you will go a wrong way. Most people do not even know which way they have to tread upon, and you will only know if your energy and your aspirations are pure without fault. So first pray to the Goddess Durga within you so that she leads you on a good path.

How can I become Durga and ride the tiger instead of being ridden by it?

The tiger she rides on symbolizes mind. When you think "I am not Durga," then the tiger rides on you. If you know mind is my tiger, then you are Durga. Most of the people become something that the tiger will ride, but you ride the tiger. This is called Durga. She has a sword in hand to cut any thought that comes. She also has a garland of skulls that she wears around her neck. These skulls mean old thoughts, people who are dead. Most people dwell on past thoughts but you can use these past thoughts as your garland. Don't remember them anymore. These dead men are thoughts that have troubled you, and no other thought comes around your neck other than a dead one. The sword is double edged and so you can even cut those who come up from behind. Have this much strength and nobody will trouble you. This is how you can become Durga. Ride the tiger, keep a sword and trident in your hand, and simply see that "I am Durga."

People get in trouble only when they do not use the strength of their mind. You must use your intellect to know what will not help you and what will create problems. Use your intellect to foresee the results of things. People do not use the intellect and are driven away, driven by the instinct of their mind. This is the only way to save your Self, to be free, and to help others also.

$$\dot{\text{ॐ}}$$

Surrender

Surrender.
Let Silence have You.

Surrender to the Source.
Surrender to Awareness,
this is the only place of protection.
Surrender your heart and you will know all.
Surrender to Consciousness and Bliss.

Surrender means to surrender your bondage
and to simply Be Freedom.
Surrender is the ego bowing down to its Source.
No more demands or commands,
but just putting all in the hands of the Source.
Submit to Consciousness and Bliss and you will be happy.

Surrender the addiction to your senses.
You don't need to stop them,
but you need to have perfect control over them.

Ego is a poor driver of these five horses,
but the Atman charioteer will not make a mistake.
Surrender the reigns of your senses to the Atman.

As the river surrenders to the ocean,
surrender yourself to the Self, the Source.
And if you find you are still swimming on the surface of the ocean;
stop swimming and you will sink into depths of love.

Love: Surrender to the Divine and Keep Quiet.
Wisdom: Inquire into the Divine and Keep Quiet.

I keep hearing about surrender, but I do not know what it is.

Only one thing you must surrender: ego. Surrender means, "I hand over to you this thing and then this thing doesn't belong to me." If I give you an apple and you eat it and I ask for it back, you can't give it. Like this you must surrender the ego, the concept that "I am the body," then you are God itself. Surrender your ego and if you do I will say to put it here in my hand. Then I assure you that you will be very happy throughout your life and afterlife also. Surrender is to submit your stupidness, your wickedness, to the will of the Lord. That's all. It is like a river discharging into the ocean. This is called surrender. What does a river discharging into the ocean become?

Ocean.

Yes. Then you can't see the river in the ocean. The instant it touches ocean it is ocean. Like that surrender to your own Self and forget everything else. Surrender your ego, your mind, to your own Self. Do It! Don't just hear about it. Surrender is to just allow whatever happens to happen. Don't initiate anything on your own behalf. This is surrender to the Divine Will.

But shouldn't...

"But" is a doubt and this is the mischief of the mind, not surrender! "Lord, I surrender my personality, my individuality, my ego to you," this is called surrender. You have to decide, I won't force you. Very few people can surrender, very few in the world have done it.

Recently, so many issues of survival have been coming up along with a lot of fear. I have nothing to hide. I place everything at your feet. I surrender everything to you.

Your surrender cannot be done in speech or writing.
It must actually be done.
As the river surrenders to the ocean
and loses its entity, its taste,
and all its limitations.
Everything absolutely changes
when she meets her lover, the ocean.
So do it practically, not just in words.

I only have the desire to wake up and discover the Source of "I."
I have no future plans or ambitions. Please show me how to surrender.

When you have no future plan or ambitions where are you at that time? To say that you have no plan is very easy, but you must understand this as well. When you really have no plan, not even a plan to die, then you are in the source of "I." So your answer is already here in your request. When you have no plan you are already awake, and you will not ask this question. To come to Lucknow and ask me this question is also a plan. So where there is no plan you are in the Source. Simply keep Quiet, make no effort and make no plans, and have no ambitions. Then you are enlightened like the Buddha himself.

In the beginning Buddha had so many plans, but none of them worked and so he abandoned all planning and sat under the Bodhi Tree: Enlightenment! Simply he sat Quiet and like this you can also do it. It is not difficult. Just stay here for one instant.

I cannot put into words the experience I am having here in Lucknow.
My experience is that when I surrender to the love that is Self, and
the love that is self as "other," I experience what I call union,
for lack of a better word.

Union is always between two meeting people, then they are united. At that juncture it is called union. So you can't call this a union because it is already there as oneness alone, not a union. It is not like two rivers meeting at the confluence. It is oneness and you can't experience this oneness unless you remove the others from it. "Others" mean ego, mind, body, senses, and all the objects of the world. The experience of keeping all these aside is not an experience, and there is no word to describe this because it is not an experience. You have to know it and this knowledge is called special knowledge. When you know this your tongue cannot speak and you cannot experience because experience needs an experiencer and an object of experience, but this is neither subject nor object. Neither the seer or the seen. I also do not have a word for it.

This is totally quiet. When there is surrender to love my mind stops. These experiences are not continuous because the I-thought reappears. I see this reappearance as doubt coming from a deep sense of unworthiness, but this is only ego. The I-thought is unworthy and limited. But That which comes before the I-thought is...

Ah, right you are! And for that you have to wait for that time when the unworthy I-thought ceases to exist. And for the other: nobody knows. That is not a thought itself, not even "I." So the I-thought will somehow leave you and I suggest and advise that you have got nothing to do now. When the I-thought has found that you are not worthy to stay it will go away. Do you follow? It will say that you are unworthy. Before you called it unworthy, but now it will call you unworthy (giggles) and it will leave you and go and spend the night with someone else. So you have got nothing to do. No effort is ever to be made to cross this limitation, this unworthiness. You have no effort to make, simply keep Quiet. When it appears, let it appear. When it disappears, let it disappear and you do not shake from your position. Simply enjoy what is happening, Simply enjoy. Very good, very nice.

I want to surrender, but I'm very resistant to it. I have a deep longing, but I can't do it.

Actually, you have no longing to surrender, you have no longing to be happy, you have no longing to surrender to your own Self because you have already surrendered to something else! You are already devoted to something else. (speaking angrily) You have already fallen in love with someone else! How can you surrender? You can't have two swords in the same sheath. You can't have two persons in the same mind; only one. So when you are holding onto some other person, it is not a chaste longing. Either you can love the Self or you can love someone else. You have to decide! Long for that person who will give you happiness, whether this person is inside or outside. This you have to decide.

I am afraid, how can I overcome fear?

Overcome fear by loving yourself. When you love your own Self there is no fear. This is the only Friend who will help you Now and then. Every time, everywhere, always, your Self is going to help you and nobody else will. No

306

one in the entire universe will be able to help you when the darkness comes. Nobody will help you. They say, "In dark days even your shadow will not stay with you. Even it will disappear." In the dark days of fear nobody will stay with you so you must see something that is light itself!

If you face the sun then the shadow, the darkness, is behind you. But if you turn your back to the light, the shadow is in front of you!

Why am I so insecure?

(giggling) Because you are depending on something that is not secure itself and, therefore, you cannot be happy!

There once was a man meditating for a long time in one position in the middle of the forest. One day he noticed a creeper next to him that was growing up a small plant instead of growing up him. So, he thought, "This simple creeper has no trust in me, and she has trust in a plant because she knows that I am mobile and the plant is not. I will get up and she will break. She is wise to go up this small tree because the tree will not move away, it is stationary." Nobody in the world is wise like the creeper. They have faith in things that move away. They will lose their body and their life. You must learn from the creeper. Depend on something which is everlasting so that you are safe. Insecurity is depending on something insecure, something that will die or run away. Don't depend on such a person. If you want to be safe keep the eternal Happiness which is within you, close to you. Yearn only for Freedom always and you will always be in the light.

Why do I prefer these other things?

It is a good question. Always put this question to yourself and someday you will fall in love with the Self and reject everything, even your body. You can't even keep association with your body! It will only stay seventy, eighty or ninety years. *So do not depend on your body, let alone others!*

Why is it hard to love myself?

(giggling) It is not hard to love yourself, it is very easy! It is only difficult to love yourself because you love somebody else. Self is Here and Now. Nearest of the near, dearest of the dear. But you love someone else and, therefore, you can't love your own Self. That's all; finished. Thank you.

I know I must surrender to the Grace of the teacher. What does it mean to surrender to you? The love is beyond what I contain.

Surrender means that you must surrender your mind to your heart. Then your ego will leave you. Surrender is what the river does when it meets the ocean. Then there is no more river left and it is finished. Like this, you surrender to the Grace of the teacher and keep Quiet and see what happens. That's all I can tell you: surrender to the teacher as a river surrenders to the ocean and loses all identification. There is no river in the ocean, no personality when you surrender to the Grace. The traditional way to come to the Guru was to take some Ganga water and say to the Guru three times:

"I give you my mind, I give you my mind, I give you my mind."

Then walk around the Guru three times. This establishes the relationship. That's all I can say to you!

Would you suggest the method of surrendering the personal will to the Divine will?

Surrendering is only surrendering ego to Self. Surrendering money or possessions is not surrender because it doesn't belong to you anyway. But if you surrender your ego, you get rid of everything.

There was a very good and kind king of India who was growing old and wanted to give the kingdom to his son and focus on enlightenment. Since he did not have a lot of time to go to the Himalayas and do a lot of practice he invited about five thousand saints and sages from all over India to come to his palace.

When they all gathered before him he said, with one foot in the stirrup of the saddle on his horse, "If anyone can give me enlightenment in the time it takes me to put my other foot in the other stirrup, I will give him 31,000 cows with gold coins on their horns and half of my kingdom."

In their minds the saints thought, "How stupid a man this king is. We have all grown long gray beards trying to do all the practices which lead to enlightenment. How could he expect to get it in a fingersnap. Even we are far from it!"

Then one mad looking boy walked in. He was nude and his body was twisted. All the saints and sages started to laugh at him and he was told to go away.

"What are you laughing at you fools?" said the crippled boy, "Are you nothing more than just a bunch of leather merchants and butchers who can only see my skin and bones?"

Then he said to the king, "I will give you enlightenment by the time you mount your horse, but this must happen between Guru and Shishya, between teacher and disciple. But I am not your Guru and you are not my student.

Since knowledge is only given to the student as a prasad from the Guru, you must become my student and give me a gift to show that you are my student."

"Okay," said the king, "I will give you 31,000 cows with gold coins attached to their horns and I will give you half of my kingdom."

"O King, these cows, coins and kingdom do not belong to you. Who had them before you?"

"My father," said the king.

"And before your father?"

"My grandfather," he replied.

"So all these things do not belong to you, next you will give them to your son. You are just the caretaker of all these things. It all belongs to the public. Give me something that belongs to you."

So the king thought and said, "I will give you my body."

The mad looking boy replied, "How many queens do you have?"

"Four," said the king.

"So a quarter of your body belongs to each queen. Your body has been given to the public as its king, to your queens as their husband, and to your sons as their father. Your body does not belong to you. Give me something which belongs to you!"

The king was clever and he realized there was only one thing that he had that was his to give and said, "I will give you my mind."

"Okay," said the boy, "Here is the Ganga water, now say three times that you have given me your mind."

The oath was taken and the king put one foot in the stirrup, but the young boy just walked out of the gathering and went away.

Now everybody is laughing, and the king doesn't know what to do, but he does know that he is not free. Suddenly, he realized that this thought, "I am not free" is in the mind and that he had given his mind to the mad boy and so he was not fulfilling the oath. To fulfill his oath he could not think!

At this moment the boy walked in and touched him and said, "What do you want? What about your other foot? Don't you want to put it into the stirrup now?"

The king could not speak. He was finished, he was enlightened. This King was Janaka and the boy was the Sage Astavakra.

So, this is what you must do. You must surrender your mind, your ego, your thoughts to that Supreme Power and then It will take care of you. This king then remained a king, but surrendered to That which was executing his duties as a king.

ॐ

How does one develop faith in that Divine will?

Faith is not needed now, neither is Divine will nor individual will. You can do anything without the will because it will happen by itself. For faith you need another person to have faith in and who is that person? The same marble that you use to stand on as a floor, you make into a statue of God and worship it. It is the same stone, and you ask the stone for Grace! So all these wills are just concepts in your own mind.

Even Divine will is a concept?

There is no Divine, you have created it. It has been imposed on you by the priests of the church. Therefore, your faith has been borrowed from someone else!

God is your creation. You even create yourself as being separate in order to speak about god. God cannot be objectified, or seen. He is the seer beyond objects. Go back to That Supreme Power and That You Are. That I Am.

Be independent of the concept of god which gives hell or heaven after death. Have heaven Here and Now by knowing "I Am That."

For one instant I felt no separation.

This absense of separation is surrendering to That and when you surrender to That you become That. There is no separation. There is no jiva ever born, no individuals ever born. There is no two. Where there is duality there is falsehood. No duality appears in That, for That Alone Is and That Isness Is Me!

I do feel existence is looking after me like it looked after King Janaka.

This is the highest faith, that existence is looking after you like a mother does. So, fully surrender to existence. Just relax and there will be no fear. This relaxation is only knowing your own Self. When you see other you are not relaxed, but when you see your Self this is relaxation. No fear.

The whirlpool is pulling and there is no way out. Papaji, please take care of me.

People are afraid of whirlpools because the boats that go into them do not come back to the surface. So I give you one piece of advice: When you see a whirlpool, and you are a strong boatman, then throw away the oars and break the mast. Then the boat will be very safe; no more rowing, no boatman, no oars, no mast. Then this whirlpool will take care of you and nobody else will help you. But you have to throw away all these things; like the ego that says "I have to row across" and "I have to stay out of the whirlpool." These imaginations and desires of your hands, arms, oars, and workmanship of the boatman you must leave aside. Now you will see how safe you will be. This whirlpool will take care of you if you surrender everything into it. Now you can't go down. She will keep you on her chest.

This universe is a whirlpool. Everybody is in difficulty. This samsara is a whirlpool. Everybody, even the most clever boatman like Alexander the Great, have all sunk down. The only way not to drown is to go to a person and learn from him how not to use your force and how to surrender. That will save you.

How can I make bliss shine unimpeded? So many hours I spend in silent happiness, but unbroken surrender is calling. Please help me surrender completely to Self and make the poisons of the snake of pride harmless.

It is absolutely necessary that you surrender to the Satguru. Your surrender should be like that of a kitten. The mother cat holds and carries the babies wherever she wants. The kitten has nothing to do with it.

On the other hand, the baby of the monkey must hold onto its mother by itself from the birth itself. It clings to the waist of the mother and is always in fear, you can see it in their eyes. When the mother jumps from one branch to another the child is afraid that it will fall and sometimes I have seen them fall. So surrender like a kitten.

This surrender doesn't take time, it only takes an instant. In this short time all the mistakes of millions of years are washed away, this is the beauty of attending Satsang. Satsang is the raft to carry you across the ocean of samsara. Don't worry about the sharks which are waiting to devour you. This raft is a very sure and certain vehicle. No misery will touch you.

I feel that there is a great difference between complete surrender and simply being passive. I desire to completely surrender to love and truth, the source. Nothing else matters in the universe. Can you guide me to complete surrender? Please accept the gratitude from this heart which has been forever changed by gazing into your eyes.

If you love someone and nobody else at the same time, this is called complete surrender. An example of half surrender is surrender to a girl giving her all your money and promises of commitment and fidelity, but you do not speak the truth because you say the same thing to your neighbor's wife. This is partial surrender. One night both of your girlfriends meet together and discover that they are sharing you and that your promises were false. This is dishonesty.

> At least with your Self, always be honest.
> Because it knows everything anyway,
> in all the states of waking, dreaming and sleeping.
> How can you hide your guilt from One who sees every activity?
> So be honest and speak: "Let Thy Will be done."
> According to Its will only, activate your mind, senses, and activities.

Do you now understand how to be honest to your own Self?

I surrender my ignorance to you.

If you surrender your ego and ignorance this is all that you have to do. Nothing more. Then the Grace will take you in her arms instantly. Most people can't surrender. They only speak it with their mouth, they don't actually surrender.

I remember someone asked the Maharshi about surrendering the ego. They asked, "Is complete total surrender a must for a devotee to know Self? I cannot completely surrender because I have other responsibilities to fulfill. Though I am here in Tiruvannamalai, my mind is at home." The Maharshi replied, "If you cannot totally surrender, partial surrender will also work."

So partial surrender will also do, and slowly partiality will also disappear! Then you will get prasad, a gift from the teacher, who will bless you. But you must be totally doubtless about the teaching of the teacher, then it will work like gunpowder. This is complete surrender. Partial surrender will be like wet wood ignited by matches: you have to use so many matchboxes before it gets dry at the cost of your own effort. The wood will also burn, but it will give a lot of smoke and you will start coughing. Then you will see that complete surrender is better than this smoky surrender.

The experience of spaciousness comes and yet I feel vulnerable to ego.

Go deep into this spaciousness and don't make effort, don't think.

> Stay as you are, everything will be fine
> if you don't allow a thought to arise.

This is eternal Love, stay Here.
Everything will be done by itself.
Let something take charge of you,
let something rise from within.
It will function, just allow it to rise.
This will work within the Consciousness.
You are not to do, think, or plan anything.

Stay as Is. Allow it to function.
Nature will function without your mind and thought.
Only action and reaction; no doership, no ego.
This is the end of suffering.
"I am doing," "I have done," "I will do,"
is manifestation and suffering.
But when you really look at it,
you will see that you have never done anything at all.

But out of Nothing you can do anything
without any reward for your activity.
All activity will be no activity,
and you will have no footprints left
to give you the next cycle of suffering.
Surrender to your totality.
You have no limitations or notions of limitations,
no intentions or concepts,
Only Freedom!

Yes, yes, I see!

This seeing is Being. When you see through the eyes at objects it is distraction, but true seeing is Being and this seeing is with different eyes. It depends on you which eyes you want to use. True sight has nothing to do with eyes. It is an inner sight, an inner Being. If you do this you will always see with the same eye, whether you are looking within or without. Then there will be no difference between samsara and nirvana. This eye has no limitation, no inside and no outside. Give up looking through these two eyes and the true eye will open and you will have Divine sight and this seeing is Being!

ॐ

"I Am With You Wherever You Are"

There is no escape from Love,
there is no east or west for Peace and Freedom.
No matter where you go it is always with you.
Satsang is the reminder that you are home,
that you are the Home itself,
so you can't return "back" from Satsang, it is your nature.
This experience cannot be forgotten.
That which can be forgotten is forgotten by the mind,
but the mind has no access to this experience.

But be careful and vigilant.
You will keep the problems most dear to you
and so your old friends, your wicked habits, the asuras,
will come back and invite you to suffer again.
They are very strong and so you must be.
Break these old habits and you are free;
so only travel with those in the same boat,
only associate with those going in the same direction.
Go to Truth at any cost, always keep Quiet.

When the circumstances of vasanas arise so will the vasanas,
no matter how dormant they are, and especially if you are Quiet.
A bullet kills once but a vasana kills again and again.
So vigilantly inquire!

Expectations are illusions, so don't run after them and
don't get involved in anger, lust, and greed either.
Just don't involve yourself with them.
Keeping Quiet and content is the best weapon.

Joy will also destroy mind and the demons.
Once you bury them do not dig them up again.

You are responsible for your family and friends
so this Satsang has to continue.
Once you know the Truth you must share it.

I was staying in Ramanashram before the partition of the country in
1947. One day in the middle of July someone asked me on which side of the

315

River Ravi I was from. I told him it was much beyond this river. Then he told me about the partition crisis of the country which I didn't know too much about since I neither had time for reading newspapers, nor for politics. He said that in the middle of the next month the country would be partitioned and so my family, who was living between Lahore and Peshawar, would be massacred if I did not save them. I told him that I had forgotten everybody and that it had all been a dream: parents, family, children, country. All of it was a dream that was over now. This was how strong my detachment was and how strong it had to be. This man told the Maharshi what I had said and as we went out on his morning walk together the Maharshi asked me, "Why don't you go and look after your family?"

I said, "When I came here I had my wife and parents and children, but when you looked at me everything was finished and now You are my only relation and no one else in the world."

"If you call it a dream, why are you afraid of a dream? It is better if you go into the dream and look after your wife and relations. Why be afraid of the dream? Your dream hand is quite safe in the mouth of the dream tiger. Like this, live in the world, and call it a dream. Don't be afraid and work as you work in the dream. The dream is a dream and nothing in it is real, but you, as their son, are also in the dream. So let the dream son go to the dream country and save the dream parents in the dream."

So in this way he defined the dream for me. Then the Maharshi said:

"I Am with you wherever you are."

With this sentence he gave me the Teaching: He is the "I Am" which is with me wherever I am.

What could I say to him? He was telling me to leave. So I prostrated to Him and collected the dust from under his feet, went thrice around him and left. I went to the Punjab and through several miraculous events rescued my family from all the butchering. This is the benefit of staying with the Teacher:

The Teacher not only gives you Freedom,
but also looks after whatever you need.

When I was back up north, I saw that the train for Lahore was empty except for Muslims shouting "Kill the Hindus!" and a group of Hindus huddled together for safety. So the thought comes into my mind to go over and sit with the Muslims even though I would much rather have been with the Hindus. I even had an Om tattooed on the back of my hand and my ears were pierced like only the Hindus had them. So who gave me this thought to sit with them? I was even shouting with the Muslims. So with this savior

Om on my hand and the blessings of my teacher I arrived safely, while every other Hindu was taken from the train and killed. When I arrived in my home town no Hindus were there. Even the tonga, the horse cart, that I took was a Muslim tonga. The place where I lived was a pure Hindu colony, Guru Nanakpura, and so to not raise any suspicion with the tonga driver I told him to go to a Muslim colony nearby, Islampura. From there I walked to my house and rang the bell, but nobody answered. Finally, I heard my father's voice from the roof top asking who I was. "I am your son! Don't you even recognize my voice?" I yelled back.

"Why have you come?" he asked. "How did you come? Are the trains still working? You should take all the relatives out of here on the trains!"

The District Magistrate, who was a Muslim and a very good friend of mine while I was in the army, protected us in his own home and helped to arrange our travel back to India.

Our houses had already been taken by refugee Muslims from Amritsar who had their women taken from them by the Sikhs. Everybody in the family, almost forty people, made it out safely by train, whereas most families were partially or totally destroyed. Eventually, my parents were flown out by the DM, because by the time they came trains were no longer running. This is the Grace of the Master. Nobody could harm us and He took care of everything.

Questioner: Papaji, is it okay to leave Lucknow and go to the West? Do you think I am ready?

Papaji: Yes. There is no east and west. This is only on the map. There is no east and west for the Master. Wherever you go is the Presence of the Teacher and you will feel it. If you have surrendered it is the responsibility of the Teacher to guide you at every step.

I am afraid of changing back to my old ways when I return to Denmark.

When you return to Denmark how do you expect that you will change? When you came to Lucknow you expected something to change and so it has, but you are a different person from what you were when you first came. So don't expect any change when you return. Stay always in Satsang and do not have any fear that you will return to the previous state. You can never change. This moment has offered you silence, quietness and happiness so do not have fear. You will have Satsang in Denmark. Tell them the story of what happened here.

I have had experiences, but ...

This experience can go back to Denmark! It has to stay with you. The experience is that you are Free. You have to stay with it! How can it go anywhere? "I am Free" will remain always with you when you have an experience of Freedom. You have not to keep this experience, you are to *be* That, otherwise it is all just imagination and theory.

How come that after the revelation of emptiness a character can still arise and think of itself and the world as real and meaningful? After seeing what I have how can I even think that coming and going are possible?

Who speaks about emptiness? Who is aware of this emptiness? That person is your own Atman which is not empty and not full. It is aware of everything, emptiness and samsara, and nothing is troubled because it all comes out of That. This world of imagination is its own production and so there is no difference between samsara and nirvana.

The wave rises from the ocean and thinks that she is independent because she has a name and a form and movement. The ocean doesn't mind this and knows that all the waves will rise, play, and fall and again become ocean. What is the substance that has never arisen nor fallen? That is water. The water is always the same though it may take the differing forms of ocean or waves. The water is observing everything rise and fall, even the ocean.

Why in the light of this Emptiness does Papaji's acceptance and rejection still seem important, as if I am something that needs something from something else?

This "I" which needs something from someone is the egotistical "I" which has been separated for generations from its home which it no longer knows. This "I" travels from one incarnation to another trying to find its true parental house. She needs someone to tell her to go home and once there she will know that she has never left. But if she doesn't go home she can wander for millions of years through samsara. For the billions on earth only a few "I's" will want to return home. All other "I's" will wander and make relationships with other "I's." You have come to Lucknow and now you know who you are. You are forever in my Heart. Stay as Such.

When you go back to your country see the circumstances that you are placed in and react accordingly. You won't forget the glimpse of peace and love. Know it is the tendency of your mind to create problems and doubts. There are no problems and no doubts, so don't think about them.

"I Am With You Wherever You Are"

I want to thank you for everything you have given me in the last four months and for all your blessings and love.

Don Juan once picked up a small stone and flung it onto the mountain. Then he said, "Look Carlos, what once was a pebble in my hand has become a mountain." Likewise, you have come to Satsang, the Truth, and have become Truth and Love. This Satsang is the river Jahnavi which purifies you when you touch her. Those who have a dip in this river become one with her and they will return a different person. You came here for only a couple of days, but stayed for months because here Truth and Love are flowing. Wherever there is Satsang where a teacher is speaking to those who need this Beauty and Truth, that is a place to stay.

I will give you the name Jahnavi, that which blesses and purifies everything. She relieves all of the pains and sins which people carry for lifetimes. Just touch her, immediately they are washed away. She is so blessing and caring, she is the mother. Whoever swims in her becomes eternal. Like this, bless everybody that comes and enters your heart.

How is it possible to remain this shining ocean of love in all circumstances? With all the stress in my life in Vienna it is hard to stay as this.

This is the question that most people ask me after having the beautiful experience and I am happy that you are here for an explanation. First of all, you want this experience to stay with you all the time. This also means that you lose it at times.

Pure awareness is impossible to lose, but it is the bliss that leaves when there is stress.

When you want to keep this experience all the time it means that you want to bring this experience into time. Why should you bring this experience into the time? When this experience occurred it was beyond time. Anything that happens in time is worthless. Anything that you get in time; happiness or peace, or a person that you love, within this time it will disappear someday. So why do you have this desire that this Timelessness should come into time just to oblige you? If you don't desire it to come into time it will be an eternal experience. To make this eternal do not give rise to the desire to bring the timelessness into time. Time means death, unhappiness, past and mind. There is no difference between time and mind. Let it be as it is. You want to jump into the ocean and once you jump there

319

is no return. When the river discharges into the ocean it becomes the ocean and stays as the ocean. It is only that the river has lost its form and name.

Remove the name. Consciousness has no name. Remove the name and form and what will remain, what do you see?

Nothing, pure Being.

This nothing is always nothing; not sometimes something and sometimes nothing. (laughs) Is it clear now?

It is clear.

There will be no difference when you return to Austria or when you are in Lucknow because these are only names! Any name is in time, but Consciousness is not in time. (giggles) Very good.

No work will interfere with this peace, it won't be a hindrance to you. Don't fear, there will be no problem. You are not involved with your work as you once were, because then it was your ego which thought it was doing all the work. Now you know that there is something beyond even your capacity to understand, beyond ego, from where your ego arises, that is doing all the work. Stay in this source. See that the work is being done by your body which is activated by something else and you simply observe it all happening. Turn your face in the reverse gear to where the energy comes to even close your finger. Go beyond and look to the reservoir of your thinking and identify your self as That. Then all will go on by the Grace of the Supreme Power. Turn your face to the Supreme, not towards an object, which is not permanent. Turn your face beyond the objects to where the energy is coming. Then you will know that nothing can interfere with your work and it will go on as it is.

If there is anything that you received here that can be lost,

Let it be lost.
You have not come here to achieve what can be lost,
But to know That which you will never lose.

Don't aspire for what can be lost.
What cannot be lost, what is Eternal
is seated in the cave of your heart
Shining like a diamond,
Look within!

It is just so hard to leave Lucknow!

How can you ever leave Luck Now? You cannot leave this luck when you are in now and wherever you go you are in now itself. In now there is luck, there is happiness, there is love, and there is beauty. You can't get out of it. Luck now will never leave you. That is what people of Lucknow have been saying for millennia: Once you are in Lucknow you can never leave it. Let the body go, don't care about its movement. What will be immovable will be with me. You can go anywhere you like, all these planets belong to you. The whole cosmos, all these millions of planets are in just a small corner of your Self. Where will you go? You can't get out of it. You cannot leave me because you are in my heart!

Now I feel my leaving is like a leaf of a tree falling gently, beautifully and quietly, sinking into the embracing ocean. I bow in gratitude and take you in my heart.

Very good, very nice. When the leaf falls from the tree it has no intention to fly northward or southward. It has nothing to do. It flies with the wind, with the wind of Grace. You are a leaf falling from the tree of ego. Now you have no relation with the tree and so you are falling and whichever direction the wind blows it will take you with it.

I am very happy that you have done your job and are now returning. Thank you.

Many people say that my stay is too short, but it only took one moment. How can I best remain aware. Is commitment the way?

No, no commitment. You don't need to commit to anything. Just feel and trust that "I am what I am." This is no commitment. You are as you are. You have been as you were. You will be as you will be. This is a trust in you: "I am what I am." Not in something else. It is very easy. It is very natural. You are not to become anything or un-become anything, but be as you are.

Even if you felt incomplete as you were leaving and felt that you didn't get anything it will not have been a waste of time. If you say you didn't get anything, you are right because I don't give anything and you don't get anything. No time in Satsang is a waste of time! This will work someday, even if you have not felt benefited. It will work, nobody can be disappointed. When they are ready, all the Truth spoken of here will rush into their mind.

I feel very complete and now I see your face everywhere.

When you fall in love with someone you see the face of that one

321

everywhere. And when the love is very deep whatever you see is your beloved and you even become That. Then identification as the Beloved takes place.

Even my feet don't touch the ground.

This is also true, you will think that you are flying because you feel no weight. I am very happy for your visit here. Thank you.

Do you have to practice to get to the effortless state? I'm returning to Brazil soon and I wonder what meditation you advise me to do there.

When you are in Brazil:

> Keep your hands active as you work
> and your thought on Me.
> Keep your thought Within,
> keep your thought on your Heart.

Keep your thought on your heart and your hands on your work. Keeping your thought on Me means thinking "Who am I?" Along with this you should work. Mind can stay in only one place at a time. If you draw it into the heart it can't see anything but heart. Keep it Here constantly and you will see that it can never escape. Constantly keep your mind on your Heart.

When people leave Lucknow they often ask for advice. My only advice for you when you return home is to keep Quiet. You can speak to your friends about this Quietness and tell them how to keep Quiet, and where you picked this advice up. That is enough.

I am the dust compared to you. I am not worthy to teach them how to be silent.

Then simply keep Quiet. If they ask you what happened in Lucknow, simply keep Quiet. Then let them think whatever they want to think.

I am afraid that when I leave you to go back to Germany I will fall back into my old habits.

Don't fear your old habits, all of Munchen will be changed when you go back. You will see everything differently than before and you will not look the same. Don't worry.

As you go into the world,
always remember what you love most in your life
and don't touch anything else.

Do this for one moment and this love which you have ignored will rise
to the surface. But unlike other things on the surface which come and go this
love is the depth itself in which there is no rising or falling. Just look at it
Now and that is all you have to do. Don't fall in love with the wave because
they will not last. They move about and are soon finished.

Don't touch anything that appears
because it will soon disappear.
Look Within to where there is no name or form
and you will know who you are:
Freedom.

*I feel it is time to go out into the world with this diamond you have
given me and test it on samsara.*

Whatever the teacher has he hands over to one when he thinks he is
ready. The Guru also hands over everything to his student knowing that he
deserves it. I will tell you a story about this.

There was a saint in China who was about to announce his successor so
he held a contest: The disciple that would come up with the best gatha, the
best statement of the dharma, would win the robes and begging bowl of the
saint. So all through the day and night the learned swamis of the ashram were
writing their gathas on a board in the main hall. There was a very humble
man in this ashram who was illiterate and was always working pounding the
paddy, but late at night, when all his work was finished, he walked into the
hall and asked what all the excitement was about.

"The Guru will give his robes and begging bowl to the one who writes
the best gatha," he was told.

He asked, "What is the best gatha so far?"

They told him, "A very wise swami has said,

'Keep the mirror of the mind clean
so no dust will alight, then you will be Free.'"

Then this humble paddy pounder simply replied,

"Where there is no mirror

323

Where will the dust alight?"

This gatha was written in with the others. Around midnight the Saint came to look at the gathas and when he saw the gatha of the paddy pounder he knew he had found his successor. So he went to him and gave him his robes and begging bowl and told him to run as fast as he could all through the night toward the frontiers because if the swamis of the ashram found him they would kill him. And so he left.

The next morning the Guru was found naked and the swamis were furious and soon figured out what had happened. A few hours later they had caught up with the paddy pounder and accused him of stealing the Guru's only possessions.

He replied, "You can have this begging bowl and this old robe, but you can never take the Light that my Guru has given me!"

They could not steal what the real gift-teaching was because the Satguru dwells in your Heart and in the Heart of all the beings of the universe.

Don't try to clean the mirror because it will always get dirty again.
There is no mirror and no dust to alight!
Get rid of arrogance that you are not Self and that there is "other."
Better to throw the mirror away and realize that all is Self.
This realization is the Diamond and a gift from the Guru.

Now you need not test this Diamond. You will be the same and the world will be the same. Now just don't be afraid because there is no difference between samsara and nirvana. Go afresh and face all the circumstances that present themselves.

I am worried that I will lose the contact I have with you when I leave.

This fear is not real, as you will experience. These four walls around us now have nothing to do with our Peace. You are this Peace and you can't gain it or lose it. Anything that you do gain you will lose because it is a material gain only. Don't worry and go wherever you like. Depend on the Mother for she will take care of you.

You should go back and continue this work there, it doesn't take much. Devote just five minutes to your Self when you rise in the morning and before you go to sleep. Then you will get what you want. I have seen no results in people who have spent decades in Himalayan caves, but this will work. Just have a strong desire for it and nothing will stop you. Think of your Beloved twenty four hours a day. With this constant remembrance you will be with your Beloved and not different from That.

How can I serve you while in Europe? What can I do for you?

What you can do is always look behind you to see who is following you as you walk down the street, and who never leaves you, even when you are in sleep. Who is aware of all your activities whether you are awake, dreaming or sleeping. Find this person who gives you the strength to move your tongue whenever you speak. When you see, find the one who is behind the retina of the eye. Do this for me and you will stay in touch with your own Self.

I feel a strong urge to go back to my family and share this with them. I feel I have neglected them.

No, you have not neglected them. You will bring them the peace and love of all beings. This they never told you because they were never told. You can take this gift to them.

I want to share time with them while it is still possible. Is this a good idea or am I lost in illusion?

It is a good idea. You are a good son of noble parents. Only noble parents give birth to a son who will attend Satsang. It is so rare for this to happen, maybe one in every twenty million.

I found that when I returned to the West after being with you two years ago, that I tended not to engage in activities very much and wasn't interested in the world.

When you return from Satsang back home to your country it is quite natural that you are not as active as the people around you. You are going to be a different person.

But you were working after you met Ramana. You had an Awakening and yet you went on working and supporting your family. This didn't happen to me.

Yes, I worked as I was with Ramana and it didn't make any difference. I only visited him on Sundays and worked the rest of the week. I would leave Saturday afternoon, get there at night and spend all Sunday there with him and return to Madras early Monday morning. Then I would attend to the business of my office from 10 a.m. to Saturday afternoon again. Maharshi never advised people to stay on and do nothing. He didn't tell them to reject their life and their work.

325

You are the Absolute That
and you have nothing to do from your own initiative.
That will take care of you, That is your own Self within.
It will guide you if you surrender your will to Its will.
Don't think you are doing anything yourself
because Self uses karma to govern all.

You can't get rid of your karma and you are led to do whatever it leads you to do. You can't stop karma.

What about the responsibilities which occur as appearances in That?

The responsibilities which you speak about are from the ego-mind. Actually, you do not have any responsibility.

What comes, face it,
and do according to the command of Self.
Then you will not bear the fruits
of the activities which you are performing
because you will be That.
That will be responsible for your activities.

Keep up this experience
by always meditating with the astral body,
not the physical body.
Let the body within the body meditate.
This will instruct the physical body
how to act according to the routines of work
and responsibilities.

Everything seems to be so dreamlike after meeting you.

Before coming to Lucknow everything was so real to you, but now it is a dream. This is the lesson you get when you return home.

Things seem real only when the mind told you so.
But when mind is not present all this is a dream.

So few experience this reality as a dream. Everything looks real when you dream. A tiger which pounces on you in your dream seems very real, and it is real during the dream. Even the dreamer seems real. But when you wake up you are not afraid of the tiger because you know it never existed. It was only a dream tiger.

So it is with everybody. They are all afraid of this dream because nobody understands that it is not real.

So whatever comes understand that it is all dream,
Don't be afraid of the dream tigers.

So should I just stay home and not come to Lucknow anymore and live life as it comes?

Yes, live life as it comes. If it brings you to Lucknow then return to Lucknow.

Live life as it comes, but don't be involved in it.
Let it come, don't reject it.
If nothing comes keep contented and sit quiet.
This is a true Teaching.

Still some doubts and notions and unworthiness seem to arise.

Doubts and notions belong to the past. Now no more doubts or notions will touch you. Just laugh at them when they arise! Grace knows nothing about unworthiness or worthiness. Throw a flower or spit into the ocean and it responds the same. Unworthiness is just mind baggage. Unworthiness is only your ego postponing its destruction.

The Self doesn't mind that the mind goes to Europe because Europe is in the Self. Go anywhere and you will be taken care of. The problems arise when the ego takes the burden of controlling itself. Identify with the Self and the mind will go nowhere.

I came here to Lucknow in the first place because I heard you laugh on a tape. I love your laugh!

Here we laugh for no reason and it is fine, but in the West if you laugh like this they consider you to be not sane or on drugs or both! Once when I was in Spain giving meditation classes somebody jumped up and ran forward to kiss my feet. He started to jump up and down laughing and saying, "I am God, I am God!" Then he ran out. To say that "I am God" is fine in India, after all, it is the Truth, but to say this in the West is not acceptable. The next day I found out how unacceptable it was. This man was dancing and laughing in ecstatic bliss when the police came and detained him long enough for his wife to come and pick him up. And you know what she did? She drove him straight to a mental institution and filed for divorce on the grounds that he had gone insane. On the contrary, after having tasted what true reality is, this man was probably one the most sane people in all of Europe at that time! He had no expectation or ideas of reality, he just *was* Reality!

So I visited this man in the insane asylum and taught him how to live in society after this realization and soon after he was released. This is my experience about the social laws in the West about laughing. You can go to Holland or any land. You will be okay. Thank you.

I haven't found a niche in society where I can both work and express myself.

You need not express yourself. Just remain in innocence. Keep your life in innocence. Whatever comes for your livelihood accept it. Don't have any desire for "this" or "that." Children don't care about tomorrow. If they are given a sweet they eat it immediately. Like this, what is given, eat it and finish it off. What is your work now?

I am a lawyer.

A liar? I see. This is innocence. If a liar says that he is a liar is it the truth or a lie? Nobody would say that they are a liar, so you must not be a liar.

So how to live in the world? Like an innocent child.

What has been happening so far is beyond words.

Anything you can sense you can describe. But what you cannot describe is freedom from the words, freedom from mind, freedom from intellect. Everything is describable, but That beyond words is what you really are, but you don't believe it.

Everything you see is an object which begins and ends and it is not worthwhile. When you see something beyond description it is your own Self. The eye sees objects, but how can it see and describe itself? It cannot describe itself because it is too close to itself. In the same way, what is too close to your true nature defies all description. So, now go back to your country, to the world, with consciousness, faith and trust that "I Am Free."

This world seems like such an illusion to me now. How did this illusion ever arise? What is this illusion? How to avoid being tricked again?

The power of illusion is very strong,

so continue vigilance in a joyful play with tendencies
because when one is near Freedom
all demons will consolidate and attack.
So continue inquiry and concentration.
Continue being self meditating on Self.
Do this playfully always.

The World Is Illusion

Under every wave is ocean,
under every name is substratum,
under every appearance, this is You.
If you do not forget who you are,
This appearance is the Cosmic Dance.
The Unnameable has given you this shape
to Play, to Love, to Know Thy Self.
Don't forget this!

Narayana: The Creation of the Illusion

The ocean does not forget that it is a wave,
but the wave forgets that it is an ocean.
This is "why" there is manifestation;
for sake of play this forgetfulness arises.
The world is only for celebration.
Manifestation is just a cosmic drama to be enjoyed.
There is only play and it is not existent,
and continues because whatever you think so it becomes.
This manifestation was created by you
and it will be destroyed by you.

The first thought is "I."
Then arises "my," which is ego,
and then comes all manifestation.
Time, mind, manifestation is projected out of "I"
which is itself the projection required to manifest the play.
Undress yourself of these things and find where "I" rises from.
You are Shiva if you do not project "I,"
and your Shakti is the projection by which to play.
Consciousness is the source of this play,
of the mind, and That is all.

The ocean cannot stay alone
and so the notion of wave is created.
When waves rise ocean loses nothing
and when waves fall ocean gains nothing.
Samsara, the illusion, maya, the play,
are the waves on the ocean of nirvana.

Waves are not separate from the ocean,
rays are not separate from the sun,
You are not separate from
Existence-Consciousness-Bliss.
This is a reflection of That.

Questioner: What is creation and how does this illusion arise?

Papaji: In the beginning Consciousness is alone like a still lake. Then a ripple arises and this is name and form. From Consciousness the thought arises "I am Consciousness." This is the I-sense. Then desire arises and this is ego. The ripple thinks that it is separate and this creates limitations which are time and space. The ripple is a blink of thought and this is ego rising from Consciousness, but ripples are not different from the lake, from water. Forget this and you are in trouble. The senses rise and then sense objects and all of manifestation is created to play with you and delude you. When you say that "all is imagination" it is no longer imagination because you are awake. Awaken from this dream called manifestation. Don't go away from yourself and the ego will not rise. Objects are not other than senses, which are not other than body, which is not other than mind, which is not other than "I." Truly, this creation is not other than your own reflection because this "I" is Consciousness. Find the source of this "I" with absolute vigilance and stop thinking, for thought is the world process itself.

Is the world that we see the totality of the universe?

There are many planes of existence. The ones above ours are occupied by very beautiful beings and on the ones below the people are sub-human and very ugly. I have visited many planes where people are very handsome and you can see through their bodies. Other planes below made me very afraid because they had half faces and other gruesome deformities. Next time we will become gods if we don't have moksham here and then we will eventually come back to this plane because this is the only place where you can win freedom. Even gods must be born here if they want freedom.

Consciousness takes any shape that it thinks; just as gold takes any shape of jewelry and remains gold. Consciousness creates the universe without losing its nature just as an ocean creates waves while remaining an ocean. So there is no multiplicity and no unity, It just Is. You are not aware of this and this is why a rope looks like a snake, though upon close investigation there is no snake. The same is for the "I." Upon close investigation there is no "I" and this universe disappears into Emptiness, into Consciousness. Never did anything arise, this is the ultimate Truth. Think this because as you think so it becomes. Break this snake's fangs: Know Thyself.

Dwell in your own Self and do not look at what is creator and what is created. Simply abide in your own Self. The whole world in all its forms come from the Source in which there is nothing! The thought arises in the source: Let me be multiplied, and existence unfolds with past, present, and future. For 25,000 years the Vedas have been saying this:

> Ek Koham Bhahosham: "Let me be multiplied."
> The purpose of this creation is for Self to love and enjoy Self.
> So the purpose of human birth is Freedom.

All form is sound and arises from sound. Any name that you utter will be form, but there is one sound which does not make any form. This Unknown is the substratum of all that is known. The known will deceive you someday, so have friendship only with that which neither appears or disappears.

Consciousness experiences infinite births and creations in a moment. These creations, these lilas, are neither real nor unreal. There really is no creation and no experiencer, and yet there are experiences and experiencers. This is a paradox only for mind because in Consciousness there is no difference between object and subject. In this instant inquire "Who am I?" and this inquiry will reveal itself to itself. Otherwise, creation will go on forever. Non-inquiry is the basis for creation and inquiry is the basis of Freedom, for the realization that your nature is sat-chit-ananda.

If our true nature is sat-chit-anand; knowledge, consciousness, bliss, why did we leave it to assume this bodily form?

Why assume that you left it? This is foolish! This assumption itself is the creation of the illusion that I have just described to you! Who told you that you are not sat-chit-anand? It is only this assumption which will cause endless rebirths. Why don't you have the conviction that you never left this home? Why don't you have the conviction that "I am sat-chit-ananda," that "I am free"?

Because it doesn't feel that I am free.

Why not have the convictions that "I am not born and I will never die"? What you think is what happens, so think of a better reality like, "I am That alone" if you are going to think at all.

Is God as Self and God as lila the same?

Both are the same. What is the difference between the ocean and the waves? Where there is ocean there must be waves and where there are waves there must be ocean. Where there is ocean there must be the play of waves on the surface which eventually returns and settles back in. Say "I am the lila, the leeelaaa" and enjoy it!

> If you say that there is Self and there is lila,
> then you are not speaking from Self, from experience.
> There is no difference and no non-difference,
> there is Nothing in anything!
> There is only Self!

> Unenlightenment is a game: Lila.
> It is a game to be enjoyed, but remember:
> death, suffering, and pain are the taxes of sense pleasures.
> Better to be free of all these taxes.
> Realize freedom; let death and suffering happen to the body.
> Play with the crocodile of samsara, nothing can touch you,
> but don't end up in its stomach! Play as Freedom.

ॐ

Maya: The Shakti of the Illusion

> It is a dark path at twilight
> and you see a deadly snake lying along the side of the path.
> Suddenly someone comes from the other direction
> and, as they walk by the snake,
> they ask you what you are frightened of.
> You tell them all about the poisonous snake
> that they just stepped over.
> Then they tell you, and show you, that it is just a rope.

> The snake does not exist and never did exist,
> and yet it manages, by the power of illusion and superimposition,
> to conceal the reality, the rope.

> As the concept of a snake conceals the rope
> so maya conceals the Atman.
> Atman is everything: Pure Consciousness,
> eternally free and blissful,
> but imagination conceals this
> with non-existent name and form,

with superimposed subject and object.
Whatever you think is; whatever you imagine to be
is superimposed over reality creating a transient dream reality.
As the concealer of reality, this is the Shakti Avarana Devi!
As the projector of illusion, this is the Shakti Maya Devi!
The incredible power of maya comes from Atman only.

All name and form is this maya.
When you see this name and form
you miss the substance-substratum.
If you see the ring you do not see the gold.
Name and form dissolving into void becomes Being!
Name and form will not provide happiness;
wherever there is name and form there is something concealed
and That is the happiness!

The waking state is a film starring the ego,
directed by karma, and produced by maya.
Even the waking state is in the dream state.
Reality is always real and unreality is never real.
You only dream this illusion when you are sleeping so wake up:
the snake is always nonexistent.

Freedom is when the illusory-ness of the illusion is removed.
Doubt is the illusory wall between you and freedom.
Stop confirming the reality of the illusion
by running after it; expectation is the running.
Maya is the imagination that never ends, and never exists.
Her projected lila comes from the inside
and for the sake of her play knowledge of reality is illusive.
The world is subject-object, to know the reality,
find what this subject-object is projected on.
Find the screen which is not touched by anything!
Like this, contemplation of Self
terminates illusions of false appearance.

What is not Here and Now is not real and not worth striving for.
Anything that can go away is not worth clinging to.
Reality is always here, so don't cling to anything,
or maya has fooled you again.

Why does maya, this world illusion, exist?

> Because you need her! Because *you* need her!
> You have desires that you want to fulfill
> and so you need her to fulfill them.
> But you are walking through the burning sand
> after a river which is only a mirage,
> because she doesn't exist.
> It is just your desire which creates her.
> Very few will stop walking and turn their face within
> to the real stream, the stream of nectar.

Can you physically prove that reality is an illusion?

Concepts cannot be proven and that is all that illusions and reality are. Illusion and reality do not exist as the river doesn't exist in the mirage. Don't leave the steady well of spring water. Only those who do and go to the desert will see a mirage and suffer this illusion. The Truth cannot be proven or experienced.

Everybody is involved in this illusion, but they don't know who she is. Everybody likes her and so they are not happy and peaceful, but are suffering instead. Learn from Kabir to be happy and eternally in bliss. He sings to maya:

> You are a great deceiver, nobody recognizes you.
> But I know who you are.

You said that God helps all who come to him. You also said that you are God and so I beg you please to destroy this illusion once and for all today. Right now!

Show me this illusion and I will instantly burn it without using even a matchstick. But you have to show me. Show me this girlfriend because you want to decide something about her, not about you. I will take care of her whether she likes to be destroyed or I can purify her so that again she will be with you. First of all, you should know the meaning of illusion. Illusion means maya. Maya means: that which does not exist. So how can I destroy that which does not exist? What is projected onto the screen is illusion. You don't have any awareness of the projection when you are engrossed in the physical pictures of the movie theater. In these pictures some are happy and some are sad, some die in the ocean and some have gone to the graveyard. You are so into these people on the screen that you become one with those who suffer and those who enjoy. This is the story of samsara.

When the projection is over and another show is to be shown you will see for a moment what the pictures have been played on. This screen is not tainted at all. She is not wet from the ocean and she is not burned by the fire. All of these projections are not real. Only a few will know this and they will not come for the next show. But some people watch the same movie again and again!

If you know that you are the screen and that all the projections are illusions then only can you enjoy them. You will know that you cannot be tainted. On that screen that you are this body appears. This body, whether male or female, needs the opposite body to play with. This is the story that is going on, it will not end. Simply stay quiet and you will know that you have never been tainted because you have never been born! The one who is born and dies is only a concept. Knowing this you will become very happy. This is the start of the romance with your own Self. Wherever you are speak this to people.

In this play of maya what is the role of the human?

Human birth is so rare because it is only in this birth that you can know that all is illusion. Within the human population it is probably only ten per billion who make the strong decision for freedom. Among them it is very rare that one wins the game of illusion.

The truth is within, but you always look somewhere else in order to appease your tendency to go out after sense objects. But all of this is illusion. Know this now! Find where the illusion rises from. Find where this thought arises from. Then you will have found the love which always dwells within you. Then you will see the illusion of everything, including your own body.

What appears and disappears is not real.

Once you know it is illusion you will separate yourself from it and you are "the one who has gone beyond the illusion," like a mirage of a river in the desert. The ones who try to be fulfilled by this mirage will never be satisfied. They will just get into more and more trouble.

Some people will know that this river is a mirage and they don't go there, they know maya appears, but does not exist. When you know this you must ask where peace and happiness is. This search will bring you to Satsang.

Is there a connection with outside circumstances and inner emotional states, or is it all illusion?

It is all illusion. Mind itself is illusion. Whatever you think is illusion and so to remove the illusion you should not think. I don't want you to practice this for years; but for just one instant, one blink of the eye, one breath, one half of a breath, and then your problems will be solved. (giggle)

Is love also an illusion?

> Love is not an illusion.
> In Love all illusion is lost.
> Where there is no illusion,
> then Love arises.

I would like a new name to remember this by.

I will give you the name Madhu, which is honey, and I will tell you the story of why I am giving this name to you:

Once a man was walking in a forest when he accidentally fell into a well. As he was falling he caught hold of a creeper that was growing down into the well and he hung there. In the well below him there was also an alligator who was very hungry and above him were two rats, one black and one white, who were gnawing on the creeper. Above the well was a tree in which there was a beehive that was dripping honey exactly into his mouth, which he started to enjoy. In this enjoyment he forgot the rats and the crocodile. This is the story of maya, of life! The man is hanging in the well of death. The crocodile is death itself and the rats are day and night, the passing of time. The creeper is the individual's life which is being cut down by time. The honey is enjoyment which distracts us from death and time. This is the situation with this samsara and we are all very happy. (laughs)

Don't allow the rat to cut your life down, and don't fall into the well in the first place. See where the next foot is falling. Be cautious in your life. It is better to go out, climb up the tree, and have the whole honeycomb, and be free of the well and its crocodile. This you must decide now, otherwise the crocodile of death is waiting for you and the rats continue to chew the vine. Nobody thinks that he should immediately climb up the creeper, even though it is a very short climb. Then he will enjoy the honey of happiness and bliss.

So you take this image and keep it in front of you everyday. This is the best teaching. Everybody must be aware of his own death. Nobody has ever avoided death because they wait and enjoy the honey drop by drop. Be free and you will enjoy the nectar of life for the first time. Otherwise the sensual pleasures are honey which keep all the people in the fear of the dark well that nobody ever comes out of. This is not just a story, it is a teaching.

Is there a way of climbing up the creeper Now?

Yes, exactly! Now is the creeper and the way out. Give up all the tastes that are dropping and see that the rat is eating away your life. So, if you are wise, jump out of the well. Everybody can do it. Don't wait like lazy men. Don't enjoy anything that will finish and which will land you in difficulty. So this thought you must decide: What is good for you? What will give you happiness? Is hanging on the creeper happiness? Few people will jump out of the world which is this well. Death is the crocodile. Life is the creeper. The rats are night and day passing on. Waiting is unwise. Waiting is unwise!

Wise people jump out as Buddha did. He was sleeping with the beauty of the land and he walked away at midnight. Very few people have done it. So many kings, at the same time, were sleeping with their queens, but we do not remember them. But 2600 years have passed and yet we remember him. Like this everybody can become Buddha and wake up from the bed of his desires.

Before Satsang you always say, "Let there be peace and love among all beings."

"Let there be peace and love among all beings of the universe" is the declaration of the book of knowledge, the Vedas. They suggest that when you get up in the morning to utter this: "Let there be peace in the world, let there be peace in the heavens, let there be peace in hell. Let all beings be happy and peaceful." I have picked this up from the Vedas itself which dates back to 25,000 years ago. Yet by stating this there has been no peace or happiness, and still we speak it everyday. Even 25,000 years ago there was no peace. Peace and world do not sit together. Wherever there is a world there is confusion. But we wish well for the people because we don't want any harm for them which comes from speaking other things. So in the morning we meet and wish everybody peace, but it hasn't brought peace. People are as disturbed as they were quite one million years ago. They haven't found peace.

Everyone is disturbed. Just stay as you are and see how your mind runs! It cannot stay quiet. So when we meet here we are suggesting and working toward not caring for the mind. Let it run, for running away is the monkey habit of the mind. We can't hold it, but we can find where this monkey is coming from. This is a very novel method and it is working. Quite a few people have done it and this is the experience. When you search for the thought that has been turning you around and around to different species for millions of years, you are Here; and you will see what can be done so that you will not enter into the vicious circle again.

There is no method as suggested by religions, but simply find out where the thought is arising from. This is the number one question. When you see the beginning of this question, before even its source, you will recognize it and merge into That whatever-it-is. I don't even call it emptiness. But when you recognize That you will merge into That as a river merges into the ocean. This will be the end of all running about and this we can do in an instant of time. Then you will know that it is this instant in which the universe began two billions years ago, this is the instant where it has stayed for two billions years, and where it will stay for many more to come. And this instant has never ever existed! It is the same instant. If you don't inquire it will keep going, but if you stop it, you will see that it never existed. Quite a few among us have tried this and found that nothing ever existed. When you dream, you had a husband and three children, but when you wake up they are gone. But you remember your children and the thought is there and this is called samsara:

The remembrance of the past dream is samsara.

Once a question was asked by a very good student to an excellent teacher:

"Master you speak that everything is an illusion, but I see everything as real and solid. Can you be illusion? Can I be illusion? Can the world be illusion? Master, please help, I am confused."

The master kept quiet and then said, "Let us have a walk in the forest." After walking for awhile the master said, "It is very hot, you go down and get some water at that river there and I will stay here in the shade."

So the student goes and slides the vessel into the water of the river. He looked up and saw a beautiful young girl across the river, immediately fell in love with her, and proposed to marry her.

"This is not the custom here. All the marriages are arranged by our parents," she said. "But I also like you and so you must speak to my father. Come and follow me and I will show you from a distance who my father is. He is the proprietor of the village. We have a lot of land, cows and horses. So I will point him out and then hide behind the doors and see what he says."

So they went to the village and when they were near she said, "That man sitting there, smoking a hooka and chewing paan is my father. Go and speak to him."

He went there and said, "I saw your daughter one hour ago at the river and fell in love with her. Can you marry her to me?"

The father said, "Who are you?"

"I am a brahmin from a nearby village," he replied.

"What is your education?" asked her father.

"I have learned philosophy, the Vedas, the Upanishads, and the Sastras. I know astronomy, geology and oceanography and all the eight sciences of the world.

The father said, "Very good. You look quite young and qualified. I don't hesitate to give the hand of my daughter to you, but with one condition. She is my only child and I am very attached to her. So if you want to marry her you must stay here with me, and you can't take her to your village."

"Agreed," said the boy.

"We will announce it to all our neighbors and you will be married in one month," said the father.

After a month they were married and after three years they had one child. Then after five years the parents registered their will in the name of their son-in-law. Now, all the village belonged to him. A couple of years later both her parents died, and after ten years they had another child and then another.

After 18 years there came a flood and the river was rising. All the farms were destroyed and they went to a nearby hill to stay, but slowly the water was rising there as well. The cows were floating away and everything was destroyed.

Finally, the water came up to his shoulders and he put one child on his shoulders and a child in one hand and his wife and another child in the other. But the current was very strong and his son slipped and as he reached for him the wife slipped and as he went to hold the wife the other son slipped away.

So, now with everything lost, the river was receding. He just sits there at the edge of the river and cries about the loss of his children. Finally, the river recedes until it is at the original level.

He feels a hand on his shoulder and his teacher asks: "What are you thinking about? Your vessel is in the water. Why don't you draw it? This should have taken you one minute, but already it has been five minutes!"

He looks at his face and stammers, "Fi, five, five minutes you say! Did you say five minutes? What about my wife and what about the children?!"

The master replies, "This is the answer to your question. All this is illusion. Just now you came and you fell in love with a girl, but where is that girl now? You are just fetching water for me. All these things are just coming from the mind. They never existed! No wife was there, no children were there, no marriage was performed and no village was there. The mind creates an instant and in that instant you lived nearly 20 years and in the same instant your vessel was emerged into the water."

So this is how it stands and you have to be wise.

As Buddha said, form is emptiness and emptiness is form.

This is what I say. There is no difference between emptiness and form. If form is there, there must be emptiness in which to see the form. There must be space in which all forms are seen. These forms are seen in nothingness and so no form must be there when there is form. All of samsara; mountains, men, animals and birds, whenever you see these forms, there must be formlessness. Otherwise you cannot see! To see form you must be in emptiness, and what is form or no-form?

The same!

I don't know how you can understand this because for understanding you need the mind. So this must come by itself and no understanding is needed. If it comes it is your good luck and if it doesn't then it is your bad luck because you will always continue in your imaginations.

How to get rid of the imagination that you see a snake in the dream or a tiger in the dream which is pouncing on you? You run away and climb the tree, but the tiger tries to climb the tree and so you are in trouble and finally the tiger reaches you and pulls you down, at which point you wake up. When you wake up, where is the tiger, and where are you? Somehow you must understand. There is no tiger and no fear and you wake up as you are! Like this you have not changed. Nothing has happened to you. There has been no samsara at all. *There has been no samsara at all.* This is the ultimate teaching.

Some people here though feel that emptiness is greater than form. This seems to me that they are subtly deluded. In the longing for emptiness they reject form.

Form or no form, there is no difference. As Buddha speaks: samsara and nirvana is the same thing. So many that went to him were enlightened like Kashyap and Ananda, and so many others were also enlightened by the lineage as this teaching continued!

Now if you reject form, where will this form go? And what will you do? To reject something you must accept something else. Both acceptance and rejection must be rejected! Reject both these thoughts: neither accept or reject! At that level, who are you?

There isn't me.

So don't accept anything or reject anything because when you accept something you must reject something. And to reject something you must accept something. Both are opposites. So don't reject or accept. Let everything be there, you have nothing to do with them. If you reject something it must stay somewhere and you will always carry this rejection and you will say "I have rejected such and such thing," This will be more prominent than what you accepted.

The World Is Illusion

How can I be established in "I am not the body"?

You are simply not the body and there is nothing to be established in. Stay Quiet and think at what time you got this body. Then you will look at the calendar and say that it was 1960 or 1970. These births and deaths are on the calendar and if there is no calendar, then when were you born? To see when you were born you must look at the birth of Christ, and from his birth you count yours. You deal with someone else and then calculations start! These calculations are the habit of mind. If you don't look at the birth and death of someone you will see who you are!

ॐ

I have no peace in the waking state, or the dream state or the sleep state. I have nowhere else to go. Can you help me?

This is a very good experience. If you don't have any peace in these three states you must go to the forth state beyond these three. This is your heart. Come here and stay Here. This can be done in any state. The activities of the body do not hinder the heart at all. Some people here are enjoying this state now.

I know I am this heart. So how can water be thirsty? How can I want to be free?

You have good merit to give you this experience. It reminds me of Kabir who makes a good joke: "How can the fish cry 'I am thirsty' while living in the water? When opening the mouth to say this the water is in her mouth!"

> We are all living in the nectar of the Self
> and yet we all cry: "We are suffering!"
> Everybody is in Divine Grace.
> Grace is around everybody,
> inside and outside and everywhere.
> Yet we are not satisfied.

So Kabir only laughs! He looks at the fish and laughs. You are not that crying fish, you have done it. You need nothing else.

How can the body be a thought? And whose thought?

Only when you think is there a body. Before exhalation or inhalation there is no thought. Every six breaths there is a pause and if you are aware of it, you are enlightened. This I-thought rises from there: in between inhaling and exhaling, and rises because you have some desire for a person or object. Also, when you sleep you do not think and you do not see the body because Maya shakti drops away in the sleep state, but still you do not realize who you are because Avarana shakti remains. So the body is just a dream object, a thought. Inquiry is to find whose thought this is.

You can stay in the dream with your dream body without generating thoughts and still do everything that life demands. Keep a thought inside that I am always Here and then the body will simply act according to its reactions and you will not be responsible for this because responsibilities and liabilities do not enter there. It is only when you are in relationship with other, on account of your identifying as a body and ego, that you are responsible. So wake up! After liberation you will see that there is a point in which nothing exists and in which there is no non-existence either. Know the body is a transient thought and simply keep conscious of this point. This is called complete liberation.

I know that I am not totally in sleep, but I know I am not awake either.

It is good not to sleep. Four persons do not sleep: One is a lover because he is not with his beloved, another is a thief because he is out robbing houses, and a third is the sick man who is awake due to disease and pain. All these are awake to their desires: lust, greed and suffering. But also the yogi does not sleep for he is concentrating on when he will be free of this illusion. All the rest of the people are sleeping even in the waking state.

When you are going in the desert and you see a very beautiful river and this is called a mirage. Since you are thirsty you want to go to swim in it and to drink the water from it, but the further you go toward it the farther away it shifts. Now, however, you have known that it is only an illusion, a creation of the mind.

The whole world is running toward this river to fulfill its desires. They are running fast, for the last two billion years, to have a swim in it. A few here and there have decided that they cannot reach it, they cannot fulfill their desires, they cannot remove their thirst. So it is better to stay Here, wherever you are. When you decide this it will rain from the skies and this will be the rain of Grace. You will not need to run anywhere because everything will be fulfilled Here. Going there you are sucked in by the heat, and nobody is going to help you. But if you stay Here, even the clouds will fall on you. So you have to be Here and have no desire in your mind to even speak and everything will be provided for you.

Nothing is real. Whatever you see is not real. One day will come when you do not see object and what was object will not see object either because both are illusions. This is special knowledge. There can be no knowledge without knowing that all is illusion. When you go back to the West you can teach your children and friends what you have learned in Satsang. They will be very happy and you will be a very good mother giving them right knowledge in childhood. They will be thankful to their mother.

Why does the mirage keep arising?

Where does it arise from?

Nowhere.

What can arise from nowhere? What is it if it arises from nowhere? What arises must arise out of somewhere, otherwise it could not have arisen. What is the mother of this "I," of this illusion? Ego is the mother and desire is the father. Don't have these parents, run away from them. Love is the best mother and emptiness is the best father.

Is it important to remember all the layers of the onion or should you go beyond all the layers?

There is no difference between the first, middle and last layer of the onion. They all smell the same, so it is better to avoid everything. Don't even put the onion in your pocket because you will still smell! (giggles) The whole onion smells and the center will be garlic! So don't touch it. Reaching the core of the issue is to not even utter the name of this onion. No name. No form. Drop this mind and you are in the cave where the smell of the mind does not reach you. This cave has no layers, there is nothing outside and nothing inside. This is available to you if you do not think of the past onions. Don't think and you are in the cave.

To realize the Self you say the mind must get dropped, but how can the mind be separate from the Self. Isn't mind a creative experience of life?

You have to see something to drop it, just as you take off your locket before you swim in the ocean, and drop it in your purse. How can you drop something that doesn't exist? It is only your concept. You need not drop the mind because it doesn't exist. Let it be there, it must be useful to you.

Is the human form precious because it is the only way to realize the self?

There is no form at all. It is a concept that there is a universe with men, animals and birds. In this concept you evolve for 35 million years to become a human. But most humans are not humans, they are just animals who have somehow disconnected with their tails and walk on two legs like a gorilla. So the human incarnation is precious because you can have doubt and you can question "Who am I?" A pig or donkey cannot ask this but are taken to the butchery of death. Everybody who is born must face a butcher, the God Yama, who will not leave any man unless they realize what he is. So it is the human birth which gives you the opportunity of "Who am I?" But it is very rare. Of six billion humans maybe only sixty know who they really are. Here in Satsang we represent so many countries, but why such a few people have come? Not even one percent in a country knows who they are.

If we want an example of an enlightened person we must go back 2600 years to Gautam who became Buddha. But this Lucknow Satsang has made enlightenment easy. You don't have to meditate in Himalayan caves, you don't have to repeat mantras, you don't have to go on any pilgrimages, and you don't have to support any charities. Just spend a second out of your life span and I guarantee that you are free. Do it this second, why postpone.

In ancient times the kings would leave their kingdoms and go for penance. After penance some Manika would come in front of them in the form of a beautiful woman and there would end their penance. But here in Satsang many Manikas are here and they too are getting free! It is no problem to love with a Manika because enlightenment has to do with your own Self, not physical contact with your own Manika. If Manika comes, live with her, but you remain untouched.

Mind: The Movement of the Illusion

Mind is Shakti, Power, Manasarovar Devi.
Use this power to find the origin of Shakti
which is Shiva, Awareness, Being, Bliss.
Simply be Quiet, make no effort,
start no thought and look Within.
Mind is a tremendous power
which causes all of manifestation to arise
out of just a single thought: the I-thought.
When you don't look at this thought it is all real,
but when you look at it manifestation vanishes.
Mind is the drug which takes you out of your natural state
and makes you trip in the realm of duality.

Mind is the appearance of limited Consciousness:
Once consciousness is conditioned it becomes the mind,

and name and form is that imaginary conditioning.
Only in the conditioning of mind do we not know each other.
You will know that we have always known each other
when mind is empty and pure without ripples.

The origin of the universe is centered on the I-thought.
If you forget the substratum of the "I" and you get lost
and then "I" hangs around your neck like a noose.
Go to the origin of the I-thought
and do not get lost in the magicians tricks.
If you identify with the wave that moves in the emptiness
you will get lost, so let notions appear and disappear
and stay as emptiness.
Birth, death, and suffering are notions.
They are not the ocean.

You wear your mind like you wear your dress.
Mind is that which is desire, is past, is graveyard,
is name and form, is transience, is describable.
"I" is a wave, is mind, is samsara, is desire,
is arrogance, is wickedness, is confusion,
is snake, is not rope, and is all of manifestation.
Identifying yourself with the "I"
is identifying yourself with past and future.
Cling to it and you will suffer and be there stuck in it.
Abandon it: Liberation!

The creation of hells is the mind turned outward
saying "I am the body."
The creation of heavens is the mind turned inward
knowing "The kingdom of heaven is Within."
Mind turned inward will see its Source and
then never return because you stay with what you love most.

As conditioned consciousness, mind is like the banks of a river.
The notion of "I am river" dies when you realize
the ocean of Consciousness.

All that you see is the five elements:
Water washes away earth, fire evaporates water,
air blows out fire, and air disappears into ether.
All of this is mind and mind is the "I."
Inside thought is called "I" and outside thought is called space

but there is no difference: It is all mind, all Self!

ॐ

I have some questions regarding mind. What is it?

A bundle of thoughts!

What is the substance of the mind?

Show me the mind and I will tell you the substance! (giggles) If you can't show me then you don't have one. If you can't find it leave it alone.

How will it disappear forever?

First of all (giggles) It is not there! If it is not appearing how will it disappear? Mind is only your desire. When desire is there then your mind is there. When you don't have desire there is no mind at all. There is no difference between mind and desire. To test this don't have any desire in the moment. Every desire belongs to the past, so don't desire for one instant of time and tell me who you are!

Nothing.

Nothingness is a very good mother. Stay with her and you will find her love and beauty.

Don't you need a mind to function in the world?

When you were not in the world all this business was there and it will continue after you go. You have no effect on its continuity and your body and mind are part of this continuity. It will run, it has been running and endlessly it will be running. You can't stop it or change it because it is all imagination. It is like a river of the mirage which moves farther away from you the more you move toward it. You don't get any water, and on the contrary you get more fatigued. But a wise man doesn't run after a mirage and this samsara is a mirage! Who is satisfied with the samsara? Everybody is thirsty and thinks that samsara will quench their thirst, but the thirst stays because the samsara is a mirage. The rare one will know this and sit quietly under the tree and enjoy it.

If I am the non-doer, who is the doer?

Your mind. Your thought "I want to do it, I want to have it, I am attached to this." This is your trouble. You are not the doer. The doer is the intention in your mind of need. Don't give rise to any intention, including enlightenment and peace, for only one second and see what happens. You will be beautiful. I offer this to everyone constantly, but nobody accepts it and they only jump to their next question. You should say, "Stop!" but you depend on the past because all these questions are from the past. You have had them in your mind. So when you are happy give up everything like the enlightened kings did.

One king was sleeping on the roof of his palace in the summer time. He was sandwiched between his two queens. What luck! (giggles) Then he looked up at the full moon as two birds flew by it and twittered. He rose up naked and left the palace because he had to stay with the beauty of the instant, the beauty that the queens, and the palace, the kingdom, and the diamonds could not provide. He disappeared into the forest.

> So once you have it, reject everything else
> because all you need is this love, this beauty.
> When this happiness comes, don't reject it.
> This we learn from the prince who became Buddha.

He went and sat under the Bodhi tree and found It due to his intense desire. He rejected all that was and now 2600 years later we still remember him because he was beautiful. We don't even remember our fathers and grandfathers, but we remember him.

ॐ

Dreams: The Nature of the Illusion

Papaji, I had the experience that everything is within me, that there is no outside.

This is a very good experience. Suppose you are living on the twentieth story of an apartment building and you are sleeping. Then you dream of a wild elephant coming at you. You also see mountains and rivers and forests. Where are all these things? Are they outside? No they are inside projections of your mind. First the space has to be projected, inside and outside, and then time is projected. The ego is projected next and you start believing that what you see is real. But as soon as you wake up the elephant and everything else disappears. In the very same way this waking reality will also disappear when you Wake Up. This reality will disappear! Your dreams are as real as anything else, though this waking state looks more real. Therefore, your experience is a very beautiful one.

I also had a dream where Vishnu and Shiva came to me five times.
It was all about dissolving karma and I awoke feeling very different.

The first time Shiva came to remove your concept of physicality, the
waking state, because nothing is physical. The second visit was to remove
your imagination, the dream state, where nothing is reality. The third visit
was to remove the transient bliss and emptiness, the sleep state. The fourth
visit removed the fourth state, the turiya state, the Sahasrara and Agna
chakras. The fifth visit was the last because then there is nothing to be seen.

Can we be awake and dreaming at the same time?

When you are dreaming it is not possible to be awake. Some people are
asleep in the dream and some are awake. Some people tell others, "Now it
is daytime, look at the sun." In the dream some are awake and some are
sleeping. Yet those who are awake in the dream also are sleeping. Their
wakefulness depends on your wakefulness because when you are awake
everybody is awake. So wake up yourself and everybody will wake up. Who
has created mothers and daughters in the dream? They are there because you
are dreaming. In this sleep there is a dream, but you must wake up from this
waking and dreaming process. Know "I am awake." Even if you say I am
waking and I am dreaming, still you are really sleeping. You are not yet
awake. Wake up to your own true Self where there is no waking, no
dreaming, or sleeping; beyond all that. This state is called the fourth state, the
Turiya state.

In the West they think there are only two states; waking and dreaming.
There is no sleep as they have seen on the EEG. A team of psychologists came
to Rishikesh from America and tested many swamis, from Sivananda Ashram
to Mahesh Yogi Ashram. They came to make graphs of the thoughts and no
swami was silent in Rishikesh. One swami offered himself and was found
that he was not quiet even for a millionth of a second. After this ninety
percent of the students left him, except for those who were paid to stay.
(giggles) This is the result.

Freedom has no-face. Don't look to any face, not even your face. Look
at the facelessness as you do when you sleep. So always sleep when others are
awake and stay awake when others sleep. This is facelessness.

Why do my night dreams constantly change, but not this world dream
of the waking state?

They both change, the difference is that while in the dream you don't say
that it is changing. Only when you wake up can you see that it changes from
one dream to another. The waking state dream also changes. Today is

different than tomorrow or yesterday. This state is real only because you call it real and have this conviction of its reality. But during a dream you don't call a dream a dream. Only when you wake up can you say that it was a dream. In the night dream you see rivers, mountains, people, and relations. In this dream you see the same thing so how can you call one real and the other unreal? You have the conviction of reality and so you call it real. But if you call it a dream and have this conviction it will be a dream. You don't look at the dreamer, who also is your own creation. The dreamer is different than the dream so now find out who is the dreamer. The dreamer and the dream and the dream objects are all the same. Now find out who dreamed, who is dreaming. Find the "me" who has dreamed. Find this now and waking, dreaming and sleeping will disappear. What you call reality is not Reality.

What can we learn from our dreams?

Learn that this is the nature of the illusion. Learn that all name and form is a transient imaginary dream that you must wake up from.

Papaji, I had such a powerful dream last night. Can you speak about dreams? Thank you very much. There were ten killers in my dreams!

Dreams can tell you that something is going to happen as the clouds tell you that there will be rain. Dreams also tell you what has happened because they are the activities which are unfulfilled in the waking state. For instance, if you are slapped in the waking state you will seek revenge in the dream state. Actually, truly speaking, everybody is dreaming because they have not spent their waking state in a peaceful way. If they had they would not appear again in the dream called samsara. Everybody in samsara has dreamt a lot and has collected millions of lifetimes worth of memories in their mind. Now they can't stop it.

You can stop it though, if you have a burning urge for freedom and if you have very good luck. Then you will see a master who will tell you the difference between a dream and the waking state. Then you will see that all are sleeping, and you are awake. Sleeping is being unaware of your true Self. Wakefulness is being awake to reality, Consciousness, truth. What others are awake to, you sleep to. They are awake to lust, interests, persons, concepts. Have nothing to do with these things. Sleep to them. This is the difference between wakefulness, sleeping and dreaming.

The killers in your dream are the senses: eyes deceive you, whatever you hear is of no use, what you smell is no good, and so with touch and taste. But, if you know this the senses lose their strength. If you know the objects of your eyes are not real then they won't affect you. Whether you hear praise or blame it won't matter. There won't be any difference between perfume and rotten things. When you know who you are you become very strong and these killers, these enemies, will lose their strength. Now complete your work. The sooner the better.

> Just stay Quiet, whatever happens is perfect.
> It is the unending game of the one
> who was Here before the beginning.
> It is the dream of the creator
> It is the magic of the enjoyer
> in whose dream we are objects.

When your love brings you very close to him he will give you the same techniques and you also will enjoy! Then you will not question what is happening. The waves of the ocean ask the questions as they rise, travel and fall. But the ocean, the substratum of the waves is resting and enjoying his own activity. Yet he knows he is not active! All those who have understood this will remain quiet as if nothing has ever happened.

ॐ

Karma: The Script of the Illusion

"The doer must pay for his actions." This is karma.
No doer is no karma and this is freedom.

Memory is the storehouse of this karma.
Each impression in your mind is an incarnation.
Millions of thoughts are equal to one "I."

Reincarnation, as governed by karma, happens to you
when you do not know that you are Consciousness,
because anything else is imagination
and this imagination has no beginning or end.
Reincarnation is in the mind only.
How can That which is never born be reborn?

What is the relation between the Absolute and the perfection of destiny?

The Absolute has nothing to do with destiny. Destiny is the reactions of your karma and is not fixed by the Absolute. Whatever you do creates fruit for tomorrow and tomorrow it is called destiny.

The World Is Illusion

Today's actions are tomorrow's destiny.

Today you earn $100 and put it in your pocket and go to sleep. The next day you see $100 in your pocket from yesterday. This $100 is called the destiny of yesterday's work. Like this all the karma or actions that you committed last life are brought into this life by you in your own pocket. You cannot change them.

Are active decisions just an illusion? Is it all controlled by destiny?

All the saints, sages and wise ones in India say that everything is predestined. You can't make any decision by yourself. Ramana Maharshi also believes this. Once a German professor asked this same question to Ramana who said that even the question about predestiny is predestined!

So everything is predestined?

Yes, sun will rise, sun will set. As orange trees will grow oranges and apple trees will grow apples, so all beings move through the dream exactly as destined. You can't change it. Everything is predestined, there is no doubt. Even an ant cannot walk without its step being predestined. This secret will come to you when you have light. But when you force things to happen your way, then you suffer. Things happen as they happen so do not imagine that they have to happen a certain way. Everybody wants their own will to be done, but when you surrender to the Divine you have no cause to worry. Depend on the will of the Mother. Where she goes, you go. When she suckles you, suck the milk! Instead of doing this most people get involved in circumstances.

Is it true that destiny can be altered by the Guru's Grace and by chanting mantras?

The Guru's Grace can do anything!
It can alter destiny also.
This Grace is also predestined.

What use is sadhana then to obtain freedom?

This sadhana also is predestined.

If it is all predestined why does the Guru get angry sometimes when we make mistakes?

You make so many mistakes, but I never get angry with you. In everybody there is anger, but you must express it only on yourself for your misbehavior. There is no other way that anger is to be used. Do you understand? Okay. Everything is predestined. Your coming here is predestined. Those who do not come here are predestined not to.

Is liberation due to prarabdha karma?

No, liberation has nothing to do with your karma. Karma occurs when you are sleeping and have desires for other objects. When there is liberation there is no prarabdha. Prarabdha is for those who are sleeping, not for those who are awake. When you dream so many things come in front of you, but when you sleep all these things vanish. In sleep there is no person and no object and no desire. All desire comes when you are dreaming or when you are awake, therefore there is no difference between waking and dreaming. In sleep though nothing exists: only bliss, love beauty. Where do you get this love from? From the absence of desire. Then you are happy. You can learn how not to have any desire so that you will be happy in all the states: waking, dream, and sleep. By sleeping when others are awake you can be without desire; when they sleep you keep awake.

This waking state is a sleep state because people are not happy because they do not know who they are. So question to yourself "Who am I?" and all that you desire will vanish. Keep this question in your mind all the time whether you are sitting, standing or walking. Inquire into the source of where these desires come from. This is not different than sleeping to the desires.

If whatever happens is destined, is our reaction to this free will or destined?

What is your reaction to a slap in the face?

Things just happen, there is no question of destiny
or of free will, things just happen.
and you are just one of those things.
All is a dream and is known to be a dream
only when you are awake.

All forms, all two-ness, is falsehood. How to understand this? Wake up from this dream, and you will know free will and destiny. Free will is used by a very few people. In Satsang you will know that all is illusion. Then you are a witness and are beyond dream and suffering. You will get a third eye, a single eye, to see the illusion from a perfect man who will open it. Two eyes lead you to untruth and form. To see formlessness the third eye must open.

Sit quiet for a moment and you will know what Truth is.
Look at what stirs in your mind
and find where this concept rises from.
Look at That point.
Then you will see something which is unbelievable
and which will fulfill all your desires.

So even the freedom of choice to choose right and wrong in the moment is predestined?

You have no freedom of choice because you are Freedom itself. You have no choice to be free or not to be free, because you are always Freedom.

Choice is illusion because only Freedom is.
The "who" that would choose
and the choices to be chosen are all concepts in mind.

The One in the Heart of all beings,
even the beings yet to be conceived and born,
directs all karma to be done.
Find who created the universe in his thought only.
All beings are a concept in his mind.
Nothing has ever been done
and there is nothing to do.

Find who you are a concept of.

You dream of climbing a mountain and resting, but when you wake up there is no mountain, no climbing and no rest. But you have performed this activity. It is all a dream and all your responsibilities, liabilities, and activities are just illusion in the dream, like a mirage in a dream desert, like an imaginary diver taking an imaginary dive into imagination. Stop chasing the mirage and wake up. Even the thirst which drives you to the mirage is a mirage, is imagination.

Wake up and know that peace is Within.
Then your illusion will vanish, disappear.

I see honest people suffering so much while so many dishonest people flourish. Why is this? Why are the honest punished and the dishonest rewarded? This is an obstacle to total surrender for me.

It is true; innocent people often suffer and the dishonest people hurt the public and flourish. This is due to the desire of some to fill up their cup of sins faster, in order to enjoy the fruits of their merits.

Look at Ravana; he would spoil the yagnas of the righteous all over India and steal all the beautiful woman and make them join his harem. The result of this is that he could build his houses and much of Lanka out of gold. He had no care for anyone and troubled everyone, he even kidnapped the wife of Rama. Rama was in exile and he was already suffering. Rama is God and *he* was suffering! By uttering his name you won't be reborn, but he himself was in a lot of trouble and Ravana gave him more misery.

Rama was in exile due to the trickery of one of his father's wives. His father was the king and at Rama's coronation as the next king the youngest queen asked for previously promised boon to be granted by Rama's father. The boon was to have Rama sent into exile so her son could be king. The king was bound to agree and soon after he sent Rama to the forest he died from being separated from him. This kings name was Dasaratha, and the whole country suffered because of this. But in the end look what happened. Ravana was killed and today we still repeat Rama's name, though he lived 7600 years ago, in this state, not far from here.

So many saints had a lot of trouble during their life.

But sometimes extreme suffering is inflicted on the innocent bystanders.

What appears to be innocent bystanders!

What do you mean? Is such suffering random or is it prarabdha karma? How would an Enlightened being view such expression of karmic law?

This question deals with total Consciousness. If I speak that it is prarabdha karma it is what is normally believed. I will explain in two ways.

First, whatever you do becomes prarabdha. Whatever happens now is due to the past. Some portion of the past has been attended to, but some portion is left. What happens now is the balance of your previous activity. But actually there is no prarabdha karma. Actually, you have done something previously, but nobody knows. If you believe in the stories of the Upanishads, there is one story that is pertinent.

There once was a saint living quietly in the forest near a muslim village. One day a cow came running into his hut and a few minutes later a man came by and asked if the saint had seen the cow that he was going to butcher. The saint said "yes," and pushed the cow out of his little hut and gave it to the butcher.

This is a happening, and it just happened.

The next life the saint again became a saint because he did nothing else. He decided to go to the village of Pandhapur in Maharastra where there is a very good statue of Lord Vitthal. On his way, about ten km before the temple a very strong storm came and he couldn't see which way to go. A man living nearby invited him in and told him he could spend the night there and the next day he could continue on to the temple. The saint agreed to this compassionate and generous offer. This man, though quite old, had a very beautiful young wife who quickly fell in love with this pure boy, and expressed to him that she wanted to run away with him.

"No, I am a sadhu, I never touch any woman."

"But I have fallen in love with you, lets run away, I have collected all my gold ornaments and it will be enough for us," she said.

"No, I cannot stay with you," said the young man, "I am going to Lord Vitthal. You are already married and if you go away your husband will be in great pain."

So she went to the house and killed her husband and threw him into the well. Then she said, "Now I have no husband. Now come with me."

The saint was astonished and absolutely refused and so the woman went out onto the road and started crying that this man had killed her husband and was going to steal all the gold.

People and police came and took him to the magistrate. The woman told her story about this stranger to the village magistrate. The judge was baffled. Since a crime had been committed the magistrate decided that there must be punishment, but since there was no witness he decided it could not be death and so he had the hands of the 'innocent' young saint cut off.

The saint then continued to Lord Vitthal who then appeared before the boy and said:

"Ask any boon: Kuch Mangalo Meray Say!"

The saint said: "I am very happy with you. I have always worshipped you. My tongue has never uttered any other name and my hands have never committed any crime, they have only clapped the rhythms of songs in your praise. Lord, if you are gracious, tell me why these hands, which only worship you, have been cut!"

The Lord said: "Look at the Devadarshan before you and see what happened in the previous life."

The saint saw the previous story of the cow, the butcher and the saint and he saw that the cow is the wife, the butcher is the husband and he is the saint. The cow had to take revenge from the husband who had killed her. That action and reaction now is over. His own hands had to be cut because he had pushed the cow out of his hut which had come to him seeking protection.

So it is with prarabdha. Nobody knows the root of what happens in the present life. We only see what is happening now. All karma must be undergone. You can't lift a step by yourself, so surrender to the One who knows what must be done.

So can we learn from our past lives?

You can learn that human birth is very rare and very precious and it is not to be wasted. Through out millions of years you have gone through the 8.4 million species and now you are human, the species where Enlightenment is most possible.

Is past life therapy or repression helpful?

With this therapy one is taken to the past to some event which is the apparent cause of present psychological disturbances. I don't reject this, but here what is told is to not go to the past. Mind is past and you should not go to the past with it, but bring it to the present where its effects are weak. This present presence is Satsang.

I don't understand reincarnation, what gets reincarnated?

No answer will satisfy you unless you see for yourself the roots of the tree whose branches are this present reincarnation of yours. What is reincarnated is any thought or desire unfulfilled. This you can't avoid. If you don't have a thought you are free. Otherwise, you will have to reincarnate to fulfill your desires again and again. Your desire will take form into that person who will help you to fulfill the desire.

Do you have a vision of the spirituality of humanity in this point of history?

I do not have a vision or a view, but trust! I trust that this spiritual evolution of humanity is not a history, but a mystery. (giggles) Unless you see that it is a mystery you're not a teacher and you cannot teach. As a history it is not a mystery, but you cannot understand. The mystery is very mysterious and secret. It is very secret and sacred.

Will Westerners have a specific role?

Definitely the Westerners have a specific role and they are playing it the best they can. What has been taught for thousands of years in India is no longer wanted by her people. Indians want things of the West and therefore they are going to the West to fulfill their desires, their Western desires. Spiritual desires will be fulfilled by spiritual people who want truth to be realized. So therefore the desire for freedom herself has gone to the West. This very beautiful girl from India has come to those who have gone in this lifetime to the West to fulfill their desires! This is why the Westerners are here: they know what is beauty. All the physical beauties they have seen and have been kicked in the back by all of them. So now they are here for something else which will not kick them in the back, but hug them.

Papaji, how to be in this illusion? How can we live in the illusion skillfully and be free of its traps of suffering?

Don't forget who you are! We are alive in the world because we have not yet completed our work: Know Thyself!

Thieves in an Empty House

Always remember:
The thieves of Peace are thieves in an empty house
because only imagination suffers.
You are That which remains untouched.

Peace always is,
find and reject the imaginary rejecter of this Peace.
The I-thought is this thief of Freedom,
and inquiry is the best way to destroy it and its tendencies.
You don't have to look at the tendencies;
The only way to get rid of them is Freedom
and inquiry is the best way to Freedom,
so always stay toward the Self.
This is the abandonment of painful conditioning.
Abandon vasanas and mind and you are Peace.
Abandon the notion "I am bound,"
and always face Self.

Desire

Before the wave rises it is ocean,
Before desire moves it is Emptiness.
The entire universe is your own desire so enjoy it
but don't be destroyed by it,
because anything you desire you are a slave to.

The thief of peace is the desire for the transient
so aspire only for the permanent.
Here, this eternal moment, there are no desires.
Just keep Quiet and then see what you really need.
Without an object there is no desire,
without desire there is no mind,
without mind there is only Self.
Desire is the veil over the face of Truth.
Remove it by finding the source of "I."

You are the totality of Being,
desire simply does not become you.
Any desire makes the emperor a beggar
because desire is only begging.
"I am not Self" is the beggar.

You miss your kingdom due to your petty desires
which take you to destruction.
So just inquire to whom do the desires arise?
Then discharge yourself into the Emptiness
which has no demarcation.

No object of desire is real,
no object of desire is worth your peace.
If your house is desires, burn it down.
It is only the absence of desire that makes you happy,
so allow no desire to rise.
Just allow yourself to be dissolved by Love.
When there is no desire there is Love and Beauty.
If you do desire then only desire Peace
because what you think you will become:
Water poured into ocean becomes ocean.

Other engagements conceal Self.
"I want this and that" conceals Self and is other engagements!
As a pot of honey with a single drop of cyanide is not honey,
so awareness with a single desire is not Awareness.

Any desire is an alligator, any attachment is a crocodile.
Being free from desire you are God, you are Ultimate.
Just stop your race and see!
Heart is always open, only desires close it.

Desire is samsara, the prisons you feel are prisons of desires.
Be always empty and let desires dance as they will.
This is true sannyas which is not a matter of cloth or circumstance.
Sannyas is not clinging to desire for the transient
because desire takes mind out of Emptiness.

Desirelessness is Freedom,
so look at where the desires rise from.
Without desires you are peaceful and
this perfectly still mind is Freedom.
The desire for Freedom will destroy all desires.
When this desire arises don't wait!
Do It Now: Sit down quietly and follow this desire.
Do not desire to have Freedom in the future,
and do not make effort to have it Now.
Between these two, what do you see?

ॐ

Questioner: Will you help me to love this emptiness that I am and to know true happiness?

Papaji: Happiness does not come from meeting your desired object, and it doesn't come from fulfilling your desires. When there is no desire at all for anything then happiness is. When you are empty of desire this emptiness is happiness. So give up the thought of any desire. When happiness comes you are alone. These two go very well together: aloneness and happiness. You need a very good guide or you will get lost in the forest of the world. You need a guide and this guide is Grace.

I am a man of many desires and they won't stop bothering me.

Let them be fulfilled, who stops them? The desires in your head will break your head where they themselves are located. Wait for some time. There is no hurry! First try what you are liking and loving and fulfill your mind. When it gets lost and sunken then it will know how to reject everything and sit quiet.

When you have the desire to inquire,
No other desire can trouble you.

Desires seem so endless. Do all desires need to be destroyed or can desires be bypassed by self-inquiry and stillness?

Desires are endless and even survive death of the body. Always the mind is busy with desires. These desires must be fulfilled or you will be born again to fulfill them.

By the Grace of the teacher and by self-inquiry
desires can be bypassed and fulfilled.

Taking desires one by one will take millions of years and still it will not work. But by the Grace of the Guru the desires will be fulfilled in dreams and mind will be satisfied. In self-inquiry you go under the source of the desires. Here there are no desires because there is no mind at all. When mind is in contact with objects of senses the arising of desires is accelerated. Going into the source you will find that this world never existed, let alone the desires. That is the place of total emancipation.

I had a desire in my last life to be with a particular woman, but I couldn't be with her because I was a big swami, so big that all the banks and shops closed on my Mahasamadhi day. What happened? I had to be born again and this woman had to be my wife. So it is better to fulfill your desires, especially your desire to be free.

I also have the desire to be realized.

Let this desire bother you! If you really have this desire, it is the end of all desires. This desire will release all other desires. Keep this desire up to the time of your death and you will be Realized. All desires must manifest, whatever you desire must be fulfilled.

Is it true that all my desires must be burnt and laid at your feet, not just the bad ones?

Do you know what the fire is which will burn everything? Devotion is the fire, devotion to the teacher. Devotion is to prostrate to the Feet of the Master and worship them. Then you don't need to do anything, this alone is enough. In ancient times many won Enlightenment only by worshipping the feet of the Master. I can tell you many stories, like the story of Bharat in the Ramayana.

His mother wanted the kingdom for him, but he had an older brother whom the king naturally had to give the kingdom to. But the king had told Bharat's mother that he would give anything to her, since she was very pretty and had helped very much in a previous war by holding up his broken chariot so that he could fight and win the war. So, when the king was about to give the kingdom to the eldest son, Bharat's mother reminded him of the boon that she was promised. So she made the king send the eldest son into exile for 14 years and make her own son the king. The younger son was in Kashmir at the time and was told what had happened when he returned to the kingdom. He refused the throne declaring that it was the place for his oldest brother. He then searched for his brother until he found him in Chitrakut and asked him to return to the kingdom.

Rama replied, "No, I must fulfill the promise that our father has made. I must stay in exile for 14 years before I can return. You must return to the kingdom and rule while I am away." Bharat said, "Then you give me your paduka, your wooden sandals, so that I can put them on the throne and worship them." The devotion of this boy Bharat cannot be measured by anyone. He only worshipped the sandals and got Enlightened. This is the reward of one who only does Padam Puja.

Meditation alone will not be good enough because even the cranes meditate as they wait for fish to come close enough to catch. The crane stands on one leg, which is austerity, in order to fool a fish. But the fish is just a desired object which you jump on when they come close. You do penance, austerities and meditation only for a desired object. Stop all this. Don't be a crane! Only worship the feet of the Lord, it is enough! Devotion alone is enough.

How happy you have become when you wash the feet of the Satguru. The Satguru doesn't want his feet washed, but he allows it for your sake, so that you become humble! Look at the feet of the teacher. This alone is enough. I challenge you to do this. It is an unfailing method. All other methods can fail. Meditations are only for something that you need, but worshipping the feet of the Satguru is to get rid of everything. Look at the Feet of the Teacher.

There is no more desire, just the bliss That I Am!

It is the desire that troubles everyone. A desireless person cannot be seen so easily. If you have no desire you have crossed over to the other shore of life and death. Now you can enjoy everything. The purpose of coming to Lucknow is to remove your desires and doubts and ego. When these are lost there is nothing more to do.

You told me to face the thieves. I did and now there is nothing. Thank you.

When things come you must face it. If you don't face it then trouble comes. Everything disappears because it is the ego facing ego. When you face ego you must be tricky because ego is tricky. So face things and the ego at the same time.

Once there was a tiger who was the king of the forest. He used to kill many animals, but he would only eat a little from each one. So all the animals of the forest held a conference to stop the killing. They decided that only one animal would be sent to him everyday so that others would be saved. So they sent a messenger to him and he agreed, but said that it must come at 7:00 a.m. because he wakes up very hungry.

That night they tried to decide who would go the next morning, but nobody wanted to go even though each of their lives were in danger every day. Then Mr. Fox said that he would offer himself first.

They gave him a party that night and in the morning garlanded him as he walked away with his tail up.

He arrived to the king of the forest at 9:00 a.m. and the tiger was very angry because he was so late.

"No sir, I started at 6:00 a.m. and I would have been here at 6:45 a.m.

but on the way I met another tiger who also was very hungry and said he would eat me. So I told him he had to wait because I had a promise with another tiger, who was king of this forest. I told him, 'So, Mr. Tiger, I will go to that other tiger and some other animal will be sent to you.' This is why I am late."

The tiger said, "There's no other king of the forest, I'm the king here!"

"No sir, I will show you. Come with me." So, he took the tiger to the top of a well and said, "Look sir, the other tiger is right in here." The tiger looked and roared with anger and the other tiger roared back!

"I told you sir, he is a very big tiger, he has given me much trouble."

So out of anger the tiger jumped into the well and the fox said "Yes! Here it is! You see! Now come up and eat me." Everybody was so happy that he saved so many of his brothers and sisters.

This is the ego; carefully deal with it. Let him jump into the river so you can enjoy.

You say leaving desire is the way to freedom.

For desires you need some object or subject and they all refer to the past. You must know whether or not that which you love is eternal. Keeping this in mind look at the consequences of your desires. Do they bring happiness, peace, and love? If they do not then it is useless to keep them, so give them up as you do every night in the sleep state. Are you not happy in this state? Why do you reject these objects and go to sleep? You sleep for peace of mind. You reject everybody, even your own body because you can't think of your body and sleep at the same time. So sleep is even better than your own body.

Why do I remain in suffering?

There is no suffering when you have a desire for freedom! You can't have two desires at the same time. When you desire for freedom you don't suffer. When you want to suffer you have to suffer because you have decided to suffer. Who has ever made the decision: "I don't want to suffer"? Most people are in love with suffering and so they suffer.

There was a woman in Paris that a mutual friend brought me to. She was suffering very badly so we went to her apartment and immediately upon seeing me she said that I could stay as long as I liked in a separate apartment which belonged to her, but that hereafter she could not see me.

I wondered why she said this. She didn't know me. So, I asked her, "I heard that you are suffering and I came and I can help you to remove the suffering."

366

She said, "Yes, seeing your face, I know that you can remove the suffering, but now I am in love with this suffering and I don't want to remove it because I have lived with it for 39 years. If you remove it then with whom will I live?"

It was a strange story and I decided not to stay there. So, like this everybody wants to suffer. Everybody is definitely deceiving themselves. How can you expect to stop suffering when really you like to suffer. This woman's life was based on suffering and so many people are like this. They don't want to be normal and enjoy life. They just want to suffer. You are so attached to suffering, but Here, how long can you suffer? You can't suffer Here! Here you must smile and be happy, and sing and dance. Don't worry, I will remove your suffering without any pain to you.

Will you help me to stop suffering?

You have to decide to stop suffering. Stop suffering and be Free of suffering. When the mind comes tell it that you won't go and tell him of your decision. Refuse him. Don't open the door! If you don't open the door no guest will come in. The mind which troubles you only functions when you desire, so stop desiring, and when you do, all the world is given to you.

I have such a strong food vasana that disturbs me. I want to be free of it.

Animals also share this vasana with you, but what they don't have that you do is the ability to make a strong decision to be free in this life. Don't waste this human birth or a minute of it. So many people die young.

> Spend all your time meditating,
> and find where the Satsang is and go there.

I also like to eat, but you shouldn't eat too much. Eat moderate food, keep moderate habits and sleep moderately. This will keep you healthy and maintain what you want. Like the river, keep on going toward the ocean. Eat to live, don't live to eat.

You have to fulfill all of your desires. It is better that you fulfill them in this lifetime or you will be born to fulfill them next time! Since your desire has come on the surface now you must go out and fulfill it, but you must promise to come back because we like you. Eating is the main desire so eat first and fulfill this desire. Kabir says physical hunger is a bitch and that she should be fed.

🕉

Mind, Thoughts, and Mental Baggage

Pure mind rises from Heart
as no-mind and this is Consciousness.
Impurity of mind is when the mind moves and desire arises.
This is bondage, this is wanting something not permanent,
something that is not abiding and not blissful.
Even the movement of thinking "I am peace" disturbs Peace.
You don't move, you can't move, only mind as intention moves.
When the mind is still, Freedom is Here!

Where there is mind there is two-ness and past.
Where there is no mind there is Freedom.
Mind is strong in other-ness
because mind is mind only when it touches an object.
Mind is the worst pollution because
it is the concept of time which steals you from Love.
Mind is samsara, the cycle of hitchhiking through wombs.
Mind is description so see
what cannot be described by thought.

Mind is your desire!
It is not the mind's fault because it is you who trouble the mind.
Your old wicked habits of disturbing your own beauty
with your thoughts and baggage are slow to die.
You are agitated by your own notions,
but know they are empty, they do not exist.
So it is most important to know mind is thought only
and it can create anything that you want.

The mind is a beggar because
the concept of want makes you a beggar!
Be only "I Am" and try to lift the begging bowl.
Throw away the begging bowl of ego for the throne.

Freedom is when the mind is cremated:
absolute destruction of the mind is Freedom.
Then mind is no-mind.
Decide that you want Freedom and surrender mind to That.
If you offer your mind you must stop thinking,
and make a firm decision not to fall back to suffering.

When you give rise to any notion
you start sliding back toward the graveyard.
This graveyard is the dancing hall of ego.
Ego subsides Here and Now in Being-Bliss-Awareness.

Mind is movement and creates desires
so that it has something to move toward.
When there is relation to the past and to the future
the play of the mind starts.
Let the mind play, it is water,
it is the wave which is not different than ocean, it is perfection.
But untold misery and suffering arises
from the demon mind-ego when it is identified with.
So play as ocean and give up the arrogance
of thinking you are the individual wave.
Stay awake to the ocean, to Self,
and the thief ego will not enter your mind's house.
Mind is a playful friend when you give him good work
and a dire enemy when you direct it to sense objects and pleasures.
Directing mind toward Self is good work.

Nothing will arrest mind except inquiry, all else is mind itself.
So use the mind to introduce you to this Moment.
This mind is this Moment and this is the Self,
as there are countless reflections of Light, but only one Sun.
To be bound or free is up to you
because you are what you think.
So inquire, stop thinking, and
leave the association of the mind entirely,
and just play in no-mind.

*I was deep in an experience when I realized that my mind was playing
tricks, creating spiritual experience.*

This is good understanding. Now you are after the mind and you have
known its tricks. When you know who is playing the tricks then he cannot
cheat you. If there is *any* kind of experience it is the trick of the mind! You
will be very happy with this experience and tell it to friends and Gurus and
they also will appreciate it only because they have not seen a place where
there is no experience at all! Therefore, everybody will want to hear how
your energy is rising from your bottom and going to your heart and beyond!

Then they will assure you that this is the last thing to be done. But when you go after the mind it will disappear.

I notice that these experiences happen when I am peaceful.

This is an incorrect statement because nothing can happen when you are peaceful. What more can happen when you are peaceful? This noticing that you are peaceful is a trick of the mind. Otherwise, how will you notice? You can only notice when something is in front of you, when you have subjectified yourself as a body and objectified the peace as being something in front of you to be noticed. This is a trick of the mind. You have not noticed correctly because now you are not to notice inside or outside. Check the trick of the mind by not looking anywhere, neither within nor without! If you understand what I speak then it is all over: Look Nowhere! If you understand what will you see? There will be no trick Here!

Nobody anywhere is taught where the "I" comes from and so here you must find out. Turn your face to the source of the "I." Do it. It is not to meditate. It is not to be engaged in any effort. Do it and tell me what happens next.

ॐ

I experience so much mental disturbance. Can you help me?

You experience mental disturbance when you experience something that you don't like. Try to fulfill your desires because if you suppress them they will just dwell somewhere in your brain and you won't be able to sleep. So don't keep anything in your mind. Enjoy your life as much as you can and when you have enjoyed everything you will know that there must be something else beyond the transitory enjoyments of the world. All those enjoyments need the bones and leather, but there is a happiness which does not depend on them. When you find this happiness you will sit Quiet and you will not go back to the cemetery which is filled only with bones. Most people stay in the cemetery everyday. Once you know this you will be attracted to the bliss which will continually pull you deeper and deeper into it. Don't worry. Simply stay Quiet here and don't let your mind go back to the previous disturbances. Whenever the mind goes out pounce on it so that it doesn't go back to the previous disturbance. Be a lion.

Don't let the mind go back into the past, that's all.

I surrender to you in the same way that I surrender to life. But still I experience a lot of trouble.

Trouble will eat you up. Any trouble of the mind becomes your enemy and will not leave you. If you want to live in a happy state of life face this enemy and don't allow it into your home. Don't allow the past to enter into your mind. Then you will be free and happy.

Most people are too attached to the trouble to part with it. But when you get fed up with it perhaps this trouble will go to someone else. Even then you are still attached to it. You are advised to give up the attachment with the past friend who has troubled you. Stay here and I will show you how to check this attachment.

I feel I should acknowledge thoughts instead of suppress them.

This is good, don't suppress thoughts, face them whatever they are. If you run away you show your cowardice and weakness and the thoughts will just follow you and become stronger. Now stand and look at the thoughts and they will disappear. You don't have to run away anymore. Face each thought and use yoga techniques to gain strength.

I want to be free of it.

You are on the threshold of success, but you have to be bold and strong. It is a strong one who will win so put your whole strength on this: "I want to be Free." This is quite enough.

I have had so many plans to travel all over, but I keep canceling them because I can't leave.

Wherever you go eventually you must stay Here for your final Realization. Your best guide is your true desire to be Free. This will take you to where you have to be which is where your mind will be killed. But she doesn't want to be killed so easily and will appear as your friend. Know she is your enemy!

ॐ

I am tired of my mind and I feel so helpless. I don't know what to do.

How long have you stayed with this "boyfriend"? If you are tired of it then stop, sit down and rest. When you walk it walks, when you stay quiet it stays quiet. Don't let this "boyfriend" of yours into your home and eventually it will go away.

I have not experienced the source of thought, though I have tried many times.

Suppose you own a house and you notice things are being taken from it at night. So you stay awake one night to catch the thief. As the thief enters the house you cough and so the thief sneaks away because he knows you are still awake. Soon he comes back and steals more things. You know he is there, but you pretend not to so that he is not scared away. The thief leaves your house and you follow him for several kilometers to his den. You enter into the den and catch the thief and restore all your stolen articles. Like this, follow the thief which is thought! Thought is the thief which steals your peace. The thief's den is your own Self and you enjoy it.

You say I should face the thoughts and feelings. How to do this?

Stay in the present and look at it and don't run to the past. Stay absolutely in the present. This is facing the thought.

When I do this then...

"When" is future and "then" is past. What thought is between these?

It seems that...

What do you means by "seems"? This is a rose (shows her a rose.) Will you say, "It is a rose" or will you say, "It seems like a rose"? Be clear of what is before you, and all thought will disappear and you will be happy and peaceful.

I want to be happy. I want to give my neurosis and all my perceived problems to you. I am disgusted at how often I get disgusted at how often I am seduced by my mind.

To remove all of this just look within your own Self. Do it as I say. Look Within, not without. I can see from the face the neurosis people carry for ages. Yours comes from childhood. You are lucky that you are here because it will go. Only sit properly anywhere and look Within, not out at your neighbor.

> The more you look Within,
> the more beautiful you will find yourself to Be.
> This beauty has been hiding for decades,
> you have to do nothing to know it.
> Simply do not think,
> and you will know who you are.

I do this, I try to look within, but my mind seems to be busy like never before. I want to allow more non-doing to take place.

Mind becomes busy when you are in front of something to which you are attracted, not otherwise. If the object of attraction is not there then the mind does not find anything. If you see a handsome boy your mind will be busy.

> When there are two the mind is busy.
> But how long can mind dance
> when there is only one?
> It will get fatigued, keep quiet, and sleep.

It is not difficult to solve these problems. Non-doing is possible when you don't have desire for any other object, person or idea. Then your mind will be at rest.

ॐ

I feel stressed and nervous and I always create problems in my life. I do feel quiet in Satsang. Can you help me be quiet?

What kind of problems do you create?

Just to be busy and restless.

Just to be dizzy? (laughs) It is good to be busy because otherwise you will sleep. The best "busy"-ness is to find out where you come from.

I try to be closer to my Self, but the noise of this mind keeps me out!

Your name is Matwalli, and I gave it to you because Matwalli doesn't care for anything, whatsoever happens. If the mind troubles you, let it trouble you. If the mind doesn't trouble you, let it not trouble you. What difference does it make? Simply don't care what is there. Whatever appears let it appear and whatever doesn't appear, let no one sit in front of you. Don't even ask the question of who you are. Don't care about anything.

I am quieter now, but thoughts still come up, though they do not seem so important.

Thoughts become important when you speak about it, when you utter it. Then it becomes important, otherwise...(giggles)

(She smiles and laughs.)

You see how easily the obstacles are removed! Look at your face! It is not the same person who came here.

You are not to handle these troubles at all. They will all be handled by the Self. Just surrender to the Self and it will take care of you. He looks after the whole cosmos, why shouldn't he look after someone like you who is on the right track?

ॐ

I feel I have met a person who is beyond time and space and mind; someone who I recognize as God and Self. Can you advise me? Should I take them as my Guru?

Beyond mind there is no distinction. Beyond mind there is no difference between a pig and a man. Your thought of distinction, that one man is superior to another, is mind.

You say he is beyond mind, time and space. Then how will you trace him? You will only find him when you are beyond mind, time and space. Then these two beyond-minded people will meet in space. (laughs)

Help me to remove my ignorance and to totally silence me. I have had experiences of bliss, but I guess I am still too influenced by the world and by my concepts.

If you have had a glimpse then let anything stay with you, there is no problem. No world or events will trouble you. Keep this glimpse in your mind and what can happen? Your father is the Lord of the universe and he cannot disown you. You can do whatever you want as long as you remember that you are the son of the Lord of the universe. All these things are for you to enjoy. Like the prince of a king can do whatever he likes. No one can touch him because everybody knows he is the prince. And if anybody complains to the king it doesn't matter because he is the prince's father, and he will not punish his son. Just do not disown your father. Otherwise you will become a beggar. It is up to you. Everybody is a prince and those who are in trouble have only forgotten that they are a prince.

You once said that, "Even the most excellent concept is still just a concept." Is there any real reason to try to understand words? They just seem to have put me into trouble.

You don't have to try and you don't have to understand.
Whatever you understand is concept only.
Whatever you will or have understood is concept only.
Whatever you see around you is your concept only.

> The concepts of your mind can become so strong,
> that they appear to be real.

Without concept you cannot recognize anything. So all that you see is that which is previously stored in your memory. Like the dream tiger who pounces on you in your dream. It makes you feel very frightened. You don't say, "You are a dream tiger, purely a mental concept only, I am not afraid of you." The dream tigers are as fierce in the dream state as they are in the forest in the waking state.

> Like this everything seems real.
> Everything you see, or touch, or taste, or hear, or smell
> seems real, but actually they are not.
> They are all concepts.

You will remove these concepts, these dreams when you wake up. Only then you will say that it is all just your concept. For so many years you have been adhering to this waking dream. Now it is such a concept that you call it real. But when you are in the sleep state nothing is there. This you can also experience in the waking state. Just stay asleep in the waking state and stay awake while others sleep.

> As you sleep stay awake to your own Self,
> and you will know it is all a concept.
> There you will find your True nature which is Eternal.
> It is neither waking, or dream or sleep.

The entire waking state is a concept just as the dream state is. When you know this you will say "Now I am looking in a very new atmosphere," and you will know who is always awake, who does not sleep. I will give you a hint on how to do this: Find the concept on which all other concepts are based, find the "I."

Thank you for taking this baggage from me.

Leave your burdens aside. All surplus baggage must be thrown away. This I learned from my army life. You can't be slow in the army or you will die and burdens make you slow. Sometimes when I see people who are too serious about some foolish thing I think of something the Maharshi used to say:

> When you are traveling on the train
> will you keep the baggage on your head or under your feet?

This is the difference between the Wise
and the rest of the universe.
The Wise do not carry their baggage,
but almost everyone does.

Thinking of friends and finances and things not even come or already gone is carrying your baggage. This is the difference between living in peace or suffering. It depends on where your baggage is.

If you feel that the baggage that you are carrying is of no use, drop it down. Then walk away Enlightened into the realms where very few have gone. Don't carry anything. This means do not think. I will tell you a story about this.

There was once a guru who had a very young disciple. They had to go to another village, but on their way they had to cross a small stream which, due to the rains, had risen and become neck deep. They both could cross the stream because they were able to keep their small bags on their heads. But there was a prostitute standing nearby who had to attend a wedding function and couldn't cross the stream because of her nice dress and make-up. So this saint said she should sit on his shoulders and he would carry her to the other side, and so she did. Then she went her way and the two sannyasins went theirs.

Now the student was very confused and troubled. His Guru had always said not to touch a woman, but then he had told the prostitute to have a ride on his shoulders! After about ten miles he humbly asked, "Sir, I have a question. I am very much annoyed with your behavior. You teach me not to see or touch any woman because we are monks, we are sannyasins, and then you touched that girl."

"Yes, yes, I lifted the girl because she wanted to cross the stream. Then I let her down and we went our way. Now we have been traveling for ten miles, why are you still carrying her? I carried her ten meters but you have carried her ten miles! Why do you still remember her? That is over now!

Like this, whatever comes in front of you take care of the circumstances and forget about it. This is the guidance.

Don't avoid anything that comes!
Don't invite anything that you don't need!
Attend to circumstances as best you can,
and forget about it!

My old habits keep coming back. Can you help me to get rid of them?

The old habits that you had before you came to Lucknow may still exist, but their strength is greatly diminished. Don't worry about them.

Just keep your mind on the formlessness of your Satguru.

Actually, there is only formlessness. The elephant that you dream about seems real in the dream, but is not there in the waking state. It is formless as all forms in the dream are, even though they may represent a person or an animal or whatever. When you wake up everything in the dream becomes formless. Similarly, when you Wake Up everything becomes formless because form is falsehood and Self is Truth.

Whenever you see form it is because your eyes, mind, intelligence and understanding are not clear and you are dreaming. So, if you see form ask yourself if you are dreaming and with these words you will wake up. Then you will not see any existence at all. Most people will never see this. They are just driven by their desires to go through womb after womb, each selected according to the desires of the person. All of you here are lucky and merited and have had holy births with holy parents.

Are the vasanas, mental tendencies of the mind, so strong that they can pull me out of peace?

When the tendencies drag you to enjoyments you can't enjoy this Peace. But once you enjoy this Peace, the tendencies no longer have the energy to pull you out of Peace. You may think you are happy when you are enjoying the objects that your tendencies bring to you, but the most happiness arises when there are no tendencies or desires.

Once you know this there is no problem of enjoying your friends, restaurants, movies or whatever you want to do. You will not be able to forget this real peace and It will not forget you. You will even be able to go to the fishmarket, but you won't smell the fish.

I just worry that the tendencies will take me back away from Self.

There is no back and no forward in the Peace that I speak about.

What causes emotions and thoughts to arise?

You have to inquire "where do these thoughts come from?" I will tell you how to stop thoughts; if some thought is arising it must come from somewhere, isn't it. So go to the root of thought, from where it is arising. If you are doing it tell me if the thought is still there. Find the source of the current thought, the one occurring in this instant. As the wave rises from the ocean, find out from where whatever is in your mind rises from. You have to tell me.

Can one really develop this awareness to such an extent that they know where thought arises from?

That is what I am asking you to do. Be vigilant. Be watchful of where every thought rises from.

How do I recreate the suffering in my mind?

When the ego is removed you will feel tremendous happiness. It is only because of ego that you suffer and feel unhappiness. But once you throw away the ego how can you let it return? Why did you pick it up again? It means that you have not thrown it away. This happens most of the time. Most of the time when people feel in peace they have not left the ego behind. Once you are clean you will not smear your clothes again with mud. Having had a bath in the Ganga how will you again smear yourself with mud?

So you have had intention to take a bath, but you have not done it. Intention is something else, but you have to put your intention into practice. If you are hungry you must go to the restaurant and not just look at the menu. You have to eat! Don't just take the menu and lick it. (giggles) You have just been licking the menus. Once you have eaten you will not go to the next door restaurant. All you have been doing is collecting menus, but menus cannot remove your hunger, you must eat! You must digest it. Freedom will take you to the proper restaurant or will even take food to you.

For the last few days I have been consumed by familiar emotions ranging from hurt to frustration. I have not been able to escape this with my safe insulated American life. Occasionally I have experienced...

Not "occasionally," always! You must always experience this. When you think, there is the world, when you don't think there is no world. This is reality. There is no world, no body in sleep because there is no thought. The world is there when you think, so do not think and you are happy.

It is hard not to think.

When your mind is going to the past, stop it and bring it to the present. Mind itself is past. Mind itself is thought; look at it and it will stop spinning. Look at any thought in front of you and concentrate on it. No thought will come if you look at it, so anytime any thought comes, simply look at it.

If someone is sleeping they do not know what is happening, but if you wake them up then everything is finished. Thought is the whole universe, and so looking at the thought will cause everything to disappear, keep on looking always. Question "Where is the I?" and you will see there is no thought. When "I" rises you look at where it rises from.

I feel that I am caught in a whirlpool and I don't know how to get out.

There is a technique for getting out of whirlpools. I also was drown in whirlpools in the Ganga and I know this technique. If you make effort you will not be able to survive because your effort will, ironically, keep you in the whirlpool. But if you don't make effort you will be thrown out of the whirlpool by the whirlpool.

Nobody in the world is successful in getting out of this whirlpool by their own efforts. The one who doesn't make effort will come right out. In fact, he can jump into whirlpools whenever he likes and he will not be in danger because he knows this technique. So know this technique for yourself and you can go back to your home.

My home is in America where I am an educator. I would like to raise the consciousness of the Americans by using the media of videos. What is the main thing that I should tell Americans about thinking?

Tell them not to do it! (giggles) Americans have learned enough, in fact they are the teachers of the whole world. People from all over the world go to America for their advanced degrees. Tell them that they have learned enough and it is time to keep Quiet! They can learn everything in America except how to Be. For this they must come to Lucknow. Tell them this and tell them to always be faithful to themselves and to others.

Tell them when this thought of, "I am the body" comes, check it, and keep it away. Again and again they are to do this. Then something new will come. Something which is not the body will appear. When the billion year old thought, "I am the body" comes, check it. Again and again check it.

I don't have a lot of success in stopping thinking.

If you can't check the thought, then just let it come.
If it comes, then don't run after it.
It will come and it will stay and it will go.
Just watching may be easier than stopping it.

If any thought comes treat it like a car coming down the road toward you. Do you run after the car? No! So like this let the thought come, let the thought stay and let it go. It cannot stay for more than an instant because another is waiting behind it. (giggles) In this moment there is no thought. Only in the last moment is there thought. What do you think in this moment?

Nothing.

In this moment nobody can think. Everybody thinks in the graves of the graveyards. This moment is the moment of love and peace, but everybody misses it. Thought is the last moment, not this moment.

In the present there is no room for thoughts.

So stay Here! What difficulty is there?

Attachment and Past

The only way not to have Peace
is to be engaged in something else,
to be attached to something other than your Self.

Any beauty other than Self is a dead corpse in a nice dress and
attachment to these things is living in a grave with dead bodies.
When you live in the association of mind you're in the graveyard,
but when you do inquire you are Free.
Doubting this Freedom is clinging to bondage.

We cling to our own attachments,
but we can fly away and Satsang is this open door.
It is your choice: old patterns are your own cage.
Befriend something permanent and unchanging
and you will be happy; this is wisdom, the Guru.
Give up your old patterns of life
which are kusanga, bad associations.

You need the past and thoughts to suffer,
you don't need anything to be free.
The boulders of the past rest on your chest
and destroy your life and freedom.
Remove them by finding the origin of the I-thought.
Freedom waits but most are engaged with something else.
Don't tie yourself to anything in the past or the future,
because it will not work!

Be attached only to this Moment.
When you hold to something other than your true nature
you will be disturbed.
By holding attachments to transient things
you declare to yourself that you are not the Fullness in which all is.
Self is totality and therefore cannot possess or desire;
so possessing is a veil, a lie!

Everyone is a Buddha, you have to break attachments!
You have to renounce because otherwise you trap yourself
in samsara and death with your own attachments.
Attachment is a demon, attachment is trouble,
because our attachments become our reality.
Only in Satsang is this removed.

ॐ

How can I stay in Awareness without being troubled by old habits?

What will you do with your old boyfriend who is always abusing you
when you have a very fresh handsome and beautiful new boyfriend who
worships you and gives you peace and contentment? (laughs) What will you
do?

This happiness seems desirable, but it is just another attachment.

This is philosophy! Suppose a prisoner is set free after twenty years, but
he refuses to go because he thinks his freedom will be an attachment.
Everybody loves to live in the prison in fear, but intellectually rationalizes it
by saying Freedom is an attachment. You are asking me if to have your legs
free of chains is an attachment! You are only philosophizing!

Will you help me experience what is real right now?

Stop hiding in the bushes of thoughts and attachments and burn them
instead. Everybody likes to hide in these bushes.

I seem so addicted to trying to find happiness in my partners.
It doesn't work anymore.

You don't need a man to give you happiness and if you try you will get
fed up with it. That will be the time to search for your own Self because your
mind will not go to the past enjoyments. The mind wants to be happy, but
those sources of happiness which cannot satisfy the mind are in the end

destructive. So after enough destructive experiences it will settle down as it has in your case.

> Forget about what you have been doing once it is gone,
> and win the happiness of Here and Now.

I have such gratitude for the Grace of your presence. You dissolve all my questions, and most without me even asking them! I just still have a yearning to be empty of all attachments.

> Only when you are empty of all attachments
> are you beautiful.
> When you have anything in your mind,
> you are in the graveyard of past thoughts.
> Anyone attached to the past
> has an ugly mind and is ugly themselves.
> Because your mind is not clean, you have fallen to the past.

> If you live in the instant Presence,
> this is called Beauty and Love.

The whole world is lost in these outside attachments, not just yourself. If any of these attachments give you happiness and peace of mind then stay with them because it isn't time to leave them. But if you see the snakes in your sleeves biting you it is time to reject them. It is no use to experience what has already been experienced. If you know the fire burns there is no need to be burned again. Like this, avoid attachments like fire because they will burn you. But don't be attached to non-attchment because just as the ocean is not effected by the waves, so thoughts and attachments have nothing to do with Divinity. So let them be there.

Have a firm decision that you do not want to suffer and that you are here to win happiness in this incarnation. This is the number one decision. If you make this decision you will have Grace. Just don't go and enjoy any object, stop it. Do this practice here and you will be successful.

> Don't let your mind
> go outside of your Heart!

I see no calm, no joy. How to stay in the non-abidance?

Stay as Such! If you look back you will not be calm or joyous. If you stop looking back you will be happy. Stop even speaking of the past.

Even when my mind is quiet there is tightness and cramps in my heart.

When you are Quiet you should be joyful. So, it means that the mind is not quiet when there is a cramp or a knot in your heart. This knot is not a present knot, it is old, very old. It has gone to your sub-conscious mind. This knot is there because someone has not treated you well, they have cheated you well. (giggles) *This is for you to forget and you have to forget it.* Don't remember any person who has cheated you and this will open the knot. Untie the knot by not remembering. The old is the old, the past is the past. Of course, it is difficult to forget the event, but you have to concentrate on the present day to day events and not go back. Try it. Tighten your fist also so the mind does not go back to the past affair. Tighten your fists and even clench your teeth. With that much determination you can stop it yourself. Otherwise, it is of no use living this life.

Enjoy this life. Nature has given so may beautiful things; we should be open to it, and enjoy it. Those who are always going to the past cannot enjoy the beauty of the present life.

You are here, and we have to help you. This is the responsibility of all of us to help that person. If someone is not happy we have to force happiness on them whether they like it or not!

I am sad because so many places where I once was able to hide are crumbling down, but I am also happy because I want to stop drowning in it all. So sometimes I am happy and sometimes sad.

What do you mean by sometimes this and sometimes that? If you are sometimes sad it means that you want to have one pattern of life which you like. Don't do this, this is a game! Let anything happen to you, let it happen. If something does not happen to you, let it not happen. This is relief.

If you are happy when someone loves you and not happy when someone does not love you then you will always suffer. For who is there to love? People don't love others as much as they love their own interests regarding others. It is only for the sake of interest that people love you. Will someone who loved you fifty years ago love you fifty years from now? This is only time, and when the time is right everybody is a friend. It cannot remain the same. You are the same and everybody else will change. You can't check the time and it is eating away at everybody in the world. Time is enemy number one and nobody knows it, but you love it.

Sometimes...

There it is again, do not use the word "time" again. Do not use the word "time" at all, for one second, one moment, and have this experience of who you are. The trick to be always happy is not to be too friendly with time. Time will kill everybody. It has killed all sages and saints. So it is better not to speak of time. When you sleep you do not speak of time and how happy are you? Try this now.

Whenever you are not happy it means you are holding onto some past person or concept. Past is time. When you are attached to the past you are not happy, but this is the habit of everybody. All relationships, all objects of the world are past. Even your body is past. But don't speak of time and you are ever young. Nobody can touch you, not even fear or death. Try this from now; don't let your mind go to any person, object or concept of the past. For one moment try this and experience your Self now. Do it now, and tell me if you are not happy. Don't let your mind drift to the last moment or day or year. Then speak to me.

How not to be drowned in the past?

Look at any thought that rises just now. All thoughts belong to the past, what doesn't belong to the past?

Just Being Here.

These three words do not belong to the past. Being is this instant, but don't use words for this moment out of time. Find out what the words point to. Seeing the Self you don't keep any other name, object, or person in your mind. Don't keep any person in your mind and tell me what do you see?

There is always an object in my mind, what keeps me from being free?

Nothing else can prevent you from being free except that you are holding onto something in the past. If you don't hold onto any past you will see that you are always free. Holding onto the past is what prevents you from knowing that you are free. Do you understand and do you agree? For one time in Lucknow decide that you have to be free of all past concepts and relations; just for one second give yourself this. Then you will know that always you have been free.

But you are from New York City aren't you? So you must be remembering your 8th Avenue. (giggles) Whosoever has gone to 8th Avenue can never forget it. I used to live nearby there also in Greenwich Village at 14th and Bank Street.

The past is like a dust storm in my mind!

All these storms of the past mean that still you are holding onto the past relationships with others. That is why it is not very clear. I think these storms will cease when you get rid of your attachments to the past. When you get attached to Presence it will be a very different affair. So don't be discouraged. Keep it up.

Fear and Fear of Death

Fear manifests as death!
"I am the body" is the basic fear.
Meditate everyday to remove this fear.
When fear comes love it and when it goes don't cling to it.

How to deal with my deepest fears?

Do not be afraid of the fear
but go to it and embrace it.
Go to the source of the fear and dance with it.
You have no fear in the sleep state,
you only have fear in the waking state
when you bring things from the past into this moment.

I have made many changes in my life I still have arrogance and fear. Now I will try to embrace this fear.

What changes did you make so that you still have arrogance and fear?

The changes were in my morals and behavior. I stopped taking drugs and alcohol. I want to be free, and free of fear. Please show me the way to release all of this.

You say you have fear, arrogance and pride. I will tell you how to remove it.

Look at fear, arrogance and pride
if you want to remove it, look at it!
Pride and arrogance is doership and this causes trouble.
They have never paid you, so be humble.
Anything that you "do" conceals Self
with the arrogance of doership.

Arrogance is not recognizing this timeless moment,
arrogance is "I am the body."
Remove arrogance and Enlightenment is instantaneous.
"I am so-and-so" is the first arrogance,
and "this is mine" is the second. Look at it!

When you look at something you objectify it and you establish the subject as different from the object. So look at the fear and pride and they will become the object and you will become the subject, or the seer seeing the seen. Do it now. Anytime something is objectified you become the subject. You are the seer, not the seen. Find out who the seer is.

To sense something you need five senses: eyes to see, nose to smell, and so on. But for the eyes to see they need an object of sight. You are not the sense object and not the senses, you are different from these. Simply understand this, but don't make any effort to do so. Simply separate yourself from all the objects. You must discriminate and know that you are not all the things you see. Once you have done this, your purpose of life is fulfilled: to know who you really are.

Most teachers divert your attention. They don't tell you that you are not anything. And preachers just dwell on the past. They will tell you about somebody who lived one thousand nine hundred and ninety five years ago. They don't let you find out what is in this present moment and they themselves have never tried this.

The Teaching here is very old: twenty five thousand years. It is the teaching of the Vedas:

Find out who you are, nothing else.
You can find This.

But people have lost this Teaching. They don't care about it; therefore, they suffer. Once you have done this you won't call it a glimpse.

So do it now for an instant of time. This is all it takes to realize it. Don't postpone like you do with other things. People say, "I will meditate when I am retired and old." But perhaps you will not see old age, perhaps you will not even see the next moment. So do It Now. It is available now because it is wisdom, it is light and you can always see this light in Now, in Luck-Now. Don't postpone it:

To see the Light, the Wisdom;
don't make any effort,
don't give rise to a single thought in the mind,
and just keep Quiet.

This is the trick I tell you and
It will not take more than an instant.

People have done it. You can do it now. Don't postpone, and don't try! If you try it means this trial will be something to be done in time.

I will try!

If you say "I will try," it means that you are postponing for the future. So don't try and don't make effort and don't give rise to any thought and don't care about whether you have done it or have not done it. What is this then? Nothing is left for you to say, except for the declaration that "I Am." Come on, speak up!!

I Am! It is true!

ॐ

I have so much fear and anger.

You have to be Nischala: That which does not move. Let there be fear and anger, but you don't move. This is enough. Repeat your name: "I am Unmovable, I do not move." Let the fear and anger come, but they will not enter you. When you become weak they enter you, but if you face them they will not trouble you. Stand like a mountain, like that which does not move. Wind in the form of anger will come, strike and subside. Waves come and drown the rock, but when they recede the rock is unmoved. So don't move. You can't fight anger with anger. Keep quiet and don't move. The wind troubles a weak sapling; uprooting it, but the mountain cannot be uprooted. This is how you will succeed in controlling the anger.

There are so many things in my life which keep me from peace, including so many of my friends. Can you help me?

You must have the joy of your own real Friend first. Then your face will change and so will your friends. Just stay here for a few days and it will happen. Now your face and eyes show so much fear. You are too young to be afraid.

When I was young I came face to face with tigers and elephants in the forests of the Himalayas, but I had so much mental and physical strength that I was not afraid even of them. I was convinced that if they attacked I could kill them with my bare hands. And often I could not even look people in the eyes because they would not be able to take it. This much self power was there. Why are you afraid? Even if you don't tell me I will go to your childhood and find out. Your parents gave you this fear. I will discuss it with you in private, after the cricket matches, or we can continue now.

Now! How do I stop the fear? How do I detach from the ego? I tend to abuse others and myself.

Fear comes from the mind. To stop it find where the mind comes from!

My mind is in my head.

Where does this head come from? When you sleep do you see your head?

No.

So the head also is not there. So where does the mind come from? Mind means thought, thought means "I." There is no difference between "I" and mind. When "I" rises the mind rises. So find out where the "I" is rising from. From birth you use the word "I." "I" am attached to this person, this person is attached to me. Which is this "I" who is attached to and abuses others and abuses itself. All this will instantly stop when you find the source of "I."

It is not there.

Are you thinking?

No!

You asked how to stop thinking; this is how! When you stop thinking there is no fear and who can you abuse? It is very good to ask your questions. Everybody must remove their doubts. Don't be shy. Without asking how can you realize it? Since you are here finish your doubts instantly.

I used to have such fears, especially of being killed by burglars.

It is the fear which will kill you, not the burglars. This fear is inside you and is the real thief of your peace. It is probably due to a childhood experience, probably a death in your family.

My sister died when I was young.

This fear of loss has grown now, and if I tell you to just stop it it will not work. When you lose a near one you lose your balance and you are shaken. Even J. Krishnamurti was very upset when he lost his brother and he had to work to get over it. So work on your own Self by knowing that this fear is your own creation and that it is rooted in your childhood. It may take a long time to go, but you must see that you live a happy life anyway.

I haven't been able to sleep and this is becoming a distraction for me.

If you cannot sleep this is because of how you have spent the waking state. If you have spent the waking state in a good way you will sleep, but since you do not sleep you have been very active for things which are not necessary. Your face shows an introverted mind which is concentrated on one fear that has happened early in childhood. Maybe some kind of abuse which has now gone into the sub-conscious mind.

Yes.

So, I think if you extrovert your mind you will be better. Go out on the town or to the forest with people, not alone. Don't fall back into the black hole. This can be cured, it is not a big problem or a disease. It is a state of mind, the overworking of the mind always going back to the past event of the childhood. So a new chapter has to be opened for you to live in the present life, present way, present things, and then you will get well.

If you are not able to sleep on account of some reason, make use of this time by making inquiry: "Who is not sleeping?" If you find the good answer it will be "the one who has never slept." "The one who is always awake, and always conscious." Let your mind sleep; let your body and ego sleep; but You stay awake! Look at them. If you don't make this inquiry and you don't sleep then you will have to consult another person!

Is the fear and insecurity at both an inner conscious level and on an outer conscious level.

Fear and insecurity can only be at the outer conscious level because there is no fear at the inner conscious level. When you see the inner conscious level you have no fear at all. You have to look at your fears. When you are aware of them they vanish, because you are the witness of the fear. Where did you get this fear? You are carrying fear from the past, not from the present. This fear is from your childhood! Nobody can help you to throw away your fears, you have to do it yourself by going to the root of the fear which has disturbed your mind. You will find out what is the cause and how to deal with it.

In the last year I have had a growing awareness of fear of the world, especially other people.

It means you are hiding something, otherwise you would not be afraid. If a robber goes to the forest he will suspect that a person behind him is a policeman who is after him, because he has something to hide. He always has the policeman in his mind. So something is there that you are hiding and so you are afraid of people and the world.

I feel I am hiding anger.

Anger and fear go together. Both are robbers. What crime have you done? What have you done to others that you are angry with them? Your anger is to wipe somebody out. Both anger and fear are very fierce enemies of a man. You are probably hiding something from childhood, but if you don't know it, it is good luck. Now you are on your heals to face fear and anger. Everybody has come here to face these enemies: lust, anger, greed. Everybody will be harmed by these three enemies.

I am just arriving from France and I am in a lack of trust and I can't let go.

What do you want to let go of? There are many things to let go of.

My fears and my tensions.

Oh, so you are always thinking about your country? (laughs) If you don't let go it means that you are attached to something and that you are afraid that it will leave you. You must be attached to something of the past, and it will not leave you. If you understand that there is no real friend and that everybody is after your flesh for their own interests and enjoyments, not yours, you will get fed up and search for the Friend who is always present, but hiding. Find the Friend who is always hiding in your own Heart. Did you ever turn your face to your own Heart? You have been looking at others, but you have not looked to your own Self. Don't think and don't make effort.

This is what I can't do.

If you don't do it yourself then whose problem is it? You must solve this for yourself. If you are hungry you must eat because it won't help you if others eat for you. So if you want peace you must find it yourself. Tell me if not thinking and not making effort doesn't make you happy!

Anger and Dissatisfaction

Anger, greed, attachment, and aversion
are the diseases of the mind
which make meditation, knowing who you are, impossible.
Anger arises only when there are two and this two-ness is ego.
Anger, greed, hypocrisy, lust, and jealousy
all are mighty enemies on the battlefield,
but conquer ego and you will conquer all of these.

Do not get involved in anger, greed or lust,
these are the ego, don't let yourself be involved.
If greed interests you, be greedy for Freedom!
If you are angry then be angry with God,
and if you must lust, desire the union with your Heart.

Check the flowing river of mind by damming it
and then channeling it or the dam will break
due to floods of anger and greed.
The channels must irrigate in the right direction.
Then anger, greed, and grief will run harmlessly.
So let them arise and as they do
know that you are the Source and forget about them.
Remember only your true Self,
like this you can face all circumstances!

*I am sorry to ask you such a personal question, but I am experiencing
so much anger lately. What can I do?*

Anger is a curse which cuts short your life by burning the entire nervous
system and troubling your breath. Express your anger and kiss what makes
you angry. It is no problem to get angry. Just don't remember the
circumstances which made you angry. Don't carry anger or love. Forget
everything. Don't worry about asking personal questions because I must take
care of my children and see to it that you are happy!

*Why do I get so angry when I think of certain people in my past,
especially my father. These old thoughts are like prison walls.*

These thoughts are not you, they are the creation of the misbehavior that
you experienced from others when you were a child. Now they do not leave

you. But by good luck you are here and so slowly they will leave you. Others are driven to suicide by this, you will be free! Simply sit and listen. Your old thoughts will be overpowered and destroyed and a new fresh way will take root in your heart. Don't try because if you do it will not happen. Simply keep Quiet and don't make effort. This may be difficult, but it is possible. Activity will leave you and you will be Quiet.

> Stillness will remove the concept of activity.
> Activity has never given anyone
> a peaceful and loving state.

Keep repeating "this is not for me," when you are suffering. "I want Love, Peace, Self." Turn the mind this way.

There seems to be so many opposing forces.

You will see that these opposing forces are actually helping you. The direction that they take are for your own good, they are not your enemies. What is destructive is your desire for objects. You will see that there is no difference between stillness and activities. Know you will succeed. Do you have any other questions or doubts?

I have been unsatisfied with my life even though I have been given so much, including this precious Satsang. I can't open up and be happy and feel joy!

The cause of your unhappiness is that you want something to enjoy and that something cannot give you satisfaction because what you want is from the past. But you have to understand that nothing of the past will give happiness to any person. Happiness and Peace are Here Now. Look for something that will give you rest, Peace and Happiness instantly and you are not to work for it.

Now tell me, doesn't this dissatisfaction belong to someone who has deceived you!? Everyone will deceive you and is deceiving you. Remove this concept from your mind and tell me if you are satisfied. If you are not attached to any person or object or idea for just one second, tell me how do you feel?

I still feel attached to persons.

Ah, but I told you not to do it for one second. You may be thirty years old and involved with your dissatisfaction for so long, but I only want one fingersnap of your time unattached to anything. Afterwards you can go on being attached! But why not just try this now. Give this second to your Self. You haven't done it and therefore you are dissatisfied and disappointed and you will die in this dissatisfaction. But do what I tell you and death will not touch you. All your pain is rising from physical relationships, but tell me how you will look in fifty years and how attractive you will be.

I don't want that.

Then stop looking into the mirror that will show a beautiful girl one day and an old hanging woman the next. Instead, look into the mirror that I am showing you. The way of the world is that everybody wants other people only for their own benefit. But you can change this now because by your merit you have won the opportunity to come to Satsang. Now at this moment are you satisfied or dissatisfied?

I am satisfied!

In this Now you are satisfied and in this Now you can run about as you like. You can stay with those things that you are attached to, but do not forget This Instant. Sit with the person with whom you are attached and speak to him about this and see what he speaks about to you. Just look into his eyes. That's all.

ॐ

I am lethargic and dissatisfied. This comes after three months of what seemed to be divine clarity. Can you shine the light on me and alleviate this painful condition.

Tomorrow we will play music and you will have to give a song. Are you prepared or do you have to make some rehearsals?

No, I will make some rehearsals.

You must finish your thoughts. If you are hungry you must eat. How did you get so lost in this musical program after saying what you just said? I wanted to see how easily you could get lost and distracted. I wanted to see how hungry you are. If you are hungry you will first go to the restaurant and not play soccer with your friends. I simply tested you, but you got so lost! I could have given you some guidance, but you must not need it because now you are making rehearsals and two things cannot happen at the same time.

I do want to be peaceful. Recently I was meditating at your home when somebody told me to leave. This really upset me.

What is that meditation if you are disturbed so much right after it?

I don't know.

Then who should know on your behalf? Find out!

One king went to see a Pir with sweets, cloth and food loaded on elephants. He also took his queen, and the ministers of the state followed on horses. This procession went to the thatch hut in the forest where the Pir stayed.

When he arrived he asked one of the Pir's attendants to inform him that the king of the country would like to pay him respect. So the disciple went in and informed the saint.

The saint told him to sit under the tree and unload all the gifts and he would be called later. The king waited for the call and sent the queen back to look after the children and the ministers to look after the kingdom.

Night passed and he stayed under the tree. The next morning he asked again if it was time to see the saint, but was told that he would be called later, and so three days passed. All the sweets and fruits were rotting and a rain started. Again the king asked that the Pir be told that he was waiting to see him.

Now one week had passed, then fifteen days, and finally the Pir said that he only has one more hour to wait. After one hour he asked if it was now possible to see him, but was told he had to wait another five minutes. After five minutes there still was no call from inside, but the message that he had to wait just one minute more.

But he couldn't wait and ran inside to touch the feet of the saint. The saint asked him why he came in without permission now and not before, and told the king that it has taken twenty nine days to erase his ego. You had the ego of a king and wanted to be received like one, but that will never happen. You had an ego, but now you came without one and fell down at my feet. There is no one to tell you no! Immediately upon arrival you could have come in!" said the saint.

So the king had stayed one month, but you have been here in Lucknow for so many months and your ego is still here. If someone tells you to go you are disturbed and so there is no use for meditation. If someone tells you to go you should because there is no difference between coming and going. If you have been told to go outside the room, go and I will call you again. Many cases are like this.

Papaji, is this deep discontentment that I feel another layer of mind or is it something else?

Discontentment, of course, is a layer in front of you so that you cannot see the clarity. You must remove all layers. Look at this card, (he shows him a painting of the gopis swimming naked in front of Krishna.) They have removed all the layers between them and the Self. This photo is the explanation. What is the layer between Self and you? This layer you must remove. This dress that they are wearing is the layer between you and the Self. In your case it is discontentment. So, remove everything, remove all the thoughts. Denude your Self and you will see the Self. This is the photo explaining it. Undress means not wearing any thought or concept, no ego, no past in your mind. Then it will be clean.

I have also been feeling such a deep dissatisfaction lately.

You are not satisfied because you are trying to measure the depth of the ocean with a yardstick. If you want to see the depth throw away all your yardsticks and dissolve into the depth of Love. Throw away your yardsticks, your calculations, and your expectations of what should and shouldn't happen. Throw away your concepts of what will happen.

I have been so trapped by these depressions and disappointments since childhood.

You have to make a strong decision to be free of these depressions and disappointments and then you can do it immediately. One very strong decision is enough. Decide where you want to go and what you want to obtain. Decide this here and now. What do you want and how far do you have to travel to get this? So there is only a confusion about deciding because once decided you have already traveled the whole distance. So take care of your decisions first. Decide to be Free!

I used to have so much anger and so many problems, but now I have a hard time remembering what they are!

Oh, you are a very good boy! This is a very good experience and I can appreciate it.

Even in forgetfulness, anger, and sleep there is an awareness of the embrace.

When you don't mind what state you are in, whether it be anger or arrogance, then your state is beyond these. These states will come in front of you, but you won't make any differentiation because you have found something else and have no time to think about the states. It is good to have crossed these hurdles such as anger. Anger raises your temperature and doesn't allow you eat or sleep peacefully. Some people are agitated with anger for their whole life. Anger is the dire enemy of Peace.

Being with you has removed all this anger and has given me so much peace.

A glance of the Guru is compassion and removes the darkness of those who really want to be Free. In the proximity of the teacher it doesn't take time or practice. Instantly, light is here, like you touch the switch and the light is on. Only your honest and sincere dedication is needed.

Can you tell me about expectations?

To be happy you should not expect anything. Have no expectations about reality, just Be reality. In sleep you are happy because you don't expect anything from anyone and you are left alone. When there are no expectations, this is happiness. Do your work with no expectations for the results. They are not in your hand. Someone else decides the result. Your dharma is to perform activities which are needed to your standard and not to seek results. This will give you happiness. Nobody can fulfill these expectations. Even when people are old, their expectations are still young. So don't get involved in any kind of expectations.

I came here to face my demons, all the unresolved dark fears, like the ones that Jesus had to confront in the desert.

If you think, "I have done this sin," this thought manifests as a ghost, as a demon.

One man from New York came to me in Rishikesh claiming to be followed incessantly by a woman demon. I saw that this demon was the guilt that he was carrying from killing his wife. By sending blessings to his wife, by the purifying effects of the Ganga, and by spending time with me he became all right. His wife's soul was pacified and his demons of guilt were removed.

Sadhana: There is no Becoming Being

There is no becoming Being.
It is simply a trick of the mind to think
that you need to be established in Self.
You are That!
Just stay As you Are wherever you are.
Be there and you need to think.
Be Here and you need not think or use mind.
This is Peace, this is Beauty.

It is a joke to look for peace
when really there is no escape from it.
Search and practice is sheer ignorance,
because only being stupid requires practice.
The river makes no effort or practice to come to the ocean.
Cease thinking and making effort and you will get it.
Don't complicate yourself with thought and practice,
don't even practice non-practicing, just stay Quiet.

The Traps of Search, Practice, and Process

Everything you do is for stillness of mind, for happiness,
and yet anything that you do disturbs your mind
because "doing" is mind, it is a trap,
whether it is a samadhi or bliss or whatever.
Anything that you try to do conceals the diamond
with the arrogance of doership.
You have been doing for 35 million years
so Now simply keep Quiet.
The Self is not seen during effort,
nor is Freedom the result of effort, it is already Here Now.
You miss bliss because you search for the transient,
but Truth cannot be seen, It is the seer!
Find That through which you would search
and you find that Being is Bliss.

Trying and searching comes from all directions
like mosquitoes to distract you from knowing Self Now!
Make no effort, for doing is mind:
The brush that cleans the mind is the mind!

So it is better to just give the ego-mind away
because you will speak of cleaning the mind
only when the mind is unclean.

On three accounts searching and practice
are foolishness and misleading
and are only the clever mind postponing Freedom.

The first is that it creates a searcher.
This reinforces the concept of an individual sufferer
that is separate from Freedom, and
that Self is something "other" than that Here and Now.

The second is the search.
Searching is a distraction which causes postponement
and endless needless suffering.
Searching promotes religions, traditions,
and paths to be adhered to,
which serve only to trap you deeper in illusion.
The Truth is only Here and Now,
but the search says it is tomorrow.

The third account is that search creates an object to be found,
and this can be the subtlest and most misleading trap.
As you start a search you conceptualize
what it is that you are searching for.
Since the nature of Maya, of illusion,
is that whatever you think, so it becomes;
whatever you think the goal to be you will attain it.
There is no doubt about this: as you think so it becomes.
So because of your search you will create and then attain
that which you think you are searching for!
Any heaven or high spiritual state that you long to attain
you will attain after you conceptualize and create it.
Then you will rest satisfied in this trap
thinking that you have attained your "heaven."
This is pie-in-the-sky freedom custom made for you
out of your very own thought and conditioning
of what the Ultimate is.
The Truth is beyond thought, concept, and conditioning
and this Truth is what you are, and only the Truth Is.
So stop your search, simply be Quiet,

definitely do not stir a thought or make an effort,
and the Truth will reveal Itself to Itself.

Practice takes ego which reinforces subject-object relationships
and all practice is through body mind and senses
which reinforces body mind identification.
Any identification is misidentification.
Whatever you think you become
so thinking of name and form
is thinking of ego-mind-world-senses-illusion.
If you must think, think of Existence, Consciousness and Bliss.
Best is to simply know "I am That Brahman."
Direct practice is Now itself, just Being itself,
not waiting for the next moment or the next thought
or the next life to accomplish something.
Direct practice is the bliss of turning your face to Self,
direct practice is Existence.

Prescribed sadhana requires and reinforces ego
to become something special when really we are One.
You cannot practice Being, you are That.
Have no pride, just simply Be Self.
You have to strike at the root of ego,
but not with sadhana which is by the ego for the ego.
Offer this ego pride to your own Silent-Peace-Self-Being.
Only going to the source of ego-mind with inquiry will do,
and once you ask this question do not come back.

Stop thinking and surrender all name and form to Silence.
Mind is movement and this is a wave.
Self is Stillness and this is the ocean.
To know yourself you must stop the movement
for one moment and Be Quiet.

The concept of "I am the body" is the concept of time.
Leave the time concept behind by facing the Source of all.
All concepts are borders: take on concepts
and you take on borders!

Another trap is thinking "I am empty" which is ego
because it is only relative to the lack of ego mind
that the concept of emptiness arises.
Therefore, there is no bliss in this Emptiness.

"I am" must be dissolved for only Emptiness to Be.
All is Emptiness so how can there be process toward it!
Most attempts to remove the wall serve only to fortify it!
So effort, method, doing, and process are the deceiving mind.
It is not even not-doing so why waste time to clean the mind!
Mind is only desire and you are only satyam,
Home is Here Now.

ॐ

Questioner: Thank you for the love and light and for making yourself so available to all. You say that enlightenment is Here and Now. In the past I have tried very hard to wake up from the dream, but I have failed.

Papaji: And this was the cause of your failure: your trying! To find this Enlightenment you are not to try for even one second. Trying is postponement which is time, this time is mind and mind is ego. That is what we understand here in Lucknow. So right now do not desire for anything or try to do anything and tell me who you are. If you don't try you won't fail! Why not get it right now without doing anything. Do not make any effort, do not think. Then you can see who you are.

Is effort important on the path of enlightenment? (He gives Papaji a lotus flower)

What effort does a lotus flower need to blossom in the lake? The lotus does not touch the lake even though it lives in the lake. Only the legs touch the lake, not the head. So make effort with the legs and no effort with the head and you will see that you will not have any connection or relation with that in which you are living. This samsara is the lake. If you want to live like a lotus, live in the world with no relationship to it. Most people are drowned in the lake and are not called a lotus. They are the creepers growing from the bottom. This is a very special method for the few who want to live free of any relationship and yet be involved in relationships totally. This is the secret. If you are aware and if you need it, you can get it, but not otherwise.

I don't advise you to make any effort for Peace. It is not the result of effort. The best way is to keep Quiet and not to make any effort. Better to be like the gopi and make effort to forget him. You must be so much in love with your own Self, That place, that you must make effort to get out of Peace. This is something that you cannot understand. If you want to make effort make effort to forget your effort of making effort.

To go somewhere you need effort, but to go to your own Self you don't need effort. Wanting to make effort is just putting it away for future where you will move to reach your own Self. But just understand what you want and how far this something is from you. Then make a choice of what process it will take to reach him. It is inside of the inside, nearer to you than your breath. Once you understand the effort will drop by itself. If you don't understand where your Beloved is you must make effort to reach him. When he is behind your retina, how will you look for him? You can't. The eyes will see some object and not the eyes themselves, because they don't need to be seen. That which is within is so near and dear is hiding in your own heart. If you don't make effort It will reveal unto you Itself.

I am so glad that I have come to you because I have been searching for a long time. I have done Vipassana meditation for 27 years, hatha yoga for 22 years, I can easily go into samadhi and have gone on pilgrimages to over 300 sites in over 40 countries. Still, though I have found some peace, I come for your help.

You have done many practices and gone on many pilgrimages and have even found samadhi and peace, but going places and following methods will never pay you. Now you have exhausted yourself and have come here. Here you will not get any method to practice or any teaching. I will not give you a way to practice or a samadhi to enter. The highest way to enter your own Self has not been visited by you. You have never questioned who the "I" is that has done the practices and who has gone on the pilgrimages! Here you have come to find out where this "I" comes from, and this no teacher will tell you. Now give me a straight answer: where does the "I" rise from?

(Silence)

You can't say? When you are searching for the source of "I," where is your mind? During this short period when you search for the source of "I" upon which practice or pilgrimage is your mind on? Where is the mind?

Again you do not know. Then perhaps you can conclude that there is no mind. If it was there you could have seen it. There is no difference between mind and time and space. It was mind that was taking you to the spaces and places and it was the same mind which did all the practices and it was the mind that entered into samadhi! It has cheated you. This mind has cheated you for lifetimes. You must have developed some merit, this I accept, and this merit will pay you, Now! The ego has been hindering you by suggesting that you go to a shrine on the top of the Himalayas like Badri, Kedar, Gangotri, Yamnotri. Actually, the people who go there return with inflated ego, more than what they went there with because they will just say that they have visited the temple there. They don't say what the god of that temple has given. The prasad that they get from those temples is not peace and happiness, but sweets, poras and coconuts. They are happy with this when they return and distribute these things among many friends and family.

There is no place in the world which will give you peace and no god which will give you Enlightenment. You have been visiting so many temples, but never did you visit the *Temple in the cave of your own Heart, where I am taking you now!*

We started with trying to find the source of "I," but when the previous "I" could not find it, "I" disappeared. Mind was finished, space was finished, time was also finished. Now, for the third time, without thinking of the places or persons or mind or time, and staying in this without thought or effort, if you see anything, tell me what it could be.

I do not know.

Ah, you do not know. Who is the one who says that "I don't know"? "I do not know" is knowledge itself. What is this "I" which can even see that there is no knowing, nothing, emptiness? What is this "I"?

I don't know.

Again you do not know. I will tell you why you do not know. To know or see something you must have mind because "I" must be there: "I see the handkerchief." Some observer must be there, some seer. You are the seer of the object that is seen. Now, who is the seer? Find out! When you see the object you are observing and the object is observed, now find out who the observer is.

This is my difficulty.

Why is it difficult? You have observed three hundred pilgrim places in forty countries. Was this difficult? Maybe you had some physical difficulty, but with this you can ask who has been fatigued? The body is fatigued. Who is the one who observed the fatigue of the body? What must you do to see the seer? You can't because then you need two observers and the observer is one! If you can't see the observer what are you to do? The answer is very simple! The observer has not been seen or touched by anyone so far. So what are you to do? I will tell you that the observer cannot be body because this is seen. It can't be mind because it thinks and you are the knower, the seer of what it thinks. Now you can't deny and so you must accept that "I am the observer"! That you have not done. You have searched someone else, but not your own Self who has been sitting quietly patiently in peace. This doesn't take anytime, because it is so near and dear. This is why you miss it:

It is too near! Your eye can see the finger, but how can you see the eye?

Only in a mirror.

Yes, a mirror gives a reflection of the eye, but if you remove the mirror you remove the reflection. So remove the mirror of "I" which is a reflection itself and tell me: who reflects in the "I" to see other reflections? You must go behind the retina of the eye.

How?

As you get a message from somewhere before the retina to see through the retina, so the "I" is a reflection and the retina of the observer. Again go back. All that you see comes from your own Self. Know "I am the Self, I am the Self." Can you doubt this?

I don't doubt, but I do not know.

"But" is a doubt. There is no difference between doubt and "but." Hell, seventh hell, is the result of doubt. When Shiva walks up to you, doubting whether or not he is Shankar is a straight elevator to the hell where you will stay until the next kalpa; where, after the creator is born again, you will be given another chance to come to Satsang. This is the result of doubt.

I feel that I am at the banks of the river and I have not jumped in.

All the retreats and practices you have done have been done on the banks of the river. You are not to move anywhere, you are not to retreat anywhere.

> Why go on long retreats?
> Abiding in Now is an instant retreat!

You are not to abandon or renounce anything anytime. Here you are wherever you are! What you have to do is to remove the notion that this is not real or prove that it is real. So don't move anywhere and don't renounce anything, just find out what is real and don't be attached to what is not real.

All the meetings with teachers and visits to holy places are yet on the banks of the river. If you go to the Satguru he will look at you and keep Quiet, but if anyone else does this it won't work because they can't make any money this way. This best and closest Mecca is within you. It is here, you need not pray for it. You need not travel anywhere. Just stay Quiet and see that your mind is not racing. If your mind is racing in the beginning, bring it back. Again it will go away and again bring it back. Slowly it will learn how to keep Quiet, because otherwise it will just receive beatings.

This is how you have to train your mind. It will not be happy today or tomorrow, but eventually he will be happy with whatever you give or don't give. So don't let this "bull" run and plunder other places and get beaten. Keep him home and he will learn how to keep Quiet.

All the methods are only intellectual, psychological, but not practical. Non-method is practical. In no-method everything will happen. In this no-method you don't aspire or desire for anything. Let go of the search. It is neither effort nor non-effort. It is neither thinking nor non-thinking.

I just can't believe that it takes no effort. I always feel that the only way anything will happen is if I push my way into it.

Once you stop your pushing you will feel the power of the Pull. Give up all your efforts because only this pull will move you within. Pushing in is not very effective. It is like a whirlpool that pulls you into itself and allows you to sink down. Throw away your oars and break the mast and just keep Quiet. The rest will be done for you.

I can't trust that this will happen if I do not do it.

It is happening by Itself! What do you think you are doing Here? Just keep Quiet and throw away everything that you have and it will be very smooth sailing. Your rowing and sailing has brought you into so many accidents. Throw away the oars and go along with this river. Give time for this heart to open. It will not open if you are making effort. Be Quiet, turn your mind within, and let this heart speak and guide you. When there is no thought heart will open. Let it work, don't interfere by making effort.

I feel this, I feel an energy, an opening, but it feels like it comes and goes in waves. There seems to be a block to the energy.

The "coming" is the opening. The "closing" is your resistance to it in the form of your effort. You have been making effort for millions of years and suffering. Decide Now what you want: effort and suffering or an open heart and happiness? It depends on you!

There is no block, there is only Now.
There is nothing to be completed so make no intentions
because practices to avoid blocks are blocks.
The Silence always Is, always is complete, beyond notion.

I want to end it.

Then end it Now. Who is stopping you? It is all right, don't worry and don't be disheartened. It is happening.

ॐ

I have been doing spiritual practices for over twenty years, but I just feel all the more lost in a new set of concepts. I am tired of all this. Can you show me my true nature? I am tired of struggling.

> For Enlightenment you need not struggle.
> You only need to struggle
> to continually carry your concepts. ⁻

For instance you may feel that the son of god will give you peace and happiness, but this will not happen. This son of god is a concept from the past. Forget all that you have read and all that you have heard. Your parents have told you that you belong to a certain religion and through the Christ of the religion you will be saved. This is all foolishness! Come out of all these stupid concepts of the old people, be brave and simply be Quiet. Then all is over. In this Quietness you will find peace, not by attending the masses for centuries. I have met so many monks in the monasteries and people in the churches and still they are hanging onto a two thousand year old cross. They have no peace of mind. Rest assured you have to find peace within your Self Here in Lucknow. Instantly get rid of the old concepts of all the sons of gods. You can do it, just don't think about it.

The thinking is the burden.

> When you think everything will come.
> When you don't think you are with your Self.
> Do it now and whose love is in your mind,
> and who is the lover, and who is the beloved?

So no spiritual practice is needed to do this?

You need practice when you find you are missing something. For instance, if you want to be an engineer you must make practice and spend seven years in the college and get a Masters of Engineering degree. But here you do not need practice because it is already Here. What you gain you will lose, but what is already here you have just to see. See who and what I Am is. Don't find it through some method because the mind will cheat you for millions of years and therefore do not listen to your mind, just keep Quiet, and it will reveal Itself to Itself.

You don't need the mind at all. Mind will cheat you and nobody is happy with the mind, not even kings and emperors. You are happy only when there is no mind. When you sleep there is no mind and you are happy. In the dream and waking state you are not happy because of all your relationships. When you sleep you are peaceful, but That is beyond all these states. Who is it beyond sleep who experiences the happiness of the sleep state? You are That.

You need a practice to attain something that you don't have now. If you want to be a boxer you must learn boxing before entering the ring. Practice assumes an absence of something to be achieved at a later date.

> Because Self is not separate from you,
> no practice is needed to attain it.
> Self is never absent!
> Practice is postponing something
> to a later date, to the future.
> So you need no practice to know your Self.
> Give up this concept of practice and keep Quiet.
> Simply keep Quiet and you achieve everything.
> Everything comes to you when you ask for Nothing.
> But when you run after things nothing can come to you.
> So simply keep Quiet and see what happens.

All the people have done enough practice and therapy in all the ashrams and centers in the world. But here we don't teach anything, we only tell you that you are That which is always free.

How can you "become" free? How can you change from one thing to another? Self is already here, always changeless! But you think you are different and this mental concept of a difference must be removed. Remove all the concepts from your mind and remove the memory which holds only past. There is no use to enter into the memory and aspire for anything.

> Just for one instant keep Quiet
> and see who you are.

When you want to sleep what practice do you need?

No practice.

So like this you should sleep. This is the prescription from Krishna:

> When the world around you is sleeping
> you keep awake.
> When they are awake, you keep asleep.

What a prescription this is! When the universe is awake you keep asleep. This means that you should "sleep" to all the things that the universe is desiring. Not desiring all these things is called sleep. "When they sleep you keep awake," means that you are awake to your Self, you are awake to the secret of Truth: I am Self. But they are "sleeping" to this secret. This is a very good prescription. The whole world is sleeping, but the wise man is awake. He knows that it is all a dream and that all the dreamers will repent later.

So when all these people are flowing downstream, you go upstream. It may be difficult and you may not have any companions who are swimming upstream in the Ganga, but you can do it! This universe is the current going downstream taking everybody with it. To go against this current of this ocean you need the might of the decision, "I have to do it!" This is quite enough. Thank you.

ॐ

I have been doing Kriya yoga and I have found some peace, but...

What do you mean some peace? You haven't found any peace. Peace doesn't come a little at a time. When it comes it comes in abundance and devours you making you peace itself. No individuality is left! Peace attacks you in full force.

I just want to go deeper into the Peace.

There is no depth at all, because in Peace there is no division. When it comes it comes. When it doesn't it does not.

You practiced intense sadhana before Realization. Doesn't this mean that you must practice some sadhana to purify the mind?

How can you purify the mind by practice? Look at the water in this glass. What is the impurity in it? Impurity is something foreign. Water is pure itself and some dust has entered it. So if you sieve it, water will come out and the dust will stay. This is what I tell you to do. Originally you are pure like water and you have not to do anything to be pure. Some foreign element has entered the water and this is attachment. Just sieve the attachment out of the Self which is already free.

You cannot become what you originally Are.

So you can't return to your original state by practice. You are the original state. Just don't touch what is foreign to it. The foreign entity is attached to something which is not eternal and permanent. Remove this and see what is left. It is what you have been always, even before death.

"This is mine," "I belong to him," are attachments. These thoughts should not come in your way. Freedom is already Here. If you win anything it means that it wasn't there before you got it and after getting it you will lose it, because anything you get you will lose.

> So you have to be as you are always.
> Don't touch anything which is not eternal
> including your own mind, body, senses
> which do not belong to you.

If you don't touch things you will see that you have always been free. Freedom cannot be won by any practice. Practice only brings the transient, the material, not the eternal freedom. What was not there will not be there.

> What is Here is always Here.
> A firm belief in this is realization.

Often you use Buddha as an example. As I understand he attained Enlightenment through meditation. But you seem to imply that meditation is limited. Can you speak about this? According to Buddhists you must meditate.

According to Buddhists, not according to Buddha. The man passed away and then his students couldn't do it as he did. They couldn't renounce like he did. So they have to do what is easier for them to do. They don't sit quiet. He sat quiet because he rejected everything, even meditation. He simply sat Quiet. His Freedom wasn't the result of any meditation. Buddhists often don't think about what Buddha was all about: Enlightenment. Most are so busy with their religious practices and paths that they forget to sit Quiet as the Buddha did.

So be wise and solve this question, "Who am I?" Then you will know. No teacher can tell you this. Even Buddha kept quiet when Ananda asked him what he found under the Bodhi Tree. This silence cannot be explained, but everywhere you go you will find a play of words of the teacher, not Silence. Don't run away from the Truth. Buddha didn't run away, but stayed. Unless he got it he would not eat. This strong decision must be there. Don't run away. It is your problem, I can't say more. If this isn't enough you can see me in your next life.

After the Master dies, the students don't follow the Teaching. There was one teacher who had a lot of rats in his room who would pinch his legs during meditation, and disturb him. So for this reason he got a cat and then all the rats disappeared. He had two main disciples. One of them decided to keep two cats tied to his legs during meditation because he thought it would be twice as good as his master. But when the other student saw this a rivalry arose and he kept four cats tied to his arms and legs. Now the number of the students was proportional to the number of cats and so they each started to keep more and more cats, and their students started keeping cats, but there was no meditation.

So to remove the rats the Master kept a cat. This is quite reasonable, but cats are not the source of Enlightenment. This is what happens.

Yesterday you guided someone to Self so beautifully! Can you give me this same road map?

I have thrown that map away.

Can you then put a little current in the stream that my little leaf can follow?

There is no map and the little stream will just go wherever she will. Throw away all maps and just let it flow. Then where will you discharge into? She will discharge back home, in the ocean.

My home is here.

If your home is truly Here then there cannot be any "there." If you are there then you need a map to get back Here, back home. But if you are Home you do not need any maps. So just stay as you are and throw away all maps which have been misleading you.

But I don't want to throw away all the maps. This would be like saying that all I have done has been a waste of time, but I do not feel this way. I feel that all I have done up to now has been beneficial.

Yes, up to now, as you say. Now you have arrived at Now and all is over. You are up to Now, you are Home! Throw away all your maps! You don't need a map in Now because Now is what you are! Now is home and you are Here and you are That!

Give up all notions of maps, destroy all notions, they are absolutely not needed Now that you are "Up to Now"! Stay as Thus! That is all! Wherever you go and whatever you do you are Free. This Here has no corridors, frontiers, or demarcations you see!

Go on expanding.

This Here is expanding, expansion itself.
It is never ending and expands wherever you go.
It is Space and this is what you Are!
You are not in space, but you are Space.
This is all that you have to know.
This is already yours.

Ah hah! I just caught myself looking for my glasses through my glasses. So it is with Freedom; people say "I want to be Free, I want to be Enlightened." You are searching for That through That! You search for Consciousness through Consciousness. If you give up the search you will see. It will come to you that you are wearing your glasses, you will know that you are Consciousness. Don't search for anything and don't expect anything and you will find it. It is already Here and is not an object to be found, It is the subject searching for itself. When you stop searching you will know "Who Am I"! If you give up your notions and intentions you will immediately understand. The only impediment, the only hindrances are your notions and concepts and intentions.

You are searching for the glasses through the glasses,
searching for Freedom through Freedom.
Freedom is not an object to be found,
but is the subject which is searching.

I feel that I have one foot in the water and one foot out, one eye looking for the diamond and one on samsara.

Your feet will be together. You can't have one foot in Satsang and one foot across the street with the pigs. If one foot is with the pigs then they both are. If you are here, then both your feet will be here, and both eyes will be on the diamond.

Under the ocean of samsara
there is a diamond, dive for it.

The one who wears this diamond
is in Peace, Love and Beauty,
but if you wear any other diamond
you will be in fear.

This diamond is very close to you, very near. How near? I will tell you a story!

There was one very special pickpocket who would never touch gold or money. He would only steal diamonds. He came to Delhi, which had a diamond market for centuries, with the Moguls as the main customers. This pickpocket went to the shops posing as a customer until he found his victim. He found a man purchasing a very costly diamond worth about $50,000. He followed him to the Delhi train station where they both purchased tickets to a deluxe First Class two-berth coupe bound for Calcutta.

The diamond merchant, who was a clever man, suspected that he was being followed. He has seen this man at the diamond market, at the booking office and now in his coupe. Now as night falls he goes to change his clothes in the bathroom and is very careful to keep the diamond in a safe place.

In the night, when the merchant slept, the pickpocket searched through everything, including the clothes that the merchant was wearing, and the bathroom, but he couldn't find anything.

Finally, the next morning Howrah junction came and both of them stepped out of the train. The pickpocket introduced himself to the merchant and said, "I am a pickpocket who picks up only diamonds. It is below my dignity to touch gold. I saw you purchase a diamond yesterday and in the night I searched everywhere for it. Even in your shoes and your underclothes. But I didn't find it anywhere. So will you tell me where you kept the diamond? I saw a lot of money, your checkbook and your gold watch, but I didn't touch anything."

The merchant replied, "I smelled that you were a clever man, but I am also very shrewd. So when you went to change your clothes last night I put the diamond into your coat pocket. I knew that you would not search your pockets, but only search my pockets. Then this morning when you went to use the bathroom, I took the diamond out again, and here it is!"

So what this story tells is that you will always look to other places. Everybody has the Diamond, but we search the pocket of others. We go from ashram to ashram, from swami to swami, from Satsang to Satsang, (laughs) but never will you get it because it is in your own pocket. God himself has kept the diamond in each Heart and yet we search for it elsewhere. The Diamond is Here. If you do not think or make effort you will have it. In between these two conditions of not thinking and making no effort is a Diamond!

Everywhere else you will find commercial business. Yoga teachers and other teachers will charge you money, but here it is all free because we are not commercial!

The Diamond I speak of cannot be sold.
You can have it in an instant,

You can do it.

You remind me of the musk deer who wanders through the forest looking for where the smell of musk is coming from, not knowing that the musk is in his own navel. You have smelled Freedom and have come here to find it like so many have, and they are all like musk deer. The musk is within you. Freedom is within you! Stop your searching; Freedom is within!

> Put yourself in That
> between past and future.
> The mind has been hanging you for lifetimes.
> Now hang the mind between past and future
> and see what happens.
> Don't touch your mind to any object
> and see who you are.

Keeping quiet is much easier now and more blissful, but still I feel there is a layer separating me from myself.

Don't look here or there for anything and you will find that the goal is already arrived. This layer is a desire and you will be happy; the only thing you must do to be happy is to stop having and holding desires because this will give you trouble. If you do get it you will lose it and then you will be troubled. Just keep Quiet and don't hold any desire.

It seems that one develops detachment and relaxation after years of spiritual practice. Is there a process or progress before realization?

It is beyond attachments and detachments. When one detaches from that which he is attached to he gets attached to something else. So detachment needs attachment to something else and therefore it is not detachment. Attachment depends on detachment and detachment depends on attachment.

The Essence is beyond all notions and is untouched by imagination and there is no progress or process in it. To progress is to be given some method from the past by somebody. Any method that he has followed gets dumped on you, and then you start practicing. So whatever method you start you have in your mind what you want to attain. This attainment is preplanned attainment that you plan to get after a number of years of practice. This planning is your own thought creation. Actually, there is no process because it is already Here. If it is not already Here and you get it through some method you will lose it. Any gain is lost someday or another. But if it is not attained you will not lose it because it is Here and always will be Here.

You say no book or practice is necessary, but you yourself have read many books and have done thousands of hours of practice in this lifetime. Why then do you give this advice?

Because I was just a boy of seven or eight and some experience came and revealed itself. I didn't work for it or do any practice, it just revealed itself. No one could explain this to me and it was not described in any book either. Later on I tried to read the books written by many saints, including the Gita, Bhagavatam, the Upanishads, and even the Vedas, but I didn't see anything that tallies with my own abidance. I found that nobody ever spoke of That which I Am is. For this reason I read many books and came in contact with many gurus from north to south. But everything that they spoke about was all in the books and they followed this like sheep running one behind the other. No one that I saw had realized the Truth and nobody spoke about it. Therefore I rejected all the teachings, all the books, and all the statements that anybody so far has made about That. Then I met my Master!

Now when I speak it is not the object of speech that I am speaking about. Some people catch it and they cannot explain what has happened. For sixty years I have asked people to describe it, but they cannot. Because the intellect and mind, which is the basis of explanation, does not accompany you. You are quite alone. There is no mind or intellect, you are just alone. It can never be explained though many people say they got it. They don't know what they got, but they know they got it. It is not even an experience because experience depends on the mind to create an experiencer, an object of experience, and their connection which is the experience, all of which can be explained. But what is beyond the mind cannot be explained. Even the Book of Knowledge, the Vedas, say "Neti, neti," after four Vedas. This book, written by Vyasa 25,000 years ago, is very honest to speak that it is not that which they could write. The best explanation is Neti, Neti, "Not this, not this, I do not know."

You said I can drop my search. If there was no search then why wouldn't all the lazy people become enlightened?

When I say drop the search, it means the search that you have carried all of your life and in many of the previous incarnations. This search must end because you must realize that you can't search for it because you have not lost it. So those who go to Satsang will realize that it is not by searching that they will be free. For them it is advised to give up the search.

Lazy people are also searching for things, but not for the Self. Sincere seekers search from place to place for where to truth is available. But when you know that you are not to search and you know "I am That" Here and Now, you don't need to be a sincere seeker, but you need a teacher. This seeker needs a Teacher to tell him that it is not by laziness nor by activity that it is found. Only know who you are. So understand "I am already That."

You can understand this but since birth you have been an extraordinary being. Is it really possible for an ordinary person like me to be free? What should I do to understand this and what should I not do?

It is neither doing anything nor not doing anything.

So sadhana is just a waste of time.

Sadhana can be a complete waste of time or, if you are with the best people, it can be the best use of time. Then you are spending time where there is no time.

I have had such a proud mind, but in the last week you have exposed all th.? parasitic tendencies of pride in the mind. Going through this experience has been like going through an illness, and I am very thankful for this. Papaji, is full realization a process or is the idea of process just a form of postponement?

Your essence cannot be achieved by any process. This idea of process is just to postpone the precious present time to be realized. Everybody wants to make a process and postpone. They go to pilgrimage places, they become pilgrims in the expectation of getting peace, but they don't get it. They go to temples, but they don't get peace. They make charities and build temples, bridges and wells, but they do not get peace. All of these activities which they have done will pay them a reward in the heaven after death, it will not go to waste. But as he strains in the high altitudes of the Himalayas on his pilgrimage, he will not find peace, even if he is at the top of Everest at 29,000 feet. The people who went there did not find peace, but came back exhausted!

Peace is not found anywhere, neither down in the ocean nor up in the skies. You will spend many ages looking for peace until you will know how easily peace is available in no-process. Simply attend a Satsang once or twice and you may be Enlightened in this life, in this year, this hour, Now.

If you make up your mind that you will be Free in this lifetime you will find that it is fiction that there is a mind.

Sadhana: There is no Becoming Being

This mind is postponement. There must be mind where there is postponement and there has been postponement for generations. Someone here or there will make up their mind to cease the postponement and do it at any cost. When this strength comes It reveals Itself; not through a process and with none of your effort involved. Some call it Grace; win this Grace by being very beautiful inside. Outside beauty will not give you peace. You have seen the skin beauty of the outside on the Miss Universe pageant two days ago. This beauty fades in a few years. So first think of the inner beauty. When you see your inner beauty you do not need judgment and you do not need to compete. People will be drawn to you by this inner beauty.

This Maharshi of Tiruvannamalai did not get a title but he is the most beautiful person to whom all the beauties were attracted. The queens came to him and all the diamonds and jewelry and everything was offered to him, but he didn't even look at it.

I was there when Queen Sofia of Spain came. She approached the manager of the ashram to introduce her to the Maharshi. Then gold jewelry and diamonds and baskets of fruit were carried in to the Maharshi. The manager, Maharshi's own brother wanted him to have a look at the presents and to bless the queen for the thousands of dollars worth of things that she brought, but he didn't look at her or her things. I was watching this. If there is so much money and a queen walks in front of you, will you not look? Everybody would look at her and the money and at least give a word of thanks, but he was unmoved like a mountain. Then this Driganada Swami told the queen that he was blessing her. But she didn't know this Indian blessing: not moving, not looking, the eyes open but not seeing her. This is true Beauty.

Papaji, please show me the way to this beauty, to ultimate freedom?

Who told you that there is a way to freedom? Where did you get this map? There is no way!

There is no way to Freedom.
"Way" means that you start from somewhere
and arrive to somewhere else,
and that there is a distance to your destination,
but you don't need to go anywhere else.
The creation of distance is the deception of the mind.
So forget about any way and any Freedom also.
If you do this, stay wherever you are!
You are not to run anywhere else.
Somehow you must get rid of

417

This concept of the mind.

Stay as you are wherever you are.

If you do this instantly you will know
that you *are* what you have searched for for millions of years.
There is no search because search is only for the lost.
But when nothing is lost there is no meaning
to searching for an object.

Here simply keep Quiet.
Don't stir a thought from the mind,
then you will know who you really are.

Should I abide as the pure "I" and have faith that purity will come?

Don't waste your time in the purity of mind because mind cannot be pure. Even the desire to be pure is the trick of the mind. You will spend many lives purifying the mind, but it will never be pure. Look at the story of Vishwamitra and Manika. After purifying his mind for 10,000 years he still falls for her instantly. It is better to just allow your desires to arise and not let them touch you. Let them arise and let them be fullfilled. You simply stay Quiet. Don't try to become anything, don't go anywhere and don't do anything and don't undo anything. Find the source of these concepts and stay there. This is bliss, nothing else. This knowledge is bliss.

The Trap of Deceitful Gurus

This is the Kali Yuga,
even Rakshashas will incarnate as teachers to mislead you.
Those who must be destroyed by these demons will be.

You must test your Guru!
Test the Guru by looking at the Guru's lineage,
it is very important.
Test the Guru by the teaching:
without inquiry there is no teaching.
Shun every teacher who does not teach Vichar!
Directly looking at your own face is the only teaching.
Preachers only speak of darkness,
the understanding of darkness, and the removal of it.
But there is no darkness, and no understanding,

there is only light!

If the Guru says "I am enlightened,"
it means the ego is enlightened so stay away.
Western teachers who say this are preachers
and only write books to load more garbage on seekers,
and more money in their pockets.
They will attract so many students,
but in Kali Yuga it is the falsehood which will draw the crowds.
The Truth and the true Gurus will be neglected.
If there is a teacher and a student for more than one second
then both of them go to avachi hell!

*I stayed with some people who said they were spiritual teachers, but I
was abused by them and now my mind stays with them.*

Why go to people that you don't know when you have Satsang here?
This pain you have now is the result of meeting stupid people. Stupid people
go to stupid people and this is the result.

*One of them once claimed to be your disciple. How is it possible that
people get corrupt and distracted even after strong awakenings?*

I don't think people will get corrupt and distracted. One who is awake
will not be distracted because all the distraction and corruption is from the
mind only. If distraction arises surrender is the only cure for this. When you
don't surrender and you think that you are the doer then this is corruption.
Surrender to the Higher Consciousness, to the Self itself, and no corruption
will be able to come near.

When you believe in That because you have had the experience I Am
That, then this doubt, which is the I-thought, will not appear. Doubt appears
only from mind and mind is only the past, and past will not affect you in this
present moment.

*I am feeling a lot of grief and anger in my heart since coming to you
because now I see more clearly how I have been led astray in the past.
Can you help me overcome this?*

Why are you sad? You must feel happy. You must be happy when you
get rid of someone who has no respect for his own teacher. He doesn't say the
name of his teacher. Here we honor the lineage. My teacher is sitting on my

head and we just celebrated his Guru Purnima. One who cannot love his own teacher is not fit to be with because that person is a rogue, a scoundrel. And he is all the worse if he abuses his own teacher.

So consider yourself lucky. My Master always prayed to his Teacher. It may be a man or a rock, it has nothing to do with anything. He worshipped this rock, this mountain, Arunachala. He was not shy to prostrate before Him. To those who questioned he replied, "A body is a corpse and when it dies nobody will touch it, but yet you always worship and praise it. I worship my Teacher, but you will see that my Teacher stands forever. It is a beacon of light. Bodies will last one hundred years maximum, but my Master is already two billion years old and is the center of the world."

So you should not be sad. You really should be happy!

You have asked many people to go and teach. Are these people messengers or masters in their own right? Can you explain this?

They are messengers. They are giving this message throughout the world of what is happening in Lucknow, so that the whole world is happy. They are just messengers, but with some of them ego crops up and so they claim to masters. They will go to a hell along with those who follow them. (giggles)

Messengers are messengers, but is it right when they are given something to give and share, that they say it is from themselves? Why not be honest? They should say, "I got this from this place and so you can go there if you want the same thing." But ego is very strong and that is why they say you have to serve twelve years so your ego is removed.

The person who hurt you so deeply stayed with me for twenty five days. In these twenty five days he stayed in Tourist Bungalow and came to me for one hour in the morning. This means he stayed twenty five hours!! And you can see the result of this twenty five hours. He says he has surpassed his teacher. Another one stayed just twelve days and declared himself the master of masters. But this Freedom is a prasad from the Teacher. He will touch your head and then he will be satisfied with you. When he is satisfied he will hand over this precious Diamond.

So all this is arrogance of the person. Ignorance and ego play this part. All the teachers of the world have this ego of being a teacher. *The teacher must be so humble.* He must be like a servant to serve the people so that they become happy. If the teacher is arrogant what can he or she teach to others? Practically every teacher in India and the West are arrogant commercial teachers. Everything is becoming commercial.

You have to be careful about the messengers. When India sends out ambassadors they cannot say, "I am the Prime Minister." Ambassadors are ambassadors and must get instructions and consultations of the Prime

Minister. But if they behave like the Prime Minister they are called back.

There seems to be cases of where people have a mistaken conviction that they have attained the ultimate Truth.

Many saints, sages and teachers *think* they have attained ultimate Truth.

Is it possible that someone is established in a state of ultimate Truth without knowing it?

This, of course, holds true for everyone. Everybody, every being is established in the ultimate Truth and are aware of the ultimate Awareness, but they do not know. They do not know It because when they try to know, this is done through the mind. To know that you are an ultimately Realized person you must use the mind. But to use the mind in this way means that you have a doubt about it. Mind itself is a doubt. Mind is the doubt! Another name for mind is doubt. When there is no doubt there is no mind and when there is no mind there is no doubt.

Awareness is beyond mind, much beyond it.
Mind gives you doubts, fears, and worry,
and keeps you unaware of That beyond the mind.
The role of mind in the play
is to keep the person in the dark, in the past.
Where there is no mind there is no time or past.
This is the ultimate Truth.

Merely reading the book is not sufficient! If possible find a person who is still in his physical form and clear your doubts with him while he is still available. But most of the teachers are preachers who teach only dogma and have no teaching. This preaching is heard mostly in the West. These preachers who are often Indians have mushroomed in the states, making money. They are just business people and they know not what to teach. None of these teachers and preachers are the Satguru. The Satguru has no teaching or method to give you. He directly reveals within your own Self and doesn't prescribe any method to you.

How can I regain this innocence with which I started this spiritual journey before I was betrayed by so many teachers?

You are born in the world to see that you are free of this cycle of births and deaths. This is your number one purpose.

You are very careful at the market not to buy anything that is not good.

But the only thing that you bargain with is a few dollars or francs. So why aren't you careful when your life is at risk? How can you risk your life? You must test your teacher first of all! Find out what the lineage is. Go back several generations. Find out who his teacher is. You have to be careful. In India, to find a mate for your child you go back seven generations of the mother and of the father. So don't sell your life just because you see the handsome teaching of a person. If you want good words then the professors in the universities can express it better than the sages and the saints.

You can't sell your soul to unsafe hands and so you have every right to test the teacher. Some ashrams even kill you if you try to speak about the teacher, like the one in Frauenfeld, Switzerland. I have been there and have seen this. Don't be lost with the beautiful sweet words of the teacher. If your heart accepts him then you know. Don't be fooled by a big beautiful ashram. The teachings you are not to get from the cement, or the bricks, or the iron rods. The teachers have always taught from beneath a tree. What can you get from walls?

Your heart will accept the teacher. Not you, not your ego, not your mind, not your consciousness. Sit with the person. If your heart is dedicated to a person only then he is your teacher. The teacher doesn't ask anything from the student. He only sees that you are in peace and beauty and love. The price he gets from you is seeing you happy. That is all! There is no price, no donation. I give you this advice. You take care.

Why do some teachers teach and display so many tricks?

Don't get involved with them. The true teacher is one who doesn't allow you to do anything, but simply tells you to be quiet. Then everything of the world will be presented to you. The true teacher has few requirements: just a little food to maintain his body, in which he helps everybody.

I want to go visit a famous guru near Bangalore.

You can go if you really want, but like going to a restaurant where you pick what you eat, choose carefully what you want to take away from there.

What I want is to reach God.

You don't need the help of anyone to reach God. Don't be fooled by famous gurus who are not easily seen and who charge money. Be wise and smell the place and see if it will give you peace. God brings you to the place where you get what you want. You want freedom; this is why you are Here.

Sadhana: There is no Becoming Being

*As I try to integrate your teachings into my workshops in the West
I often do not find success.*

To teach meditation is not so easy because you must find your own Self
first. If you have not found your Self and try to teach meditation, you are
just deceiving people! Telling what you don't know yourself is only cheating
others, it is deception and you would be better to avoid this. So next time
when you go to the West, tell people what you have gained from Satsang.
That's all!

But I want to give Satsang.

Okay, you can start with me. Just practice looking into my eyes...Oh, you
are very good. Now my ego is gone! Now go to the States and look into the
eyes of girls and fax me the results! One other man who asked me this same
question is doing this job very well. Daily he transforms two to three girls!

*I have been working so hard on cleaning the shoes of those who come
to Satsang just as you have told me.*

I told you to do this in order to remove your ego, but it hasn't worked.
You are proud of this service, which was given to remove your ego.

Go to any temple and you will see the Indians cleaning the temple. They
clean it and forget about it. They don't tell people that they swept the floor
of the temple as you are saying. Even the women in their saris clean the
temple. This doesn't work on Western people, only on Indians, so I have
given you a wrong prescription. I will tell you something next time.

*Papaji, in Satsang a few days ago my father's image occurred within
me. I could see that he was happy that I was here. He died when I
was eleven which caused a deep part of me to shut down. A search
for a new father figure led me to a swami near Bombay, but he
betrayed my trust.*

First of all, your father has died so why keep a man who is no longer in
the world in your heart to disturb you? A man who is born must die, this is
his nature! So don't keep him in your heart, everybody must die. You are
not a graveyard where the dead are kept! Don't be a graveyard, which means
don't remember the past. Forget about your father. Your true Father, your
Eternal Father is the one who will give you peace and happiness. Your eternal
father is your own self! It is of no use running here and there. What could

this swami give you when he himself did not arrive at that state where he could forget others?

Once in Paris I stayed with a friend named Annapurna. She was a devotee of this swami and organized his Satsangs in Europe. She wanted to ask some questions, so at dinner she came down dressed as a swami, and asked some very good questions. I won't tell you about the questions because they will trouble you because some people stay with teachers who have no right to call themselves teachers. They have stolen things from the books or have not stayed with someone who is a Master. If there is a Master you must stay with him all the life until he sheds his mortal coil. Then, if he picks you up, go and teach the world. But you must stay with him for twelve years. It is better not to teach and spoil the life of the students. It is better to stay Quiet, go to the Himalayas. Teaching is very important, but as long as your ego is there what can you teach? Egotistical teaching will trouble you all the more. This teacher who steals the teachings will go straight to hell number eight along with his students! Seven hells are defined, but this hell is beyond conception. This hell puts people into the fire each moment and each moment they survive and this will continue for another 12,000 years.

So I gave the answers to this girl. She was very happy and said that she could never get the answers before and now had gotten them over the dinner table! Though she wanted to quit working for the swami I told her she could continue since it was her work. But her heart was so clear and so she quit. She wanted to come with me, but I was going to Caracas. So instead she opened up a center in Southern France to share what she got with people. So now you have to find out where the eternal Father of all beings is. Do it in just one instant, do it now, not in years and years that you have spent with teachers. Spend just one instant. This instant is not in the time, it is out if time. As Saint Kabir says: One instant, one half the instant, one half of the half of the instant, if you are with a real Satguru you will no longer have to return to the ocean of samsara.

All the teachers who say you must postpone it are butchers, not teachers. You don't need to spend any time here because you have no distance to go. To go from New York to Lucknow you need to know the distance and take a plane, train, or a surface road, whatever is needed. But if you know that it is no distance from you, that it is deep within and nearer than the breath, in between two breaths, then how much time do you need? No time! Time is mind. Mind means postponement. In Now there is no mind. Look right Into Now! That is what the teacher says! That is what Kabir and some of the ancient teachers have said.

Turn your face toward the eternal Father and say: 'Oh, Father, I want to see you, have Grace upon me, I cannot live without you, this is the time which I should give you!'

Why is it that when the guru leaves his body it causes so much strife and separation between his disciples? Some go to other teachers, some become teachers themselves, some become babas and mas, and usually they all speak badly of each other. Can you talk about this.

Most of gurus are businessmen. They are not enlightened and they cannot enlighten any other. In all of India I do not know of a single guru who has an ashram and is enlightened. Therefore, it is of no use to stay with them. You yourself have stayed in many ashrams. Have you seen anyone who has been benefited?

No, not really. After the guru leaves the body who will declare when the vision is realized?

Those who have not lived with a perfect saint will not Realize. They will live in a game of imperfections because they have been misled by some guru and will carry on this misleading all their lives. The vine which gives sour fruit spreads quickly, but the one which gives sweet fruit has a short life.

> The Truth will be held by the honest
> and the honest will not be followed.
> Only the dishonest will be followed.

The Traps of Religions, Traditions, and Ashrams

> Religions, traditions, and ashrams often start good but turn bad
> when they fall in the hands of those who want gain and fame.
> Enlightenment is not the product of these religions.
> As you can see throughout history
> the work of religions is fear and death:
> fear of hell and death to the infidels!
> Take the hell out of religion
> and it will not be a religion!
>
> Religion is fear and fake.
> Fear is the very foundation of religion.
> Religion is a hindrance to Freedom
> and has even banned "I am Free!"

so walk out of them because you Are!
You are complete Here and Now!
You do not need the sheep's fold,
you do not need any religion,
you are always Free.

Are there some traditional things that must be done in order to proceed on the inner path?

On the inward path there is no tradition. You need no traditions at all.

Outer traditions are outward.
The rudraksha beads have nothing to do with it,
though they help with physical problems
and may give you a tranquil mind.
You can wear the same cloth that others do, but
tradition is outside, only physical and mental.
Inside you are simply to sit Quiet
and not allow your mind to touch the outside.
Sit for just one second like this,
and you have fulfilled the purpose of your life.
Just don't let your mind touch any tradition
and you will be finished with samsara.

I had a dream where a panther with green eyes ate me, except I was in the form of a sheep. I realized it was Self dissolving my sheep-like mentality.

Everybody in the world is a sheep who is always looking for a shepherd. This shepherd usually is the founder of some religion. You are a Catholic priest so you know this. The shepherds don't allow the sheep to go away from the herd and so the sheep stay as sheep. But some have escaped the shepherd and the sheep herding dogs, the priests, and are no longer controlled. There have been some good saints in these traditions who spoke of the Truth and their different scriptures have some good sayings, but for the most part I have seen very little benefit from them even though I have traveled all over the world for decades looking for it.

I am glad you've come here and crossed over the religious barriers. You have come here as an independent person. You need independent views and understanding to know yourself. Don't depend on the past or anything you have heard or read in the past because the Truth is Now. Get Free yourself Now and then you can understand what the saints have said and written.

Sadhana: There is no Becoming Being

Can one find the truth through any religion?

Yes, one can find final Truth in any religion but they must be ardent, true and honest to really love God. It is not about going to church or to a temple. You won't find God there, but only within. Religion doesn't have much to do with the life of men except for giving fears. So if you live without religion at least you won't have any fear. Live independently, it is better for you. The god of religions is a projection of security to take care of your projected fears, desires, and possessions.

It seems that spiritual communities are filled with hierarchy, formality and control. This seems to contradict what Freedom is. Hierarchy and power struggles seem especially common around spiritual masters.

You have had a taste of Freedom, but then you started censoring other people and judging what is good behavior and what is bad.

> Stay with the experience of Freedom
> and don't look at the inadequate behavior of others
> or you will lose your chance.

Don't push Freedom into the background by getting involved in what others do or don't do. Let them do whatever they want and whatever is in their karma to do. Who are you to check them? How long will you spend finding faults with them, one hundred years? People will always have faulty behavior and you will have to keep being born over and over just to judge them, there will be no end of it! It is far better to take care of yourself, and to fulfill your purpose.

> You have come for a definite purpose.
> Don't look here and there!
> Just sit Quiet.

You are like the man who found a diamond and tied it around the neck of his donkey and kept working hard carrying bricks. This foolishness happens to everybody until they come to Satsang and are appraised of the fact that they are a valuable diamond. This diamond had been shown to you, but again you tied it around the donkey of your mind! This will never give happiness!

> Mind your own business,
> and let others do what they are destined to do.

You can't put your finger in this process.
It belongs to someone very intelligent
who knows how to look after the people.

Take care of yourself. If you ever have the experience of Self again forget everything! Even the kings have rejected the kingdoms and have gone to the forest quite satisfied. Your ultimate desire must be Freedom whether you are with a saint or not. Now you have become lost because you are in the company of people who do not speak of Freedom. Ashrams do some good things, but most of them are just interested in the social relations of their guru brothers and sisters, they don't sit Quiet. I don't recommend that anybody waste their time with useless activities and not sit quietly. Don't just create social relationships with people all over the world, sit Quiet. You have to see whether or not your mind is peaceful in your ashram situation. It doesn't pay to just socialize or to just gossip about other people or to just read books.

Sitting Quiet is most essential.
Don't waste your time
by not doing this.

ॐ Guru ॐ

Useful Sadhana and Dropping Practices

There is no sadhana better than just staying as Peace.
If you must do any practice, then do Vichar.
Joy is also a good sadhana because
it destroys mind, so always be happy.
Always think of It and be happy:
spend the rest of your life knowing
you are Existence-Consciousness-Bliss.

Some practice is better than getting lost in samsara
and is good in that it sometimes fatigues the mind,
but typical sadhana is usually important only for the ego.
All sadhana is projected by ego so it is on a sandy foundation.
This ego projection is samsara so search only for the seeker.
"I" is ego so when this meditates there are no good results.

Choice of practice depends on the choice of results.
Brahman has no attributes and is beyond mind
so no practice will take you to that: It is self revealing.

Ramana says "Simply keep Quiet for it is Here and Now."
This is the nearest practice because
Brahman is your very nature.

Though I do not prescribe practices, some of them are prescribed in the scriptures as being of benefit. Since you have some questions regarding them I will tell you about them but they will not necessarily give you Freedom and will seduce most people into the trap of process. First know who you are. Then do sadhana if you wish.

Dropping Practice

How to stay more stable in Self? Does formal practice help?

Simply witness the circumstances, don't be touched by them. Don't receive them. Simply witness and keep separate from the circumstances.

I've been practicing purification techniques given to me by Tibetan Buddhists, but you're helping me be the practice, not just do a practice.

Yes, you must *be* the practice. I don't tell you to practice anything but to get into the practice. This is very hard to understand for those who are not serious, for those who want to continue in samsara. Even if you tell them they will not be able to see that this is all illusion. It is as if they are in a desert and believe that they see a river which will quench their thirst. So they run after it but it just continues to shift farther away.

Everybody, six billion people, are running after their desires wanting to have a nice swim in the cool waters of the mirage. Above them is the hot sun on their heads and below is the hot sands under their feet and still they run toward it. So this is your own creation, it is illusion, there is no river. But when somebody tells you this you do not believe them. Only a few believe that it is a mirage. Buddha rejected it and still 2600 years later he gives us peace because he rejected everything and won everything. Like this you must sacrifice all things that trouble you.

You gave me the name Sadhana one year ago. Can you tell me what it should mean to me now?

Sadhana means practice. Any kind of practice: dancing, singing, running, swimming. All of them need practice. Keeping Quiet also means sadhana and this is the meaning for you because keeping Quiet is the best sadhana for anything that you want to do. Sadhana has one more meaning that few know.

keep Quiet and I will tell you.

I have let go and I am waiting to continue my meditations.

What kind of letting go is this? Why do you want to continue your meditations?

Because it feels good.

You have let it all go, even your meditations and the meditator. Even let go of the desire for meditations and the desire for emptiness.

I trust that my mind and desires will disappear.

You have to disappear! So many people go off to some cave to do their sadhana but their minds follow right with them and their practices increase their bondage. If you disappear where will mind be?

I met one such man as I was on my way to Badri. It was a very rainy night and so I asked a baba in a small hut if I could sleep in his hut for the night. He said yes, and so I gave him some money to buy vegetables and dal and we ate at ten o'clock at the banks of the Ganga. Then I saw a hut raised above the Ganga and offered to sleep there, but he insisted that I sleep in his hut which he thought would be more comfortable.

He had been living here for thirty-six years, supported by a man who sent him twenty rupees a month. His bed was made out of sand and covered with burlap cloth and, of course, so was his pillow. You could really see his renunciation of the world. I thought it was better not to have such a hard pillow and when I removed the pillow there was a magazine of sexy film fare with nude photos of women.

Why live on the path to Badri Narayan if this is what you are keeping in your mind? What is the use of his meditation? Better to keep yourself in the house and don't hear it, be it. Surrender to His will. What comes, comes by His will, what goes, goes by His will.

You have spoken about several ways through which Self can be realized, like Self inquiry, devotion, service, surrender...

You have left out many other ways which I speak in Satsang. For instance, painting. The painter becomes one with the paints. I have seen some good painters in Germany and France and when I asked them what they were going to paint they said that a good painter doesn't know what he is going to paint! One man even said "I don't think, only the brush is working."

Dancing is also a way to realize the Self. Tukaram danced and found that God would come. He was from Maharastra, and when he was about to die the chariot from heaven came down to get him because nobody is dancing in heaven. The chariot was waiting and he said to his wife and friends to come but they all made excuses and so he flew away and never came back.

He was a devotee of Krishna and would sing and dance, but his wife would get angry at him for not working. Once spring season was well underway and Tukaram had not yet sown his fields but all the other crops of his neighbors were one meter high. So one day she took up some sugarcane and beat him in the head with it saying, "This will not do, you have to work, you have to plow, you have to till the soil! Everybody is laughing at you!"

He didn't care and instead every morning would go to the quiet side of the mountain. But she was a good wife and would find him in time to serve him his lunch and then eat lunch herself. Once on the way to find him a thorn went into her foot and so she couldn't walk to find Tukaram. A young beautiful boy appeared and offered to dress the wound, but she said, "No, no you go away to my husband. You have spoiled him and now you are going to spoil me! I am not going to listen and you cannot dress my foot."

"No mother, let me do something for you, you can't walk otherwise."

So she agreed and he dressed the wound with the yellow cloth that he always keeps on his shoulder. When he finished she told him to go away and not to follow her.

When she found her husband she told him the story. "This man who has spoiled you has come to me but I kicked him away and told him not to touch me because he had already spoiled one member of my family."

"You are such a good lady that you have seen God with your eyes earlier than I have!" he exclaimed.

A few days later a cyclone came and destroyed all the crops, but at this point he sowed his fields and he was the only one with a crop that year.

This is how God will help you if you are serious and sincere.

Sculpture is another way to realize the Self and also music. Many saints have found themselves and become Free just by singing, like Mirabai and Kabir.

This is why we have a little of everything in Satsang. We speak about "Who am I," but when you get bored, we have music! (laughs)

So there are many ways, but you have to be *sincere*.

I want to be a better musician and artist and I want to know silence.

When you play the flute you don't think and when you don't think you play the flute. Any painter, dancer, musician is silent at that time. The dancer is not acting, he is not moving. He is absolutely immobile, with no mobility at all. Then he is the perfect dancer. You won't understand this unless you are near an expert.

I have read of all of the hours of practice that you have done and I don't think I can do it. Enlightenment feels so far away.

Practice is needed when you have not come across any teacher. I had been practicing on my own accord since early childhood and I continued because I did not find any guru in Pakistan. So simply it came into my mind to meditate, due to some previous samskaras. I also had a vision of Buddha and like Buddha I sat in meditation and fell in love with him. He was very beautiful. I wouldn't tell anyone in my class or in my house what I was doing and I myself didn't know why I was doing it. Simply I wanted to be as Buddha was because he was so beautiful and for this reason I started to meditate, not for any definite purpose. Day or night I could not forget him and as best as I could I was always meditating.

This is how my practice started, I was doing it for fun only. It came to me from birth. But luckily, I have seen the Master. Perhaps very few people can meet such a Master who showed me the no-way of keeping Quiet. He used to say, "Only keep Quiet." This was his only teaching and this is what I speak to you. He himself was Quiet and therefore I say to you keep Quiet.

After intense meditation gods and goddesses visited you. Why?

These gods have been visiting me because a man who is Enlightened is superior to God. Gods can live for thousands of years, but eventually they will fall back down here but the Enlightened one is Free of everything. The gods have unfulfilled desires like being with their goddesses. This is why gods and goddesses are always together. Therefore, to remove their attachments they come to see people who are realized.

I used to have a meditation room with only one mat, where no one else was allowed to enter. I would return from my office at five o'clock, have a bath, hang my clothes outside and enter the room wearing only a loincloth, as the Maharshi wore. I would not speak to my family, but keep quiet alone in my room.

One day before my usual wake-up time of 2 a.m. I heard some voices outside and so I went to look thinking that perhaps some relatives had come from the Punjab and their train from Peshawar had been late. When I opened the door I saw Ram, Sita, Lakshman and Hanuman standing there. I thought

Sadhana: There is no Becoming Being

I was dreaming, but I wasn't.

So I quickly went in to my wife's room and woke her up saying that they had arrived and to please bring them some fruits. She came to where they were, but couldn't see them and so she went angrily back to bed.

Rama said, "Hanuman has told us that there was a Krishna bhakta here and so we have come for your darshan."

This was too much for me! Garuda was there as well and eventually they all left on him as I watched. That day I did not chant the mantra or meditate for the first time in years. I kept standing there until my wife told me to go to the office. I had spent about six hours looking at them. I can still see them and read the palms of their hands as they held them up in blessing.

That weekend I went to the Maharshi and told him what had happened. In Tamil he told me it was "very good."

I asked him, "Why did Rama visit me when I always worship Krishna?"

He replied, "There is no difference between Rama and Krishna. All gods will come to worship you."

So Hindu gods and goddesses really do exist?

Gods of all religions really exist because they live in your faith. When you have faith in someone that person loves you. Jesus was real for St. Teresa of Avila and Krishna was real for Mira because they loved them so much. I also have seen Krishna so many times and I saw Jesus on the Jordan River with Peter once when I was sitting quietly on the Ganga.

After Rama's darshan in Madras you couldn't practice Krishna meditation anymore. What exactly happened when you went to Ramana for his advice?

This happened in my residence on Lights Road in Madras. Rama left an impression on me of what God looks like. No longer could I chant the name or meditate. So I went to a temple in Gopal Puram near my house where there was one Gauri Mission. I used to go there in the evenings to take part in the Arti and to sing bhajans and kirtan. That day Bhaktivedant was there and I told him that I had no interest left to chant or to meditate. He told me I had to keep chanting because sometimes demons visit a man to keep him from performing his rituals. I wasn't satisfied.

Then I went to Ramakrishna Math in Mylapur where I would go every Sunday. I asked the swami there about it and he told me that it was the dark night of the soul. I wasn't satisfied with this either so I went to Ramana.

I asked, "Bhagavan, I have been an ardent devotee of Krishna, but now I can't say his name anymore. What is happening?"

"How did you come here?" he asked.

"By train."

"And from the station to the ashram?"

"By bullock cart," I replied.

"Where is the train now?"

I said, "The train was at the station and now it has gone. From there I took a bullock cart to you. I sent the cart away once I got to the ashram."

Then he said, "You made use of the train, but then you left it behind. Then you took a cart and also left it behind when you arrived to see me because it was of no further use. Like this, all the things you performed are of no use now and they will be left behind. It is most important that you keep your intention in mind. You wanted to see me and now you are here only because you left the train and cart behind." The Maharshi continued:

> What comes and goes is of no use;
> all your bhaktis, meditations and chanting
> was to direct you to some Light
> and now are of no use.

Then I said "okay" and went to the other side of the hill where I played with Krishna. When I returned to him he asked me where I had been and I told him what I had been doing.

He asked, "Do you see Krishna now?"

"No sir, I don't, but I have played with him since childhood, he is my friend," I replied.

Then he said:

> What appears and disappears is
> not eternal and is not Truth.
> What does not appear or disappear?

Then he stared at me a beautiful glance, retina into retina and all my doubts were cleared. Something happened and my body shook. *I knew what had to be known.* Maharishi transmitted it to me and in that instant also permeated me with the power to transmit this to others. Now, by his Grace only, I am able to help people all around the world. He is forever my Master and when I speak it is him speaking, have no doubt about this. If for just one instant I thought it was Poonja speaking I would surely be destroyed, and I would have no right to sit here because whatever came out of my mouth would be false. It is my own Master who speaks, it is your own Master who speaks, it is your own Heart speaking, it is your own Self speaking to you.

ॐ

Meditation

I am practicing Vipassana. What is your opinion about it?

You can continue this, but actually you don't need any practice. Practice makes you dependent on practice, but you are That which is not dependent on anything. Practice also is something taught to begin and continue but nobody teaches you how to stop. Practice is the past. Just stay Quiet Here.

Why did you continue your Krishna meditation after you first met Ramana? Is it beneficial?

Meditation is always beneficial, even after Enlightenment. What else can you do?

Meditation means that you don't have to be attached
to anything that is not everlasting.
This keeps you at home.
Sit Quiet and meditate always,
as much as you can.

Why run around when Peace is found only when you meditate. Don't waste your time with the talk on the road. Just Now you can find the difference between the faces in this house and those out on the road. It is better to have meditation always. In the time before your departure spend meditating; then your departure will be beautiful.

How long should I sit in meditation?

Meditation has no time, don't look at the watch when you sit. If you do you are not meditating, but you are concentrating on time only. Meditate whenever you can, but don't think of time. You can think of time in your office, but not in the time when there is no time. Then it will be like sitting quiet for thousands of years. Simply sit and when something pulls you go and attend to it. There's no restriction to how long you should meditate and my advice to you is to always meditate. Nothing else will bring you Peace.

All your life: waking, dreaming, sleeping,
just meditate.

As Krishna said, "Do whatever you want, but always meditate on Me." This is the teaching. If you have a teacher concentrate on Him and if you don't, concentrate on your own Heart and work. Work is your duty and you can't avoid it, but the results are in my hand. You will get according to what you want. This is the advice that I can give you.

I know that you say that meditation will not enlighten anybody, but it does help me to get some control of this monkey-mind.

˙ You can continue your meditation, but along side don't forget to find out *who* is meditating. Before, your meditation was focusing on some past object. And so all meditation belongs to the past, not the immediate present. But asking who the meditator is will lead you to the immediate present.

Why dig in the grave of the dead and try to feed them bread and wine? This is what meditation on any object is. You can spend years meditating, but it only takes one second to give up the concept of meditation. If this one second doesn't pay you then you can return to your graveyard. Not digging the grave is not touching the past. Try this and tell me if it doesn't work.

I ask only for one second, one second devoted to your own Self, though you have spent millions of years devoted to others. You have lived for the happiness of your parents, of your teachers, of your spouses. For one second don't belong to anyone and find who never belonged to anyone.

(A woman gets up and sings a beautiful song. A man, sitting in fron. of Papaji, who was in a seemingly deep meditation during the song, suddenly jumped up and applauded loudly.)

This is what happens to the people who meditate. One man meditated for ten years in a cave of the Himalayas having no food or water, until one day a girl started to dance in front of him. Instantly ten years of meditation was finished. He starved for ten years and in seeing a very rich meal in front of him...(laughs) Look what can happen! All samadhis will be disturbed and so it is better to listen to the music and don't confuse yourself by meditating. You should be true. When you meditate, meditate. If you want to enjoy music, enjoy it. Why meditate when there is music going on?

Spend five minutes in twenty-four hours. No problem! That will give you a rich reward. For just five minutes keep Quiet, and don't look here or there or anywhere. Just five minutes! If you can't then two and a half minutes is quite enough. Decide this sometime in your life span.

Even the thought of meditation is a thought and, therefore, I do not suggest what most people call meditation. Just keep Quiet by looking at the thought and the thought will disappear and what remains will be silence. Silence is most important for you and this is the meditation that I speak of. You can keep silent when you are doing your activities by just looking at the thoughts that arise and knowing that these thoughts belong to the past. Mind itself is the past, it is a thought, it is time. So when you look at the thought time is gone, past is gone, mind is gone. The no-mind state is a state of quietness and if you stay here you are always Quiet during your activities also. Chello.

ॐ is the name of God, of Reality,
and is always chanted to cleanse body, tongue, and mind.
Chant Om at the beginning and end of the waking state.

ॐ is that vibration in which millions of planets hang.
Inquiry is only through the mind and this mind is in the vibration.
Om is vibration taking you to your Source,
Om takes you to Being.

To chant ॐ as long as possible is one way to empty the mind
because it pumps all the vasanas and desires out of the heart.
Then sit in meditation as long as possible
and you will win freedom.

This ॐ was picked up by Christians and called Amen,
and by the Muslims who call it Ammin.
They are both forms of Om.

ॐ is Brahman is Sat-chit-ananda,
contemplation on Om is contemplation on Self.

ॐ

I want my body to say Om every second. I want to have a cave to be in Peace. Please show me the path with love.

Are you chanting Om or simply wanting it? You have to do it. Chant Om always and this is enough. Then you will be happy and in peace also. Don't try to understand, simply go on chanting day and night, from when you wake up until you go to sleep. Om should always be in your mind and on your lips. You won't lose anything. Even if you do this for only one day you will know what it is. It is meeting the Self because this word is the Self itself. Unless you do it wanting it is of no importance.

Start from now. Chanting by tongue will do. Then I will teach you how to chant this from tongue to throat, which will give a better result. Then mental, then transcendental. I will show you that, but you start with chanting. Not very loud and in a low tone in your mind. First do this and come tomorrow and tell me what happened when you slept. You can't find the answer unless you simply do it. Om will take you and not let you see anything else. If this lasts it is Realization itself because Om is Brahman. You are not to chant Om, you are to Love Om!

Is this why the Om symbols are hung on the walls here?

Om must be inside and outside because this symbol of Om forms into the emptiness of the space when you repeat it. It is not a word at all. When you breathe out listen to what it is speaking. It is speaking Om. The first word of the baby when it is born is Om. Om is everything. It is not a word nor is it a non-word. It is how the creation was created. With the word Om creation was there. Om is a soundless sound. It created everything and after the dissolution of everything it will be there. It is eternal sound and it has no form. You can read Gaudipada's Karika. He comments very well on Om.

In 1972 I was in Cannes in Southern France, where I saw a TV interview of the Cardinal of France and Bhaktivedant. The Cardinal was insisting that in the beginning there was sun, so the light was first, otherwise, no creation could be found and no souls could live. So, he said, "In the beginning God sent light, as is written in the Bible." But Bhaktivedant said that sound was first, and this sound was Om, as Hari Krishna, Hari Rama, whatever it is. He said that there was sound in the beginning and not light, but the Cardinal was not happy, or satisfied with this. The people I was with asked me if I could speak something regarding this. I said, "Yes, and I will silence him!" So a time was made for me to meet with the Cardinal, on a Sunday about ten days later from four to six p.m.

When I arrived there were monks and priests and local people and again the same question was asked. So I said, "When your God said, 'Let there be light,' there was sound! This 'let' was sound and so light was after sound. Out from Om comes 'Let' and, therefore, this sound is before light." Then he didn't speak, but quietly in French he said, "He is a very clever Indian!"

Mantra

Mantra is used only to concentrate the mind
to bring it back again and again.
"I am Emptiness" should be your mantra.
Reaffirm "I am Consciousness,"
not, "I am body" or "I am suffering."

What is mantra meditation and how does it work?

It quiets your mind by engaging it in something so that it won't follow objects. It will help you concentrate by its sound. Chanting any mantra is usually for beginners. As long as you chant the mind is busy, but immediately goes to outside objects when you stop chanting. Chanting is good but not the end in itself because it doesn't give you happiness, but only engages your mind. This mantra can continue for some time until it is of no use. Mantra is used to give only one occupation to the mind. You can't think of two things at the same time and so it is necessary to chant a mantra in the beginning, unless you see a teacher.

When an elephant is taken in the market the mahout takes a rod or a log and gives it to the elephant to carry with its trunk so that the elephant will not pick up the fruits and vegetables at every chance. Mind is like that, so if you give something for it to hold in its trunk it will stay quiet. This mantra will take you to a teacher so that you will find out who you are!

If you do not get an answer, simply go on chanting and someday you will see that this mantra will leave you and Quietness will be there. Simply keep Quiet and let the mind repeat this mantra, the mind, not the tongue. Then you will be quiet, for it will give you Quietness. Your purpose is to be Free and not to go on chanting the mantras. When you sleep you don't chant, this is only in the dream and waking state, but if you chant long enough you will also chant in the sleep state. At that point the mantra will leave you.

Most mantras will give you some name or form as the mantra "Ram" does. But, "Who am I?" does not give you any name or form so this is the best mantra that can be given. Without repeating this mantra one cannot be Free, and you only need to say it once! This mantra gives you liberation

439

because it doesn't take you to any past and doesn't represent any name or any form, it keeps you in the immediate presence. Therefore, this mantra is invisible and will give you peace all the time: Just keep Quiet and don't make any effort. Chanting takes effort, but in keeping Quiet don't use anything or make any effort. Try this now and if you need more advice ask me.

You chanted a Krishna mantra for 25 years. You said mantra quiets the mind. Does mantra also purify the disciple's mind?

Yes, absolutely. Repetition of a mantra will allow you to see God who is within your own Heart. He will see that you are calling him to you from within. The mantra purifies your mind by engaging your mind away from distraction which give suffering and eventually frees you from all attachments. Eventually you will chant all the 24 hours of the day. At this point, your mind is attached only to God, the one whose name you are chanting and That manifests in front of you. Then you will see in a vision the one whose name is chanted.

A guru I had fifteen years ago gave me a mantra to repeat. I prefer to just sit quietly. What do you recommend?

As I said, mantra is usually a preliminary stage, but because there isn't much quietness in the way the world is today it can benefit you. Kabir was always chanting the name of Ram as did Tukaram and Namdev. This was their path and it obviously worked.

There are two main ways: Vichar and devotion. The way of Maharshi is Vichar. In Vichar you must inquire "Who am I?" In devotion you sacrifice your ego to Peace. You are lucky to be sitting quiet because so many other paths become traps of doing which you can't get out of. Truly being Quiet will give you much more benefit than chanting the name of God. When chanting the name you chant the name of someone who is not there, but when sitting Quiet you are That.

Whatever practice suits your temperament do it. But beware, you can be so attached to it that you lose the original intention. Surrender to your teacher and he will take care of you.

I cannot say "I am free" because freedom is everywhere and so these words feel so limiting. Can you say something about this?

You cannot say "I am free" because when you have this experience you don't need to say it. Just as you don't say "I am a woman," because it is something that you definitely know.

This is a slogan for these people who are battling for the victory, just as the soldiers in the battlefield cry, "Victory, victory, victory," even though they do not know that they may be defeated, or victorious. So this is a slogan to always keep in the mind, "I am Free," just to check the mind so that it will not go some other way and into bondage. "I am Free" will break the limitations and when the limitations are broken even this will fall back. So always say, "I want to be Free, I am Free, I want Freedom" and this mantra will take you to a place which does not come from your mind.

So, if you don't have the experience of freedom chant the slogan as a mantra to the mind so that it is defeated because otherwise the mind likes to stay in bondage. But if you have this experience you need not speak about it. Freedom just is always there. This is what I speak everyday.

ॐ

I was introduced to yoga and meditation early in my childhood by Swami Venkatesananda. He gave me the mantra Soham which, I am told, means "I am That."

No, Soham means "That I Am," not "I Am That." "I Am That" is Tat Vam Asi. That is the difference. It is not a mechanical thing to repeat. It has a very deep meaning and you only have to say it once: "That I Am." Why repeat it? It means that you have not understood. It is not to be repeated, but to be trusted and known: That I Am God. That is all.

Should I chant the mantra "I-I" instead?

Why waste your time chanting a mantra? If you have extra time spend it looking for a teacher instead because if you spend just one moment with a teacher you will know who you are.

How can I deepen this inquiry into "I"?

What people call meditation is really concentration because there is an object in the mind concentrated upon. In meditation there is no thought in the mind, and one is very beautiful. So don't make this "I" an image to concentrate upon. Simply know and have great trust that Soham.

Since Ramana has the same root as Rama, would chanting this name help?

Chanting can help in the beginning because it brings attention to the person whose name you chant. "Who am I?" will take you to the source of all mantras, the source of all Quietness and Peace. Once in the Source there is not purpose of the mantra and it will drop by itself. You will not disturb this Peace by any sound.

I was in Anandashram doing Ram nam, but to no avail. What was I doing wrong?

You can chant this name Ram, but nobody knows how to chant it. It will work to some extent if you don't know how just because it will keep your mind off distractions. But if you know how it will be much more powerful than this. The first thing to remember is this:

> Chant the name on the breath, not with the tongue.
> Let the breath chant the name, not the tongue.
> Don't put a pressure on anything.
> Just let the breathing in and out happen
> without your notice, naturally and habitually.

Then this will continue while working, walking, shopping and sleeping. I have seen people who have chanted this name for crores of time with no effort. Do it this way and within days you will see the one whose name is chanted. In the Kali yuga there is no time for penance, but the power of the word is tremendous. Ram purifies. The word "Ram" will enter your heart. It is a raft to cross the ocean. Let it be the last word of the last breath. Ram will confer Freedom without practice.

Beyond everything there is nothing to do and no appearance of anything there is only the Self which is neither subject nor object. This is the highest experience because there is no experiencer, just Peace. Then you know that:

> I am That seated in the center of the Heart,
> and this is Om Mani Padme Hum.

Master, can I have a name?

I'll give you a name and you can chant this name as a mantra because there is no better mantra for releasing you from the suffering of samsara. It will work even uttered once, but it is a name so you will use it many times a day and the merits that you earn by using this name will work because the name will penetrate to where it belongs. This name is SitaRam. Sita is your wife and Ram is her husband. Everybody can chant SitaRam. Even once uttered, even once uttered it gives liberation to a person. Thank you.

Karma Yoga

*Will you speak about the yoga of knowledge and the yoga of action.
I have read the Bhagavad Gita, but still I am confused about them.
What path should I take?*

The Gita is the book which removes doubts and confusion of everyone
who reads it, but you are confused by reading it. You are confused because
you don't know how to react to the circumstances before you. This Gita
arose when a man was in doubt about fighting his own family and teachers.
He asked the advice of a wise one, Krishna himself, who drove the chariot of
the doubtful one into battle.

Krishna even advised Arjuna to fight against his own cousins when they
wouldn't divide the kingdom of Hastinapur, which is now Delhi, between
them. Krishna told Arjuna to fight for his rights, especially since his cousins
were not good dharmic people. Krishna not only told Arjuna to fight but told
him he must kill all of them. Arjuna said that if he killed his cousins and
gurus that he would certainly go to hell, but Krishna replied that those who
even join with the unjust must also be killed. Krishna told him: "Your
profession is to fight because you are a Kshatriya, a soldier. Your cousins have
not been following the true path and don't deserve your compassion so rise
and fight.

Abandon all your duties and dharmas and surrender to me.
I will take care of you. Surrender your mind to me
and I will give you salvation. Do not worry."

So Arjuna took up his bow and arrow and he killed everybody and he
won the battle. His confusion was removed by his teacher, so he fought and
he didn't run away. The killing did not send him to hell because he was
fighting for the good of the people and for the peace of the country. Krishna
fought for this and so did Rama.

Karma yoga, the path of action, is to not run away from anything that
comes in front of you. If a fight comes then fight. If love comes then love.
This is the path of karma: don't run away. Simply react to the circumstances
that are in front of you.

Your dharma is to fight and the result is not in your hand. Leave this to
me. Just perform what needs to be performed and don't imagine any result.
The result is not in your hands. You can plan all you want, but may simply
die the next moment. Then what use is all of your planning? So simply react.

So this is how you could be both an anti-British freedom fighter and a Krishna devotee?

Krishna himself carries the Sudarshan Chakra on his finger. This is the greatest weapon of all. He also killed many people and demons who were bringing great harm to innocent people. An example of this is when he killed his uncle Kamsa because he troubled the entire state. There is no trouble in fighting unless you kill innocent people, which of course is a sin. You can fight so that all beings may live in peace, but not for selfish reasons.

Yoga and Pranayama

Yoga and pranayama
will give you a fit body and mind and this is needed.

Is pranayama necessary for inquiry?

It will give you some relaxation as long as it is there. In pranayama you can stop the breath for sometime and during this time no thought will arise. Holding the breath inside or outside in retention is called kumbhak. The mind cannot think anything in retention of breath because mind and breath rise from the same source. When the mind rises thought rises, when the mind ceases thought ceases. So pranayama is next best to inquiry. Pranayama with long retentions is a very difficult process and I do not advise it because it has a very definite code of life. Food, environment, behavior, responsibilities all have to be taken care of, but now it isn't practical so let's not think about it.

True kumbhak is making no effort and staying quiet. A yogi who knows how to perform kumbhak does not die. Inhalation. Stop. Exhalation. Stop. You don't need effort. Simply be conscious of the retention between inhaling and exhaling. That point is twelve fingers from your nose after exhaling and on the Heart after inhaling. You only have to be conscious of it and that will be your fixed place where nobody can enter.

Watching the breath can help your inquiry at first because then your mind can't go anywhere else. Just watch, witness from where the breath rises and to where it returns.

I would also like to know what you think about Hatha yoga and Vipassana meditation since these are two methods which I practice.

The word "yoga" also means union and is explained by Patanjali, who began the Yoga Sutras with 'Chit vritti nirodha iti Yoga.' Chit means the mind; actually something more subtle than the mind. Vritti are the concepts of sensual desire or any sensual activity. Nirodha means to cease. So what Patanjali is saying is that 'yoga is the cessation of the vritti of the chit,' or 'union is the cessation of the movement of the mind.' When you abandon all the vritti; or all the desire for anything of the universe and when they do not rise, this is the union of soul with the Self, which were separated for so long. This is an indirect explanation and a direct explanation is not yet to be found.

Yoga is the reunion of the jiva with the Paramatman. So when any tendency arises about anything in the mind, even God, reject it and be Quiet. This is what Patanjali says. Hatha yoga means the eight limbs: yama, niyama, asana, pranayama, pratyahara, dharana, dhyana, and samadhi. But nobody practices the first two, yama and niyama, inner and outer purity, which are the foundations of yoga. Without these practices how can you even sit?

I once was invited to a yoga center in Lisboa which did not teach yama and niyama. I asked the director how can they practice yoga unless they are clean in mind and in habits? The director said that since teaching yoga was his profession, he couldn't afford to deal with purity because then no one would come to his classes. The main interest of his students was to stay young, strong, and attractive, so that they would remain attractive to their partners. It seems that so many people in the West practice yoga for sex only. There are books just for this.

Yoga is a very good method to control the mind but you have to be pure and you have to go to the right teacher who will teach you properly. Otherwise there will be no benefit.

Do you recommend that I continue my yoga practice?

If you do yoga and pranayama correctly then no disease will touch you. You need good prana and a healthy body and so I recommend that everybody do some yoga.

What form of pranayama do you recommend?

Before sitting for Vichar or meditation you can have three nadi shodana pranayamas, which will purify the mind. This helps meditation and concentration, and helps to do Vichar in a right way.

Bhagavan said that we have to meditate on the spiritual heart and not on the space between the eyebrows. In which way should I do it? You say just to be Quiet. Can you help me experience the spiritual heart by your grace?

Whether you concentrate on the Heart or in between the eyebrows, it is just to arrest the outgoing tendencies of the mind. Concentrating on either place you are thoughtless. This leads you to Quietness. But I don't tell you to do this because if I did you would be body-minded instead of searching for your Self. So when I say keep Quiet I don't want you to concentrate on any part of the body, I only want you to keep Quiet as you keep quiet when you sleep. Simply keep Quiet and don't let your mind touch any object. This means Quietness. Look at the rise of thought and it will not rise. This means vigilance, simply watchfulness. Simply keep aware of what is happening.

Between the ages of four and six I had the ability to walk on water and to levitate and I had other powers.

There is no doubt that in your previous life you were a great yogi with lots of siddhis. But, if these siddhis really were of any use why did you come back to this world again and embrace suffering? It means that these siddhis are only magic of the mind and not worth having, much less striving for. They did not give you peace of mind. I have seen some yogis in the Himalayas who had most of the siddhis, but were not happy and peaceful. Their teachers had taught them so much and also taught that it was not the end, that they needed someone to teach the real Knowledge because all of these tricks are nothing before the sun of real Knowledge.

This life you were born in the West to fulfill all the physical attractions that you could not fulfill here in India. That is also a must because otherwise you are not complete in your experiences. Now you have come back to your own land to continue further.

Kundalini Yoga

How is kundalini shakti related to sexual energy?

Kundalini shakti, sexual shakti and Shiva Shakti are different names for the same thing. But it is not true experience. Sexual experience you will forget, but you can never forget True experience and you can never describe it. Anything that you can describe is false and stupid. True experience has been had by very few and none of them describe it, so you need to find a very expert teacher who can give you practical lessons in this.

You are the Master.

Yes, "You are the Master." (laughs)

Since practicing kundalini yoga I have a pain in my first chakra.

This kundalini is lying dormant in everybody in the muladhara chakra of the astral body which is in the heart of the physical body. This energy is sleeping and you give rise to it by concentrating on different chakras one after the other. If you are interested in it I don't advise it because it takes special guidance and it can be dangerous. Focusing in the chakra will cause the energy to start traveling upward through all the chakras. Finally, it reaches the top and then you will feel that you are not the body, but that you are out of the body. This is a difficult process and takes at least twelve years in a quiet place with a good teacher. And the benefit is that you will have power of the mind to levitate and manifest anything you want. I remember one yogi that I met who had these powers. I was on my way to a place which enters directly into heaven that I had heard about in a Lahore Urdu publication. This was the same place where all the Pandavas had gone after the MahaBharata war. Though they all tried to make it, only Yudhishtara was able to do it. All the others fell into their deaths on the glaciers. So on the same route in the high Himalayas, I came across this yogi.

He had been living in Jammu Kashmir as the son of a sub-postmaster, but ran away and met a guru who taught him all he knew, but also told him that it was not the end. Before his guru died he told this man to find someone who could give him knowledge of the Self, Brahman yoga.

He had left school very young and found a guru who taught him kundalini yoga. He spent twelve years with him and learned everything, but his guru told him that it was not the end. The end was Jnana yoga. But there is no guru for Jnana yoga. I asked him what his training had done for him and he started levitating. He could sit on the earth or he could sit in the space.

So I said, "What is the use of this? Any sparrow or crow can do this. You are a man, but you are trying to become a bird, so you will be born a bird in your next life!"

Then he said, "I can manifest anything, and since we are both hungry I will manifest food."

So he said, "food" and there was a lot of food including chola bhatura and gajar halva, all according to my taste and served fresh from Kashi by a brahmin. I said to him "You worked for twelve years for this? Why not just work for money so you can buy food or use the herbs that are here in the mountains?"

He then told me, "I can go to different planets and realms!"

But I said, "To be in this one planet is troublesome enough, why visit so many places?" He did say that there was one realm which he was not allowed into; Brahma loka, the plane of Knowledge, threw him out!

He could also speak any language by just praying to Saraswati. So I tested him with Persian, Karnat, Tamil, Telagu, Malayam and Bengali and he could speak, with the grace of Saraswati. He traveled all over India looking for a guru who would teach him Jnana yoga, but wherever he went people, yogis, gurus all wanted to know what he knew instead. Even in the Kumbha Mela, where there are eight million sadhus, he could not find a Jnana guru.

So I told him to sit down along side the small hot spring-fed river which was totally surrounded by snow. He had a magic staff in his hand, which was from Yama loka, the realm of death, which made him immortal and which was the source of his powers. His guru had given it to him. I took the rod and threw it into the river. This staff that he was so proud of and worked for so long to get was thrown away. Actually, it was his pride which I threw away and all his powers were finished. Then I told him, "I am going back to the plains. I have only come here to find Swarga where the Pandavas had gone, but I couldn't find the way. So now I am going back."

He said that his guru had told him that whoever gives you Knowledge you must serve for the rest of your life. I replied that I always travel alone and that though I was going back to the Punjab, he could come as far as Rishikesh. I told him to stay in the mountains and that I was a householder, not a yogi, and that he should go his way and I will go mine.

So, if you want to practice this go out and buy the book *Serpent Power* and practice. Many people try to practice, but they do not get it. If you want guidance I will guide you. You will have to live in solitude and have special food and circumstances. You have to be very strict. You are a very young man and you could do it. You could become another Sai Baba. (laughs)

But why not just have a simple way of living. Just make inquiry and find out who you are first. See the Divine within yourself, but don't see anyone else, don't see any other thought. Keep only one thought in your mind; and that thought should be of God.

I realize now that I am not here for kundalini.

By the true Knowledge of the Self the kundalini arises by itself. It's not that you will first feel the rise of the kundalini to the sahasrara and then you're Enlightened. It's not true and it will not happen. If you realize yourself by simply keeping Quiet you will see that the nature will listen to you and obey you, including gods. Try this and if it fails I'll teach you kundalini.

There is no path, no person to tread on the path and no mind to think about all these things, and there is no time and no space. This is called Jnana yoga. There is no practice because any practice is in the time. When you sleep there is no time and you don't make any practice. All these things you must avoid. Don't stir a thought in your mind, and don't try to attain anything. If a thought comes reject it. Whatever is left you should speak of to me. I will wait for the answer.

ॐ

Kundalini has suddenly arisen in me.

I don't believe it. Your face doesn't show it. Maybe you are experiencing the impact of a new culture, but not the kundalini. When kundalini arises the face changes and the decisions are no longer made, but they come by themselves. These are symptoms of the kundalini. She gives light and wisdom, confidence and contentment.

I don't advise working on kundalini sadhana because this usually only brings magical activities like levitation, multilocation and manifesting objects. These siddhis have nothing to do with Freedom or with dissolving your desires, in fact they can trap you deeper into desires. I don't advise it.

I advise you to do no practice, but to simply sit Quiet and watch the movement of the mind. This will give you such strength that you will feel that when you walk the world walks with you. When you breathe, the world breathes with you. That feeling you will have; oneness with all beings, and this will not be an up and down experience.

ॐ

Yatra

The true Yatra is returning Home to Here and Now.

I want to go on a yatra to some sacred places.

It is better to just sit where you are and ask yourself "Who am I?" Most of these sacred places are sacred because there your mind is focused on the saint who is related to it, like Buddha in Bodh Gaya. This focus benefits you by strengthening your decision, not the place itself. Most people who live in Bodh Gaya or Tiruvannamalai are not affected, but those who go there focused on the saints and teachings of these places are benefited.

Find where the "I" rises. There is no better education for only this brings you to no past object, but to your Self. "Who am I?" finishes your relationship with time and in this timelessness you know who you are. Go to the sacred places, but the main purpose must be to know who you are. After inquiry, the two places I usually recommend for a yatra are Arunachala who is Shiva and also my Guru's Guru, and the Ganga, who is the Divine Mother. By drinking her water you will remove all your physical problems and diseases. She is a heavenly nectar, and therefore, Ganga is worshipped. If you keep her in your room it is quite enough to purify the atmosphere of the whole room. This is why we keep containers of Ganga in our houses and this water will stay unpolluted for one hundred years. Also, when people are dying a tablespoon of Ganga is place on their tongue and then they are not reborn if it is the last sip of water that they have.

You can go to the source of the Ganga, Gangotri, and there you will see that there is no river! Like this, go to the source of your mind which has become a river of so much samsara and time. Don't forget that going to Gangotri is symbolic of something that few people will understand.

If you do want to find another sacred place besides these, go to where you can feel the peace. Adi Shankaracharya was traveling into the forest once when he saw a frog and a snake together. You know frog is the food of snakes and so they can't stay together for long, but he saw a female frog giving birth and a cobra using its hood to protect the frog from the rain. Shankaracharya thought that this must be a holy place since there was no enmity there and started an ashram there which is Sringeri in Karnatak state.

Whenever you see enemies living together you know that it is a holy place. Somebody must have lived there who removed hatred from the beings, as wherever Buddha walked all the animals: deer, rabbits, lion and tigers were peaceful with each other. Where Buddha walked there is only love, no hatred even among the animals. This Buddha still lives in your heart. If you have no hatred for anything you are the Buddha. Then there is no hatred for men, animals or birds. You can try. Everybody is a living Buddha.

I want to sit with you and connect in our hearts. I've been traveling all over India going to sacred places and now I want to connect with you.

Where have you visited?

The Aurobindo Ashram, and Vrindaban,...

What did you do in Vrindaban?

I sat and listened and just visited the temple.

Which kind of Vrindaban did you visit?

I don't understand.

You don't need to understand when you go to Vrindaban. You have gone to see structures and buildings only. That is not Vrindaban. Vrindaban is love. Didn't you find this? You said you wanted to connect. Did you connect with the dust of Vrindaban where the devotees sang, danced, and played with the Lord himself in form? That is Vrindaban!

It doesn't matter. You just stay here now and learn how to stay in Vrindaban. You have to dance in love; that is called Vrindaban. Not simply running from temple to temple.

For that Vrindaban you must look into your own heart just for a few seconds. Then you will find your way to Vrindaban! If you can enjoy within, then only you can enjoy outside.

This is the connection you speak about: connect yourself with your own Self. If you do not, no other connection will give you peace. So how to have this connection? Do not think of anything from the past, just for one instant, and you will have connection with the presence. All the past connections will disturb you so look into your own Vrindaban, which is inside you.

Yantra

I bought a Sri Yantra in Rishikesh. Can you tell me how to use it?

Keep it in front of you and do puja with flowers, and use the mantra that is written on it. Concentrate here, clockwise around petals and rings of triangles in a spiral, until you get to the center. When you can concentrate here it is another way to stop your mind. I will tell you the mantra before Shivratri.

(Someone gives Papaji a letter with a swastika written on it)

You have drawn this swastika backwards. It must start the other way. Drawing it backwards is the German swastika which Hitler used and he lost the war. It makes all the difference and this is how Hitler was defeated. Swastika means intelligence and it must be used correctly. It is an ancient symbol of intellect, Ganapati, and it must be worshipped.

Tantric Sex

Some people use union with a partner as a means of liberation.
Do you think it is possible to use sex as a sadhana?

For the Westerners it is very suitable according to some teachers. They say the bliss of sex is the bliss of Self. I don't have any objection to this, but I also don't see any results from it. I have not seen anyone realized through sex. This is because they have not been taught in a true way.

At a certain point in sex there is rest, there is peace, there is no desire. But people miss this chance and stir another desire for another activity again and so this has not worked. This peace and realization does not come from the union, but because of the dis-union. After the sexual activities you get some shock of weakness which you call peace. This peace comes because the desire for union has left you. During the desire for union you are disturbed and you search for someone to have union with. When you meet with someone you are no longer desiring and this absence of desire gives you peace. If you know this you can do anything that you like. But only if you reject everything will the happiness come, as Buddha rejected everything and the result was Enlightenment. So do not forget this:

> When an object of desire appears in your mind
> you are not happy.
> When it leaves you, you are happy.
> So if any desire touches you do not accept it.
> Then you are happy.
> Allow the desire to fulfill itself
> without touching you.

Are the tantric yogis wasting their time?

Tantra is a worship. It is their way of worship. The idea of tantra is to take you beyond the mind and beyond sexual activity by worshipping the goddess. It is meant to take you out of sexual attachment and not to get you more attached. The original book which describes this was written by a rishi about 3000 BC. In it is said that the staircase that you have descended out of bliss is the same which you must ascend into bliss again. I think he was wrong because the staircase must be rejected, and not continued forever. Most people just use a meaning of tantra that they like the most and lose the original intention of the rishi.

ॐ

Living Skillfully

Living Skillfully:
If you know it, play in the lila.
Inside abide alone and yet play in the lila outside.
Manifestation is a play,
Never forget the "I" is a transient actor,
whose friends are body-mind-elements.
Identify as That, keep aware, and play the game
in lila as you wish, but do not leave the Source.

World is here to enjoy!
There is so much to it.
Open your eyes and live wisely:
The world is so beautiful and exists for you
because you want something to do with it!
The wise will aspire for something else,
for what sees the beauty,
for who decides what is beautiful.

Essence of Skillfulness

Whatever comes let it come,
what stays let stay, what goes let go,
always keep Quiet, and always adore Self:
this is the essence of living skillfully
in the world appearance.
During all activities of life
always know that you are the Self.
The way to live a happy beautiful life
is to accept whatever comes
and not care about what does not come.

Things will come so enjoy them and be happy.
Let the play happen by the Supreme Power;
you will be taken care of.
Be free to be happy, love has no traps.
If you are happy all will be happy,
if you suffer, all will suffer,
if your mind smells bad others will be affected.
Keep yourself happy in Peace,

Light, Wisdom, Consciousness.
This is your responsibility.
Be happy and have compassion
and live hand in hand with nature.
This makes birth worthwhile.
Start from Heart and see that all arises from Heart.
Always do this, Always *be* This.

You cannot be skillful and arrogant at the same time,
but without arrogance all will be skillful.
Face the One, seeing everything as one is no-mind
and this is the pure state of Being, of Self.
When you are one with all
do not hold or possess and It will Be.
When you are connected to all things
do not hold onto the connections
because this makes them separations
and you will have divided yourself by creating "other."

As the lotus does not touch the water,
so do not let the world enter you heart.
Being busy in the world is no trouble
unless you are troubled being busy.
Then the only trouble is the trouble.

Let attention go to manifestation,
just know that manifestation is Brahman.
Let there be creations and destructions,
All is Brahman and you are beyond even that always.

Your environment is very important
so stay where there is no tension.
Make sure that the circumstances within and without
are not disturbing, so be with peaceful beings in peaceful places.
You need a place of love and beauty and peace,
even your own apartment and body must be peaceful.
Love and Quietness is enough.

If you speak ill of anybody else, you speak ill of yourself,
if you speak good, you speak good about yourself.
Words have great power so use only appropriate words.
Speaking from the head is pain and from the heart is pleasure,
so shut your head and your heart is open.

Don't trouble any being and do not let any being trouble you.
Don't get angry with anyone:
the tongue doesn't get angry with the teeth when the teeth bite it,
and this sometimes happens when the food is good.

Contentment is absolutely necessary
because whatever you will be in the next state,
or in the next life is whatever unfulfilled desire
that you have in the present state.
Therefore, desire only the Infinite.
Let the other desires arise and see that they arise from me,
from Emptiness, and then let them fall, as waves must.

Don't run after projections on the screen, be very wise.
Do not lose your peace at any cost.
Things *will* rise and fall so not do be caught!
Peace is most important, you have to be happy in the lila,
no-mind-limitless-happiness with Freedom in your mind,
not problems. Here in this moment there is no problem
and daily life is within this moment, you cannot walk out of it.
Just try to invite past and future problems into this moment.
They cannot touch Here so do things of Now Now,
and do not touch yesterday or tomorrow.

Remove all becoming, you are Being.
Becoming is effort, Being is no effort.
You are always That so be like the breeze
that is attached to neither the garbage nor the garden
that it blows over.

Do not run away from worldly activities,
only always keep in the "I am Self," stay as the screen
on which all the projected activities take place.
In all activities simply keep Quiet and know "I am home."
Your business is to keep Quiet!

You cannot say that it is a dream unless you are awake.
So in the true waking state, the state of Wisdom,
it does not matter if there are dream objects or not.
Emptiness is not affected by any dream object, not even duality.
Ocean does not complain about the dance of ten million waves!
So don't be concerned about the rise and fall of thoughts.
To be nowhere is home, not allowing thought to land is home.

Allow thoughts to arise, but do not let them land
because thought landing is an object
which brings desire for the object,
which bring possessing of an object, which brings insanity.
There are only two choices: Freedom or insanity.
Choose "I am free and happy."

Bad moods are either past or imaginary future,
in the present there are no moods at all.
Moods belong to circumstance, to the past;
Face the Sun and there will be no shadow of moods.

Give up all concepts and remain what you are.
Identify yourself as Cosmic Consciousness;
don't accept name or a form.
Detachment is your own nature
so the wise are not attracted to the transient.
Only the foolish cling to that which brings unhappiness
and are thus butchered by time.

This world is a garden, a game, play this divine game very well.
See things only as they are but do not possess them
or you will be in trouble because even your body is transient.
The next breath is not guaranteed so do what you have to do Now:
play well, play wisely, by first finding out who you are.
Yoga only, no bhoga, first finish your work,
then go to the world with a heart that is dancing.
Don't use words for this dance because the game is tricky.
Just be silent.

The world is like a tail of a dog, its nature is to curl.
The best you can do is to stay Quiet
and not let anything bother you.
Visitors will come and go, don't interfere with these waves.
Be always empty and let desires dance.
Being asleep in the waking state is
being asleep to desires and aversions.

The avalanche of vasanas
which may happen as you approach the summit
is notions, intentions, and ideations.

With no intention, there is no summit and
That is Here.

Hidden tendencies arise to leave when you are Quiet,
so it is a good sign when vasanas rise.
Do not be dismayed because they are Self.
Let vasanas arise, they do not exist.
The world is a playground for the wise
and a graveyard for the foolish.
Let the vasanas play, they are transient imaginations
and even the "I" to which they occur is imagination itself.
Abide as Substratum and allow circumstances to come and go.
Stay Quiet with no intention, or notion,
not even to inquire for Freedom, and don't utter the word "I."
Then the gods and demons of the vasanas will vanish.

Your True nature does not come and go.
Play with what comes and goes.
When they arise they will disappear.
Allow them to go away.
Let things happen through mind-ego
and just stay Quiet as they happen,
with the firm conviction: I Am I Am.
This meditation is absolutely necessary to clear tendencies.

Only in the dream do you see objects.
Know that all objects are dream objects
and that the dream snakes are not real.

You have been ignorant for years
so when you know the Truth
you must focus on staying as such for some time.
What else is important.
If you find that you are still in the mind,
never mind! Don't remember!
Then you will not forget.

Though name and form and place and fields are different,
Consciousness is never different, so let there be these differences,
but do not accept and reject anything or you divide yourself
and there is no love in this division:
take a cent from a dollar and you no longer have a dollar.

A fool doesn't look at foolishness and so is foolish.
The wise one looks at foolishness and so is wise.

Have no individuality:
Surrender to space or dissolve the ego with knowledge.
Just keep Quiet and watch the ego.
Keep vigilantly alert; aware but not involved.
Doing is trouble.

Clinging to non-eternal things is arrogance,
No clinging is loving all,
so don't cling and don't don't cling
because both conceal the Truth.
What you have, you have to lose,
there is no water in the mirage, only dry sand.
Be attached only to That
which is impossible to be separate from.

If you have to think, think "I am pure consciousness."
If you have to speak, speak about the Self.
If you have to read, read what the Enlightened have written.

I advise you to keep good company, a pure sattvic diet,
attend Satsang, and live in harmony with nature.
Be as you Are and allow no concepts to trespass into your peace.
Your foremost duty is to remove concepts and engagements.
Love all beings, love all beings, love all beings.

Treat the ego and mind like shoes:
wear them when you need to go out
and take them off at the door when you are home.
Otherwise the seat in which knowledge would sit is occupied.
The thought "I am the body" is enough to occupy the throne,
so keep the mind and ego out with the shoes
until there is no in and no out
and no one left to wear them.

Buddha nature flows from simple doing,
not doer-thinking-doing.
Allow things to happen, you just stay here.
What has to happen is happening
Just remain here as Peace, just remain as Peace,
just remain as Peace.

ॐ

Questioner: How to live in the world?

Papaji: When you are strong in the experience of That you can live in any circumstances. This is the end of desire. How to stay with desire without disturbing our Consciousness, our Awakening? Simply do not touch what disturbs you. Be aware and drop back to this pure I as pure Consciousness at an individual level.

If you have this experience you'll help other people by simply Being and not necessarily speaking about it. Waves radiate from this One and others are benefited, as a silent rose attracts by its radiant beauty. Eternal Love is the perfume that attracts people. Try it, you'll find people pulled to you.

Does one need to live in comfort or in austerity? India doesn't offer the comforts of life.

India has everything, but it doesn't allow you to use these things as bodily comforts. It may not be the same comfort that they speak of in the West, though. A true comfortable life is very simple living and very simple things. This comfortable life is only available in India, not in the West.

How do I let go of control and be natural and let existence guide me?

Many people ask this question. You must know this answer for yourself. I will tell you this though, when you say "let go" you imply that you have "let in" something. How did you allow this "letting in"? In and out is the same gate. This is what the Bible means when it says: "From dust it comes and to dust it returns." From where something arises there it falls too. Who did you allow in? It is of no use to keep an old habit.

> Keeping an old troublesome habit
> is like keeping poisonous snakes in your arms.
> Now is the time to hold this snake by the tail and throw it out.

This snake is someone that you love. If you feel the bite of this snake, throw it away. This doesn't take time. Unless you throw out the old habit you will not see the beauty of the fresh habit. This fresh habit will bring tears of joy from your eyes.

Let go by knowing the pain of holding. There is no struggle in sleep. Who does not struggle in sleep and who struggles when awake? Everything that happens, happens naturally. What is born must die. It is only that you want things to happen in your own way and that is the trouble.

How can I add more peace, bit by bit, to my life?

I don't believe in bit by bit like the sparrows eat. The crocodiles swallow the whole thing. You just slip in and stay comfortably inside. Millions of people are inside the stomach of the crocodile of death. Every minute a person is dying and is being chewed by this crocodile, even a day old baby, but nobody knows.

Avoid this death by knowing that there is no crocodile and that you are Free; swimming in the ocean of Freedom. If you say, "I am so and so" then you land in the stomach of the crocodile. But if you don't use any name then who are you? Don't land on any name of the past, present or future.

You have to abandon everything for Freedom:
god, mind, and especially "I."
Then when Freedom comes it comes instantly,
It comes immediately, all at once.
The only impediment is the indecision
of not removing the arrogance of "I am not That."
This is saying "I am suffering,"
which is like a fish in the water saying: "I am thirsty!"
So simply say "I am."

In this dream is it better to act with love, kindness and generosity as so many spiritual teachings suggest or doesn't it matter how you act?

These are suggestions from the teachers. Those who have truly experienced Emptiness have no teaching or suggestions. They simply say, "Keep Quiet."

How can I be non-identified when suffering and emotion comes out?

Suffer when there is suffering and be happy when there is happiness. Just don't accept and don't reject. Be like a breeze which just flows through the gardens and garbage equally. This moment cannot be separated from air. Learn from the breeze and don't stay at a particular place.

And what to do when a desire arises?

Fulfill it. When there is an unfulfilled desire you are in difficulty. Why not finish it?

How can I always be happy?

There is a state between waking and sleeping and between sleeping and waking where there is no time. Stay like this state and you will be happy. Stay with no desire for any person, object or concept. This is called sleeping, but nobody knows how to do it. Waking state is the attachment with persons, objects and ideas. This is called the waking state. Keep up the state with no concepts which is the sleep state of a realized person. The suffering state of the unrealized person is the state of persons, objects and concepts.

> Stay in-between the transient, in-between time.
> Don't ignore the zero-time between waking and sleeping,
> between inhalation and exhalation, and between day and night.
> The first and last thought should be: "Let there be Peace,"
> so stay aware as you transition between waking and sleep.
> In this moment simply be Existence-Consciousness-Bliss.
> Spend time with Self at this moment.

Your homework is to always feel happy. Leave aside the I-thought and all other thoughts and just keep happy. The past is hell so the secret of happiness is that nothing touches you in the moment.

> The human life is celebration:
> welcome to the planet,
> plunge into this moment.
> This is happiness,
> all the rest is suffering.

You have nothing to do. Simply stay as you were, like a lotus in a pond. You may live in the dirty water, but you are above it and you don't do anything about the circumstances. Don't touch the circumstances, don't be attached to anything, and yet live with everything.

Would you advise me to go to Ramanashram and inquire there?

The Grace is there as it is here so it doesn't matter. What matters is that you make the best of any circumstance that you are in. Your time must be utilized in a perfect way. Don't look behind, but have a strong decision that you will do it.

Soon I plan to leave and ...

This planning is not in your hands. You came for three days, but have stayed three weeks. Just react to circumstances. Planning does not work: Simply Be!

You are right. You will always be in my heart because I don't exist.

And this will be your name: "I don't exist." This name is Maina.

Maina was the mother of a king in India in ancient times. The king had four queens and once she was sitting in the balcony above where the king's four wives were giving him a bath in milk and honey mixed together, as was the custom then. She should have been happy, but she wasn't and a tear dropped and landed on the body of her son. Though the king was covered in milk and honey and the hands of the queens he still felt this one tear because it had so much power.

"What is this I have felt?" And in looking up he saw his crying mother! "Mother you should be happy. I am enjoying my bath and you are crying."

She replied, "Yes, my dear son, the body you are looking after and that which the queens are rubbing is not worth it. It is not worth it because every next day it becomes older and it will lead you to death. Don't only look after your body; look toward your happiness because the body stays only eighty or ninety years, and after that what will happen? So do it now! After the bath, sit down and meditate."

Then he prostrated before his mother and left the palace to go and win Freedom. This is the instruction of a good mother.

The only way I can thank you for what you have given me is to be still.

If you are Still you can't lose anything. When you are Still everyone will think you are attentive and awake and they will not come near you.

> Stillness is the greatest achievement
> one can have in life.

Stillness is not so very easy and so few people will opt to be Still and among these a rare one will be successful. Now you have started losing objects. Next you will lose your desires. Then you will lose your ego and finally your ignorance. Losing all this only Stillness remains.

Papaji, I have a letter for you, but it is very confidential and I don't want you to read it out loud.

I have no privacy. Don't keep anything confidential or secret because the day will come when everything will be known. Keeping anything confidential will trouble you. You are here with your own family, your own friends. Kabir says this also:

Don't keep anything confidential
because if you do it will revolve in your head
and at the time of departure it will be your next birth.
What you concentrate on will bring you your next birth.

I want to serve people from my heart, from essence to essence. I don't seem to be able to do this in my present occupation as a doctor. Tell me what to do and where to go. What is the number of my flight?

The number of your flight 000. Your destination is Here Now. Just don't get attached to the transit lounge as you wait for your flight. Your neighbors to the right and left are coming and going and now you are left alone; where nobody is on the right flight.

I have heard that people like Ramana and Ramakrishna had to give up their studies and games in order to develop spiritual strength.

You don't have to give things up to develop spiritual strength. I don't teach to stop your studies and to meditate.

You can keep up your natural interests, whatever they are. I have played cricket and now this is my interest. To see cricket I don't lose anything. The games and studies can be carried on without any difference and you can still realize your Self. Ramakrishna did it as did Ramana, you see. Though Ramana had only a high school education the doctors and Ph.D.'s bow down before him. He was not an illiterate and he didn't give up his studies. He was as common a man as anyone, helping in the kitchen to cut the vegetables and playing with the monkeys and cows. He didn't leave his interests. He studied very well and was in love with everything; including rocks, monkeys and cows. He didn't leave anything. What Ramana has taught me I am teaching to everyone and everybody who truly listens to me will become Ramana.

I want to be silent.

You can always be Quiet, no matter what you are speaking or doing. Inside you will still be silent. Silence is always there, no special time is needed. I make everybody Quiet without disturbing their routine of life and wherever you go you can keep this Quietness because one is always Quiet. In your own place, in your Self, no one can die. But the fisherman which is the mind will try to take you away and bring you to the market. Then in the evening you will be on the table. Therefore, stay in the water and don't become enamored by the food of the fisherman because underneath the food is an angle that you do not see! Whenever you enjoy there is a hook, but you don't see it. All enjoyments hook you, but now be aware and do not go near the easy food or you will be angled. Beware! Stay in the deep waters and food will come to you by itself. No fish will die in the deep water. It is only the greedy ones who go for the quick food who die. This is how to keep Quiet.

What should I do with my judgments?

Don't judge at all and if you do, judge your own self. Give up the concept of judging. If you want to judge, judge what the purpose of your life is. Judge yourself, judge your intention and judge *your* mistakes, not those of others. Allow others to do what they are doing. It is not your problem.

Though I am a devotee of Shiva and have been chanting his name for years, I have recently been having dreams of Krishna. Why is this?

Shiva lives in the cremation ground and you have gone there and so he is very happy with you. Because of this he has sent you out of the graveyard, to enjoy the gopis with Krishna. When God is happy he fulfills your desires that you are carrying buried within. In your case he is removing your allergic reaction to women. Don't carry anything of the past. Let it happen and then forget about it. You have come from the cremation grounds so now enjoy yourself. Krishna teaches you enjoyment.

Shiva and Krishna are the same god. Don't care about which one is before you. In the Shiva aspect he says to go and meditate in the graveyard and have fierce renunciation and determination. This means that you should go to where nobody can interfere with you, go where your mind is not disturbed. Stay alone in the graveyard.

Then when you have everything, enter the universe because it is beautiful. This is the Krishna aspect. Why shun it? Why run away from it? You only need to know the proper tact of handling the serpent either by the tail or by the tongue and fangs! That tact you must learn from me because it has two tongues! And one simple prick of its fangs is quite enough. So handle this serpent by the tail and shake it and you will break its bones. Then it will still be a snake, but it will be harmless because it can't move.

Like this you must know the tact to handle everything: not from the front, but from the back.

How to kill the serpent demon.

You must kill the demon as Ram killed Ravana and Krishna killed Kamsa. Kill the demon by purity.

ॐ

Few people can create what they want in their lives.

Are you speaking on your own behalf or on the behalf of the planet? Look after yourself first and then look after your neighbors if necessary.

It seems that since we are made in the image of God that we could have that creative power or will to satisfy our desires. But instead we live in fear and frustration.

If you believe you are made in the image of God then it will be alright for you, but you don't believe it. If you believe that you are the image of God then there will never be a problem since God will look after you.

But this image is running after something else, not God, but demons, hence, your fear and frustration will never end. But your fear and frustration will vanish when you come to Satsang and stay with the teacher. If you try to do it yourself you will only listen to your ego and mind and you will be frustrated. See that you don't touch the ego and mind. Never touch it. Only then will you be happy.

Don't follow the foolish.
Follow the footsteps of the sage and you will become a sage.
Only one in a billion on earth are really wise and Know.

Know that you are being pulled up from the millions of pigs on earth to be eternally happy, and to challenge death, to be untouched by death. On this side this is the reward, on the other side is the slaughter house. Pick up what you want.

You won't find satisfaction to the physical desires of your physical embodiment. Nobody is happy, not even the kings and certainly not the beggars because they are all ordinary people governed by the mind and ego.

How can we make our universe a more colorful and happy event?

The universe is given to you to play in, not to cry about it. You are not to cry, weep and suffer. There are so many beautiful things like the forests, rivers, animals, mountains, and birds all for your happiness. But you are suffering, and so the mountain gives you suffering.

Find out how to sing like a small sparrow sings for the joy of everyone. Why can't you do this? Who stops you? The only problem is that you want to do things the way you want them done.

> Leave everything in the hands of the Divine
> and your activities will be Divinized.
> Surrender your will and you will be happy.
> Surrender your will to the will of God.
> Let it be done!

This will give you happiness though nobody ever does it. Just try it, for a day at least.

I thank you for your love and compassion. How can I be like a bird who leaves no footprints?

If you are always in Satsang you will not leave any footprints because you will not look to the past attachments. When you are free of attachments you have no footprints. This is very simple. Don't be attached because it will land you in difficulty even if they seem to give you happiness at first. No attachment ever gives happiness because both the attachee and the attached are in the attaché case! All attachments close you into a box and you are carried away by your desires.

> Don't follow any attachment, and get rid of the company
> of those who give you chains of attachment.
> Keep the company of the Free people who desire Freedom.

Think of Freedom, walk in Freedom, stay with those who aspire for Freedom. This is the only way not to have footprints.

Is there more to it other than just being and accepting what appears?

That is enough, accept what is presented to you and reject what doesn't come to you. If something comes accept it. If something doesn't come to you do not aspire for it. Don't desire what your neighbor has, don't think of it. Be contented with whatever you have. Don't look at others. This is the best teaching that you can have and you don't need any other: contentment.

Everybody is greedy and jealous and hateful, because they are not content. They do not know the simple trick: Keep happy whatever is given to you, wherever you are, keep happy.

How can someone make a decision based on dharma and not ego and the I-thought?

The supreme dharma is to reject all dharma. This is your dharma. All

dharma of doing things and not doing things don't care about. Supreme
dharma is to reject all the dharma of the world. If you reject everything what
will happen? This dharma will reach you to the perfect Peace and Love. Your
supreme dharma is to reject all dharmas.

Will you change my name?

Govinda dances with illusion, Radha, but he knows he is dancing and
keeps as a witness of both of these dancers.

> Dance with the circumstances
> but keep aware of the dancers
> and of the purpose of the dance.

I will give you the name Govindas, the devotee of Lord Krishna. Krishna
is responsible and will give you all you need. Being a devotee of the mind
everyone is proud. Don't sell yourself for the sake of pleasure and then suffer.
How much time do we have and how much of this is for sleeping and eating.
Don't waste your time. Make the best of it. Depend upon the Lord who looks
after the creation. Surrender to the Divine will, not to your will. So I give you
the name Govindas! A servant of the Lord only.

I have met many crocodiles in my life, but you are the only one I trust.

You are becoming a crocodile yourself, and are even learning the
language. You become like the association that you keep, you become one
with them.

*I was living such a dark life of theft and robbing before coming here.
What snapped me out of it is when I started to plan a murder. I am so
glad I have come.*

You look like a good boy, where did you get all these bad habits? Bad
company? Don't worry about your past and live the rest of your life in service
to man, not killing them! Humans are a good species! They don't have tails.
But those who do not behave like humans are really animals, they bark and
bite others. You are a beautiful boy so behave like a good human being and
not like an animal.

Relationships, Marriage and Sexuality

The relationships you keep have a great effect on you:
you become what you associate yourself with.
So stay only in holy company,
only travel with those in the same boat.
Nothing is better than Satsang so keep your friends here.
Associate only with those going in the same direction
and go to Truth at any cost.

Be the One, for One is None.
This is the basic good association.
Where there are many, there is falsehood.
So send all your thoughts away.
Shun their bad association.

A friend is one who does not disturb your mind.
Maintain no friendship with ones who disturb your mind,
no matter how close they are, be it a person, a place, or idea.
Do not accept the invitations of foolish persons
because when you live in their society
Truth will not kiss you.

Wicked habits and society will come back to you.
They are very strong and so you must be.
You are going upstream to the source,
they are flowing downstream and will drag you along.

The love that any two beings share
is the Love of Self for Self.
Keep away all notions and intentions
and you are meeting all beings in this Love.
This is Self meeting Self.
All attraction is for the Self only,
though appearances are deceiving.

If you use this word love
for what goes on between skin and skin,
it must be replaced by the word lust.
Relationship causes separation, anger, fear, and grief,
it does not cause love.

Understand that you are not in love with a body.
A body, be it man or woman, is a corpse.
Know that what appears to be love for an "other"
is really Love of Self because "other" doesn't exist.
So this innermost Love can be given to no "other."
Love of friends is for the sake of Self, not for body to body.
True Love has no lover or beloved
because all love is Love of Self.
If you want to really Love,
Love the Supreme Self right Now,
Love the ultimate Truth.
This Love is Freedom.

Wherever there is two there is fear of separation
and this separation must eventually occur
because body meeting body is transient.
Only marriage with Freedom will last.
Any friendship with anything else
will not abide and will bite you in the end.
This isn't to say you should run away from relationships,
nature is not foolish: man and woman together is okay,
being a householder is not a hindrance to freedom.
Even all the rishis and gods are householders.
You just have to be with the right person,
going in the right direction
so that you keep focused on Self.
Just remember Freedom first!

How can loving be more natural?

Loving is natural. It is hating that is not natural. Love cannot become natural because it *is* the natural state. The unnatural state is to hate those who irritate you. This unnatural state will create so much trouble for you in this life and it will create more lives in which you will be troubled. Be free of this by begging forgiveness of those who have insulted you lifetimes ago. Love, who will not like it?

Love everybody because Love is God.
If you Love everybody you will become God.

As God, you'll never hurt your own creatures. This makes the difference.

Love is natural.
Console your mind and make it listen.
Love all or it is not Love.
Make your mind love this way
and you will see the magic of this everyday.

Then other people will come close to you. When they do don't hurt them.

Is the feeling of love for a loved one a creation of the mind?

Love of "other" is mind. Love for the Self is not a creation of the mind.
To love someone else is a creation of the mind and will not give you a good
experience. You can only love Self. Mind is destroyed when you Love your
Self, and you can't Love your Self with the mind.

Papaji, my husband is a spiritual seeker and wants to focus on that,
but I still want to have sex and a baby, can you help?

All activities are possible in no-mind.
Actually, when you are meeting so close together
it is a form of natural meditation,
though this is a different yoga than what I speak of.
Do everything with no-mind.
Sleeping together with no-mind is called meditation
and this is called the beauty of Love.
You become one, you are one,
and you will see that you are one.
You are not meeting anyone else,
you are not touching the physical forms of each other.
This happiness does not arise from your body,
but from another reservoir.
Don't forget about this reservoir
which gives you the bliss of this union.
Go to this reservoir during every activity
and you will see that the bliss is the same,
whether there is no activity or the best of activities.
You have to understand this secret.

I want to share my life with a woman. Is this a distraction?
Can you advise me?

Why don't you enjoy life like that famous teacher recently taught. He taught people to enjoy sex now because you didn't know what will happen tomorrow. The example he used is that the same ladder you used to come down you must use to go up. So it is sex which brought you into samsara so it is sex which will take you out and the bliss of sex is the bliss of Brahman.

My teaching is different: Neither coming down or going up! You don't need an old bamboo ladder which will break. Now there's elevators that bring you to the top floor of the Empire State Building in seconds. Get in this express elevator and press your own buttons! You don't need anyone else.

Inquire where you have come from and you will not be able to say. Stay Here. Here doesn't mean anywhere. Know you are always beautiful and fresh, shining everywhere. Understand this. Those who Love are the wisest of this world's six billion. Very few will know it:

> Because you are not to do anything and
> not to think about anything. This nobody knows.

Here there is no teaching, no past, no time, no future. Just know who you are and that is all. This is what you hear in Lucknow. You came from all nations here to Lucknow because there is no country which you belong to. You are the Self Within, untouched by earth, water, fire, air and ether. Instantly you will know this and this is why you have come.

Is it wrong to want to stay in duality in order to love?

If you love your own Self is it duality? If the wave loves the ocean is this duality? (giggles) It is not duality, but there is a way of thinking otherwise. Unless you know your Self, even your own body is duality. But in sleep there is no duality at all. Even your body is not there and is not duality. No relations are there because you are simply sleeping. So if you want to remove this duality feel that you are sleeping. Sleeping means not looking at others as others, but all as One. When you dream the duality arises. So many mountains and rivers arise when you dream, but when you sleep where do they go? It means that you create this duality. Otherwise all things are One. You create duality! I am here, somebody is there! I am a woman, somebody is a man. This is your own creation. When you wake up, everything at the first instant, instantly rises in front of you. Just an instant when you wake up from the formlessness of the sleep, everything is there in just one step out. Why should it be there? Where did you bring it? It means you create the universe! You create the relations! Where were they in the sleep, you don't even see your own body. No gods, no teachers, no students are there. Are you not happy without all these things?

ॐ

I feel that my boyfriend and I can help each other toward Freedom, but we both are so fearful of abandonment that we cannot commit to each other entirely.

You want to help each other toward God, and toward Freedom, but how can you do this with so much fear in your mind? I don't understand this language at all. Most people love each other and yet this fear of abandonment is there. This fear I find only in the West. Here in India we don't have this fear. So I advise you to be united with the very strong bond of marriage. The people who are afraid are those who are not married to each other, so they have fear. In India we marry and then it is finished. (giggles) You can't leave each other, there is no fear. You have to stay with each other until the end. This union will bring you very close to Divine Light. During the marriage ceremony the Vedic mantras will be chanted with the meaning that you have to walk together step-by-step, hand-in-hand, consulting each other before you do anything. Each one of you will give love and happiness to each other and not be interested in one's own self. You will live for each other. These marriages are permanent and eternal and with each other these people find Peace, Love, Light, Wisdom and everything. Don't have fear.

I had two friends who stayed in Paris for thirteen years without marrying because the man, Michael, would not agree to it because he thought he would be dominated and not allowed to see other girls. So, I scolded him and told him how special this girl was and that she had lived with me in Rishikesh. I was very angry with this boy, very angry, and so I pushed him out of his own house! (giggles) I had forgotten I was his guest! It was the month of December in Paris and you can imagine how cold it was. So his girlfriend asked if she could give him a coat, "He will freeze Master, he will freeze, can I give him a coat?"

I said, "No, he is a very bad boy, a very bad boy." I didn't care. When I woke up the next morning I saw a sign on the door:

"Thank you Master, we are going to marry now!" So we performed a Vedic marriage with a yagna and homa. That was seventeen years ago and now they have three children. It is a very good marriage.

You have to commit entirely if you love someone. If you have fear you can't even meet God. So you must decide. This is my only advice. You can also live together without marriage if you have this understanding. Most of the sages, like Janaka, Vashishta, Maitri, Krishna, and Rama were all married. The problem with being unmarried is that people usually think and dwell on the opposite sex more than a married person does. Though outside there may be a yogic posture, inside there are disturbing thoughts. So why not be side by side? You can do whatever makes you happy.

ॐ

My partner causes me to suffer so much. I want to be free of this distraction!

As the ass kicks the donkey and yet the donkey keeps following behind her trying to smell under her tail. Again the ass kicks and again the donkey with a bleeding nose continues to follow her. At this time the donkey doesn't try to ask any questions about realizing God. It just keeps trying to smell under the tail! This is exactly how most people are! *Exactly!*

So you'll get what you want. You must be very sincere and honest. Then you can get it. It'll come if you have a pure heart. Then you'll get everything and all will be offered to you by nature. Try now or today or sometime during the span of human life. You will see how easy it is, but if you want two things at the same time it will not happen. Touch the nectar of love and see what is offered to you. Two things though, cannot go together.

We just can't break out of the rut we have developed together.

Forgive and forget. Look at your own mistakes and not to the other's mistakes. Then you can lead a beautiful life. But most people make the mistake of finding the other person responsible for the trouble while they themselves take pride in their own purity. They believe that they don't make mistakes themselves. To forgive is Divine, look at your own mistakes. You will see that it was due to your own mistakes that the misunderstanding arose. If a man makes the same mistake day after day then it becomes his nature and you must accept it.

Now stop thinking about your girlfriend! Enough is enough! You are in Satsang for two hours a day. You can give your girlfriend the other twenty two hours of the day to suck you, but give these two hours to Satsang, to your own Self. Do this and you will not repent later. This is Wisdom. Spend two hours for your purpose. Don't let your mind go out while you are in Satsang. Slowly you will see the prize you will get for keeping Quiet for two hours. More and more you must get attracted to what you actually are, the eternal Self, and not to body-mind-ego or anything with name and form which comes and goes.

> Discriminate between transient things
> and the Eternal Love that you Are.
> Then do whatever you want, whatever you please.

My heart is so filled with love and gratitude. Even though this love is always there it is sometimes covered up with fear, and disappears.

Love doesn't disappear at all,
but this word love is mistaken for lust.
Love is pure, it cannot change.
If you once fall in Love with your own Self,
there is no escape from it.
But when it comes and goes,
some person must be involved in it
and that is called lust, not love.

Several years ago I had a husband, a house, a job, and a child,
but the child died and the husband left, and I left the job.

This is what I say, your husband was involved in this "love." Here you
have the difference between love and lust.

Losing everything is a good sign. Otherwise, you never would have come
here. For the sake of Freedom everything can be lost, and in your case it was
in your stars to happen. You could not and cannot change anything and so
you should not think about it or worry about it. After all, what benefit can
you derive from relationships and for how long will you have these benefits?
When the sparrow which twitters in you flies off they will get rid of you as
fast as they can. This has to happen, so if it is going to happen tomorrow then
understand it today; then you will be happy. Otherwise you lose the game
that you are here to play. So take things as they come and be happy and lucky
on this occasion.

Now I experience an emptiness, but this emptiness keeps me apart from
others, especially males, though I long for a man.

There is no male or female in Emptiness. You must be experiencing
something else. You have been given some trouble by a male, but this doesn't
mean all males are bad. You can try to satisfy yourself with relationships, but
the time will come when you know that you don't need any relationship.
This is why kings get Enlightened: They have no more desires. Beggars are
not Enlightened because they are attached to their begging bowls and their
robes and malas. The kings have so many queens, and gold and diamonds
and elephants and maidens. The night comes when they realize that it is all
not enough.

There is a story in the Upanishads of a king who had two queens. One
was Maitri and the other Katiani. The king was sixty, Katiani was forty and
Maitri was twenty. Just imagine the taste of the king. Maitri was the beauty
of the land.

One night he saw a glimpse of the Truth and told the queens, "I have decided to leave the kingdom; tonight I divide all the kingdom and treasure and ministers and servants and army evenly between the two of you."

Maitri said, "When I came to you you said that I was the most precious thing in the world, and that you were more attracted to me then to anything else. So your desire to leave me is confusing. There must be something more beautiful than me because otherwise you would not be so foolish to leave me and the kingdom. So I will go with you and serve you and together we will find what is so beautiful. I give my share of the kingdom to Katiani."

They went into the forest together and both of them attained Freedom. This is the resolve that is needed: that you would even give up your kingdom. Not less than this will do and therefore the kings have done it and not the ordinary person who is so filled with desire.

Get this and you will be the king of the kingdom of heaven. If you attend Satsang with only the desire for Freedom in your mind, you will be rewarded someday. This you will gain, and you will lose nothing.

I feel that my fun life of music, tennis, girls, drinking and eating is distracting my spiritual growth.

Self realization doesn't tell you to shun the things that life needs to do! This Self is not so timid to do or not do something. Self is fullness and accepts anything that you do. You say you are distracted. This distraction has to be distracted from your mind. This Self is not afraid of girls.

Is suffering needed to balance the enjoying?

If you are trained in the yoga I speak of, there is no suffering, only enjoying. If something is there you enjoy it and if it is not there you enjoy all the better. After you are with the girls you sleep and you enjoy this better than anything else, even though you are not with them anymore. So, this is the trick:

> Whether you are alone
> or busy with the activities of the world,
> you should not differentiate!
> Feel as alone as you are when you sleep.

If enjoyment is there then enjoy it. If it is not there then enjoy that. Normally when you enjoy you must suffer, but if you learn the trick then suffering and enjoyment are the same.

You must know: if things are there then enjoy,
If they are not, it doesn't matter.

*My marriage has fallen apart and with it I feel that the part of me
which was married is dead now.*

This is a beautiful death. After this death you can come to Satsang, but
only if you leave him behind. He has left you, but have you left him?

I have left him.

Then don't speak of him. You really haven't left him. You have to be
strong. The weakness you feel is from the conditioning of male arrogance.

I want a new name to begin living anew.

Name is not important, what is beyond name is important. I will give you
a name of That so you forget the world of names and forms. But if I give you
this name you will have to vow not to touch anyone who has a name. This
is reasonable, isn't it? Sometimes I am very reasonable! Very good. Chello.

Why do you recommend people in Satsang to marry?

Why should you live alone? You can help each other in this relationship
that is greater than the relationship with father, mother, brothers, sisters,
children or friends. The husband and wife relationship is a very pure
relationship. I recommend a married life because it is this life which will give
you peace in the end. The friends which enjoyed your youth will not come
near you when you are old, but your partner will because you are one soul
in two bodies. It is very special and I can't explain it to the people of the West
because they don't know the relationship of husband and wife. It seems to
be out of fashion to be married.

There so much confusion in marriage in the West!

There is confusion before marriage, during marriage and after divorce.

What is the proper way of marriage if the purpose is realization?

Realization of the Self also is a marriage of the soul with the Paramatma.
Harmonious life between two is only possible when Freedom is their

common goal. I can tell you about the Vedic way of marriage. First you have to ask some special guests to your wedding ceremony:

> Earth is your Mother and so earth is worshipped first in any puja.
> All the elements are worshipped, as are all the directions
> and the gods and the sun and the moon.
> They are all called to the wedding
> as guests to witness and bless the puja.
> Then you eat honey, milk, curds and sweets
> so that your speech is sweet.
> You are married for Freedom.
> This is what you are moving through this species for
> and why you are a human this time.

What is true trust and devotion in the context of marriage?

The husband trusts the wife and the wife trusts the husband and there is no divorce, it is an eternal marriage performed before your birth. But Western marriage doesn't last long and people hitchhike between partners until they are too old for it. In the Vedic wedding you take an oath to not even look at another person. This marriage you cannot break. You walk around the fire three times which symbolizes the fire of life. Equality is shown by each taking a turn leading around the fire and each sitting on both sides of the other.

Can one attain enlightenment while married?

I believe, and the Aryan culture agrees, that you have to marry. If you don't you will keep the "other" inside your heart, and if you do they will be at your side. Sex is very important to everybody and so married life is necessary. If a lack of sex helped you to be Enlightened then eunuchs would be the first to be Free!

Your marriage is the most important factor in your life. Brahmacharya usually is taken to mean celibacy, but it means also to be with your wife or husband with the intention to produce children. Marriage is only Vedic. All other marriage in the West is not a marriage. Staying near your Self is real brahmacharya.

You have said it is good to be married, but my experience is it is better not to be.

In your case you spend all your time trying to be together and you never found a minute to be alone. It is the aloneness that makes you happy and not the time together. When you have no more desires you are happy.

Desirelessness is happiness. This only happens when you are alone without person, concept or object in your mind.

You can stay as a couple, but never forget the purpose of your life: Freedom! Two people can be together as husband and wife if they both have the desire to be Free. Then there is no harm. The partner you have been with wanted you only for physical enjoyment so, of course, it did not work. You both have to be on the same track in order to be helpful to each other. There are so many couples here in Satsang living together and helping each other. Avoid those partners who only suck and lick your skin.

Isn't it a trick of the mind to think I need a marriage partner?

The trick of the mind is that you think you don't need freedom. Be wise. You can select a partner, but make sure they're on the same track. Marry the person who you are balanced with.

I want to be Free and I want to meet a man.

Both things are not going to happen. One at a time! (giggles) Either you are busy with a man or with your own Self. But I will give you a trick; first be busy with your Self, then if you are busy with a thousand men, you will not be touching any of them.

I am usually so blissful when I am alone and I forget who I am when I am with other people.

You can only be blissful when you are alone and not when you are with someone else. When you are with someone else you can't be happy because there is always a fear that the person may leave. There will always be this fear unless you learn how to live alone without "other."

From morning to night you are always jealous and in fear and conflict. But when you sleep the fear is gone because you are alone. Not even your body is with you. You are alone when there is no contact with body, intellect, or senses; then you are happy.

Is there a time in the life of a devotee when it is better not to have sex?

Sex and devotion can run concurrently.
Are you satisfied now?
There is no clash between sex and the search for Truth,
because Truth is beyond all;
Beyond every concept and activity.

Truth is not involved in anything.
It is absolutely immaculate and untouched.

Sex can be continued if you take care of yourself. One way to do this is to keep on laughing because then you won't get old. So when you have sex you laugh and tell me what happens. Laughter always is the best song.

Self Realization is pure and cannot be polluted by semen or any effort. It is untouched. So with all these, Self Realization can still happen. In the Upanishads there is a story of a prostitute who wanted to be free and started going to all the swamis seeking help, because she heard that peace was available in the ashrams. But the swamis told their students to turn her out. Everybody rejected her, so she decided to find peace herself.

She kept quiet, but the regular customers kept on banging at the door. When they walked in they saw her meditating and her face was aglow with light. Then they sat around her and started meditating, forgetting the purpose of their visit. This makes the difference.

You are not to specialize your habits in order to win Freedom because Freedom is free of everything. Most saints tell their student to live a special kind of life, but ask the swami if he is not a product of sex himself! None of them have won Freedom.

So there is no particular rule about it. "I want to be free," is quite enough. It has nothing to do with your circumstances as I have pointed out with the story. For sex you need two bodies, but Self doesn't belong to one sex or another, or any body. I have children and I have grandchildren, and I have great grandchildren too, and none of them have held me up. You don't need to be without sex. How can I produce children without sex? Everything was there and I didn't reject anything.

Does the quality of making love make a difference?

The quality of making love certainly makes a difference and this love is with your Beloved One. That will make the difference. Make love with your Beloved. Do you know who your Beloved is? It is someone who you have missed and that Beloved is waiting for you. So fearlessly you should go, straight away to your Beloved. This will be a very special meeting for the first time. Then you will become pure without thoughts, looking at your Beloved.

What should one do about the sexual drive?

Drive it! But make sure you remove the concept of "otherness" before you do and then look within. Then you are in Love. Now what are you thinking?

There is Silence.

Go deeper into unfathomable Silence. Don't touch mind, touch only Love.

ॐ

Papaji, I have three questions. The first one is why are the sexual experiences so attractive to the ego? The second question is, is the desire to be free of desire still a desire? Why can't ego live without desire? Can I be free without renouncing the world? The third question is why do I fear death so much?

Your questions are about sex, freedom and death, in that order. I think the second question should have been first. "How to be free?" should have been the first question. All the other questions indicate that you want to be a slave of your sexual desires.

I want to be free of these desires!

That is the second question only. You want to cling to your sexual desires. But these desires cannot be fulfilled. You need another person to fulfill these desires. How long can you stay with this other person? Could it be more than a minute?

A few minutes.

Two minutes, okay. Then after this two minutes didn't the sexual object kick you at your back? You can see this on the Lucknow roads. A donkey fulfills its desire and still runs after the ass only to be kicked in the face again and again. With a bleeding nose he still follows her! This is what will happen to everybody!

It is the donkey's nose, but your mind which is bleeding. Your mind is bleeding! It is always going to the past to remember what you had done and so it cannot enjoy the Presence. Presently you cannot enjoy the Presence! All this enjoyment comes from the past because all desire belongs to the past.

Yes, it always comes from the past.

Your enjoyments belong to the graveyard, the past. So now, desire for the present happiness.

But why won't these memories go away?

Memory! Now I will tell you how to be happy. All desires need someone else so that you can fulfill the desire. But happiness does not come from another person, though you attribute to them. It is like a dog who chews on a dry bone until its own tongue and gums start to bleed and the dog enjoys the taste of the blood thinking that it comes from the bone. So it is the instant when you are finished with your desire that gave you happiness, not the object of your desire. You need to separate from the object of desire to be happy and so if it really was the object which made you happy, you wouldn't need to separate from it. When the work is finished the mind returns briefly to its Source because it doesn't have another object. That time nobody knows because the mind is in its Source, and there is only happiness. But then you see another object and your memory is engaged and you do it again. Like this you spent millions of years not knowing that the happiness comes from within you. When you know this there is no question of renouncing anything or even getting rid of your physical desires because you know happiness is within and so no physical attachment or relation can trouble you! If you have to eat food it will not stand in your way. Like this all your body's requirements and biological desires are dealt with. They are all equally important. Don't give any more importance to the desire for sex than the desire for food. Just always keep in mind that I Am the Source of happiness, and enjoy. But don't get involved with it because that is only a body involved with another body. Just see that both the bodies are enjoying. Let them enjoy. This is a very simple trick. Just enjoy, witness it, and don't get involved in it. The one who is involved is different than the witness.

Can you answer my third question?

Look at the faces of those sitting behind you. So many people have benefited from what has been said. They have such peaceful and happy faces, but you didn't get it. You will just have to suffer for another thirty five million years. You are an Indian and you are not getting it. That is why so many people are coming from the West. You must be ashamed of yourself. (He points to woman nearby) The answer to your questions is written in the tears of joy on this girls face! Your face looks like a sheep. When there is Peace there must be rain, but your eyes are as dry as the bones of a dead ass!

Kabir used to try to help people, but "none has been helped," because nobody came to him for Satsang. Kamali, his daughter, said to him: "Father, you are wasting you time, nobody comes to you for Satsang." The next morning nobody came.

Like you they came for some other purpose. I know your purpose, but I will not disclose it because you will not like it. The people who come to find their own source of happiness will instantly get it. This is the kind of help that is available to you now if you look.

It is up to you, if you are bent upon not getting it, it is your choice, I can't force you. You are welcome to come here and I will do the best I can to serve you, but if you don't need this service I am happy with you. You can do what you want. You can have sex with 365 women like the former Sultan of Lucknow did with his 365 wives. You can still see the houses that he built for his wives and the summer quarters which were built under the river. But even with so many wives he was still hungry for sex, and he died this way.

The English came and attacked Avadh under the command of Colonel Young. Everybody ran away except for the Sultan. He just sat where he was and continued to drink. The Colonel came to him and asked him why he did not run away when he had a chance. The Nawab's reply was that there were no servants to put shoes on his feet. This is the luxury that he had enjoyed. So why don't you enjoy a woman everyday of the year. You say your question is unanswered. Well I can't help you anymore.

Papaji, I have experienced the death of my ego just now.

The depth of your ego?! Chello!

As a child I was abused physically and emotionally and it is still a distraction.

I know this is difficult, but you should not carry so much excess baggage filled with dead rats. Try to forget the past and stay here for awhile.

But I was raped by my grandfather, my father and my uncle when I was young.

Of course you can't forget this so easily. This memory will stay for a long time, but here you will come to know that you are not this body which has been abused. You will know that you are the soul, the Atman, and that nobody can touch Atman. Atman has no relations because it is everything. This is true. You are Atman, you are Untouched. Know this. It will work.

I have also always been so fearful since this. I have been able to forgive them, but this fear persists. I push the fear away during the day by keeping physically busy, but at night it comes back.

Physical activity will not help, you must keep your mind busy. It is like the newly weds at the office who can do their work but can't keep their minds off their spouse. Keep your mind busy with the question, "Who am I?" This question will keep you busy. Always investigate who you are, where you came from, and what your purpose is. Then you will forget everything else including all relationships. Keep your mind inside. Concentrate all the time on this advice. I know you can do it because it is the injured mind which is more capable of reaching Peace. Don't worry. Stay Here for your stay, in happiness, and when you go, leave your baggage of worries here.

All the children who have been abused in their childhood somehow should not carry this for their whole life. Past is past. It takes time but somehow you must forget. You are advised to forget the past. The parents who abused their children will reap the fruits of their sins. You have not done anything wrong, so why should you cry? They will cry here and in the hell. So you have to forget it!

I was sexually abused by my father, but now I am experiencing such clarity and the ability to deal with this and how it has affected my entire life. I had a longing for a father who would not betray me and I even didn't trust you.

Of course, when you are afraid of a snake, you will also be afraid of ropes lying in the path which looks like a snake. Many people have come here with this problem and slowly they have forgotten it. It takes time to heal, this wound is very deep. So don't worry. As a fence protects a field so the parents must protect the child and if they themselves are abusive, who can save the child? So the wound is deep.

The joy of letting this old story go is overwhelming. It has also helped to have a partner who is truly Here.

It is often useful to divert yourself and so this boyfriend is a very good remedy that you have picked up. The more you get attached to a natural loving relationship the more you will forget about the unnatural relationships of the past.

I have so much love and gratitude for you.

ॐ

Occupation and Money

Before coming to you I was a therapist. Now I am wondering what will happen when I go back.

You will be a better therapist because you will have greater understanding and much greater compassion. Simply your touch and your sight will help people and this is compassion. Before this work was a profession for you, now it is a compassion.

You can do whatever you want to do wherever you want to do it. Wherever you will be you will be Here, so all of this is your domain. Wherever you will be you will be in Consciousness. This is your abode, your place, your Happiness. Work in this peace and happiness and teach all your friends to be happy. Give them this simple secret on how to be happy and you can do whatever you want. This secret will work itself, by Itself, within Itself. There will be no doing on your part, no pride of ego. You see, you will be working in a totally different way. Your work and your actions will not be dictated by mind and ego. You will be very spontaneous and natural.

This work is not a hindrance to Peace and inquiry. Any occupation you can continue with the grace of the teacher. People of all occupations have been Enlightened: carpenters, barbers, kings, and weavers. Just stay with the teacher if you want Enlightenment and it has to happen. I wish you the best of luck. Bon voyage.

Thank you so much!

It is very good that you came here. I Love You.

I am a writer and I feel that if I pick up my pen I won't be free.

This is not what I am speaking! To work you need your physical body to carry on your physical activities. These activities you carry in the waking and dream states, but you don't have them in the sleep state because there is no mind in the sleep state. You don't need mind for Enlightenment and you don't need any activity. Let your hand go on working, but know that inside there is something which is always Quiet. This Quietness is never disturbed.

You can love That in your heart, but it will not interfere with your daily activities, so these activities can be continued. It is like a woman who is in love with the neighbor. Her husband goes to the office and her children go to school and she takes care of them better than other wives so that they do not 'smell' that she loves the neighbor. But as soon as they are gone she jumps the wall to be with her beloved. Like this you must love your Beloved. Keep this love sacredly and secretly in your heart and nobody will know, but outwardly you can be busy with so many things.

ॐ

Papaji, my job in Germany is very 'minded.' I have to think a lot. Is there any way to combine this work which requires so much thinking with being quiet in the mind at the same time?

You can look after your projects better when you are quiet in mind. If your mind is disturbed you can't do a good workshop, you can't even teach. Suppose you came to work at ten o'clock, but before you came to work you had a fight with your wife and she showed you a chappal on your head. How will you teach? You can't. But if you are Quiet you will have forgotten about what happened in the house when you enter into your workshop. Whatever you do you are Quiet, but you do not know it. You can test it yourself: before any manual work, before speaking, before thinking, you are quiet. Do you follow what I speak about? Before any activity, mental or physical, you are quiet, and so the activity comes from Quietness. If you remain quiet throughout your work it will be very beautiful. You only forget you started from Quietness just as a child starts with laughter, but forgets this joy as people abuse him more and more. But if by good luck this child attends Satsang he will remain as he Is. This is the beauty. You are not to forget your inherited nature and your nature is Quietness. With Satsang train yourself so that you are always happy and Quiet, because unhappiness, suffering and tension is not your natural state. To have good work you must combine this Quietness with it. Good work will always happen when you are Quiet. When you are not disturbed. Then only the goodness will come out of your work. So many of the great discoveries of the great scientists occurred in this Quietness. Even things which are beyond hope of success will be successful when you are Quiet!

Sometimes I feel I must give up my work and become a real seeker.

This is not necessary. A real seeker does not mean that you have to leave your family, your house, your country, and go to the caves of the mountains. Nothing will happen. It is not that the cave will give you Freedom, it is your ambition! Your ambition that "I am going to be free in this life" is quite enough. Keep this ambition alive! Whether at work or out of work. This will pay you in the end. Even while working it will remain the same. Suppose someone has a toothache and they meet a friend going to the beach. They will say "first I will go to the dentist and get my tooth fixed, otherwise, I will not be able to spend good time with you on the beach because I will be in too much pain." So remove all your troubles if you want to enjoy on the beach. Remove every trouble that you have in your mind.

So, you can combine your work with this Quietness wherever you go, but your decision must be firm like a rock that "I am going to be free, I am going to be in peace, love, and beauty in this life span, in this year, today!"

I am a lawyer, but I fear that this will succeed in distracting me from the Truth.

Do not fear and continue the work which has come to you. You are an advocate, so help the innocent people when they are in trouble. Advocates are needed for this. Know the laws and give advice accordingly. It is a good profession, don't worry.

> Whatever profession is given to you,
> do it with full consciousness and awareness.
> Perform it as demanded of you.

In ten days I am going to join the Israeli Army. I do not know if it is the right thing to do, though it is compulsory.

Go to the army and practice what you have learned here in Lucknow. It will work. I was also a soldier in the army and it didn't make any difference.

An army man is better placed because he has a weapon and understanding side by side. Lift up your rifle only when needed. It is a good safeguard to ensure that no one attacks you. Also in the army you must be alert, like you are in Satsang, and you will also learn concentration and meditation better than a typical civilian. They will also teach you concentration when you align the sights of your rifle with the target. Then you will practice pranayama, breath control, because you must shoot between the breaths and the heartbeats.

You can be helpful to your country. They have a reputation for having good soldiers. The country with a strong army will stay independent and not become dependent slaves. I always feel that man should be as brave as a soldier. You cannot meditate if you are not strong enough. Freedom is Freedom. Freedom from invaders, freedom from the ego, freedom from mind and everything else. You have to win freedom for yourself and it won't work unless you are strong and your circumstances are favorable: unless they are peaceful and lovely, you can't practice anything. First look at the neighborhood, it is more important than your apartment.

Kabir was a weaver living among a community of rascals and thieves who would spit on him as he walked by. Though he tried to help them, eventually he just kept quiet. He said:

> Kabir you are living among the stupid people.
> You just keep quiet and let others reap what they sow,
> the fruit of their karma.

Ego is more wicked than any men you will ever fight, so you have to be careful. When you have to meditate, sit Quiet and search for Freedom, see to it that these enemies do to touch you. This neighborhood of mind, ego and senses is not good. We are all living in the company of these wicked enemies and we do not know when they are going to attack us, though most people are happy with these attacks. You have to be like a warrior and fight the traps and tendencies set by the ego. Fight by totally surrendering yourself to Peace. So let go! Keep Quiet. Sit down and don't worry who does what. They will reap the fruit of their karma. This is how to live wisely in this world. Very few people have lived this way.

> Always face the Self.
> If a thought comes let it come,
> if it stays, let it stay, if it goes, let it go.
> If you are on a battlefield, fight.
> If you are in the forest, keep Quiet.
> And whatever you do, forget it, and focus on Self.

When I was twenty years old I was drafted into the Australian Army and spent a year fighting in Vietnam. Now twenty five years later, the nightmares still haunt me and my nervous system is shattered. I often consider that life is not worth living, though I also feel very close to a beautiful void which I know is my True nature. Please guide me home.

Why do you fear fighting? Every soldier has to fight as you did. I also fought, but I was not troubled if I had to fight or I didn't. Fear arises when you are in front of a soldier of another country. The void that you speak about is the same as when someone is pointing an LMG at your chest and you are pointing a Three-naught-three at theirs. At that time there is a void. (giggles) Nobody knows who the killer is and who is killed. You need not be afraid of either. Your duty is to fight for your country and you did this. It is better to die fighting for freedom than to live as a slave.

How do you come to this void that you know that you are? Void means that you don't see any person, concept or object.

> There is no difference between Freedom
> and the place with no person, concept, or object.
> So then you must stay as such always.
> This is your fundamental nature,
> don't be afraid.

> Here is Beauty, Here is Love, Here is Eternity,
> why be afraid of it? Here is Peace and Bliss.
> No one can taste it because they fear the void.
> This is your home and it is where all must return.

> Let it not be too late or you will repent later.
> Therefore, now is the time.
> Just spend an instant on you, on this void.
> An instant, a fingersnap, a second, half a second,
> half of a half of a second is quite enough.

You should ask how you didn't get it. Nobody has spent this half of a second. Though people may live for one hundred years they cannot spend an instant on themselves because they are hunting something else. They want some person or object to be with. Now you do it here; in this second that I speak about do not think. For one fingersnap do not think and do not make any effort. Then tell me what happens.

I said don't think! You are still thinking. When you do not think your face will be very different. Try to do it now, though trying is not really needed because you will only try those things that you have heard of or read about. Trying is always for something of the past, not for what is immediately present. The present doesn't need any thinking. When you don't think you will see that you have achieved everything worth achieving. Then you will not repent even in the face of death! And when death does come, she will be afraid of you! Try it. (giggles) Do you have anything more to ask me?

I do not know what not trying means.

The trying, the trial, must belong to the past. Tell me what does not belong to the past. Tell me what you have tried that you have not heard from some person. It comes from the past and so your accomplishment belongs to the past. But This is not the past because it is not time. There is no past, no future, and no present. So you will get it by not trying, not making any effort.

Living Skillfully

Now do you understand the meaning of trying?

Yes, Yes!

When you do not try you are Quiet, but when you try you are in trouble!

I so enjoy being in your presence. How can I live in the world without throwing away things and without holding on to them. It is like the choice of either throwing your money out the window, putting it in the bank, or giving it to friends.

I will tell you how the wise use money by taking you to the banks of the Ganga in Calcutta. There was a man there who had some coins on his right side and some pebbles and stones on his left. With his left hand he throws a stone into the Ganga and with his right he throws a coin. Then he saw whether or not there was a difference. Like this he threw them in everyday. Whatever money came to him he would throw into the Ganga. Finally, he found no difference between the stones and the money. This man was no other than Ramakrishna Paramahamsa. See money for what it is and don't be trapped by it. We must learn from these stories. I was in Madras in 1945 when I read this story of Ramakrishna. After I read it I went to Marina Beach and threw everything I had into the sea, not even saving the bus fare home to Mount Road where I was also working.

One day my wife and children wanted to come with me. Generally, I went there alone on a Saturday night and would spend the whole night until dawn meditating. So I said to my wife, "When I come here I throw away everything that I have and so you must do the same. Throw away your jewelry from your hands and ears and feet and neck." But she didn't want to do it because she couldn't understand why.

About a week later our house, which we rented from a school teacher who lived below us, was robbed. This man below us had six daughters and a boy with polio who couldn't walk. Just look at the fortune of this man! We were coming home from the temple where the Krishna Janmastami celebration was going on. As we approached our house I could see the school teacher descending on a ladder down from the balcony of our house. We went into the house and discovered that all my wife's jewelry had been stolen along with all the money, all the saris, and the rent receipts. I knew that the landlord had taken them, but I assumed he took them to keep them safe in his part of the house.

After a few days I received a legal notice from an advocate that I had not paid the rent for a year and I had to pay. But since he had stolen the receipts what could I do? He was very much in need of money and I had actually paid three months in advance!

So I appeared before the magistrate and explained everything, and how this teacher was so in need of money to support his family and to pay the necessary dowries for all his daughters.

The magistrate asked, "Did you lodge a police report about the theft?"

I replied, "No, I saw him take the items and thought he would return them."

The magistrate understood and could see that I was honest and so he said, "Poonjaji, in these days you take care because this kind of honesty does not help you." The case was dismissed and as we were moving out of the house the neighbors told me that he does this with every tenant.

So you must use your discrimination and do the right action at the right time. We have discrimination and we must use it before we do things. This is what this story is about.

On the seventh day of the dismissal of the case the only son of the teacher died. Soon after this man was bitten by a snake and died at the age of fifty. If you cheat someone the nature is not going to leave you alone. You will experience the consequences.

I asked his wife and children if they knew that this was the result of what he had done. He could not bear it and had to die. Then I asked them about the stolen jewelry which I knew that she knew about because she had been holding the ladder for her husband, but she totally denied it. I couldn't believe it, even though her husband had died and the case was dismissed she still spoke lies. Yet I offered my help to her. So this is the world!

You are helping me to get rid of my attachments with money?

You may be attached to money, but money is not attached to anyone. It comes, stays and goes. This question must have come from the money because it does not want to stay with you. Money never stays with anybody.

Just be Quiet and don't worry and the blessing will be with you.

I feel that I have come home and so I would like a new name to celebrate and to have for guidance.

I will give you the name which means wealth, but you must use this wealth wisely and not like some foolish rich people.

When the Shah of Iran fled to America they checked his hand baggage and found a huge fortune of diamonds. Now what will he do with all these stones while in exile? He can't eat them! If he would have used some of this money to help his people and his country he would have stayed the Shah and

Iran would have been a happier place. This is the duty and purpose of the rulers and the rich. But instead he was greedy and look at what ruble Iran and the world has now! Just because of greed. Like this so many people have so much money and diamonds and think that they are rich. The truth is they are not rich at all, not at all!

So be wise with the money that is given to you and know what true wealth is.

ॐ

Raising Children

When do we first start to become aware of the ego and when does "I" first start to rule our lives?

This is a very good question that nobody asks, "When does the ego start?" How and why does the ego start is a very good question.

It starts with the parents, I think. They introduce relationships and hence the ego starts to separate and the child belongs to sisters and brothers and relations! Then a priest baptizes you and tells you that you are a Christian or Buddhist or a Muslim. And the ego starts to think that it is superior to others because a priest said that others will go to hell, but you will go to heaven. So there is a religious ego as well as one of the country, thinking that your country is somehow superior. Like Americans who think themselves superior to all and this is true in terms of money and warfare. This just supports ego, like the way the world goes to America for food and education. The ego "I am German," or "I am American," or "I am Indian" is a barrier that is very hard to remove. But when you do you will be a person belonging to the earth which is common. The sun is the same in Asia, Africa or Alberta. It is the same sun and the same mother earth, the same sky and the same breeze, but we don't accept this which is common to all. If our relationship is based on wisdom we will know that we all belong to one earth, one world, one universe. Then you will be able to understand the environmental oneness and you will sit in peace within. How can you sit in peace when you are afraid that your neighbor is attacking you? When this fear comes you can't sit Quiet, you can't meditate, you can't have any Satsang. So you must ward off the ego before you can start to be peaceful. Have no fear.

My daughter is just starting the terrible twos. Is this the point where a person develops ego and moves away from a natural state of consciousness?

I think the natural state of consciousness does not exclude your children, your relations or anybody. Rather it includes everything. It includes everything and you are not to exclude yourself from anyone to be consciousness yourself. This Self contains everything and yet you can advance towards it.

Some people don't understand and think that they shouldn't love their children and their relations so they run away to the caves to be alone, but they are never alone. So I do not advise that one must reject everything. To realize your Self, you are not to take such a step.

Sometimes she demands things very strongly, like toys or ice cream.

So you are identifying as that "sometime." Why not identify time as time. You consider it your time and so in this time you have to do such and such thing. You have not yet understood how to see from a larger perspective. So if anything comes let it be done through you. Then you will have no problem with "sometimes." Whatever comes just react, just react. If a child is there then kiss her. If she needs food then give food. This is the way of living wisely.

You express a fear that she is going to leave her natural state of cons·iousness. Truth does not leave you. You can stay. From Truth we came and ;o Truth we will return and in the Truth we live. If you have this understanding you will not hate anyone, but you will love everybody.

How can I help guide her? Will you help me so that I can help her?

You must have full faith in yourself that you can stay wherever you are and that all action is done by That which is within. I am glad that you are taking care of the child and that you ask your questions. So many people keep their doubts but do not open their mouth. There are so many mothers, but they do not speak these things that you do. You are a lucky mother, because coming to Satsang is Absolute good luck!

Stay on here for some time and you will know how to raise your children, how to raise your own Self, and beyond all how to raise something else which you do not know. It is not your children or your body but something else. Slowly you will know what this 'something else' is which you have never known or heard of.

Health and Healing

Why you need a healthy body

Being a temple of God,
the human body is a very rare gift of nature.
It is a raft by which you can cross the ocean of samsara.
Respect and adore this human birth, do not waste it.
Take very good care of your body and mind,
don't put the Diamond in a plastic bag.

You have to take care of your health
because it takes a strong body and mind to be Free.
This strength and health has to be channeled:
a strong body can sit in a strong posture
and a strong mind can make a strong decision.

Keep the blessed form of your body in good shape.
Healthy mind and body is important for freedom
because when the body and mind are sick
the focus goes toward sicknesses and hospitals.
Sickness and weakness steal too much attention
to allow focus toward That.

No pain is bearable or permissible!
You should keep your body and mind
as pain free as long as possible.
This is very important.

Good health, strong mind, and desire for freedom
is an excellent birth. Your body is your boat,
don't let the water of samsara in.

How to keep a healthy body

The worst pollution to the body is bad thoughts
and the worst thought is "I am the body."
Your diet is also important so eat sattvic food.
Simple food cooked with love and eaten with friends
is tastiest of all, so take good care for your food.

Know Consciousness cannot be touched,
it cannot be sick and it can't meet with an accident.
Only the body becomes sick and meets with accidents and dies.
Truth has no beginning or end.

The Causes of Disease

You need a healthy body as a vehicle,
but if you take yourself to be this vehicle you will suffer
because "I am the body" is the origin of pain.
All diseases are minor complications of the disease
of not knowing the Atman.
So first take care of yourself, know your Self,
and then take care of others.

All diseases are from previous births
and are carried into this life in the genes.
The exception are those due to accidents
which are carried in by karma alone.

A mind attached to anything becomes a sick weak mind.
A weak mind will keep going to the garbage of attachment
and this causes the nervous system to get squeezed and weakened
so it can not handle this very energetic decision for Freedom.
A strong mind is needed to make the strong decision
and handle the power that will come with it.

Do not fault beautiful nature for your poor health,
it is your responsibility to stay healthy
and to keep your body and mind in harmony with nature.
Sickness is not the fault of the rain or dampness or heat,
but is the fault of your poor habits and foolish decisions
and your weaknesses caused by these habits and decisions.
Otherwise, there would be no sickness.
Mind engaged in the past will make you sick.
The body itself is a sickness.
In this living Moment no one is sick.
Know "I am not the body"
and you will be free from disease.
Leave behind everybody, even "I,"
and who will jump into this Freedom,
and where is this Freedom?

All pain belongs to objectification.
Pain is only in the head, not in the heart.
Heart needs no healing because nothing touches it,
only memory hurts, not heart,
only concepts suffer, not reality.
"I am body" is "I am suffering."
The body itself is a pain, "I have a body" is a pain.
The body is inert, it itself cannot suffer
only the concept of "I am the body" can suffer.
There must be past if there is pain.

Mind uses life-force to fulfill vasanas and desires.
Too many vasanas and desires can drain the life-force out of you
leaving you weak and open to disease.

What you think you become and so
consolidated vasanas become the physical body
and dormant vasanas manifest as the cycle of birth and death.
Pure thoughts lead to pure vasanas and tendencies.
Pure vasanas lead you to health, Satsang, and Freedom.
Impure vasanas lead you to disease, mischief and destruction.
It's not in the lot of everybody to be happy and rid of old habits.

The Healing of Disease

First you must decide
that you want to be free of pain and suffering.
Without wanting this nothing else will work.

Inquiry is simply looking unto your own Self
and this is how you will remove your illness.
Direct your mind to Consciousness and do not stir a thought.
Here and Now look unto your own Self.
Stay Quiet: no reasoning, no understanding.
Looking to "other" brings misery and sickness.
Give up all notions, mind is a notion itself, so get rid of it
and you will be free of pain and suffering.
When "I" has dissolved into the Self
then everybody is healed.
So heal yourself before others.

All diseases can also be cured by prana,

even the disease of bondage.
Prana is an energy which can be utilized for Freedom
but with prana you still need an "I."
With Awareness you do not.
Though we usually use the mind and awareness for Freedom,
prana also will work but it needs special food and circumstances.
Prana should not be disturbed by poor food and circumstance.

Physical ailments and mental diseases must be removed.
The firm decision "I am not sick"
will cure you because you are what you think.
So whatever you think you will get:
think you are fine and you are fine,
think that you are in hell and you are in hell.
Think "I am suffering," and you are suffering.
Replace the thought "I am suffering"
with the thought "I am free, I am Freedom,
I am Consciousness, I am not the body."
Do not kiss your ego by saying "I am suffering,"
rather kiss yourself by saying "I am Free."

Healing your body is like doing the laundry.
First know your Self and then your body will be healed.
Body is just a state of consciousness,
know the Substratum, this is Reality.

You can use therapy to heal when needed, but don't get lost in it.
Just find the source of sadness and mental suffering
and Innocence will reveal itself.

To forgive and forget is the best medicine for curing all pain.
Let the thought that causes pain come into the present
and discharge into Emptiness.

Do this Now!

*Why do we have to give up the world of forms in order to be identified
with Self?*

I do not tell you to give up form to be identified with Self. This form is
the temple of God, you have to appreciate this form as you do god in the

temple. This body is the temple. You have to worship it and keep it up very well. Don't waste this life and body by fasting. Don't be like some people who are so weak and unhealthy that they can't even sit in an asana to meditate. When they do sit they fall asleep because the are to weak. So eat well and live well. This form is a gift from God so that you can recognize That within it.

Can meditation help physical ailments?

Yes, I have seen it many times. One woman who sat just once with me was cured of juvenile diabetes. Meditation will cure, but you must have full faith in what you want out of your meditation. Wisdom, light, and love will also be given by this meditation when you have a strong desire to get rid of physical ailments, because mental ailments are also cured.

In some physical and mental diseases people seem to go into a space of no-thought. Is this also no-mind?

No. No-mind gives you happiness, not suffering. The state of dreamless sleep is similar to no-mind because sleep gives you happiness. The dream and waking state have mind, but not the sleep state.

What you talk about is when the mind is in so much tension it can't function. This is a sick mind, not no-mind. With a healthy mind your body, thoughts and activities also are healthy. Be with those who have a sick mind and see that their needs are taken care of. This is all you can do. If there is something bothering them you can change their circumstances. Whenever something old bothers you, you can do this. It helps a lot. If you are in a situation that is peaceful, then carry on. But if you are somewhere which disturbs your health, your mental health and your neurological health then you should stop it. Think about the consequences that the affair at hand will give you.

Most diseases are brought from previous incarnations. Health is a matter of karma. Good health is good karma and poor health is bad karma. If someone doesn't use their good karma and health to win enlightenment it is bad karma and they are stupid, foolish and wasting their time. A sick person's mind is attached to fear and sickness so they cannot get Freedom. But those who are fearless and free of disease can devote this whole life to Freedom. It is best to spend this life in the pursuit of Freedom. So many people pursue sex and other short term satisfaction and not permanent peace; they follow in the footsteps of sheep. Be healthy and strong and follow your own path like a lion. Don't let yourself be herded. People get so unhealthy by thinking and even kill themselves by thinking. They never just do something. When they walk they think, when the drive they think and get into accidents. You seem to be young looking and healthy. How old are you?

I am fifty-three, but with a light in my heart it is very easy to look young.

And what food? Food is most important! You must have a vegetarian diet and spend your time with good people. The most important aspect of your life for living happily is your partner. They should be nice, sweet tongued, healthy and listening to you as a peer, not commanding you as a superior. This will relax you and give you a good life. To remain at peace select a person who is very nice to speak to and to live with. They must be equal. If you ignore this you will suffer. Together take good care of your habits and you will look younger than your age.

I prefer that you have vegetarian food. This diet will give you a peaceful mind because vegetables are sattvic. Eating animals can be very unhealthy because people take on their diseases and their unhealthy states when they kill and eat them. Use vegetables instead of meat and you will have a peaceful mind because your mind is the essence of what you eat. You can give the gift of this diet to your parents also.

ॐ

I have such a painful back injury that I am not able to sit or walk.
I have been weak for three years and several times I thought I might
die. How do I step out of body identification, especially when there
is such constant pain?

You cannot get rid of body identification when you are sick, so you have to get well and after taking care of your physical problems speak of other things. When a man is sick he is always identified with his pain whether he is in bed or out on the street. His mind is always on the pain. How can he inquire into his Self? It is not possible. Someone who is having a toothache may be working in the office, but he cannot forget his toothache. After work he will go to the dentist and so all day this dentist is in his mind. So it is not possible at all unless your body is very strong and your mind is still. Both body and mind must be very healthy and then you can speak about the realization of Truth. Otherwise, it is not possible. You are advised to take care of your problems. Show it to some doctors.

Sometimes I can watch and know that I am not this passing form...

It is not true, it is not true.

Living Skillfully

How do I break free of this physical pain?

You have to consult a doctor. Take good care of your body and mind so you can cross the ocean of desires. Take care of your body first and don't speak of Enlightenment before this. Pain must be removed or you concentrate on pain. When the vasanas and pain arise, be strong and look at it. Pain only leaves by discrimination, when you know what is real there is no pain.

The more pain there is the faster the thoughts arise. What can I do about this body that tortures me?

What is this pain about? Where did you get it and why did you accept it?

It comes from my mind.

And you accepted it? Do you like it?

No, I don't.

If you don't like something what should you do with it?

Throw it away.

So why don't you throw this out? Admit that you love it. If you truly do not like it it will instantly go away. If you vomit do you put this vomit in your pocket? Do you keep what the stomach has not accepted?

This is what suffering is:
Clinging to what should be let go of!
Nothing can bother you unless you cling to it.

Most people like pain and suffering and death and this is why it is there. You have to decide that you want happiness and it will be, because it is your nature and it is due! First you have to decide to be rid of this pain or nothing else will work. If you want to keep it no god can help you.

Everybody has been suffering for millions of years. Now you have a beautiful body so don't waste it. You may not have another chance for a long time. Simply say "I want to be free of all pains, all sufferings, and all deaths." All of us are here to make this decision here and now: "I want to be Free." Don't wait.

I get so angry and frustrated from it sometimes.

Anger is a curse which cuts short your life by burning the entire nervous system and troubling your breath. Express your anger and kiss what makes you angry. It is no problem to get angry. Just don't remember the circumstances which made you angry and don't carry anger or love. Forget everything.

I had no intention to come here, but suddenly I find myself in your Satsang due to my leukemia.

If you have a deep will for something it is fulfilled by good or bad circumstances. If you would have been a healthy woman you wouldn't be here. Six months ago the allopathic doctors gave you three weeks to live, but Ayurveda has kept you alive this whole time. I know for certain allopathy could not cure this disease, but in Ayurveda it can be cured if the doctor is experienced. I have seen it. There are some herbs which can cure it.

Now you are in Satsang and you will understand what life and death are. This understanding removes fear. I will give you a method that I use on people who are dying from a disease. This may even totally cure you.

Sometimes I feel very disconnected with everything and there is a great sadness because all suffering just cries out.

This body is connected with objects, but when you are ill those connections get cut off. It is the body which has relationships which come and go, not the Atman. Body means sickness. There is nobody in the world which is not sick. Even the babies have sickness following them. Body is disease itself and so it has to die. So it is better to give up the identification with the body. You are untouched and cannot die and you have no relations with anybody. This you must realize and then you will be free of sickness, whether the body is thrown out or not. Don't care for that.

I so much respect your unshakable commitment to Satyam, Shivam, Sundaram and how you destroy the darkness. In the last two and a half years I have not always been a good boy and often did not follow your good advice. Finally, all my bad habits led me to hepatitis which shook me up like never before.

You had hepatitis?

Yes, it was a good disease.

You had to stay in bed and look at your body, and your Self!

*Yes. I realized that if there is no body then there is no Buddha.
So now I am taking care of my body.*

It is good that you learn even from hepatitis. It is good to get a teaching
out of everything. You can learn from the disease also. It is a warning to a
person that someone has done something that he should not have done.
Perhaps drinking water or eating a food that he should not have. This
warning must be taken care of and treated as a lesson so that you do not
make any mistakes.

> Any disease that you get
> has something to do with your decision.
> Wrong decisions, wrong food, wrong association,
> and wrong environment are the causes of dis-ease.

You have to change them to get good health. With good health you can
do many things. With good health you can meditate, not otherwise. You can't
sit quiet if you have trouble in your eyes, nose, ears or anything on your skin.
Many people are suffering here and they say that they cannot keep peace.
Other than this you have a healthy happy body.

*I have always been connected to you beyond mind and world, though
we rarely had physical contact. May you be in your body longer than
any Buddha before. This world needs people like you who hold the
torch of Wisdom so well.*

You have been named after the Buddha and so you are well looked after
by your own Truth, but you wear Shiva on your chest.

It is a love affair.

Yes, learn about this. He has a trident in his hand and a dumulu in the
other. This dumulu, this drum, is the dance of Freedom he dances when the
world is destroyed. He is very happy after destruction. The snakes around his
neck mean fearlessness and the ability to drink the poison of the universe and
yet keep happy. The snakes are desires and he is fearless and immune to their
poison. This is his jewelry, his decoration, the trident in his hand and the
snakes around his neck and arms. He wears only a tiger skin and when I saw
him and Parvati on Badri Narayan they were sitting on a bear skin.
Everybody must be Shiva to be free of all the species of the universe. This is
not only a symbol, not only a legend, but everybody must be Satyam, Shivam,

Sundaram.

I am Shiva, I am the most beautiful person in the world.
I am peaceful. Satyam, Shivam, Sundaram:
This must be your wish in this life.

I am very happy to see you so happy and healthy.

I have been genetically tested and it has been confirmed that I have a fatal hereditary disease of the nervous system. I want your help.

You have fear in your eyes and it has spread throughout your body. Your skin is pale and it shows the fear also. You have to remove the fear. I will tell you a story of fear.

In the springtime in India we celebrate a festival of colors called Holi. What most people do to celebrate it is to throw colored powders and water on each other. One boy kept a bucket of blood red water in the bathroom that morning to throw on his friends, but his father accidentally used it to wash himself after he used the toilet. When he saw the toilet was all red he was instantly horrified because he thought it was covered with his blood due to some bleeding cancer. He thought he would be dead soon. He raced to the hospital where the doctors agreed with him: he was dying quickly. The scalpel was inches away from his stomach as he laid on the operating table when the phone call came explaining the Holi blood-red water. Instantly his fear was gone, his cancer was gone and his dying was gone. After all, only fear had made him sick.

So you have to remove the fear by disbelieving what the doctors say. You can remove the fear by meditation or by a mantra that I will give you.

I have been diagnosed as having cancer. I don't know if it is worth fighting, but also it doesn't feel right just giving up. I have been doing Vipassana meditation and reading books like I Am That. *Can you give me guidance?*

Would you have come to Lucknow if you had never had this disease?

No.

Would you have done Vipassana or read the book by Nisargadatta Maharaj?

Maybe.

Maybe not also. "Maybe" is doubt and those who doubt are not decided and they are not here. So this disease is welcome because it has brought you the understanding of how your life should change and it brought you here. Without this disease you would have just enjoyed your life with your partners and not turned to your Self. So this disease is welcome because it will make you fearless of death.

Life must end, and whether it ends today or tomorrow doesn't make a difference. You must know that this body is not so important and if it gets worn out you should change it with another body. It is like a t-shirt: once worn out you just throw it out and change to a new one. This life is a blessed life if you know you are not the body and not the mind. Knowing this where can any disease land? Disease comes only to the body and if you know you are not the body it cannot trouble you. So now forget about anything that is attached to your body. Leave everything. Forget all senses and objects of senses. What is left then? What is left if you forget about everything that is connected with your mind body and senses? What is left?

Just here.

So always think of "just here." Walking, talking, waking, dreaming, sleeping; only think of "just here" and the result will be that you will know "I am This" and not that. This is the purpose of life. We all have come here to know who our Father is and where he lives. We all have come to return to him.

This is what we do here in Satsang. We remind each other that we are only our own Self and nothing else. Find out who is your own Self. So think of this and talk about this and it will come forward to you and reveal itself to you. You must, however, be very true and pure in your desire to meet it. You must decide that you will meet That which you have missed for generations. This desire must be very firm. Stay here and see what happens.

Healers

I am a therapist working on the energy of people. Sometimes this gets out of control and goes spinning into pain, sadness, and anger.

Most therapists are not happy and not healthy because as they relieve others of their pain and suffering this all goes into their own minds and bodies. The therapist takes the pain and suffering even if they don't want it.

This is a trap of the attempt to have compassion.

It is better if you shift your profession. I can see that the pain of others has migrated from your mind to your face. The face is the index of mind. Get a profession which gives you happiness. Don't suffer at any cost. I feel that it is the business of the creator to look after the world. He can cure everybody of anything and everything, but what will you help?

Also this world is meant for a place to suffer and indeed everybody is suffering except a few like Saint Kabir. If you want to be happy and peaceful find another job.

ॐ

I own and direct a medical center in Berlin which keeps me very busy, but what I really want is the peace that I find with you. Do I have to sell my center in order to have this peace?

You don't have to close your clinic. Doctors are very useful to people and it is a good way to serve. This was originally a profession of compassion, though nowadays it is a profession more interested in making money than in showing compassion.

You can live a normal life and carry on with your center without compromising what you have found in Lucknow.

How can I use Satsang in my healing practice?

Do not forget your Guru. Whatever you do is not your responsibility but his. He will take care of everything. Just remember that it is the Guru that takes care of everything.

Is there a difference between healing and teaching?

When you are healing you cannot teach and when you teach you cannot heal. Healing takes a healer and a patient. The Teaching takes no teacher and no student.

Do you have any other advice for me as a doctor?

"As a doer," did you say? Remember that you are not the doer! You are a tool in the hands of the Divine. Stop inflating your doctor arrogance and serve people instead. Remember that you have the power to heal people by simply verbally consoling and reassuring them because they trust you. This trick is in the hands of the doctor: smile and tell them that they are all right.

Doctors may help people after they get sick, but if they eat the right food and breathe clean air they won't fall sick in the first place. So tell people how to stay healthy in the first place. Eating simple food prepared with love is one of the best medicines you could prescribe. This is even better than meditation.

I am a midwife. How can I remove the feeling of guilt and the fear of fighting with the 'authority' of the allopathic doctors. They have no respect for the midwife and say that using a midwife is irresponsible.

Don't listen to what they say and go on with what you are doing. It is a very good and compassionate job. Don't get afraid. You should also experiment more with water births.

I see colors on the faces of people which seem to indicate their inner spiritual and emotional state. What is the purpose of this? Can you tell me about it? I have been using this talent to give people advice.

These colors that you see are your own imaginations. There is no significant reason for it. What you are inside you see on the outside. If you are happy and loving you will see that the people are happy and loving. If you are sorrowful you will see that everybody is suffering.

So maintain your own health first. Maintain your physical, emotional, neurological, and your social health also. Social health is not very well known, but it is responsible to keep you healthy. If you are living among the sheep you will bleat like sheep only. So change your environment. It should be a good environment of like-minded people. Then you will be happy and you will see the same colors on all the faces.

Death and Dying

The reason why everybody wants to avoid death
is because Eternity is our real nature.

Death is not to be feared
because it is an enjoyable and happy occasion
and it only hurts one who has
anger, greed, attraction, and aversion.
Death only comes to an active mind.
Even the gods must face death.
All die but there is no grief because the Indweller lives.

Death is only the five elements returning to themselves.

The essence of wave, ocean, and raindrop
is still Water: nothing can be lost.
When a raindrop touches the ocean it becomes ocean.
So do not fear death for nothing can ever be lost
and nothing can ever be gained.
Death only takes those who have become something,
death only takes the body, the dress.
Death is a foolish notion.

Samsara is desire, desire is samsara.
Desire creates the dream and propagates it.
At the last moment of being in this body
all dormant tendencies, fears, and anxieties of the dream
will manifest before you.
The one that you are most interested in,
the dearest thought that you see in this stream of mental events,
will be your next birth!
Any footprints in your memory will be your next birth.
At this moment remember only Self.

Then when the heart stops,
the eternal Heart will take over.
So don't worry:
When death comes, go laughing!

*I am having such a hard time being free of the trauma of my
daughter's death.*

You are not in Satsang if you are thinking about your daughter. Let these
things be there. Who doesn't know the grave of a loved one? While here stay
here and not connected to the past. Make use of the present and what is
presented to you in the present.

*It seems to me that death is permanent and the focus of love is gone.
Is this so?*

If you remember that death is permanent then you will know how to deal
with things when they leave you someday. Even when your child was just
born the death was following her and one day or another she would be

swallowed by this monster as will all the other beings.

There is only one way to avoid death.
That is: Know Thy Self, Now.

Everybody is in a coma. Everybody is senseless and sleeping. So the best way is to not waste time. Don't look for tomorrow. Do it now and find out what the reality is of the beings that appear to you. In the dream you have a relation with a beautiful girl and you love with her for years. But when you wake up where is this wife? Like this you have had wives and husbands for many births, and brothers and sisters, where are they? They are a dream. Anything that appears and disappears must be a dream. What does not appear and disappear must be real. Find out what it is, within yourself. What is that something which has neither appearance nor disappearance? Find out now. Chello.

I want to die!

You can't! Your body may dissolve, but you cannot die. You are not the body, you will not die! This is the experience you will get here. You are beyond birth and death. You must settle this before the death of the body takes place. Understand what death and birth are. Stay here a few days and you will understand.

The idea "I am not the body" is totally theoretical to me. Can you make it practical.

You have to know that death is for the body and that you are That which will never die. There was a man and wife who lost their only son and so they took the corpse of their son to a saint and asked him to bring him back to life. The saint said it would be very easy to do. All that they had to do was to bring a handful of soil from a house where nobody had died. So the husband and wife traveled all over looking for a place where nobody had died, but of course, they could not find such a house. Everywhere everyone had experienced the death of loved ones. Finally they returned to the saint endowed with knowledge of death: whoever and whatever is born is born to die for death follows all name and form.

When there is Satsang there is no death because the one in Satsang knows that death is for the body only and they know that they are not the body. Death is for the name and form. The nameless and formless one will never die. That is the one who had no attachment with the body, mind, ego, senses or objects. Make this theory into practice by knowing your purpose. Is it to enjoy attachments or is it to be Free? Then your eyes will open and you will not be afraid of death.

I see some other fear in your eyes. What is this fear?

I fear that I will die right now. I feel that if I don't leave Lucknow I will die, but I feel like I can't leave.

This fear of death is in the mind and it is genuine because it will be the death of mind. Don't attribute the death of mind to yourself. When the mind dies you will live and you will be Free.

Mind gives you this fear and compels you to run away because it is the death of the mind that is immanent! The death of desire happens in Satsang, but this is mind only. Do not fear. Persist, persevere, stay here and let your mind die. Stay here and overcome this death. Don't give your mind anymore company. Don't be a coward. Invite death to come and you'll be Eternal.

> You have only two choices:
> Allow the mind to live, or let your Self live.
> This is your decision.

What has happened to make this fear of death so overwhelming to you?

Last month my mother, my father and one of my closest friends died in England while I was in India. It feels like I want to avoid death because I am afraid of it.

Nobody has ever avoided death, from the beginning to the present date! Everybody who is born must die and since it is so natural why be afraid of it? Why be afraid of death? Everybody must die and by running away you will not save yourself.

There is only one place where you can avoid death and it is This place. Knowing that you have never been born you are not going to die because you know that you are not the body. The body is born and so it has to die. Inside the body is something Eternal that you do not know. If you be That who is going to touch you? If you know that you are not the mind or body or senses, that you are something within, who is going to touch you? If you know this then your fear is gone.

Actually, nobody is born and nobody dies. It is the mind that gives birth to this whole world. In the dream you are sick and the doctor says that you have only one week to live and so you are afraid. This doctor, the disease, and the body all were in the dream, but when you awake the next morning where is the doctor and the dying patient? This you will know in Satsang: it is all a

510

dream! Wherever there is fear you are dreaming!

> When fear arises you are dreaming.
> All fears belong only to the dream.

When you wake up there is no fear at all. Waking up means no fear at all and this is called the waking state. Then you will know that "I am Eternal, no death can touch me." This is fearlessness.

So instead of running away it is better that you go and console your family by telling them how to be free from fear. First remove the fear yourself and then tell your friends and countrymen. Death will only take away something which has a form. Therefore, all form will die but you are That which has no form, you will never die, so don't carry any form of fear!

There just seems to be some terror about death.

Simply understand that whatever is born must die! You cannot avoid it! Everybody is dead: gods, sages, and saints, everybody is dead and will die so do not be afraid of death. Death is a time of rest, when the bird flies out of its old cage. Death is a supreme Mother, a loving Mother for all beings who do not know that she really is loving and who fear her instead.

The problem is that everybody speaks about death without ever experiencing it. Very few people speak about death and post-death from direct experience and those who do are not afraid, but describe it as awesomely beautiful. This is the difference which generates so much fear of death. It is only the living that are afraid of death, not the dead! People have no authority to speak about something that they themselves have not experienced.

Science cannot understand death, but once you know Her you will know that she is the Mother Supreme who gives you the rest that you couldn't give yourself. So don't be afraid of death. It is a very lovely contact. No dead person complains that it is not good! Sit with them and perhaps you also will have peace!

I have been praying for peace.

Go to the source of prayer and there is no need to pray. People who pray are atheists because they pray to stones and concepts.

What happens when a Self Realized person leaves their body?

There is no such thing as a Self Realized person because only when there is no person will the Self be realized. When there is no person there is no question of coming or going! The person is just a temporary appearance in the unchanging Self.

Is this person the jiva, the soul?

Yes, and the jiva is the doer, a bundle or accumulated desires, doubts, and fears.

How to avoid death?

Have you ever been Quiet without thought? This is the way to avoid death. Do it now, don't think of past or future and I will find out if you do. Saying you do it will not do. Doing it is to keep Quiet for one instant of time. In between past and future tell me who you are.

I can't tell you.

You say "I can't" but yet you are speaking. Who is it that says "I have done it" and "I can't say it." You have never done. You lie!

I try to do it.

This trying is for the future. You have been with some stupid people who taught you this.

Can you talk about what happens to Consciousness at the moment of death and after the death?

What comes after death I will speak to you after death. How can I speak of things after death when I am now alive? You should have written to me after death. Don't forget now! Chello.

My mother recently died, but I am not upset because it is clear that the Self she is is the Self I am and the Self all around me. I do miss her, but I realize that I miss and loved her ego. I so appreciate your grace on the day that I found out that she died. You touched me so deeply.

I am very happy with you. This is the Teaching! Everybody who comes must go and this nobody can change. But the fact is that nothing comes and nothing goes, this is the Truth.

As far as loving her ego, these are not allowed into Satsang. Just as you leave your shoes outside, so you must leave your head there as well! Losing your head for Enlightenment is a very cheap bargain, don't wait. This bargain has Peace and Wisdom on one side and ego on the other.

Take my head please!

When you say this I can see the person who has no head. It is very beautiful; a few people are here who are very beautiful and are without heads. Satsang is of the most benefit to those who come without a head, without ego.

Can you speak of death and dying and heaven and hell?

These are notions imposed on you. Along with the notion of heaven you have the notion that you are not in heaven. That is the impediment. You have to rid yourself of all these impediments in order to be free. You have to be rid of the impediment "I am not free." This is why you have come here. It is not to be Free, but for the affirmation and confirmation that you have always been Free. Your whole life has been a long string of repeated affirmations: "I am bound," "I am suffering," "I will die." These are the notions that you have entertained. Simply get rid of them! Freedom is within just waiting for you, ready to hug you, but you turn your back. If anything is death it is turning your back on your Self by carrying your own notions, ideas, and intentions of bondage and suffering.

Now find who is bound and who is suffering. Find out who you are. You are not the dress, not the skin or the hair or the nails. You are not the bones or the muscles or the brain. You are not the ego or the mind or the senses. Reject all these just for one moment and what is left? Reject what you are not and what is revealed in front of you? If you are not all these things which appear and disappear, what are you? What remains?

Just "I."

"I" will remain and this "I" will not die. What you have rejected will die but, what remains after all is rejected is before the concept of death and birth. Arrive home and recognize yourself simply by getting rid of all these notions that you have entertained for so long: "I am a body, a mind, an ego, senses, I am this manifestation." All these are notions and vanish in the sleep state. But since sleep is an ignorant state you do not see what remains after these notions vanish to allow sleep. So find who is awake in the sleep state. That you are, That you must be, and That is Free! Even the states of waking and dreaming and sleeping do not touch That, let alone death and dying and heavens and hells. That will never die and That you are.

Even if you say, "I am not That," who is it that is conscious to know that you are not that? What is conscious of ignorance and doubts? Who is conscious of suffering and happiness? What Consciousness is here which is needed to even raise a doubt that you are Consciousness! There is nothing you can do to escape the Truth because It is what you are.

What is unreal is not even here now, even if I try and pretend!

Exactly, once you know that the rope is not a snake it can be hard to imagine it to be the snake even if you try. Yet the rope has never changed. It has all been your notion, including the sticks and stones you picked up to kill the snake! Go and see for yourself that it is a rope. Keep Quiet and abandon all notions and ideations and intentions.

It seems like a lot of unlearning.

It is getting rid of all the things you have been keeping in your bags and then getting rid of the bags. Then what is unlearned will reveal Itself to Itself. Speaking of bags I am reminded of a sannyasin who visited me about twenty years ago.

He was quite famous in the south and had seventeen ashrams, but was obviously not satisfied. He had come to Haridwar with two bus loads of his disciples on their way to Badrinath. This swami was eighty years old and I was sixty. He came alone to my hotel room after hearing from some friends that I may be able to help him. He strolled in and announced what we were not going to talk about.

He said, "Poonjaji, I have been a yogi all my life. You may have seen my picture in the papers. I was buried alive underground with no food, air or water for forty days in a controlled experiment with scientists and doctors to prove the power of yoga. I simply went into samadhi and that was it. So, I know yoga and there is no need to talk about it."

He continued, "Also, for decades I have studied in depth all of the Vedas and the Upanishads, the Mahabharata and the Ramayana, the Brahma Sutras, Bhakti Sutras, and the Yoga Sutras, and all the books of all the religions, so we are not going to talk about all these. I teach all of this in my ashrams so there is nothing in any scripture that you can teach me. Furthermore, you are not to say anything about tantra, yantra, or mantra. And don't mention jnana or nijnana either. So Poonjaji, I have come here for your help. Is there anything that you can say to me?"

I said, "Yes Swamiji, there is. But first, please, the garbage that you just hauled in my room with you, will you please take this bag and put it outside and then enter again. Then I will speak about something that you have not mentioned."

He just looked at me not understanding what I was saying, so I repeated, "I said, Swamiji, I am here to help you, but will you first bring this bag of garbage outside the door? Then when you come back in just leave it all out there." He went to the door slowly and turned around shocked. He looked at me and I looked at him. Then he came into the room and tried to touch my feet.

"Oh no Swamiji," I said, "you are a sannyasin, and a scholar, and also you are twenty years my elder! I have no right to accept your prostration."

He replied, "For the first time I know what Enlightenment is, I know now that I must leave understanding and all that I learned behind. Then I found light, then I found my Self. I have been fooling and cheating so many people. Right now I am going to tell all my devotees the Truth! When can I come back to see you?"

"Swamiji, you don't need to come back!" I replied.

Later, I heard that this arrogant swami was totally transformed and happy and had gone into a long retreat somewhere.

So get rid of all the notions that you have entertained and just be Free. Freedom is already waiting for you for millions of years, but you still entertain doubts and fears like, "I will be born, I am suffering, I will grow old and die." All these are notions and when you get rid of them you will know who you are. Do this now, don't postpone it even for a moment. In between the past and the future, who are you? You are not to do any exercise or any meditation. Here you will feel Light! Can any death enter this Moment?

This is your own place, your own abode, stay Here.

My father's death took me to a deep timeless silence and my mother died as if dancing, and as she said goodbye to her body we were one flame of love. Both of their deaths gave me so much love and freedom. Being with you brings me back to this beautiful gift. Papaji, can you tell me the secret of a beautiful death?

It is an excellent death when somebody can die in full consciousness, and say goodbye to the relations. This is very beautiful because most go crying and suffering due to attachments.

At the time of death it can be a very painful affair for the person who is dying if they are attached to things. Then it is like tearing a sheet of cloth off a thorny bush. The thorns of attachment stick to the sheet of your mind and cause great pain. I saw one man who was dying and he was fighting with those who came to take him away. He even had a revolver and fought for one hour until he lay down dead.

But a rare person without attachment only feels that the breath has stopped. Like this he doesn't feel anything, only that the breath has stopped, and it is finished. This is the death of an easy person, one who has been devoted to their own cause. They will have a beautiful departure from this universe. Even animals can have this beautiful death.

Once an elephant who had three wives and five children went to the lake for a bath. As he entered the lake immediately a huge crocodile caught his leg and started to pull. He looked at his wives and children and cried for their help, but they just stood and watched. So he was dragged into the deep waters and he lifted up his trunk above the water to breathe one last time. As he lifted his trunk he saw a lotus flower and picked it and offered it to someone unknown to him for help, and looking toward the skies cried for help!

Now, of course, someone who the elephant had never thought of before, instantly appeared and crushed the crocodile's jaws and released the elephant. The elephant went back to the bank of the lake, but did not speak to his wives and children and went alone to the deep forests, realizing that the attachments that you are so involved with are of no help, but This is going to help you. He never returned, but after his death he went to the heavens. The last thought, the last breath can help anyone.

I am afraid of death and I feel like I am dying.

Everybody will die. Every body. Are your grandparents still here? Are your parents? This dying will go on as you become the grandparents of your grandchildren, so don't worry about the death of the body.

What is born must die, don't worry about it.
There is a pleasure in death which cannot be found in life.

Don't have the desire of keeping your body because when it gets old it is good that it dies. Bodies which are alive after they are too old are not good bodies to have. I will tell you a story about a group of people who wanted to keep their bodies young.

There is a tunnel, or cave, near Taxala. As the death of Alexander the Great was imminent, though he was only thirty-two, he came to visit this cave. He had been told by a yogi on the banks of the river Jhelum that he would die young and so he came to this cave which had a lake of the nectar of immortality in it. The only problem was that whoever went to investigate this lake never returned. Alexander, of course was very clever and so he rode a mare into the cave and kept her newly born colt at the entrance of the cave. He entrusted his life to the mare's sense of smell and her desire to return to her colt.

He eventually found this lake which had about twenty-five people living on its shores. He asked them who they were and they replied, "We once heard of this lake and came to drink its nectar. But now we are 10,000 years old and though we are sick of this life we cannot die. We cannot die the blessed death." As I said, he was very wise, and so after speaking to these living skeletons, who didn't even know what Yuga it was, he went back without tasting the nectar and tasted his natural death instead.

So your body will live in this market for a hundred years or so. But don't worry, the market does not belong to you. It belongs to another "person" and it will be taken care of as it was taken care of before your birth and will be taken care of after your death.

> Your focus and responsibility is only to the One
> which has created this world and who will look after it.
> By not believing this we fall into trouble.

Do not fear death.

ॐ

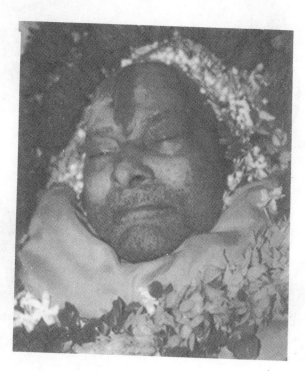

Freedom

Freedom, Liberation, Enlightenment:
This is your own fundamental ultimate Self,
this is Being, not even "I am Being,"
Just Being! This is a still mind.
This Stillness is the greatest achievement.

You will spread the vibration that you are to everyone,
so keep your Self a blossom of Love.
As Freedom you always leave good vibrations wherever you go.

Enlightenment

Enlightenment is to know your true nature,
which is Silence. This is knowing everything.
Freedom is knowing this with every breath.
This Liberation is Silence, not touching duality.
This Silence is no doer and is the language of Peace.

Freedom is aloneness, Oneness, not two-ness.
When there is no object in Consciousness
there is Stillness and this is Freedom.
If you think at all that this world is real and
as long as there is "I" and "you" there is no Freedom.
Freedom is knowing the "I" in me is the same as in you.
This me is you, there is no difference.

Remaining as presence is Freedom,
remaining in past is samsara.
Freedom is always Here in the heart of all beings.
It is in front of you, inside, outside, everywhere!
What is bondage when Freedom always is?
What is not the Truth?

Freedom is free from all modifications of the mind.
Freedom is when the mind is cremated, absolutely destroyed!
Then mind is no-mind, and anything that comes and goes
does not change you because you are always full.

In Freedom there is no right and no wrong.
In Freedom there is freedom from right and wrong.

In Freedom there is no process or way,
no here, no there, no this, no that, no in, no out,
no wall, no depth, no understanding.
Nothing has happened, Nothing is happening,
Nothing ever will happen.
No mind, no bondage, no freedom.

In Wisdom there is no phenomena,
there is no giver and no receiver and so
life is very beautiful, the world is very beautiful,
and relationships are very beautiful
because they are all with your Self.

The Supreme is concealed by name and form
but when the Truth is known it will conceal name and form.

When all is lost then you are Home.
This is Enlightenment! When you are awake
you possess nothing that can be lost.

Being is the dissolving of all notions.
All is dissolved when you meet this Source,
all questions, answers, and experiences
are only on the way to the Source.
Questions are in ignorance
because Enlightenment leaves no questioner!
When you wake up you will know that nothing ever existed.
When there was subject-object, or any duality
you were in a dream.

Realization is uncovering that you are already Free.
It is always Here and only relieves you of bondage.
It is throwing the bucket of your individuality
into the well of Being, without the ropes
of desire, intention, thought, or attachment.
Don't try to go anywhere, just simply Be.
The only "need" is to Be, not even seeing.
It is so simple that it is difficult.
It is Here and Now this very instant.

The secret of Freedom is Satsang,
which is to undress your Self of the mind.
This is giving up beliefs, notions, desires, and illusions.

After they disappear Consciousness remains as Freedom.

There is no today, yesterday or tomorrow in Now.
When nothing ever existed what is there to be free from?
Emptiness has to be emptied of Emptiness,
Freedom must be free of Freedom.
In Freedom there is nothing to do and nothing not to do.
It cannot be imagined or touched.
Human birth is for this Freedom,
so smell Freedom, inhale Freedom, be Freedom.
Every moment Freedom is Here to hug you.
Eternity is living moment to moment.

The sun wanted to see the night,
so it showed up at midnight.
But it still could not find any night or darkness!
So it is with ignorance: one look and it is gone!
There is no ignorance, there is only Truth!
There can be no darkness in the light!
With the dawn of the Sun, mists of illusion evaporate.

When the beggar is put on the throne
there is a great shock, but indeed, you are Free!
The body can stay in the shock of this happiness for only 21 days.
This is why so many saints die young.
Only those with a special appointment
live long in the body.

When mind is pure and there are no ripples
you will know that you have known all beings
from the beginning of creation.
One glimpse of this beauty is enough for Freedom for life.
Remove name and form and you will see
and this seeing is Being!

I am pure Awareness!
Stay as such.

What is Enlightenment?

Enlightenment is the substratum of all states. Realization is the firm belief: what is Here is always Here.

Are there different levels of Enlightenment?

There are not levels of Enlightenment, but levels in your approach. Serious approach, moderate approach, and the level of doing it in old age.

When Ramana found it, he went directly to the place of Lord Shiva and not back to his old circumstances. Levels are of decision only. These levels are for the ego, not Enlightenment. The light is there and if you only half open your eyes you will not see the sun. The sun is always there and does not turn its back to the earth. The earth turns her back to the sun and the result is night. There is no night or levels in the sun. There are no levels in Consciousness. It is like the ego of the king which kept him away from the Pir. But when ego was gone he immediately rushed in. Your own Light and Wisdom waits for you, but you have been postponing it for a million years.

Does Enlightenment change the body chemically or energetically at all?

Ramana Maharshi said that the power of the Self was surging through him so strongly that he couldn't keep his head still.

Are there any indications when one has realized the Self? Is there a change of behavior?

Yes, there are definitely some indications by which you can know that One has attained the Ultimate. The main indication is that if you look at them or are near them your mind will be at peace. When you see a photo of the Maharshi, or when you go near him you sense something that you do not sense with any other person.

Sometimes the mind is quiet due to fear, for instance, when you meet a tiger face to face in the forest. The Quietness that I am referring to is not from fear, but from Love and Peace. So test someone if you are not sure. You must test them! Whosoever went near Buddha had a Quiet mind.

To this day, 2600 years later, even the dust of the earth
wherever Buddha walked is giving people peace!

See for yourself in places like Bodh Gaya, Sarnath, and Lumbini. Every grain of the earth in these places is sanctified.

Regarding behavior, the actions of the Jnani are perfect because there is no doer. Judgments of right and wrong is for religions only, not the Jnani.

Do you foresee a time in the not too distant future when there will be many people on earth who are Enlightened?

There is no future, there are no people, there is no earth, there is no one seeking Enlightenment, there is no one gaining Enlightenment. This is the final Truth. Time is just a concept and if you do not think about it, it does not exist. This earth also is your concept. If you keep Quiet then there is no existence, and no one ever existed, and there is no time. Time is mind. When there is no time there is no mind. When you sleep there is no time and no world. This is up to you. Mind is a thought, mind is past, mind is everything. If you do not stir a single thought from the source tell me what you see and what is there. Even you do not exist.

Does Enlightenment mean that you are always happy and never angry?

Happiness always is! You will know this if you identify with That which never changes. About anger, if the situation arises for it I can be ferocious, like a tiger (laughs) and I will not leave the person alone.

Is it only possible to love each other when both people are Self realized?

In Self there is no other.

When is a person ripe for Enlightenment?

The force of merits pushes you toward Enlightenment, towards contact with the Holy. Whatever contacts the Holy becomes Holy.

> Those who are Holy will attain Truth.
> Holiness is the main condition.
> Purity of mind is Freedom, free of all desires.

If you remember anything you are not ripe for Enlightenment. You have to be free of all desire for sense objects and the dependence on them for happiness! Desirelessness is the only happiness. If a sense object comes let it come, if it doesn't, don't wait for it to give you happiness because nothing in the world will give you happiness because nothing can give you happiness. This is certain. Nobody can get happiness from anyone except your own Self, and this is available only when you have no desire. How simple, you see.

Does the destiny of a Self Realized person end with the departure or is there a continuance of greater revelation beyond Mahasamadhi?

The Enlightened one is not born again and so there is no destiny for him. Destiny is for those who are not realized. They are in its inescapable grip. But the Realized man has no destiny from the day he is Realized. All the karma committed by him has no effect or reaction, so future karma is dead. The present actions are governed by the Divine and so nothing he does is other than Divine will. Therefore, he gets no karma from present actions because they are not attributable to him. The past karma cannot be undone, but it cannot act on him in the next life because there is no next life. Therefore, they will come to him in the form of dreams. In this way a whole lifetime of karma can be burned away in just one minute of dream. The good karma that remains will go to those who love him and the bad karma that remains will go to those who think and speak badly about him.

You seem to be a Hindu. How can an Enlightened person be bound by a religion?

After Enlightenment one has no hatred or judgment toward anyone. The Enlightened one is a Hindu, and a Buddhist, and a Muslim, and a Christian, and Hebrew, and everything else because this One knows the Essence of these religions, this One *is* the Essence. The Enlightened one finds no difference at all and so you see representations of different religions on the walls of this Satsang because we don't hate anyone. You need no brands or labels of anything in Freedom.

For myself, I was born into a Hindu family and that tradition is very well maintained. But inside of you your Atman is neither Christian, Hindu, Muslim, or Buddhist. In this regard let it be called by any name, it doesn't matter. Take one hundred cups and fill them with one hundred different colors of water. The sun rays that touch this water are not affected by the color. Remove the water and the white porcelain of the cup and the pure rays of the sun remain. This color is "I am a Hindu," or "I am a Muslim." When you remove this thought from your mind you will see the Atman shining everywhere in the world. That is the difference.

In modern physics it is clear that the experimenter affects the outcome of the experiment. How are things affected whether seen by an Enlightened one or seen by someone not Enlightened? What is the relation between prakriti and the collective consciousness viewing it?

The views are different. The Enlightened one views from behind the observer and the observed, not as the observer in the case of an unenlightened being. The Enlightened one knows the observer which is the ego and transcends the observer, observed, and observation. Nobody except the

Enlightened one knows who the observer is and knows who is looking at the observer from behind. So you must turn your face to that one which observes the observer.

This is my question to you! What is the consciousness by which you can know that, "I am conscious of everything"? That supreme Consciousness looks at the individual consciousness and what is done via the senses.

There are objects of the senses. Before that there are the senses. Before that is the mind which command the senses. Beyond the mind is the decision making intellect. Beyond intellect is ego. Go now beyond the ego. What Consciousness is aware of the ego and where does this arise from. From Here all is done and Here is not affected by anything. Here you are not the doer and not the done. This is Enlightenment and Freedom and beyond karma. The karma we spoke of before is all in the framework of the mind and it is in the recollection of the mind that these activities of karma arise. Beyond mind there is no arising.

Advice is given to those who are on the mental plane, but if you rise above this you will know that there never existed anything. This is the fundamental Truth: there never existed anything, there never will exist anything. This is the ultimate Truth.

What is seen is seen only through ego. This manifestation that you see is only what you needed to see, what you wanted to see and is all related to your individual identification.

Just as all of this disappears when you go to sleep, so it will disappear when you know the Truth. All you can see or say is in regards to the waking and dream state, but who is it that witnesses the soundness of your sleep? All your suffering belongs to the waking and dream states, but what happens to the silent happiness of sleep once you wake up? How will you utilize this happiness wisely in the next waking state? This silent happiness is where you come from. This Consciousness is aware even when you are unconscious. Why do you forget this happiness when you wake up? You must honor this happiness. You must know That which is awake while you are sleeping. Stay awake while all others sleep and sleep while all others are awake and you will never be affected by the suffering of life because you are beyond that.

This understanding doesn't need any practice. You just absorb it and be It. Practice just strengthens the mind. Practices begin and end and so are not the Truth. What always is, is the Truth. Practices give you gains, but all gains will be lost. Your own nature you can never lose and you are That. You are That which is awake while you sleep and which sleeps to what the world is awake to. This That cannot be explained.

Your disciples talk about you as a Realized being, are you one?

I do not say that myself and neither do I have a name plate which says, "Here goes an Enlightened person." There is no difference that I find between you and me. I never say that I am Realized.

Many speak about this, saying that you are Realized. Is there any difference between realization and enlightenment?

Many people say that I am a realized person. This is due to their notions about realization and, therefore, they think that I am realized, but I don't see any difference between them and me.

And yes, though we usually use these words interchangeably, there is a difference between realization and enlightenment. Realization is realized after some sadhana or practice or method and what is realized was not there before. To realize through a method is called realization.

Enlightenment is to be aware of something that was not clear before. Like a diamond that you think is a pebble, but later on you find out that it is a diamond. Light comes after knowing that it is not a pebble and thus you start giving value to it.

It is beyond awareness and enlightenment. This is the Essence. Who could be aware and who could be enlightened because there is no darkness at all. It is already there and it is revealed when the dust of your notions is cleared away. Then it will come up itself and you and It will merge together and you will not see a difference between you and It. You will not see anything else. No words can explain it.

In the West people either believe in god or they don't. Is there any god and if there is what and who is it?

Let people believe or not believe. Self is not affected by any belief or god. God is your thought and is your own creation of the mind. You even created the creator. Creation, preservation and destruction is just a thought.

You have said that Ramana looked into your eyes and showed you the Seer. Can you describe what happened then?

No, any description is past, not the instant Knowledge which is not past or future. Nobody can describe it.

The behavior does change though, and some become quiet like a mountain. This was the Maharshi. Some become childlike and innocent. In this case people don't believe that they are Enlightened, but this behavior is the exact outer behavior of the man who knows It.

What was the effect of this experience on your life?

It was not an experience. Experience needs an experiencer and an object to be experienced, but this was not that. Something was pulling me inside. This something was not a personification of anything, it was just a pull within. I don't even know what this "within" is. Since this pull I have always been happy for no particular reason.

Why were you unable to continue Krishna meditation after the Divine experience of darshan of Lord Ram?

I cannot continue that meditation because I feel I am Him. I need not be his devotee and he need not be my Lord. We are the same. This is the Essence you must understand. If you have complete total Love for That you become That as the Gopis became Krishna.

Does Papaji have an ego?

Yes, I have! I have ego. She likes to serve me as a maidservant. Without a maidservant the house cannot run. She is very helpful and takes care of arising situations without even telling me. I have no complaint against ego. Let her live in my house, I have no problem with her. I don't find any enmity between her and me. She is quite happy.

Some people are surprised to see me eat ice cream and Coca-Cola because no swami takes Coca-Cola and ice cream. But the ice cream has nothing to do with Enlightenment and Enlightenment is not affected by ice cream. Ice cream goes from the tongue to the stomach and my Enlightenment doesn't dislike ice cream, so when the ice cream comes I take it. I have no trouble because I have no restrictions. I don't have any do's and don'ts as the swamis practice. I don't belong to: "you shouldn't do this and that."

Do whatever you want to do and live a normal life, not trying to become something different and separating yourself from the society. Wearing malas and dying your clothes has nothing to do with That. It doesn't matter if you wear white or black or orange or how you behave. These things belong to religions. Do's and don'ts are religions: "If you go to church you will go to heaven, if you don't you will go to hell after death."

I don't tell you to do something after death, I just say to make use of the time before death and live and act as you like, but in a way which doesn't touch you. No body contacts will interfere with your understanding, so I do not prescribe to wear this or that kind of dress or behave in any one way.

Do you still have thoughts?

They do rise when the occasion rises, but I don't run after them to pick them up and utilize them. As the car on the road passes by and I don't grab it. But most people do run after the car and try to hang onto it. I let the car come and I don't worry when it disappears. I am not the car!

Enlightenment has nothing to do with neither positive states or negative states of the mind. Enlightenment simply has nothing to do with the mind.

Why does the "I" stay with you after Realization?

You fail to understand the difference between the "I" that you use and the "I" that I use. That makes the difference! The "I" that most people use indicates the ego, body, mind and senses. It indicates someone who is born. You consider yourself to have a form and thus you want a name and the most basic name is "I." But when you sleep there is no "I." Then who is there when you are sleeping and when you are awake?

> Simply keep Quiet and do not look at the Quietness
> or the form, or the name. Then you will see
> that some sort of Awareness is still there.
> This is called Aham Brahmasmi,
> the one mantra for all, but don't repeat it,
> get into the Truth of it.

Don't touch any object, place, or concept for one second and you will see that there is a super Consciousness without name and form. It is That which is the true "I"! When you go to It you are no longer there and It speaks "I"!

Swami Rama Tirtha speaks of this "I" so beautifully. At the age of twenty-four he realized himself and said:

> When I wake up the whole world wakes up.
> When I eat the whole world eats.
> When I sleep the whole world sleeps.

> Let this body go, I do not care.
> For I move as the breeze
> and kiss the flowers and plants,
> and touch the Himalayan waterfalls.

It is this "I" which I refer to. The use of the word "I" is simply to refer to the ego and anybody who uses "I" in this way will never be happy.

Satsang is not meant to give you anything, but only to appraise you of the fact that something which cannot be seen is hidden in the cave of your Heart. It is Light and Knowledge and when you surrender to it, It will take charge of you. Then when you speak, "I am doing this," though the words are the same, it is That which is doing it! That makes the difference.

Why do you have all these pictures of Ramana Maharshi?

When you have been benefited by someone how can you forget!? How can you forget the One who gives That which nobody can give? Nobody has ever shown the Happiness and removed the suffering, so you must be indebted to that person as long as you have physical presence on this earth.

If you are helped by someone you say "thank you" or maybe you give them $100. But how can you ever repay the debt to someone who has removed all suffering from you forever? Everywhere you see that that person is following you. He even came to me in my house in the Punjab which is a miracle that not everybody believes because when he appeared in the Punjab he was also at Arunachala.

I had been searching all over the country for That which was Within me, but I did not know it. Then this Self came to me in my house in the Punjab and gave his Arunachala address to me. But how to go to him? I had retired from the army and had spent all my money traveling trying to find a Guru. Then I saw a job offer in the Tribune. It was for an ex-army officer who was needed to manage the stores of a supply company near Madras, in Avadi. So I applied and got the job and also some advance in pay. Instead of going to the job, I went straight to Maharshi and reported for work a month later.

When I went to the ashram I saw the same person who had given me his address in the Punjab. So I didn't enter the hall because I felt he had only been advertising himself. I spoke to one Parsi gentlemen who said, "You look to be North Indian."

"Yes, I am," I replied.

"But how is it that you have just arrived and now you are leaving already?" he asked.

So I said, "This man came to me in the Punjab and told me to come to this place for the answer to the question I had asked."

The Parsi replied, "You have made a mistake, he has not moved from Here for the last fifty years since he came here from his house. He has never left Arunachala once since he came and you can ask anybody here!"

This is how it all began.

I have experienced so much and now am left just full of peace.

Now go and share this experience with your friends, family, and country. First receive help, then digest it well, and then give it to others. When you know this you know that you have always known it. All other experience is fresh and new, but this experience always Is. This Knowledge means "I am Buddha."

I want to thank you for this gift of Self that you have given to me.

When you have this experience of being Home, throw everything away and serve the Teacher. The best way to serve the Master is to stay Quiet and serve the devotees.

You have awakened the 'Christ-mind' in me and now all is seen as One.

When you came here as a priest I told you I would show you the Love that Jesus has for the Father. Then you did not believe it, but now you have to believe it because you know that:

> Everybody is the son of God.
> If you love God,
> you will become One with him someday,
> because there is no difference
> between God and the son.

I experience such a peace and a love in my heart and I cannot bear to leave now, so I have postponed my departure.

It is good that you have not left. When you feel that this experience is stable, you can leave. Often the mind cheats people and so be sure now to cheat the mind. Play with it by imposing different circumstances before it. Play with it; say "I am in difficulty," or "I am not in Peace." Then he will not come to your house.

I am very happy to see such a young woman here. Most people postpone Satsang for old age, but this is too late because in old age you get filled up with diseases which do not allow you to be Quiet.

> So do it Now!
> It is not difficult.

I feel that there is no problem with thought, only in taking thought seriously. I feel that if I want realization that it means that I am taking myself to be somebody who is not That.

Enlightenment is only for those people who think that they are bodies. For them only. Those who do not see the body or who do not think that they are the body do not need any kind of realization. Realization is to remove the concept, "I am the body."

If you want my correction it is that you are now carrying "bodylessness." This you must correct. There is no difference between speaking about body or bodylessness. The thought of bodylessness came to you and you accepted it. You are thinking about no-thought!

> Watcher is still the mind watching!
> So first watch thought, and then watch the watcher.

The smoker is in a way better off than the one who dislikes smoking because the smoker smokes the cigarette and then throws away the butt, but the non-smoker always says and thinks that they do not like smoke. Having a cigarette in your hand is better than having one in your mind!

Like this, if you think that you do not have a body it really means that you are carrying this dead body, this corpse, in your mind. So somehow avoid both the concept of body and the concept of no body. Then what will you speak about? Next time correct this.

This heart dwells in peace and bliss. I thank you so much.
Please continue this until all vasanas are removed.

When the mind enters into the Chit, the Heart dances and dwells in Peace and Bliss.

Now the sound of the birds and everything is so incredibly beautiful.

Singing of the birds, the sound of the wind, the enhanced colors of objects, are experiences that people have when their mind becomes very subtle. They listen to these beautiful sounds and experience light of different colors. Saint Kabir speaks of this experience of subtle sounds and colors.

I can't touch all the old things anymore either. I am very happy.

Then you must dance now! Dance out of happiness, not for the sake of dancing. It is not the dance that I enjoy, but something else. I enjoy That which makes you dance.

Papaji, I am so grateful to you, I would love to sing and dance for you.

For the next two days keep Quiet and don't give rise to any thought in your mind. If you keep Quiet for these two days you will automatically stand up with so much bliss and happiness that you will instantly start dancing and you will never know the end of it! You won't even know who the dancer is. Just keep Quiet and wait for what happens. This dance will be beyond words.

Once when I was in the forest near the Kaveri River I found a man simply dancing for nobody and for no reason. So I asked him to whom he was dancing. He said, "Once I saw nobody and no form, then this dance automatically started."

So if you have no object in your mind, including no object which will appreciate the dance, then you will dance a natural dance as the clouds dance in front of the mountain. What is the use of the clouds to dance in front of the mountain who does not move? Then the cloud falls in the shape of rain.

Keep Quiet and then dance. This dance is quite enough so you don't have to meditate. This is the dance of Nataraj who dances even on the day of dissolution.

> The destruction of the traps of concepts
> is the eternal dance of Love.
> Trading these traps for Peace, is not a bad bargain!

> A good dancer makes no effort
> and every step is in tune: perfection!
> Simply Know yourself and then walk freely
> and effortlessly on the planet.
> When the wave arises
> the ocean does not worry that it will run away.
> Knowing "I am ocean,"
> the waves of the ocean are allowed to rise.
> When you know that you are water
> then waves are no problem.
> Nothing is not harbored in Consciousness.

I see the "I Am" is the Cosmic dancer. Thank you so much.

I am happy with this experience. Actually, it is not an experience, but this was burned here and so you are at the last rung of the Truth. This is the purpose of your life. Now I must give you a new name. It is the name of the one who won the battle over the demon of attachments. Satyavan, the one who is truthful to what he must do. I love this name.

I love it too!

After Realization you witness everything, good or bad; and you realize that everything is just a game. If someone kisses you it is fine and if someone slaps you, you make sure their hand has not been injured.

Once there was a saint who went down to the river for a drink of water and noticed a scorpion was being washed away. So he reached for it, but it stung his finger. Now, a scorpion bite is really painful. He tried saving the scorpion several times, but each time he was stung. A man standing nearby asked the saint, "Why do you keep trying to save this scorpion when it keeps trying to sting you?" The saint said, "If he cannot get rid of his habit of stinging, why should I get rid of my habit of serving!"

So it can be a difficult game to play and there are many scorpions to bite you and many worms waiting for you to become their food. But we forget this and that is why we suffer. We don't remember that this earth on which we tread will bring us underneath her. Nobody remembers, but those who do are wise persons. So play the game as long as the breath moves through your nose. This playing, this game, this sport is lila. Play this game and witness all that goes around and you are a wise person.

A guru has been coming to me in a form which is not physical, but not non-physical. Can you tell me about what these meetings mean? And what is this 'form' that he takes?

It is a special meeting. At one level of consciousness we see a different world, a world which is born and then perishes, with short lived objects. This is our eighteen-hour waking state world. Then there is the dream consciousness and also a sub-conscious state called the sleep state. No matter what state you think that you are in Consciousness is there, awake. You know this because when someone asks you how you slept you can say that you had a very deep sound sleep. So, you were not awake, but some Consciousness was aware and in this Consciousness there is no present, past or future, and yet you can perceive all these things and everything is just as it is. Many saints live in this Consciousness. When you rise to this you will see everything as it is. In this Consciousness nobody dies. There cannot be any death in Consciousness. Nobody dies really, though there is a level of consciousness where birth and death appears to be real. At another level you were never born and you will never die. Many saints and holy cities are in this super-Conscious state, and yet everything still is as it is. Nothing is destroyed in Consciousness.

Consciousness is always Conscious of Consciousness.

Everything is there in Consciousness and nothing is changed except your view which can be called your "level." When your view is gross you see the gross creation, when your view is subtle, as in the dream state, you see subtler creations. Your view can be far more subtle than this if your temperament is very sattvic. With the tamas guna we see the world, with the rajas guna we see the dreams, and with the very subtle pure sattvic guna you see the saints.

Beyond sattvic there is a state where nothing ever existed. There is no time, no existence, and no destruction there. No creator is there, no creations, no forms, no concepts, nobody! This is the Ultimate Substratum of all these levels of consciousness. So it is a good sign to see Holy men. They will guide you. You have risen to the level of consciousness where you have seen these saints.

Ultimately, there is no past or present or future and you can experience this right now when your mind is not agitated. When there are no ripples in the lake you can see your face. These ripples are thought disturbances. If you do not stir a ripple in your mind you can see your face Now. All of manifestation is just a ripple in the lake. Under the surface you are calm and quiet, this is your nature. When thought comes and disturbs the surface you cannot see your face correctly. You are always living Here and whenever you want manifestation to cease it will immediately. You just have to decide! When you want to rest make the decision to be free of manifestations, ripples, and see instantly who you are!

Very nice. It is a good sign. It is a very rare phenomena and very good luck to see an Enlightened One. Each century doesn't have the capacity to produce even twenty Buddhas.

Since it is Buddha Purnima today will you tell us the story of how Buddha was Enlightened?

This is the day Buddha was born, this full moon day. I will tell you a little story about him.

His mother was told that the son that she was going to give birth to will be the king of the universe and that according to his horoscope he would not be staying in the palace, and actually this is what happened. So the father made all the arrangements to provide luxury to the boy so that he would stay and did not permit the boy to go out of the palace grounds. Within the walls of the palace young beauties from all over the country were kept so that he would not have any time to think of anything else, except the enjoyments of the palace.

One day he asked the man who was training him in horse riding what was on the other side of the wall, but the trainer said he wasn't allowed to go

there. This horse trainer was Achana, even his name is remembered.

The boy insisted that he should see it and so Achana took him. As they left the palace the gate locks opened by themselves, and so they were able to leave as the gate keepers slept. They didn't notice. The earth became so soft that the hoofs of the horses didn't make any noise. And so they got out.

The first thing that he sees is a sick, coughing old man hunched over. "Achana, why is this man not walking straight like you and me?"

"He is an old man and therefore he cannot walk straight. At around seventy years old a man becomes hunch-backed and cannot walk upright," replied Achana.

"Will you also become old?" asked Siddhartha.

"Yes, my Lord and you too!"

Next he goes and sees a man carried on a stretcher with the family members crying behind him. "Achana, why is this man being carried on a stretcher, why doesn't he walk?" asked the prince.

"My Lord, he is dead! Therefore, he is being taken away to the cremation ground."

"Will you also die?" he asked.

"Yes my Lord, and you also. Everybody who was born has to die," answered Achana.

A little while later he saw a man sitting under a tree with a radiant face. "Stop the horse!" shouted the prince as he went over to the man. "This man is laughing and smiling! Achana why is he different from the sick and old man?"

Achana said, "My Lord, he is meditating."

"Why?" inquired the prince.

"To find out his own Enlightenment within. The Light is within and he is very happy about it," answered the horse trainer.

"Will you also do this?" asked Siddhartha.

"I can't do it, my father never did it and nobody really does it."

"Achana, move the horse back home," said the prince.

Now he decides for the time being to be like this meditating man. When they returned to the palace he went to see his wife and son in case they had noticed that he was missing, although they were sleeping when he left the palace. Still Yashodara was sleeping and Raul was suckling the breast of his mother.

He decides: Let me go out! One step was inside the threshold and one step was out. He turned and looked behind, and feeling such attachment to them he thought, "No I should not go! My wife will be alone and my son will miss his father."

Now in between attachment and Light...

(tears stream down Papaji's face)
...the foot outside the threshold was very firm!
He leaves and does not look behind.

So he goes to find a guru who will teach him how to become Enlightened. He goes to one ashram where the people are meditating for years. He stayed there for six months, but did not find anyone like the first man that he saw under the tree and decided that it was not the place for him. So he left and went to another ashram. There very rigid practices and tortures were given. They were doing serious meditations, upasanas and were hanging from the trees with feet up and head down. They taught starvation and he became a skeleton until he saw that this rejection of the body would not give him Light. He went to another ashram where they were meditating the whole day and night, but there was no radiance on their faces. He had seen something that they were missing and so onward he went to Bodh Gaya where he decided to sit down, simply stay Quiet, and not get up until he was Enlightened. There he found something which was very new to him.

For a long time he had been barely eating, and so one girl who was looking after him brought him honey and milk and for the first time he took it. Then Ananda comes and asks "What is it that you have found?" But he did not speak. Again he asked, "You look very radiant, and your whole body is different. Master, tell me what is the secret of this?" Again he kept quiet. So this is his life.

The first time I knew about Buddha it was in my history book. There was a part about the life of Buddha. I saw him meditating under the Bodhi Tree in a picture of my history book. I was about fourteen years old when I fell in love with him. I didn't know what Enlightenment was, but his person was very beautiful and so I decided to become like him.

The only way to be like him that came to mind was to reject food. Then I would become like him: all skeleton with visible bones. So like this I rejected food. The food that my mother gave me I would throw out to the dogs. After a month of not eating I became like a skeleton and the dogs became very fat. My schoolmates even gave me the name Buddha because of my weakness.

It also was written that he would beg for food and that he wore a robe and so next I took one of my mother's saris and dyed it ochre and made a robe out of it. I kept the robe in my books so she wouldn't know and I would go out and beg. I would go to shop keepers and houses and though they didn't know me they would give me biksha. Then I went to beg at a friend's house to see if they would recognize me. I went to their shop first and the father gave me one paise. Then I went to his wife, but since they usually didn't open the doors to beggars I told my friend to go in and tell his mother to give me biksha. So, since sadhus address the women as daughter, I addressed my friend's mother the same way: "My dear daughter, may you be blessed with six sons." This is what every sadhu says to Indian women. Then she removed the robes from my head and said that though she didn't recognize me she did recognize the voice; the tongue which shouted "biksha" was known to her.

Then the father came home from the shop and when he was told the story of how I came and was recognized he said that anyone would recognize me since I came to his house everyday and sometimes even slept here. Then I showed him the paise that he had given to me in his shop!

Sometimes I would go to the clock tower of the town and many people would collect there to listen to me. Then one of my neighbors told my mother what was going on, but she said it was not her son. The neighbor was insistent, but when she asked me about what the neighbor said, I denied it. One day she wanted to wear her sari for a wedding and after a thorough search for it she found it behind my books made into a robe. Then she knew the neighbor's claim was true.

There is something which is there from the childhood itself and this takes time to manifest later on. Sometimes it happens in youth and sometimes in old age. So don't think that you are here for the first time. There is a reason why you have come here from all over the world. This had to happen at a given time and now is happening here, and many people have been benefited.

That star is there looking at us. We are collected here to celebrate Buddha Purnima, which means we will celebrate the birth of the Light of Asia. Tonight we are celebrating this and I am happy we are all here.

Compassion and Service

Compassion is a jewel that adorns itself on one who is Free.
You cannot practice this kind of compassion
because It is all your own Self so who is helping.
This compassion may incarnate as a human, as the Bodhisattva.
Compassion is your dharma which arises as doership dissolves.

Let your joy be enjoyed by all, don't be a miser.
Don't hold back, give everything,
love all, no matter what, love all,
and honor everybody because all is your own projection.
Any jiva must not be troubled, all jivas must be happy.
Trouble no being and let no being trouble you.
Nobody should be harmed.

Stay in Peace, this is your responsibility.
The planet will be very beautiful
if you just stay in Peace.

If you want to give to the world
give what you are: give peace and happiness.
To give happiness you must *be* Happiness,
to give peace you must *be* Peace,
to give wisdom you must *be* Wisdom.
Be happy and out of compassion distribute this.
Then "I" means the entire universe.
If you give food or blankets
the world will soon be hungry and cold again,
so just be happy, you have to share this!
What else is left except to share the experience that you are?
It must be shared. It is full of fullness so always give.
This is giving Wisdom.

Do not speak to foolish people about the Truth,
just share the Love and the Happiness,
because the greatest gift is an empty mind.
But even if you do not speak
your Silence will reach the whole planet
as a silent rose radiates beauty.
Sit Quietly and send peace from your heart
to all beings of all the worlds.
Oceans may empty, but there is no end to Love and Peace,
so share it always in selfless service; this is worship.

The time left in this body is to be used helping
all others on the planet and in all realms.
Remain Being and help everyone.
This is not a desire, but a natural surrender:
you are just a tool, like a bank teller,
it is not your money that you are giving away,
you are only the instrument.
Always give and you will never need.
If you do not give you will always be needy.

Dissolve yourself into the Self
and the whole world is taken care of.
If you want to help the planet

live that life of compassion for all beings.
Live that life of Love.

Papaji, when I inquire I go into an original and blissful state. I have been told, however, that this is not full Enlightenment because it is selfish, it is only for myself and does not help others. What is my responsibility towards others?

If you have this experience you have fulfilled all the responsibilities to yourself and to all the inhabitants of the world. How can you call this selfish? To know thyself is enough to fulfill your responsibility to all beings, to everybody. This is not selfish.

Everything disappears, except this thought that I must help other beings.

This thought that does not disappear, to whom does it belong to? You will not be benefited by any practice or meditation unless you find the root of the thought which does not disappear. This thought that does not disappear is the I-thought. Nobody knows that "I" is also a thought. When there is no I-thought there is no other thought so you have to strike at the root of the I-thought. Long meditations, staying in caves of the Himalayas, or staying with teachers is of no use unless you do it. The "I" should not appear when you meditate.

You are coming close, but you do not know who the thief is. The thief is not caught. "I" is the thief who deceives you. "I am so and so" and "this belongs to me" and "that will belong to me" is the thief that is never arrested. If you want to help others the best way is to be Free yourself. The richest man on the planet could maybe feed the whole world for one or two days, but Buddha has been feeding the world for 2600 years.

There seems to be only three choices: serve the ego, serve the "other" or serve the Divine. I have only done the first one.

I suggest you serve all three. Why have any distinction between the Divine, you and others? Serve yourself, your parents, your country, and the whole world. This itself is service to the Divine. Selfless service is worship and will destroy the ego.

After your realization why didn't you help others immediately?

You mean to say why did I immediately start helping others?! I help others without want of a result or reward. This is called compassion. All who get Light get compassion as well and wish peace to everybody. I started helping people by giving them spiritual advice when I was around twelve, in the early 1920's. People recognized me as a Yogi including the headmaster of the school. Once I even went into a samadhi because "Om Shanti Shanti Shanti" was chanted by the whole class. My teacher punished me, but the headmaster was wise and was proud of me instead. He used to brag years later that his school had produced many VIP's in the government and in business and it also produced one Yogi. So I have continued my activities as a normal person and never grew a beard, or wore orange robes to imply I was superior. No one can recognize me. You don't have to become something different than others.

How can we improve the world?

My teaching is not to improve the world, nor to improve yourself. Just understand and listen to what I speak:

> The world has never existed.
> Anything that has never existed,
> how can you improve it?

You said that I have to be realized while in this body. I also feel a strong desire to share what you have given me until all beings know it. Does there have to be rebirths until this feeling of sharing is complete?

If you think that your work is not complete in this lifetime you will be reborn in some suitable circumstances to the parents who will help you to fulfill your work. If you have not finished your business you will have to continue endlessly.

Why not finish right now? Spend one second for your Self. Otherwise, all lives are spent for others. Right from childhood you belong to parents and priests. As a young man you belong to teachers. Then you belong to your wife, children, and employers. As you get old you belong to the doctors. At the end when this sparrow has flown away, when the soul has left you, you belong to the priests and undertakers and and then finally you will belong to the worms. You belong to everybody but never did you belong to your own self!

So now is the time to understand. Dedicate just one second to yourself today, this hour, this instant! And your work will be over. Don't postpone. I don't want you to postpone because there is nothing to resolve or solve. This is only to realize that you have always been realized. Know this and nothing will be left for the next life.

Who ever knows if there will be another life at all! Nobody comes and tells us. The dead don't speak of it. What happens after death is only a problem for the living ones. So finish it up now. Then you will know the secret, which no one ever has known, and you will simply laugh.

I feel that I am dissolving and expanding, and I really feel that in my expansion I will liberate the entire universe.

This is compassion of the Self sending you to every person and being and rock to tell them to wake up. This is what Buddha did up to the age of eighty years old, up to his last breath. He was dying and one man came to see him, but he was stopped by Ananda who said the Master would only breathe one or two more breaths. With one breath Buddha called the man over to him and with the next he gave him his Teaching and his blessings. Then he died. This is called compassion. So, after your own Freedom you must see that everybody is Free. But mind you this: suppose you are dreaming and within this dream you have won Enlightenment. In the dream there are many others who are still living in very poor states. What will you do for these people? Tell me now. What could be the best thing to do for these people in your dream? Who are these "others" in your dreams? "Other" is there only because "you" are there.

This is a dream! You've won Enlightenment in a dream! Wake up and you will help everybody. "Other" will disappear, and "you" will disappear. The dreamer is no more. Wake up and tell me where the universe and all its suffering and enjoyments are. Wake up and know you're not even created!

> Nothing ever existed;
> not even the creators who created creations.
> Much beyond that. There nobody exists.
> There the sun doesn't shine,
> there the moon doesn't reflect,
> there the stars don't appear.
> That is the place for you to stay,
> where nobody else is.

I am happy that you are doing something. Three billion girls are out there suffering indefinitely, but you are chosen to be here. There must be something at your back pushing you out of samsara, giving you experiences that no one else in your family has had. Go now and transcend this experience. All that you read and think is a cheating of the mind, it is not It. Proceed further.

Proceed further and reject it, proceed and reject,
and later rejection will be rejected.
Tell me where rejecter, rejection and rejected is finished.
That is the place where all will arrive and
actually, everyone is there already.

The forgetful lover is not a lover,
so you can't forget the Love.
Your Beloved is seated in your Heart,
though you search for That outside.
You search for happiness with "others"
but when all of it is rejected,
you will merge with That love.

There seems to be something beyond compassion.

When a man is free from sorrow, personality and identification, compassion rises in his mind for those who suffer. For this compassion there is a sufferer and one who has compassion. Actually no one is suffering and no one is happy. You are beyond both: beyond emptiness and bliss.

The wave arises to know its own unknowability
in the mind of the unknown.
The known is in the womb of the unknown
and so you can't say if it is known or unknown.

Nobody is calling and nobody is called.
It is as It is.

Love: Beyond the Beyond

Freedom is the start of something
that Nobody knows:
there is no end to Satsang,
it is always new fathomless Bliss.

The firm conviction
that one is Existence-Consciousness-Bliss

is the end of the Teaching.
Yet there is a sacred secret beyond even this.
This sacred secret must be asked for in secret
and followed sacredly.

Constantly go to the Source.
Don't even land in the Source,
but forever go deeper.
Still beyond It Is.

You have to take the last half step
from Peace-Awareness-Bliss
into the Mystery beyond the mind.

Do you still progress in this final stage of evolution where you are now?

This is a very good question. Many people will say that this is the final stage and that everything is finished with no more progress or evolution to experience. This is what everybody will say.

I still have something more to do in this direction which is not mentioned in any book. There is no end to understanding. As long as there is very pure intention there is still something to be done after complete and final Realization. That I don't speak of and I have never spoken. It is not mentioned in any book. Those who know it cannot express it because it is beyond intellectual grasp. I want to tell what it is. It is a sacred secret, as Krishna says to Arjuna, "The Knowledge I give you is sacred Knowledge, it is not to be retold to anyone."

I know a Mystery so rare and sacred and secret. It has no oral description, but yet I will "tell" it to some people that I like. There are some people in the West. I am not hiding this, it is just that I cannot speak it. Perhaps the time will come when I speak. It is very subtle and can only be understood by the supreme intellect. Even if I did speak it nobody would understand. It is not what is transmitted by look, touch or word. It is something beyond that.

Can you speak something of the Mystery?

If I could speak of the Mystery how could it be a Mystery? It could be a history. You can speak about history, not about the Mystery. Nobody knows what this Wisdom is. Those who go there never return.

It seems like Self and Being rise from Mystery.

Everything arises from the Mystery so you are not describing Mystery, but the Self. Everything that can be seen and felt has for its origin Mystery. Mystery cannot be seen.

Mystery is beyond Self?

Yes.

Is creation arising due to Self exploring the Mystery within Self?

There is no inside or outside for the Mystery. Inside and outside arises from thought. Where does this thought arise from? Go toward where the thought rises from, this is a mysterious place where no one has touched and where no one can speak about. Even gods and existence comes from the Mystery. Nobody knows that the Mystery is behind creation and the creator.

Maybe it is only a mystery that we even see a creation and it may not even be there at all because it is a mysterious. Just as you dream you see so many things like rivers and forests, men, animals and birds, but when you wake up nothing is there, nor was it ever. So it was a mystery that in your short nap you see so many things. Then you wake up and nothing is there. When you wake up you realize that nothing has ever existed. To see the Mystery you must wake up from the sleep of forms and names. If you don't see any forms or names then that is not describable.

If you are in love with Mystery, really in love with the all compassionate Mystery, then she will reveal to you the Mystery and you will Be this Mystery, but you will not be able to describe what you have seen. Mystery and Beauty and Peace and Love all are the same thing.

I heard that you say that you have not given your final teaching yet. Why have you not transmitted this to anyone yet?

It is very true that I have not done this so far because the Truth exalts a Holy person. Therefore, it will go to a Holy person. It will itself reveal to him whom It will choose.

It is a secret teaching that is very sacred, so I cannot give it to everyone and so far I have not given it to anyone. I have seen that when the time comes, the person runs away. This is because they are rejected, not accepted, because the Truth is revealed to a Holy person. One must be very Holy in all respects and then It will unfold Its own Glory. So everybody must wait and see who is chosen. They are not to demand anything. The one who will be chosen is the one who will be Absolutely Holy and beautiful, most beautiful, so that the Truth itself is attracted. That beauty one must have. A person who looks outside for his beauty will not see his beauty inside. Okay, wait and see.

Love is so simple and I have been so dishonest to complicate everything.

Yes. Love is inside you, Here and Now. You don't need any center or church to teach you this. Methods are just a running away from the love that is always Here and Now. Stop avoiding it and just stay where you are. Then it will reveal itself to Itself and you will forget who was the lover and who was beloved. Love is pure and immaculate. That is All!

I have a longing to know what love is.

This longing is not long enough and; therefore, you can still ask a question regarding Love. When your head is sticking out of the water of the river then only can you speak! Keep your head in the water of Love and try to speak! Whenever you speak your head is out of the surface of Love and you are speaking to people on the banks of the river.

Love is fathomless. This word has no value compared to That which it points to.

> Love itself speaks through every pore of your body,
> you need not open your mouth,
> there is no word for Love.
> What you can speak about
> and what you can experience is not Love.
> All thought and speech is philosophy, not Love.
>
> For everything else you need to work.
> There are sadhanas and paths and ways,
> but there is no path to Love.
> There is no center which will teach you Love.
> Bones will melt in true Love,
> let alone mind and ego.
> Nothing is in true Love.
>
> In Love you are Love,
> who will speak to whom?
> Just look at It and it will happen.
> Everything is artificial, everything
> but Love.

When you Love you know how to Love,
otherwise you don't.
It comes by itself from within,
you are not to do anything about it.
Then when Love is here all the rest is finished.
There are no attachments to anything,
there is only Love Loving itself.

So long for only your own Self and you will Be That.
Taking time is just postponement
and interest in something else.
Love is spontaneous and is the indweller of your heart.

Do you know that we really love you?

Why should I not know? I am the lover! I am the lover and the lover knows how many beloveds he has. He cannot hide and you also cannot hide.

Papaji, I am home all the time, forever. It is impossible to enter what was never left and impossible to leave what was never entered. There is only this expansive unmoving peace. I love you so much!

There is always some kind of undercurrent of longing which still continues that I cannot describe. There is still this longing before the dawn of Enlightenment and after manifesting as Freedom Itself. But it is not a longing from ignorance toward Wisdom.

Some say that all is over in Wisdom and that there is no further experience, but I feel that there is a movement because it is Fathomlessness. So you are That itself and there is still an undercurrent working to bring you deeper and closer to Love. There is no end to it and if you have this experience you will agree, but it can never be described.

If it is fathomless then this Love process is also fathomless and never-ending and will just increase as an undercurrent. It is like a river discharging into the ocean: it just keeps on expanding and is ocean and then transcends the ocean-river relation. Now it is from the ocean, from the bottom to the surface of the ocean. (laughs)

I feel the love is deeper in the Emptiness.

Some people say that in Emptiness there is no Love and no Beauty. These traditions and teachers say that Emptiness is empty of everything. This is not my experience.

> It is the Fathomlessness of Emptiness.
> The very Heart of Emptiness,
> arriving at the depths of Emptiness,
> there is Love and Beauty!
> It is very beautiful.

Papaji, thank you from the depths of the Heart of all Beings for what you have given all of us. By totally surrendering your life and time and body to serve and advise us in anything we need you have shown us true surrender, devotion, and compassion. By your very Presence and by your wise words you have revealed to us True Knowledge and have given us Peace. By taking us into your daily life you have taught us how to be skillful in this world, and by taking us into your Heart forever you have drown us in such sweet blissful Love. Thank you so much. Papaji, what is this love that you are dissolving us into? We love you so much, so incredibly much. (Kisses the feet of the Master)

> There is a perpetual fathomless pull of Love into Love,
> an undercurrent of Forever expanding Self into Self.
> This is how I experience Love as the depth of Emptiness.
> The more you go into this Fathomlessness
> the more you will be pulled, attracted, dissolved into It.
> This Beauty is attraction and as you go deeper into it
> you will be more in Love every moment.
> This Moment is pure Love
> which is Absolutely Forever,
> all is Love, everything is this Love,
> there is no escape!
> Love is Self
> and this is so complete
> that it doesn't even need understanding.
> There is nothing besides Love.
> It is the source of Joy.
>
> Here, Here is the Secret of Love: Here It Is!
>
> First Be in Love.
> Then, if there is any time left, you can speak of it.
> No head is needed to speak of Love, only Heart.

In this Heart there is no need for maps to get home.
The easiest thing is to be Here in this Love,
all else is effort and takes effort.
Remove all ideas: This is Love.

Love, the Heart, this Moment, Is the Truth.
To see this Love everywhere see only from Love.
See from Heart and you will see only Heart,
but see from ego and you will see ego.
This moment of Love does not belong
to a "me" or to a "you" so therefore I am in Love.
When mind is no-mind it is Heart.
Heart is Self, is Atman, is Emptiness.

What is unknown is That which is to be Loved.
The Beloved One is before knowing.
It is Freedom, It is Fathomless Love
where Existence, Consciousness, and Bliss arise from.

This is your own creation so enjoy it!
Love Everything: Be and radiate Love.
As Love you are seated in the Heart of all Beings
and they in yours. Here within the Heart
you can see everything
because everything is projected from Here.

The rose is silent, yet it attracts.
So those in Love have faces shining with Beauty.
If you cannot hold the Love, if you cannot contain it,
then distribute it to all, for it is always Full.
Love all, no matter what, Love all,
it will win all battles.
Love is always Loving you.
Without this Love you cannot breathe,
as without air you cannot live.

Love is Meditation, Meditation is Love.
Heart has no frontiers;
Meditate on This.

You are this Love, you are That.
Simply Be Quiet and stay as such.

Thank You, I Love You

ॐ

Let there be Peace and Love
among all Beings of the Universe
Let there be Peace, Let there be Peace
Om Shanti, Shanti, Shanti

Glossary

Agna chakra	The third eye
Anandamayakosha	Bliss that subtly veils Self
Arti	Daily prayer ritual
Atman	Self
Avachi hell	The lowest realm, the worst hell
Avarana	Veiling
Baba	A man or male Sadhu
Bhajan	Repetitive hymn to God
Bhakta	Lover of the Divine
Bhakti	Love of the Divine
Bhava	Mind state
Biksha	Alms
Black hole	Papaji's term for womb
Brahma loka	The highest realm
Brahman	Self
Brahmin	The Hindu upper caste
Chakra	Spiritual center in the body
Chappal	Sandal
Chello	It is finished, let's move on
Chillum	Marijuana
Chit	Consciousness
Crore	Ten million
Dal	Lentils
Darshan	A very auspicious sight
Deepam	Light, festival of lights
Devadarshan	God's view
Dharma	Righteousness and duty
Dhyana	Concentration
Diksha	Initiation
Dupatta	A woman's scarf
Garuda	The King of birds, the vehicle of Rama
Gatha	Succinct spiritual statement
Gayatri	The Goddess and her mantra
Guna	Physio-psycho quality, tendencies which underlie manifestation
Hari Om	A name of Self
Hazrat Ganj	A retail center in Lucknow
Holi	A Krishna festival centered in Vrindavan
Homa	A simplified yagna
Hooka	Water pipe for smoking
Indiranagar	Suburb of Lucknow
Jai	An exclamation indicating greatness
Jiva	Individual soul, the ego
Jnana	Divine Knowledge
Jnani	One who has and is Jnana
Kali Yuga	The present Yuga, or age
Kalpa	Four Yugas
Karma	Cosmic law: "The doer must pay for his actions"
Kashi	Varanasi, Benares
Kirtan	Hymn to God
Ko ham	"Who am I?" (pr. ko hum)
Kschan	One forty-five hundreths of a second
Kumbha Mela	An ancient festival occurring at Prayag
Kundalini	Shakti-Energy of Awakening
Lila	The playful appearance of manifestation
Ma	A woman or a female Sadhu
Maha	Great
Mahout	An elephant driver
Malas	Rosary
Manas	Mind
Manika	The embodiment of sensual temptation
Math	A Guru's or tradition's main ashram
Maya	Illusion, projection
Mela	Festival
Mentate	Activating mind, i.e., thinking
Moksham	Liberation
Muladhara chakra	The chakra in the perineum
Namaskar	Welcome, prostration before God or Guru

Neti, neti	"Not this, not this"	Sari	Indian woman's garment
Nirvana	State of non-identity		
Paan	Betel nut and additives	Sat-chit-ananda	Truth-Consciousness-Bliss
Padam	Feet		
Paddy	Rice	Sattvic	Having the qualities of peace and harmony
Paduka	Wooden sandals		
Paise	The Indian cent	Satyam	Divine Truth
Pandavas	Five brothers and heroes of the Maha Bharata	Seva	Selfless service
		Shaktipat	Transferring spiritual energy
Paramatma	The Self		
Parsi	Zoroastrian	Shakti	Primordial energy, power
Pir	Sufi Saint		
Prakriti	Primordial manifestation	Shankar	A name of Shiva
		Shava	Sanskrit for corpse
Prana	Life-force, vital air	Shava Shuddha	Pure in body
Pranayama	Control of the prana	Shishya	Disciple
Prarabdha Karma	Karma manifesting as this present lifetime	Shivam	Divine Auspiciousness
		Shivratri	The night of Shiva
Prayag	The confluence of the Ganga, Yamuna and the Saraswati	Siddhi	Supernatural powers
		Sri Yantra	A geometric symbol of the Goddess
Puja	Ceremonial worship		
Purnima	Full Moon	Sundaram	Divine Beauty
Purusha	Primordial Spirit	Surya namaskars	A yoga posture flow
Rajas	Having the quality of busy activity	Swami	A Vedic monk
		Tamas	Having the qualities of dullness
Rakshashas	Demons		
Ram nam	Chanting Rama	Tapas	Penance, austerity
Ravana	The demon killed by Rama	Turiya	The transcendent state beyond waking, dreaming and sleeping
Rudraksha	A special seed used in rosary		
		Vairagya	Dispassion and renunciation
Sadhana	Method of spiritual practice		
		Vedavakya	Great statement of Knowledge
Sadhu	Renunciate, ascetic		
Sahaja	The pure natural state of Being	Vichar	Inquiry
		Yagna	Sacrificial fire ritual
Sahasrara chakra	The crown chakra	Yama loka	The realm of death
Samadhi	Transcending the normal state	Yama	The God of death
		Yoga	The practice for and the Union with the Divine
Samsara	This continual flow of desires, cycle of birth and death		
		Yuga	An Eon
Samskaras	Mental tendencies		
Sannyas	The state of being a Sannyasin		
Sannyasin	An ascetic; one who has no desire for anything transient		

About This Book

The Truth Is NOW, and this is not in books or cassettes! Reading books is like reading menus, the menu is not the food. You have to eat, you have to have the experience. If books gave you Freedom librarians would be the first to be Enlightened, but the banks of a river are better than a library. Don't read books, read only your open Heart in this Immediate Presence. Reading books before you know the Truth will destroy you because books pollute you with so many notions which will just distract you from your Self. Words are indicators only so follow the indication and don't stick to the words. Leave the wordiness of the world and Realize Here and Now what the words in this book are pointing to. The Truth, the Teaching which IS, cannot be spoken of or described by words. The Teaching can only be Silently transmitted from Self to Self in the 'form' of Satguru to Disciple. The words written on the preceding pages are not the Teaching, but act as mere 'fingers pointing' to the Truth.

This book is composed of many chapters and sections. This differentiation is due only to the various topics of the questions asked. The answers to all of these questions have just one power and import: You are Eternal Being, Unbounded and Undivided. Now you are with someone who has no teachings and only one thing to say and that is also not a teaching: Just Keep Quiet, all will be well, Keep Quiet. You Are God Itself! What else? Here and Now, Everywhere, You are Happy, You are Peace.

Do not entertain any notion that you are in trouble. This is all that you have to do. It is not a search but the cessation of distraction. We are here to help each other. Don't entertain the notion that I am high and that you are low. We are here to find out how to be happy, how the whole world can be happy. We can speak about this between ourselves: What is the way to be happy and how can we transmit this happiness to all Beings.

Photographs

Cover: Master under the Banyan Tree, Botanical Gardens. Lucknow, May, 1991
Photographer: Prashanti

Page 6: Bhagavan Sri Ramana Maharshi, 1940's • Photographer: Welling
Courtesy of Sri Ramanashramam, Tiruvannamalai

Page 10: Lucknow Satsang, 1993 • Photographer: Kevin Meyers

Page 24: Arunachala, 1994 • Photographer: Vidya

Page 53: Papaji in his home, 1994 • Photographer: Bharatmitra

Page 54: Celebration in Lucknow, October 13, 1992 • Photographer: Dev Gogoi

Page 85: Celebration in Lucknow, 1993 • Photographer: Unknown

Page 86: Guru Purnima Celebration, Lucknow, 1994 • Photographer: Prashanti

Page 95: Swargashram, Rishikesh, 1993 • Photographer: Prashanti

Page 96: Lucknow Satsang, 1995 • Photographer: Prashanti

Page 120: Lucknow, New Year's Day, 1991 • Photographer: Patrick Suthor

Page 152: Lucknow Satsang, 1991 • Photographer: Unknown

Page 242: The Master's Feet, 1993 • Photographer: Prashanti

Page 281: Lucknow Satsang, 1994 • Photographer: Unknown

Page 282: Lucknow Celebration, 1995 • Photographer: Unknown

Page 314: Papaji at Arunachala. Sri Ramanashramam, Tiruvannamalai.
Photographer: Unknown

Page 329: Arunachala and Sri Ramana Maharshi, 1940's • Photographer: Unknown
Courtesy of Sri Ramanashramam, Tiruvannamalai

Page 330: Papaji in Manali, September, 1994 • Photographer: Chandi Devi

Page 359: Papaji in Karnataka, 1967 • Photographer: Mr. Neginhal

Page 360: Lucknow Satsang, 1996 • Photographer: Unknown

Page 397: Papaji walking above Rishikesh, 1970 • Photographer: Unknown

Page 398: Papaji in Dandeli, Karnataka, 1966 • Photographer: Unknown

Page 453: Papaji • Photographer: Unknown

Page 454: Haridwar, September, 1992 • Photographer: Dev Gogoi

Page 517: Papaji's Mahasamadhi. Lucknow, September, 1997 • Photographer: Chandi Devi

Page 518: Haridwar, April, 1990 • Photographer: Hanuman

Page 549: Lucknow Satsang, 1996 • Photographer: Unknown

ALL TIME BESTSELLERS !!

Bejan Daruwalla

Love Signs
Bejan Daruwalla
145/-

Numerology Made Easy
Dr. Narayan Dutta Shrimali
75/-

Ayurvedic Remedies
Dr. Bhagwan Dash
195/-

OSHO MEDITATION SERIES

Love is a Free Bird	75/-
Life is a Gift	75/-
Stranger to the Earth	75/-
Be a Lamp unto Yourself	75/-
Alone We Fly	75/-
Live Dangerously	75/-
I Teach Fearlessness	75/-
Become One with Yourself	75/-
Surrender to Existence	75/-
Say Yes!	75/-
A Dewdrop in the Ocean	75/-
Meditation — An Ecstasy	75/-

VAASTU/Rakesh Chawla

Vaastu for Health Wealth & Happiness
195/-

The Pocket Book of Vaastu
125/-

New Titles from FULL CIRCLE

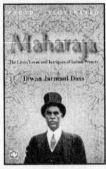

Maharaja
Diwan Jarmani Dass
The Lives, Loves and Intrigues
of the Maharajas of India
295/-

The True Name
OSHO
"Osho is one of the greatest
souls born in this country."
— *Khushwant Singh* **295/-**

De-Stress Yourself
Mridula Agarwal
A dynamic new book that will
help you cope with the harmful
stress of every day life.
250/-

**By Which We See All
Colours**
Mrinalini Patwardhan Mehra
"Will draw you in and touch
you deeply."
— *Dominique Lapierre* **295/-**

Available at all leading bookstores.

OTHER ENGLISH TITLES FROM
FULL CIRCLE

Passion India

Javier Moro

295/-

The Essential Flower Essence Handbook

Lila Devi Stone

195/-

Reversal of Heart Disease in 5 Easy Steps

Dr. Bimal Chhajer

195/-

Food for Reversing Heart Disease

Dr. Bimal Chhajer

395/-

Teachings on Love

Thich Nhat Hanh

125/-

The Prophet

Kahlil Gibran

195/-

Available at all leading bookstores.

SELF IMPROVEMENT SERIES

 The Art of Conversation

Eric Watson

60/-

 Born to Win

Promod Batra

95/-

 Correct Manners and Etiquette

Eric Watson

60/-

 The 7 Keys to Prosperity and Success

Rajesh Aggarwal

250/-

 Increase Your Word Power

Y.K. Modi

60/-

PERSONALITY PLUS

Making the Most of Yourself

Developing Self-Confidence

Achieving Happiness

How to Overcome Loneliness

Each: 60/-